Raising the Flag

Implications of U.S. Military Approaches to General and Flag Officer Development

KIMBERLY JACKSON, KATHERINE L. KIDDER, SEAN MANN,
WILLIAM H. WAGGY II, NATASHA LANDER, S. REBECCA ZIMMERMAN

Prepared for the Office of the Secretary of Defense
Approved for public release; distribution unlimited

NATIONAL DEFENSE RESEARCH INSTITUTE

For more information on this publication, visit www.rand.org/t/RR4347

Library of Congress Cataloging-in-Publication Data is available for this publication.
ISBN: 978-1-9774-0488-6

Published by the RAND Corporation, Santa Monica, Calif.

The RAND Corporation is a research organization that develops solutions to public policy challenges to help make communities throughout the world safer and more secure, healthier and more prosperous. RAND is nonprofit, nonpartisan, and committed to the public interest.

RAND's publications do not necessarily reflect the opinions of its research clients and sponsors.

Preface

This report presents findings to assist the Office of the Secretary of Defense in understanding what professional experiences and other characteristics the general and flag officers in each of the military services tend to share as a result of each service's approach to personnel management and other related factors, and how these approaches might influence the ways in which general and flag officers lead, manage, and advise.

Specifically, this report provides analysis of the fundamental elements of military personnel processes in each service and across the U.S. Department of Defense and identifies common career experiences within each service in categories such as career field, years in service, commissioning source, education and training, and duty assignments. This report further examines how these professional experiences and other characteristics might influence general and flag officers' approaches to institutional leadership and management, and the type of strategic-level advice they might provide to civilian decisionmakers.

This research was sponsored by the Office of Net Assessment in the Office of the Secretary of Defense and conducted within the Forces and Resources Policy Center of the RAND National Defense Research Institute, a federally funded research and development center sponsored by the Office of the Secretary of Defense, the Joint Staff, the Unified Combatant Commands, the Navy, the Marine Corps, the defense agencies, and the defense intelligence enterprise.

For more information on the RAND Forces and Resources Policy Center, see www.rand.org/nsrd/frp or contact the director (contact information is provided on the webpage).

Contents

Figures

Tables

Summary

The 2018 National Defense Strategy (NDS) directed a reorientation in the U.S. Department of Defense (DoD) toward near-peer competition and countering rogue states and articulated a need to rethink how DoD prepares and leverages its personnel to approach these challenges. Specifically, the NDS stressed that confronting these challenges will require military leaders to adapt and directed DoD to reform professional military education (PME) and development in strategic decisionmaking.[1] Further, Congress has taken legislative action to provide more flexibility in military officer management processes, which the services are beginning to implement, and public discourse about the way that military leaders are developed has increased in recent years. These emphases reveal a growing recognition that, as the global security environment evolves and new challenges emerge, the United States might require substantially different military leadership approaches and perspectives.

Study Objective

To help understand whether military leadership might need to change to better serve national security objectives, the Office of Net Assessment within the Office of the Secretary of Defense asked RAND to analyze how the military services' approaches to personnel management might influence the ways in which general and flag officers (G/FOs) lead, manage, and advise.

Specifically, our research objective was to analyze what professional experiences and other characteristics the G/FOs in each service tend to share as a result of each service's approach to personnel management and other related factors, such as service culture.[2] This research then enabled us to examine how these characteristics and experiences might influence G/FO approaches to institutional leadership and management, and the type of strategic-level advice G/FOs in each service might provide to civilian decisionmakers.

---

[1] U.S. Department of Defense, *Summary of the 2018 National Defense Strategy of the United States of America: Sharpening the American Military's Competitive Edge*, Washington, D.C., 2018, p. 8.

[2] Other related factors include service core missions; warfighting tactics, techniques, and practices; service traditions; and resource management styles, for example. Although leadership and management overlap, in this report we consider leadership to be primarily concerned with directing and motivating teams and personnel, whereas management is concerned with overseeing the processes that guide organizational operation. Civilian decisionmakers include, but are not limited to, the Secretary of Defense and the service secretaries. We define *strategic leadership positions* as those positions either within a service or at the joint level that require both subject-matter expertise and an understanding of political and bureaucratic dynamics. For more information, see U.S. Army War College, Department of Command, Leadership and Management, *Strategic Leadership Primer*, 2nd edition, Carlisle Barracks, Pa., 2004.

Research Approach

We used a mixed-methods approach combining qualitative and quantitative analyses that included a review of relevant literature, interviews with military officers and civilian and military subject-matter experts, analysis of available G/FO biographies, quantitative analysis of personnel data from the Defense Manpower Data Center (DMDC), and a RAND-led exercise called the Senior Leader Selection Exercise (SLSE).

We began by analyzing the fundamental aspects of military personnel processes, including

- commissioning source
- duty assignments
- education
- special training
- evaluations
- promotions.

We also compared trends across Army, Navy, Air Force, and Marine Corps officers on dimensions such as time in grade, years in service, commissioning source, and career designations.[3] Further, we identified key legislation in officer management, G/FO management processes, and basic information, such as pay grade structure and size of each service's officer corps.

Second, we conducted analysis of each service's *specific* personnel management processes and approaches to developing senior officers. Through this analysis, we identified what professional experiences and other characteristics tend to be common among each service's G/FOs and how service personnel processes select for and develop these attributes. During this process, we also identified reflections of service culture and other factors that matter in service G/FO selection but whose effects are more difficult to measure (such as personality and networks), and we gained perspectives from literature, the SLSE, and interviewees on the impacts of these processes on service G/FOs. The professional experiences and other characteristics we analyzed by service included

- career field
- time in grade
- years in service
- commissioning source
- PME and civilian education
- special training
- duty assignments (including leadership experience, broadening and joint experience, deployment experience, and high-visibility assignments)
- other factors, such as additional certifications.

---

[3] Commissioning source is also referred to as *accession source*.

These integrated findings served as the basis to then develop G/FO "archetypes" at the grade of O-7 for each service. Each archetype describes a notional profile composed of the most common characteristics for each service that we identified throughout the course of our research. Although officers' career experiences and other characteristics—and how those experiences might influence an officer's leadership, management, and advising style—might vary, these archetypes were useful to distill all the information we had gained on service personnel processes and their potential impacts, common experiences and other characteristics, and other observations provided from literature, SLSE participants, and interviewees into one notional unit of analysis per service.

We established a set of assumptions regarding service preferences in the development of service archetypes. One key assumption is that the way an officer is trained, educated, and gains experience through a service's personnel management system at more junior grades will be reflected when the officer attains a senior grade. Also included in our assumptions is the fact that officers are educated in their service's desired skills, traits, attributes, and experiences through formal systems and requirements *and* by observing the characteristics of those selected for G/FO grades. Because some characteristics are consistently replicated within the services' G/FO corps, we assume that those consistently replicated characteristics provide information regarding the strengths (and potential weaknesses) that each service's G/FO corps might possess. Based on the literature, interviews, and SLSE, we also assume that experience within an officer's service is more highly valued for promotion by the service than experience outside the service, whether through broadening or joint assignments.

Finally, using these archetypes built from our service-specific analysis, and also informed by our analysis of literature, interviews, and the SLSE, we developed our conclusions about how typical career experiences and other characteristics might influence the ways officers in each service might approach institutional leadership and management, and the type of advice they might provide to civilian decisionmakers, such as the Secretary of Defense or the service secretaries. We also utilized a set of assumptions that helped us develop our conclusions. Although these conclusions follow logically from the set of assumptions we used, the assumptions themselves are essentially hypotheses that should be empirically verified in future research.

Because we needed to limit the scope of the study, we focused on personnel processes primarily up to the grade of O-7 and on the most *common* pathways that result in O-7 promotion (and in some cases, beyond). We were also mindful of the larger question about the characteristics of G/FOs these pipelines are producing for positions at higher grades, and specifically those critical and strategic positions at the O-9 and O-10 grades, within the services and in the joint environment. These positions, such as service chiefs, combatant commanders, and major service component commanders, have substantial bearing on the missions of each of the services and their overall advisory role in setting DoD's strategic priorities. Although we do not specifically analyze personnel processes and their intersection with service culture beyond the O-7 grade, we include observations throughout the report from interviewees and SLSE participants that refer to G/FOs of all grades, as it is challenging to separate those characterizations solely by grade. We expect that service approaches to generalship continue to play a large role in how G/FOs beyond O-7 lead, manage, and advise, and we recommend further analysis of this population of officers that fills the most senior joint and service positions in the U.S. military.

We are not suggesting that the archetypes developed and the inferences about their leadership approaches reflect every G/FO in each service. Rather, they highlight the "archetypical" officer that the services' officer management processes produce and the likely tendencies that such an officer might exhibit when in a leadership position. By studying processes and preferences surrounding G/FO selection, this study allows senior service, joint, and civilian leaders to understand whether there is a gap between the characteristics and experiences their processes select for and the characteristics and experiences they want and need in the men and women in service leadership positions.

Our findings focus on two areas: (1) common observations across the services and (2) for each service, a description of service G/FO archetypes and the potential implications for institutional leadership and provision of strategic-level advice.

Service-Common Observations

While the services each rely on certain career management processes mandated by law and shaped centrally by DoD, each of the service's unique cultures, missions, and institutional preferences work to create different incentives and rewards for specific innate or developed traits, career experiences, and other attributes. Despite these differences, there are commonalities in officer career development and selection among the Army, Navy, Air Force, and Marine Corps. That some commonalities exist is expected: After all, the services all support the same overarching U.S. national security goals, are subject to the same officer career management laws, and work in the same joint organizational structures. The list below summarizes our observations regarding these relevant commonalities among service personnel processes and the types of experiences and other characteristics that enhance an officer's promotability.[4]

- **The value of command is universal.** For all the military services, time and successful performance in command (particularly at the O-5 and O-6 grades) consistently serve as the chief signal to promotion boards that an officer is proficient in their specialty and has potential to excel at higher levels. Many career fields throughout the military do not offer command opportunities, so those officers are not evaluated on the same criteria—but the

[4] At time of publication, in early 2020, the services were undertaking different efforts to evaluate and potentially modify specific aspects of officer personnel management. These efforts could have bearing on the experiences and other characteristics for which the services select, but the effects, if any, are unknown at this time.

vast majority of senior-most G/FO positions are filled by officers whose career fields do feature successful command assignments.

- **"Ducks pick ducks."** We heard repeatedly from interviewees in each service that there is a tendency for promotion boards to select officers whose career experiences are comparable to their own, and for senior officers to select aides with backgrounds similar to theirs, positions that serve as a signal of O-7 potential to board members and can provide access to powerful networks of G/FOs. We also observed this trend in the SLSE. The notion of "ducks picking ducks" serves to cyclically reinforce service culture by perpetuating the selection of officers who similarly reflect service goals and preferences. However, this observation does not mean that the officers who are selected for promotion by similar, more senior officers are necessarily less qualified; it is possible that the "ducks pick ducks" tendency in some cases occurs because well-qualified officers sitting on promotion boards are selecting for other well-qualified officers.
- **Many officers become O-7s with narrow, mostly service-specific experience.** Partly because of demanding career path timelines, officers across the services tend to have mostly tactical or operational, service-specific experience and relatively little joint or strategic experience. Thus, strategic-level experience—frequently gained from broadening and joint positions—is more often acquired "on the job," after an officer becomes a G/FO.
- **Personnel systems discourage risk-taking in career management choices and in professional performance.** High-quality evaluations are critical in promotion decisions for officers across the services, and failure resulting from taking risks might not reflect well in an evaluation, even if those risks are innovative and forward-thinking. Along with the tendency for "ducks picking ducks," the inclination to avoid risk-taking can drive even more similarities among G/FOs within each service.
- **The effects of many other factors that influence who becomes a G/FO could not be accurately accounted for in this study.** A few of these factors, which emerged in our literature review, interviews, and senior leader selection exercise, include the timing of promotions, networks and personal connections, personality, appearance, and gender, race, and ethnicity.

Service General and Flag Officer Archetypes

Service archetypes depict the most common characteristics and experiences of G/FOs in each service that result from their respective approaches to officer development. In turn, these factors could translate to the way these archetypical G/FOs might lead and manage institutions and advise senior civilian leaders. Although leading and managing institutions and providing strategic-level advice are different actions, they are related, as they derive in large part from an officer's same experiences and perspectives. While we attempt to characterize an "archetypical" G/FO within each service, every G/FO's approach to leadership, management, and advice will differ based on factors such as individual personality and preferences.

Much of the analysis in this section is based on a set of assumptions and heavily informed by common themes within the literature, the data, our interviews, and the SLSE that we have captured throughout this report. For example, we assumed that the way an officer is trained, educated, and gains experience through a service's personnel management system will be reflected when the officer becomes a G/FO; that officers are shaped in their service's desired skills, traits, attributes, and experiences through personnel management systems and requirements, and also by observing the characteristics of those selected for G/FO; that officers are provided with the necessary training and education to succeed within their service and career field, but that intangible factors (and the assignment to specific career fields themselves) influence officers' potential for selection to G/FO; and that characteristics we observe to be consistently replicated provide information regarding a service G/FO's potential strengths and weaknesses.[5] It was beyond the scope of this report to specifically measure the amount of influence that professional experiences and other characteristics have on a G/FO's advice or approach to leadership and management, and, accordingly, we do not make claims about the degree of influence that any factor might have.

The Army Archetype

The Army's current GO pathway tends to be tactically focused, command-centric, doctrine-based, and, especially for O-7 promotion decisions, influenced by an officer's reputation among Army senior leaders. In various official publications, the Army highlights its need to develop leadership experience at all levels, as well as proficiency in combined arms warfare. The Army also stresses other qualities in its formal documents, such as agility, adaptiveness, and ability to lead in joint, interagency, and international organizations, but it is difficult to identify the incentives that promote those same qualities throughout an officer's career development processes.

Typical Career Experiences

The archetypical Army GO features the professional experiences outlined in Tables S.1 and S.2.

[5] Examples we highlight in Chapter Two include the following: We assume that a lack of training in and exposure to strategic analysis could mean that a G/FO's advice would not rely heavily on strategic analysis; that tactical training (and selection for promotion based on tactical performance) might lead to an officer being more likely to focus on tactical-level solutions to strategic-level problems; and that few or no assignments in civilian environments and/or nonservice assignments might lead to officers who are either initially uncomfortable or underprepared when the officer arrives at an interagency, policy, and/or civilian organization.

Table S.1. Army General Officer Archetype Career Experiences

Category	Career Experience
Career field	Infantry, armor, or support branch career fields at O-7; by O-9 and O-10, overwhelmingly infantry or armor
Time in grade and years in service	Somewhat likely to have been promoted early to O-4, O-5, or O-6; more time in grade at O-4
Commissioning source	Reserve Officer Training Corps or, U.S. Military Academy (USMA) graduate at O-7, and more likely a USMA graduate as GO rank increases
PME and graduate education	In-resident PME experience focused on military planning, but performance in PME will not have been weighed heavily; unlikely to have civilian master's degree/doctor of philosophy (Ph.D.)
Other factors	Demonstration of tactical excellence throughout their career; minimal experience in strategic analysis or financial management but strong familiarity with doctrine; strong networks in the GO community

Table S.2. Army General Officer Archetype Duty Assignments and Related Experience

Duty Assignments	
Heavy experience in tactical and operational positions; service institutional assignments such as assignment officer with Human Resources Command (HRC), as an aide-de-camp to a GO, or in the 75th Ranger Regiment	
Leadership experience	Significant team leadership experience starting at junior grades; experience in command within their career field or in Army-heavy organizations
Broadening and joint experience	Minimal broadening or joint experience, and joint experience will rarely occur in commands where Army officers are in the minority
Deployment experience	Multiple combat tours, often in key tactical positions
High-visibility assignments	Post-brigade command assignment as a GO's executive officer or aide, with broad exposure to GOs who will serve on O-7 selection boards

Archetypical Approach to Institutional Leadership and Management

We assess that when leading large institutions, the archetypical Army GO might

- lead based on an Army-centric, ground combat–oriented perspective
- work decisively in situations for which doctrine exists
- rely on tactical and operational experiences to guide strategic-level decisions
- define leadership in terms of personnel management rather than platform management
- be unfamiliar working in organizations where the Army is not the majority, potentially affecting the Army GO archetype's effectiveness in joint organizations
- excel in J-3 and J-5 positions but be challenged to work in civilian-dominant organizations and to navigate strategic-level policy processes[6]
- emphasize tactical performance.

[6] J-3 positions are leadership positions in joint organizations that manage and oversee operations; J-5 positions are those that manage and generally oversee plans, policy, and strategy.

Archetypical Approach to Strategic-Level Advice

Based on these same factors and feedback provided in interviews and the SLSE, we assess that when advising senior leaders the Army GO archetype might

- base advice on formal military planning, meaning that the officer will be an excellent planner of military operations but might not be highly adaptable and creative, particularly when facing challenges for which doctrine does not exist
- share similar perspectives with other Army GO archetypes, based on the uniformity of their experience and lack of emphasis on strategic analysis in training and education
- rely on their combat deployment experience in providing advice, which can be a useful frame of reference but can also introduce biases formed from previous wars
- be less likely to share innovative perspectives and advice in order to maintain strong support networks and strong evaluations from senior raters.

The Navy Archetype

Across the three main unrestricted line (URL) communities (aviation, surface warfare, and submarine warfare), the Navy's career development processes tend to emphasize self-reliance, technical expertise, and "Darwinian" competition. In the surface and submarine communities especially, command at sea is emphasized. These values directly reflect Navy culture and help to create FOs who have substantial community-specific operational experience, are comfortable with executing operations independently from other services and with minimal oversight, and are used to working across multiple naval domains. Navy guidance on leadership and promotions stresses the essentiality of these attributes in its officers, and also names leader development, including mentoring, as its top priority. Specifically, the Navy's evaluation forms heavily weigh dimensions such as strategic thinking and ability to lead change, but it is unclear how those attributes are measured.

Typical Career Experiences

The Navy FO archetype profile features the professional experiences summarized in Tables S.3 and S.4.

Table S.3. Navy Flag Officer Archetype Career Experiences

Category	Career Experience
Career field	Aviation, surface, or submariner communities, especially the latter at higher grades
Time in grade and years in service	Promoted in the primary zone at all grades; more years in service at O-6 grade than any other grade, or O-6 service counterparts
Commissioning source	U.S. Naval Academy (USNA) graduate, especially at O-9/O-10
PME and graduate education	Navy Nuclear Power School graduate; science, technology, engineering, and math (STEM) expertise; completed intermediate-level education online; PME performance will not have been weighed heavily; any civilian degree will have been completed during free time
Other factors	Strong peer and FO networks, forged in part through USNA affiliation; potentially has other specific certifications, such as financial management

Table S.4. Navy Flag Officer Archetype Duty Assignments and Related Experience

Duty Assignments	
Extensive command experience in their platform along a highly specialized, technical career path; focus on operating in a naval multidomain environment; on-the-job training gained through milestone assignments intended to weed out lower performers; emphasis on learning operational independence and self-reliance	
Leadership experience	More seasoned in platform management than personnel-focused leadership; extensive command experience within their community, but not in a joint environment; comfortable with taking initiative and operating with minimal oversight
Broadening and joint experience	Familiarity with naval multidomain operations; joint/broadening experience only as required, likely at U.S. Indo-Pacific Command or related command
Deployment experience	Significant operational sea duty, particularly in the Pacific theater, but limited combat experience
High-visibility assignments	Aide to a senior Navy FO, generally at O-5/O-6

Archetypical Approach to Institutional Leadership and Management

Considering the Navy FO archetype's career experiences and other characteristics, we assess that when leading institutions, the officer might

- be relatively comfortable with decisionmaking in ambiguous situations or relatively unfamiliar situations
- demonstrate self-reliance and initiative, which could lead the officer to drive needed strategic-level changes; alternatively, self-reliance and initiative could lead the officer to rely only on their own judgment when making major decisions, rather than weighing others' opinions
- be less risk-averse in operational decisions than G/FO archetypes in other services, though not careless—although this might be more true of archetypes with surface warfare and subsurface backgrounds
- utilize formal procedures for managing technical systems, but be less tied to standardized, doctrinal approaches in strategic leadership tasks
- define leadership more in terms of platforms the officer has commanded rather than in terms of people the officer has managed

- see value in leveraging multiple communities with different equities to work together, but still favor service autonomy over jointness.

Archetypical Approach to Strategic-Level Advice

Based on our analysis and additional feedback provided in interviews and the SLSE, we assess that when advising at the strategic level, the archetypical Navy FO might

- exhibit relative diversity in their perspectives across Navy FO archetypes because they will come from one of three distinct communities; however, within a community, they will likely provide technical advice based on very similar, narrow career pathways
- demonstrate a higher degree of risk acceptance in operational decisions than other services' G/FO counterparts, depending on which community the officer represents
- provide more-intuitive advice that does not heavily incorporate strategic analysis
- offer fresh perspective and strategic advice that does not carry forward biases incurred from previous combat deployment experiences; however, the officer might not have firsthand understanding of how strategic-level decisions affect tactical and operational combat environments
- prioritize maintaining good relations with their peers and senior ranking officers, which might mean that the officer is hesitant to provide contrarian advice in an effort to maintain cordiality.

The Air Force Archetype

The Air Force's personnel management processes feature early identification of talent, compressed timelines due to emphasis on below-the-promotion-zone (BPZ) promotions, and greater importance placed on education and jointness relative to the other services. Given the Air Force's missions and culture, the archetypical GO is a pilot, and most frequently a fighter pilot. The Air Force's official leadership development goals place a premium on technical mastery, strategic analysis, and developing its personnel.

Typical Career Experiences

The archetypical Air Force officer's career experiences are summarized in Tables S.5 and S.6.

Table S.5. Air Force General Officer Archetype Career Experiences

Category	Career Experience
Career field	Pilot background, especially a fighter pilot as grade increases
Time in grade and years in service	Promoted below the zone at least twice; fewer years in service than same-grade counterparts as mid-grade officers and GOs
Commissioning source	U.S. Air Force Academy graduate, particularly at higher grades
PME and graduate education	Distinguished graduate from in-resident intermediate developmental education; possibly a U.S. Air Force School of Advanced Air and Space Studies and/or Weapons School graduate; educated in strategic analysis
Other factors	Will have demonstrated excellence by O-3; has developed networks and mentor relationships; strong communications skills

Table S.6. Air Force General Officer Archetype Duty Assignments and Related Experience

Duty Assignments	
Clearly defined, time-compressed pathway focused on developing skills needed at the senior GO level emphasizes tactical leadership, technical mastery, and communication and analysis skills; at least one staff-level position to increase visibility and awareness of strategic issues	
Leadership experience	More skilled in technical mastery than "people" leadership; minimal experience leading teams at junior levels; has held squadron, group, and wing command
Broadening and joint experience	Minimal joint/broadening experience due to tight timeline; strategic level exposure through staff and joint assignments at the O-4 through O-6 levels; possible experience in a resource management role at a joint command
Deployment experience	Multiple deployments, but might not have been directly involved in combat
High-visibility assignments	Executive officer or aide to a GO (Air Force or joint), Air Staff position that increased exposure to senior leaders

Archetypical Approach to Institutional Leadership and Management

Considering the archetypical Air Force GO's professional background and other characteristics, we expect that, in institutional leadership roles, the officer might

- emphasize technical, platform-based leadership over personnel leadership, but value officer development when they are in a leadership position
- be less comfortable with "outside-the-box" ideas and in leadership positions that require decisions without the benefit of clear order and procedure
- seek guidance and input from others, rather than executing independently, valuing broader perspectives in decisionmaking processes
- bring a keen understanding of resource constraints to leadership positions
- demonstrate openness to change and willingness to adapt
- value jointness more than G/FO archetypes in other services
- exhibit strong communications and strategic analysis skills.

Archetypical Approach to Strategic-Level Advice

Based on our analysis and feedback provided in interviews and the SLSE, we assess that Air Force GO archetypes might

- provide analytic assessments that might be less uniform with one another than in other services
- apply analysis that combines strategic analysis skills with operational experience
- bring a nonhierarchical view to planning and operations, given their familiarity with flatter command structures
- hesitate to deviate from an established course in their advice
- be somewhat uncomfortable with challenging the status quo when they provide advice
- focus on technological solutions to complex problems
- rely on strategic analysis and understand broad implications of future fights and technological changes
- favor incremental change over sudden or large changes, and weigh pros and cons carefully
- advocate for a substantial role for Air Force capabilities in a campaign, but also be comfortable advising on ways to leverage Air Force capabilities in either a lead or a support role.

The Marine Corps Archetype

Across Marine Corps career fields, the officer development process is highly prescriptive and performance-based, and common experiences serve to reinforce the Marine Corps' egalitarian culture and create a highly cohesive Marine Corps GO corps. Officers are promoted to O-7 by career field roughly in proportion to commissioning rates, but career pathways remain similar regardless of specialty. Official service guidance emphasizes the leadership and development of marines, tactical competence, and discipline.

Typical Career Experiences

The Marine Corps GO archetype's typical career experiences are summarized in Tables S.7 and S.8.

Table S.7. Marine Corps General Officer Archetype Career Experiences

Category	Career Experience
Career field	At O-7, could represent one of several career fields; most likely aviation and infantry as officers approach O-10
Time in grade and years in service	Promoted on time, not below the zone; selected to O-7 later than other services; more years in service than other service counterparts, particularly after O-7
Commissioning source	OCS graduate, in line with commissioning rate
PME and graduate education	Location and performance in PME will not have been weighed heavily; civilian graduate degree, if any, will be directly related to Marine Corps requirements
Other factors	Known for military bearing, discipline, and command presence; experiences focused on tactical leadership and team over self; multiple screening processes weed out lower performers early

Table S.8. Marine Corps General Officer Archetype Duty Assignments and Related Experience

Duty Assignments	
Career pathway is Marine Air-Ground Task Force–centric, focused on leading marines and developing discipline and tactical expertise at every grade; performance will be exceptional in every position, but very few "kingmaker" positions exist	
Leadership experience	Tactical leadership experience starting at junior grades; personnel leadership emphasized over platform management; command assignments are paramount
Broadening and joint experience	Minimal joint experience outside of the Marine Corps, but will have gained cross-service institutional knowledge in valued B-billet assignment; assigned to a congressional fellowship to advance Marine Corps needs[a]
Deployment experience	Significant overseas assignments and multiple combat tours
High-visibility assignments	Congressional fellowship will denote excellence, but no other specific signaling assignments

[a] A B-billet is an institutional assignment intended to "broaden" the service member in a role outside of their career field, such as in recruiting commands, basic training commands, and reserve component commands.

Archetypical Approach to Institutional Leadership and Management

Considering these career experiences and other characteristics, we assess that when leading institutions, the Marine Corps GO archetype might

- define leadership as personnel-based, rather than platform-based
- emphasize the importance of developing and leading marines
- equate effective leadership with understanding how to also be a good, disciplined follower—of rules, and of other leaders
- expect order and adherence to a hierarchical chain of command, but also focus on developing and utilizing the capabilities of its personnel
- be able to recognize and leverage the utility of a wide range of groups within an organization
- emphasize tactical performance
- value career fields other than their own in an organization the officer is leading, but still favor Marine Corps perspectives and capabilities over others

- chafe at sudden or large institutional reform efforts, particularly with respect to personnel policy
- demonstrate adaptiveness to operational change and commitment to evolving operational approaches to meet rising threats.

Archetypical Approach to Strategic Advice

Based on our analysis and feedback provided in interviews and the SLSE, we assess that, in providing advice on the strategic level, archetypical Marine Corps GO might

- provide advice representing the Marine Corps as a whole, rather than being narrowly focused on career field requirements
- value discipline over risk-taking
- be averse to questioning assumptions underlying existing processes, strategies, and orders
- lack key preparatory broadening and joint experiences for providing advice in senior-level joint billets
- rely on experience in tactically focused assignments
- have increased years of experience relative to other service G/FOs on which to base advice, which could add breadth and/or depth of judgment, or could further entrench specific biases and inflexibility
- place a high value on forward presence
- view warfighting strategy based on the models of those they have previously fought in
- favor investments in warfighting platforms that enable Marine Corps autonomy.

Importance of Specific Experiences and Characteristics Across Services

Although we did not conduct comparative analysis of the utility of each service's approach to developing and selecting G/FOs, we include Table S.9 for illustrative purposes. While other specific experiences matter for promotion to O-7 depending on the service, we highlight selected types of experiences here to show the range of promotion criteria valuation across the services. We base our determinations on the totality of our research described in this report and define the range of values as "not important," "minimally important," "somewhat important," and "very important." Of note, the importance of some of these factors change beyond the grade of O-7, but Table S.9 shows the importance of these experiences only in terms of each service's pathway up to O-7. The cells which are designated as "very important" are highlighted.

Table S.9. Importance of Specific Experiences for Promotion to O-7, by Service

	Army	Navy	Air Force	Marine Corps
Commissioning source	Somewhat important	Very important	Somewhat important	Minimally important
Joint experience	Minimally important	Minimally important	Somewhat important	Minimally important
Command experience	Very important	Very important	Very important	Very important
Below the Zone promotions	Minimally important	Not important	Very important	Not important
Combat-related deployments	Very important	Not important	Somewhat important	Very important
Type of PME and PME performance	Somewhat important	Not important	Very important	Not important
High-visibility assignments	Very important	Very important	Very important	Minimally important
Personnel-based leadership	Very important	Somewhat important	Somewhat important	Very important
Experience in strategic analysis	Not important	Not important	Very important	Not important
Personal networks	Very important	Very important	Very important	Minimally important

Conclusion

Looking forward, we expect that the professional experiences and other characteristics that tend to define each service's G/FO corps and drive G/FOs' leadership, management, and advisory approaches will largely remain the same in the near to mid-term, given the length of military careers and how long major changes to personnel management processes can take. Although adjustments to officer development processes, and responses to changes in the geopolitical environment, will certainly occur, the institutional traditions and cultures of each service are strong and entrenched, and therefore will evolve slowly.

However, certain trends suggest potential for evolution in the G/FO corps. Examples include

- the effects of major ongoing military operations since 2001 on more junior officer development, as well as future warfighting requirements and technological development
- current efforts across the services to reform military personnel processes, such as allowing career intermissions, during which to pursue civilian education, and increasing merit-based promotions
- the reduction of G/FOs across the force, which could, for example, lower the number of certain preparatory assignments that are frequently leveraged as professional development opportunities to prepare a junior G/FO for a position of greater responsibility, and/or challenge morale across the officer corps as leadership opportunities diminish.

Despite these potential impacts on officer development, the very nature of service culture means that efforts to change the development, training, and experiences of G/FOs in each of the services will take time and substantial effort.

With renewed focus from the NDS, Congress, and the services on major institutional reform to reshape G/FO management and military personnel processes overall, now is the time to understand more deeply how the services produce G/FOs and how they select—consciously or not—for professional experiences and other characteristics. By drawing these factors into the light, senior decisionmakers can best ensure that their reforms succeed in building the G/FOs needed by the services, the joint force, and the nation.

Acknowledgments

First and foremost, we would like to thank Andrew May of the Office of the Secretary of Defense's (OSD's) Office of Net Assessment, who sponsored this work and consistently challenged us to provide bold, rigorous analysis of topics we believe to be fundamental to improving national security decisionmaking processes. Captain Mark Seip, also of OSD Net Assessment, provided key insights and support throughout the project.

Our interviewees, who were mostly active duty and retired officers from across the military services, were incredibly generous with their time and candid views. Their perspectives were invaluable, and this report would not have been possible without their contributions.

We are grateful to the participants of the senior leader selection exercise held in January 2019, whose contributions helped us better understand service preferences for specific professional experiences and other personal characteristics, cultural equities in promotion processes, and overall management of promotion boards.

We are indebted to Bart Bennett, who provided candid and valuable feedback as this report's dedicated internal reviewer, as well as Tony Kurta and Chaitra Hardison, who also improved this report through their careful peer reviews. Inside RAND, we also thank Lisa Harrington, associate director of the Forces and Resources Policy Center; John Winkler, director of the Forces and Resources Policy Center; Christine Wormuth, director of the International Security and Defense Policy Center; and Agnes Schaefer, associate director of the International Security and Defense Policy Center, for providing guidance and support throughout the project. Finally, we thank Suzy Adler, who was instrumental in helping us access Defense Manpower Data Center data that were critical for this study, and Sarah Heintz and Kofi Amofa for assistance in preparing this report for final submission.

Abbreviations

ACC	Active Competitive Categories
ACC	Air Combat Command
ADP	Army Doctrinal Publication
AFDD	Air Force Doctrine Document
AFM	Air Force Manual
AFP	Air Force Pamphlet
AFPC	Air Force Personnel Center
AFSC	Air Force Specialty Code
AMEDD	U.S. Army Medical Department
BPZ	below the promotion zone
BZ	below the zone
CAG	Commander's Action Group
CCMD	combatant command
CDB	Career Designation Board
CGSC	Command and General Staff College
CJCS	Chairman of the Joint Chiefs of Staff
CNO	Chief of Naval Operations
COE	Center of Excellence
COMO	U.S. Army Colonels Management Office
CSAF	Chief of Staff of the Air Force
CSC	Marine Command and Staff College
CSL	centralized selection list
DMDC	Defense Manpower Data Center
DNP	Do Not Promote This Board
DoD	U.S. Department of Defense
DoDI	Department of Defense Instruction
DOPMA	Defense Officer Personnel Management Act
DP	definitely promote
E-JDA	Experiential Joint Duty Assignment
EOD	explosive ordnance disposal
EWS	Expeditionary Warfare School
FITREP	Fitness Report (Navy)
FitRep	Fitness Report (Marine Corps)
FO	flag officer
FY	fiscal year
GCC	geographic combatant command
GFM	Global Force Management
G/FO	general and flag officer

GO	general officer
GS	General Schedule
HQDA	Headquarters, Department of the Army
HQMC	Headquarters Marine Corps
HRC	U.S. Army Human Resources Command
IDE	Intermediate Developmental Education
ILE	intermediate-level education
IPZ	in the promotion zone
ISR	intelligence, surveillance, and reconnaissance
JAG	Judge Advocate General
JCS	Joint Chiefs of Staff
JCWS	Joint and Combined Warfighting School
JDAL	Joint Duty Assignment List
JOM	Joint Officer Management
JPME	joint professional military education
JQO	joint qualified officer
KD	key developmental
KSA	knowledge, skills, and abilities
LAAD	Low Altitude Air Defense
LAF	Line of the Air Force
MA	master of arts
MAGTF	Marine Air-Ground Task Force
MAJCOM	major command
MBA	master of business administration
MCDP	Marine Corps Doctrinal Publication
MCTP	Marine Corps Tactical Publication
MCWP	Marine Corps Warfighting Publication
MEB	Marine Expeditionary Brigade
MEF	Marine Expeditionary Force
MEU	Marine Expeditionary Unit
MOS	military occupational specialty
MPA	master of public administration
MS	master of science
NATO	North Atlantic Treaty Organization
NDAA	National Defense Authorization Act
NDS	National Defense Strategy
NEC	Navy Enlisted Code
NOBC	Navy Officer Billet Classification
NPS	Naval Postgraduate School
NROTC	Naval Reserve Officers Training Corps
NSC	National Security Council
OCLL	U.S. Army Office of the Chief Legislative Liaison

OCS	Officer Candidate School
OER	Officer Evaluation Record
OML	Order of Merit List
OPA	Officer Personnel Act
OPMF	Official Military Personnel File
OPR	Officer Performance Report
ORSA	Operations Research and Systems Analysis
OSD	Office of the Secretary of Defense
OTS	Officer Training School
P	Promote
Ph.D.	doctor of philosophy
PLC	Platoon Leaders Course
PME	professional military education
PRF	Promotion Recommendation Form
RL	restricted line
ROTC	Reserve Officer/Officers Training Corps
RS	Reporting Senior
RV	relative value
SAASS	U.S. Air Force School of Advanced Air and Space Studies
SAMS	U.S. Army School of Advanced Military Studies
SDE	senior developmental education
SEAL	Sea, Air, Land
SECNAVINST	Secretary of the Navy Instruction
SEI	Special Experience Identifier
S-JDA	Standard Joint Duty Assignment
SLSE	Senior Leader Selection Exercise
STEM	science, technology, engineering, and math
SWO	surface warfare officer
TBS	The Basic School
URL	unrestricted line
USAFA	U.S. Air Force Academy
USCENTCOM	U.S. Central Command
USEUCOM	U.S. European Command
USINDOPACOM	U.S. Indo-Pacific Command
USMA	U.S. Military Academy
USNA	U.S. Naval Academy
USNORTHCOM	U.S. Northern Command
USSOCOM	U.S. Special Operations Command
USTRANSCOM	U.S. Transportation Command
VCJCS	Vice Chairman of the Joint Chiefs of Staff
VCNO	Vice Chief of Naval Operations

1. Introduction

In 2018, the National Defense Strategy (NDS) redirected the U.S. Department of Defense (DoD) to prioritize countering near-peer adversaries and rogue states over the violent extremist organizations that have dominated the nation's attention for the past two decades. Underscoring this evolution, the NDS highlighted the essentiality of the human domain to achieve success over these adversaries, stating:

> Cultivating a lethal, agile force requires more than just new technologies and posture changes; it depends on the ability of our warfighters and the Department workforce to integrate new capabilities, adapt warfighting approaches, and change business practices to achieve mission success. The creativity and talent of the American warfighter is our greatest enduring strength, and one we do not take for granted.[7]

Further articulating the criticality of the human dimension in strategic competition, the NDS went on to stress the need for military leaders to keep pace with emerging technology in order to effectively counter malign actors, and highlighted the need to improve strategic decisionmaking abilities throughout DoD.[8] The NDS also claimed that professional military education (PME) has "stagnated, focused more on the accomplishment of mandatory credit at the expense of lethality and ingenuity" and noted that military educational experiences and professional assignments need to be revised accordingly.[9]

These themes reveal a growing recognition that, as the global security environment evolves and new challenges emerge, the United States might require substantially different military leadership approaches and perspectives in order to address them. General and flag officers (G/FOs), as the military's senior-most representatives, make decisions and provide counsel that have substantial bearing on the nation's security posture. Their experiences are shaped over decades of service, in large part by their professional experiences and unique service cultures.[10] The expectations, values, and perspectives gained through command and staff assignments, deployments, educational experiences, and more have fundamental effects on how officers will approach challenges, lead and manage institutions, and advise senior civilian leadership. These influences begin at the start of an officer's career and are reinforced over years of service. Thus,

---

[7] U.S. Department of Defense, *Summary of the 2018 National Defense Strategy of the United States of America: Sharpening the American Military's Competitive Edge*, Washington, D.C., 2018, pp. 7–8.

[8] U.S. Department of Defense, 2018, p. 8.

[9] U.S. Department of Defense, 2018, p. 8.

[10] S. Rebecca Zimmerman, Kimberly Jackson, Natasha Lander, Colin Roberts, Dan Madden, and Rebeca Orrie, *Movement and Maneuver: The Evolution of Service Culture and Competition*, Santa Monica, Calif.: RAND Corporation, RR-2270-OSD, 2019.

who the services develop and select today—and how—will directly affect who will lead in key service and joint positions in years to come.

Given the uncertainty of future challenges, it is impossible to know the precise characteristics and perspectives that might define highly effective military leaders years from now. However, the pivotal changes in the nature of strategic competition, the increasing adaptability required to counter U.S. adversaries, and the critical roles that G/FOs play in the design and execution of U.S. national security strategy give reason to ask: Are the military leaders being developed today the ones we will need in the future? This is a critical question to consider so that the services do not find themselves applying today's solutions to tomorrow's problems. As Paul Yingling wrote in 2007, "the most tragic error a general can make is to assume without much reflection that wars of the future will look much like wars of the past."[11]

Research Objective

To inform this notion that military leadership might need to change to better serve national security objectives, the Office of Net Assessment within the Office of the Secretary of Defense (OSD) asked RAND to analyze how the military services' approaches to personnel management might influence the ways in which G/FOs lead, manage, and advise at the strategic level.[12]

Specifically, our research objective was to analyze what professional experiences and other characteristics the services' G/FOs tend to share as a result of each service's approach to personnel management and other related factors, such as service culture.[13] This research then enabled us to examine how these characteristics and experiences might influence G/FO approaches to institutional leadership and management, and the type of strategic-level advice they might provide to civilian decisionmakers.[14]

We do not contend that all G/FOs within a specific service are identical; rather, we find that certain characteristics that are selected for and produced by service pathways are common, but

---

[11] Paul Yingling, "The Failure of Generalship," *Armed Forces Journal*, May 10, 2007.

[12] This study stems from previous RAND research, also conducted for OSD's Office of Net Assessment, which identified culture, goals, and competitive preferences of each of the military services, and analyzed the nature of the current state of inter-service competition (Zimmerman et al., 2019). A compelling theme emerging from that research was the role of personnel processes in defining and selecting service leaders, and how those processes both help shape and are reinforced by service culture.

[13] Other related factors include, for example, service core missions; warfighting tactics, techniques and procedures; service traditions; and resource management styles. Although leadership and management overlap, in this report we consider leadership to be primarily concerned with directing and motivating teams and personnel, whereas management is concerned with overseeing the processes that guide organizational operation. We define strategic leadership positions as those positions either within a service or at the joint level requiring both subject-matter expertise and an understanding of political and bureaucratic dynamics. For more information, see U.S. Army War College, Department of Command, Leadership and Management, *Strategic Leadership Primer*, 2nd edition, Carlisle Barracks, Pa., 2004.

[14] Civilian decisionmakers include, but are not limited to, the Secretary of Defense and the service secretaries.

not universal. Taken together, these pathways shape the broad contours of a service's G/FO corps and thereby influence both the direction of the force and the service's upward messages to senior defense leadership.

G/FOs are a product of each service's personnel system.[15] While G/FOs are certainly not interchangeable with more junior officers, their development is rooted in the same systems and processes. They carry the imprints of the values inculcated upon commissioning, the education received at various grades, the types of joint assignments they fill as mid-grade officers, and the characteristics they have seen reinforced at each level of promotion.

We focus on selection to O-7, but the larger question we examine is what sort of G/FOs these pipelines are producing for positions at higher grades, and specifically those critical and strategic positions at the O-9 and O-10 grades, within the services and in the joint environment. These positions, such as service chiefs, combatant commanders, major service component commanders, and others, have substantial bearing on the strategic focus of each of the services and the overall trajectory of DoD. The skills necessary to successfully execute the responsibilities of those positions are many but are often challenging to identify objectively in traditional personnel management processes. Consequently, the backgrounds and experiences of the G/FOs who tend to fill those positions are largely uniform, with some permutations, and tend to be heavily operationally focused and service-specific, which might not be ideally matched to the needs of the positions. As retired Lieutenant General David Barno noted in 2011 when commenting on the career fields of the Army's newest cadre of brigadier generals,

> We remain a military and a nation at war. Our combat commanders are carrying great weight in this long conflict, and their skills deserve our utmost respect and recognition. But their battlefield talents may not identically correlate with those skills that we will need in our future strategic leaders. Skilled tacticians are highly prized in the military culture, but they may or may not have the right "strategic DNA." These groups—great tacticians and great strategic leaders—are not identical, and they may not even overlap a great deal. And I'm not sure anyone knows.[16]

A Growing Emphasis on Senior Military Leader Development

The divergence between the needs of key strategic positions and the abilities of those selected by the services to fill them has sometimes been termed a mismatch by Congress, civilian experts, and some military officials, with potentially serious consequences.[17] Indeed, who makes

---

[15] Background on select service personnel basics including pay grade structure, end strength, and the size of the officer corps, and the distribution of officers across the services is in Appendix B.

[16] David Barno, "How One General Interprets the Army's Selection of New One-Stars: Too Much Infantry, and Way Too Many Exec Assts," *Foreign Policy*, June 9, 2011.

[17] See, for example, Major General Stephen L. Davis and William W. Casey, "A Model of Air Force Squadron Vitality," *Air and Space Power Journal*, January 2018; B. A. Friedman, "The End of the Fighting General," *Foreign*

and influences defense choices and priorities has a significant impact on the trajectory of foreign policy and, ultimately, on the nation's place in the world order.[18]

Further, this research comes at a time when the military is seeking transformation both to manage new strategic threats and to harness innovations in technology. In the Fiscal Year (FY) 2017 National Defense Authorization Act (NDAA), Congress mandated that DoD initiate reductions in G/FO positions, which included a requirement to cut 110 G/FO authorizations by December 2022, to conduct a review of G/FO requirements, and to identify an additional 10 percent reduction in authorizations.[19] This legislation came on the heels of DoD's 2015 Force of the Future initiatives, which applied to military personnel more broadly, and were intended to

> update and adapt the Department's active and reserve military and civilian personnel systems to account for new conditions affecting workforce markets, generational change, and innovative new practices in people and talent management, while retaining the professionalism, rigor, and tradition required for an institution charged with defending our Nation's interests.[20]

While the proposals stalled within DoD at the time, some were codified later as personnel management reforms in the FY 2019 NDAA. These provisions (along with the 1980 Defense Officer Personnel Management Act [DOPMA]), subsequent reform of DOPMA legislation, and other related legislative initiatives are discussed further in Appendix C.

This focus on military personnel management has entered the public domain, as well. Substantial discourse in academia and in the media, for example, has centered around military talent management and ways to improve current service personnel processes. For example, an Air Force colonel, writing under the pseudonym Ned Stark, stirred debate in *War on the Rocks* in 2018 and 2019 by writing candidly about the failures of the current Air Force talent management system.[21] Chief of Staff of the Air Force (CSAF) General David L. Goldfein responded publicly to the author, offering him a position in his own office.[22] Other debates have increasingly occurred at academic conferences and in op-eds nationwide on related topics, such as strategic

---

Policy, September 12, 2018; Robert H. Scales, "Ike's Lament: In Search of a Revolution in Military Affairs," *War on the Rocks,* August 16, 2017; and U.S. Senate, 115th Congress, S. Report 115-262 to S. 2987, the John S. McCain National Defense Authorization Act for Fiscal Year 2019, 2018; U.S. House of Representatives, 115th Congress, H. Report 115-676 to H.R. 5515, National Defense Authorization Act for Fiscal Year 2019, 2018.

[18] For example, leaders of the geographic combatant commands (GCC) almost always come from combat-focused career fields, but the requirements of some GCCs might mean that a regional specialist or a strategist, for example, would be better prepared for the position.

[19] Public Law 114-328, National Defense Authorization Act for Fiscal Year 2017, December 23, 2016, Sec. 501(c)(1).

[20] Ashton Carter, *Force of the Future: Maintaining Our Competitive Edge in Human Capital*, Washington, D.C.: U.S. Department of Defense, November 18, 2015.

[21] See Ned Stark, list of commentaries, *War on the Rocks*, undated. U.S. Air Force Colonel Jason Lamb later identified himself as Ned Stark.

[22] David L. Goldfein, "The Air Force Chief Responds: Keep Writing, Col. 'Ned Stark," and Join My Team," *War on the Rocks*, August 21, 2018.

thinking, reform of PME, and improving retention.[23] Additionally, each of the services is undertaking its own efforts to assess its approach to military personnel management, analysis that is prompted in part by the changes authorized in the FY 2019 NDAA. While these efforts are too new for us to assess what effects they will have on how senior leaders are developed, we consider their potential impact throughout the report.

Scope and Limitations

This study focuses on the major personnel management processes in the Army, Navy, Air Force, and Marine Corps that help shape the perspectives and experiences of each service's G/FOs. Because this research was intended to be exploratory in nature, we do not seek to analyze all potential aspects of the military experience that might influence an officer's worldview, but instead to identify common service approaches and experiences in a typical officer's career pathway. While other institutions and processes certainly have bearing on the nature and characteristics of each of the services' G/FOs, such as recruitment activities, they are beyond the scope of this report. We also do not seek to quantify the level of influence that career experiences and other characteristics have on a G/FO's decisionmaking, leadership, and management approaches. Instead, we aim to identify which experiences and characteristics are common among G/FOs, and how these common experiences and characteristics might shape a hypothetical G/FO's advice and approaches to leadership and management. We accomplish this using logical inference from a set of reasonable assumptions. However, we do not have empirical data with which to test these hypotheses. Therefore, the archetypes' approaches to leadership, management, and the advice we identify in Chapter 8, while reasonable, are hypotheses that should be empirically verified in future research.

In this analysis, we focus on personnel processes up to the grade of O-7, for two specific reasons. First, the distinction between O-6 and O-7 is substantial and is far more than a simple promotion. It is an extremely competitive promotion: 40.8 percent of O-5s across the services promote to O-6, but the overall promotion rate from O-6 to O-7 drops to 7.2 percent. The overall promotion rate between O-7 and O-8 then increases to 67.2 percent.[24] However, many of our interviewees and representatives in the Senior Leader Selection Exercise (SLSE) we designed to

---

[23] See, for example, David Barno, Nora Bensahel, Katherine Kidder, and Kelley Sayler, *Building Better Generals*, Washington, D.C.: Center for A New American Security, 2013; Colonel Casey Wardynski, Colonel David S. Lyle, and Michael J. Colarusso, *Talent: Implications for a U.S. Army Officer Corps Strategy*, West Point, N.Y.: U.S. Army War College Strategic Studies Institute, October 28, 2009; Paula Thornhill, "To Produce Strategists, Focus on Staffing Senior Leaders," *War on the Rocks*, July 20, 2018; Major Steven T. Nolan, Jr., and Robert E. Overstreet, "Improving How the Air Force Develops High-Performing Officers," *Air and Space Power Journal*, Summer 2018, pp. 21–36.

[24] Authors' analysis of Defense Manpower Data Center (DMDC) data. These promotion rates represent the percentage of officers that eventually go on to make the next higher grade. The chance that an officer will be promoted in any given year, however, is lower than these numbers suggest, given that officers are considered for promotion across multiple annual promotion cycles.

support our research spoke about preferences and patterns that often remain with officers beyond O-7. To a more limited degree, we include these perspectives when they are particularly distinctive.

We also focus on the *primary* pathways in each service to O-7, rather than all pathways. Officers from many career fields in each service have the ability to be promoted to G/FO grades, but we have focused on the most common pathways that result in promotion to at least O-7, because senior civilians will most often interact with and be advised by these types of officers.

We did not analyze some professional experiences that interviewees and the literature identified as critical to understanding service pathways to generalship because of the limitations in the data that were available to us (e.g., years spent in joint positions, civilian education, specific assignments).[25] Analysis of these factors would provide greater insight into additional professional experiences that each service does and does not value, their relationship to becoming a G/FO, and the effect such experiences have on advice and leadership and management styles. Further, while demographic characteristics such as age, race, socioeconomic background, and gender could affect G/FO development and promotion, they are not within the scope of this report.[26] We did not fully analyze the effect of combat experience on officer development, given that officers at lower grades during the wars in Iraq and Afghanistan will not be eligible for promotion to G/FO for years to come. Also, because we were not able to obtain completed evaluation reports, we could not analyze the comments sections on these forms. We understand that critical information is imparted in these sections, so further analysis of what language is particularly valued in those "blocks" would be very useful.

In terms of our quantitative data analysis, we were limited in only having access to Defense Manpower Data Center (DMDC) data; we could not access any service data (discussed further in Chapter 2). This means that discrepancies might exist between the DMDC data we used and other data collected by the services. Further, we acknowledge that some data might be dependent—for example, career field and attendance at certain specialty schools. We attempted to explain these dependent relationships throughout each of the service chapters, and we also attempted to control for it in our profile testing, as explained in Appendix E.

Further, the effects of certain factors with potentially substantial impact on G/FO development and selection are extremely challenging to measure objectively, such as personal relationships and networks in promotion decisions, certain personality traits, race and gender, and the role of good timing. We address these factors throughout our analysis, but we were not able to assess them in a way that enabled us to fully account for their true significance and

---

[25] Throughout the report, we use the term *generalship* inclusively to refer to general and flag officers in each DoD service: generals in the Army, Air Force, and Marine Corps and admirals in the Navy.

[26] Susan D. Hosek, Peter Tiemeyer, M. Rebecca Kilburn, Debra A. Strong, Selika Ducksworth, Reginald Ray. *Minority and Gender Differences in Officer Career Progression*, Santa Monica, Calif.: RAND Corporation, MR-1184-OSD, 2001, p. 23.

effects on officer career paths. Additional research could provide valuable insights into how these factors affect G/FO promotion.

Significantly, this study is focused on how a service selects an officer for G/FO, not how an officer decides whether to stay in the service or retire or separate. While we cover factors that might affect this decision briefly in each service chapter, this decision merits further research beyond the scope of this report. We also focus only on the DoD military services, thereby excluding the Coast Guard. This study also does not specifically focus on G/FO pathways in the special operations communities of each service. However, the dynamics introduced by distinct cultures within each of those communities, and the role U.S. Special Operations Command (USSOCOM) plays in personnel management, might have substantial effects on special operations G/FOs and make a unique and compelling case for future research.

While we refer to the traits, experiences, and abilities that specific key service and joint positions require or benefit from, it is beyond the scope of this report to identify what those specific positions are, and the qualifications and other characteristics that those positions require. Such an analysis would provide greater insight into the existence and nature of a supply-demand mismatch.

Finally, it is not the intent of this study to provide value judgments or cross-service comparisons on which service produces the "best" G/FOs or recommend ways DoD can improve its personnel processes and G/FO development efforts—though the results of this analysis could inform changes to those processes. Our research allows us to characterize the approaches to generalship the services employ, analyze how culture and other factors are reflected in those approaches, and identify the common characteristics, behaviors, and experiences observed in each service's G/FO cadre. We also do not seek to predict future G/FO profiles; we are only providing impressions of the profiles of archetypical G/FOs if current pathways are unchanged.

Implications for Officer Development in the U.S. Military

By detailing processes and preferences surrounding officer development and G/FO selection, this report allows senior service, joint, and civilian leaders to understand whether there is a gap between the characteristics and experiences for which their processes currently select and the characteristics and experiences they might want and need in the future. Both the means of selection and the ends they are selected for have strong subjective components, and therefore it is difficult to be prescriptive. The range of leadership roles for senior military leaders varies so greatly—from combat leadership to institutional leadership, political deftness, and vision-setting—that it would be challenging to make a single judgment about whether attributes of G/FOs fall short of the intended mark.[27] Despite these challenges, this report provides critical

[27] Robert H. Scales, *Are You a Strategic Genius?: Not Likely, Given Army's System for Selecting, Educating Leaders*, Arlington, Va.: Association of the United States Army, October 13, 2016.

information that the services and DoD overall can use to assess whether their current approaches to G/FO development need to be adjusted to ensure that G/FOs develop the skills and experiences that they might need to meet an evolving global strategic environment.

With renewed focus on major institutional reform to reshape G/FO management and military personnel processes overall, now is the time to understand more deeply how the services produce G/FOs, and how they select—consciously or not—for professional experiences and other characteristics. By drawing these factors into the light, senior decisionmakers can best ensure that their reforms succeed in building the G/FOs needed by the services, the joint force, and the nation.

The findings in this report also provide perspective on how the different service cultures are reflected in G/FO promotion and, in turn, how these officers might approach senior leadership roles. It provides an overall introduction to the types of officers who are promoted and the potential tendencies of those officers as decisionmakers and advisers, which we believe can be useful to senior leaders. Of course, each G/FO is an individual and cannot be fully characterized by the culture and processes of promotion to O-7 and above, so these results should not be applied to every G/FO.

Organization of This Report

The remainder of this report provides details of our analyses and their results, beginning in Chapter 2 with an overview of our research approach. Chapter 3 reviews basic concepts of military personnel management processes and compares certain career experiences across the services. In Chapters 4 through 7, we focus on the pathways to generalship and common G/FO professional experiences and characteristics in the Army, Navy, Air Force, and Marine Corps, respectively. Finally, in Chapter 8, we present our conclusions and service archetypes, and what their common training and experiences, combined with other factors such as service culture, might mean for how they approach G/FO management and advisory roles. Appendixes detail the types of DMDC data we analyzed, basic military personnel concepts and data, key legislation guiding military personnel policy, G/FO management processes, and methodology and findings from the SLSE.

2. Research Approach

To conduct this research, the study team used a mixed-methods approach combining qualitative and quantitative analyses which drew on numerous data sources, including a review of relevant literature; interviews with active duty and retired military officers and civilian and military subject-matter experts; a RAND-led SLSE; available G/FO biographies; and an analysis of personnel data from the DMDC.

This chapter describes the data sources and the steps in our methodology. It details how we researched the services' personnel processes and the characteristics they tend to value, and how this research was used to develop notional profiles, or "archetypes," of current G/FOs in each service. Further, we discuss the role of organizational culture in military officer development processes.

Data Sources

Each data source supported multiple steps of our research approach. We identified the common professional experiences and other characteristics among each service's G/FOs by looking across the data from multiple sources, rather than using one data source for a particular characteristic. Our analysis was based on the following sources.

Literature Reviews

We conducted a review of more than 100 academic publications on officer personnel management processes and linkages between professional experiences and career outcomes, official DoD and service guidance and doctrine, other official service publications, and news articles and commentary to augment our understanding of the types of characteristics and career experiences each service values.

Interviews

We conducted 37 semistructured interviews with current and former officers ranging from O-4 to O-9, civilian subject-matter experts, and representatives from each of the services' G/FO management offices.[28] Military interviewees included officers who were promoted to O-7 or higher with typical paths, officers who were promoted to O-7 or higher following atypical paths, officers who were not promoted to O-7 but had wanted to be, active duty field-grade officers identified as "high potential" for G/FO selection, and military personnel specialists. We selected

---

[28] All relevant Human Subjects Protection Committee protocols were followed in the conduct of our interviews. The breakdown of our interviews by service is as follows: Army (11), Navy (7), Air Force (10), Marine Corps (9).

interviewees based on position, expertise, and/or their ability to represent these different populations. The interview protocol is in Appendix F. While our interviewers attempted to adhere to the protocol when possible, they tended to speak broadly and passionately about these topics. Accordingly, we found that many of our interviewee responses concerned related topics about which we did not initially ask, such as the ways in which service G/FOs lead, manage, and advise, and how career experiences influence those factors; the value of jointness by service; and how certain factors whose effects are difficult to measure might affect promotions. It was further useful to our research to understand which topics interviewees tended to focus on, as interesting patterns emerged by service that informed our understanding of how service culture affects personnel processes. For example, the majority of Air Force interviewees discussed the importance of being a fighter pilot and attending specialty schools, whereas most Marine Corps interviewees stressed that promotions are based not on particular assignments or networks, but rather merit alone.

We analyzed interview notes and used them to provide examples of certain trends we identified through our other sources. In this report, we use interview quotes to underscore a point derived from multiple sources, rather than to highlight one interviewee's experience. We highlight interviewee quotes and personal experiences from military officers wherever possible. This is in response to our sponsor's direction that we explore and capture perspectives from the individuals who are most directly affected by service approaches to officer development. These quotes and perspectives lend depth to our analysis, but we do not imply that one individual's impressions necessarily constitute fact. However, it is important to note that, in some cases, perception might weigh heavier than facts since actions—such as an officer's decision not to pursue a nonstandard assignment because the officer believes it will negatively affect their chances of promotion, for example—are often based on perceptions.

Because the number of interviews was small, we were able to analyze interviews without utilizing a formal coding mechanism.

Senior Leader Selection Exercise

We conducted a SLSE to test our archetype profiles that we created using our other data sources. In addition to the SLSE being a step in our methodology, as described later in this chapter, data collected from the SLSE discussion sessions also informed our overall analysis.

The SLSE included 30 retired O-6s the G/FOs from each of the services, and the exercise consisted of three separate stages in which participants were asked to rank profiles of notional O-6s for promotion to O-7. Participants' choices, both as individuals and as part of a group, enabled us to test and refine our archetype profiles, and facilitated discussion between stages about these choices generated considerable information about why the individuals and groups made the choices they did. During these discussions, we posed specific questions that were relevant for understanding selections in each stage, and for validation of the service-specific analyses. These questions concerned topics such as which indicators mattered most and least to the participants, which factors should have been included but were not, whether the constraints posed in subsequent stages affected a participant's ranking of notional profiles, and the degree to which participants identified elements of their own career paths within the notional profiles.

Participants' experience and knowledge of service culture, preferences, and processes enhanced our understanding of key factors for promotion to G/FO, such as service promotion board proceedings, the impact of service culture on personnel processes, and specific characteristics valued in promotion decisions. Further, SLSE participants shared valuable insights we had not previously identified from other sources that helped to refine our service profiles.

Although not the topic of our formal questions during the SLSE, discussion during the SLSE elicited useful information about how service G/FOs approach strategic advice, leadership, and management and how those approaches are affected by career experiences, preparation to perform in interagency environments, value of joint assignments and jointness overall, and reflections of service culture in personnel processes.

The SLSE is further discussed later in the methodology section of this chapter and in detail in Appendix E.

DMDC Personnel Data Files

To supplement our qualitative data sources, we conducted quantitative analyses of DMDC data. DMDC is the repository of record for administrative information relating to service members. It provides de-identified data points for service members over the life of their service. DMDC data include individual attributes, such as gender and marital status, as well as service-related experiences, such as assigned units and entry into service dates. Our analysis drew from the DMDC Active Duty Master File to show descriptive trends across a number of career experiences in each service, such as time in grade, commissioning source, career field, and special training. We interpreted the DMDC data as the entire population (rather than a sample) of all officers over the period of time of interest (those individuals promoted to G/FO between 2008 and 2018). Thus, we determined that statistical inference is unnecessary, as the differences within the entire population are in and of themselves meaningful.

Appendix A contains a detailed discussion of the specific data used in this analysis.

G/FO Biographies

We conducted a semistructured review of publicly available, official G/FO biographies to understand service G/FO characteristics that were not in the DMDC data. The information available in these biographies varied by service but generally included information on specific awards, command positions, and certain schooling. Analysis focused on current G/FO biographies and was primarily based on manual reviews of biography text. We augmented manual reviews with keyword searches to identify the proportion of G/FOs whose biographies mentioned specific assignments, awards, trainings, or other topics of interest, such as "Pacific

Fleet" or "brigade commander." We validated keywords used in these searches through manual review to ensure inclusion of all relevant terms, such as both "CSG" and "carrier strike group," when examining a particular topic.

Methodology

To accomplish this research and develop our conclusions, we adopted the four-step, mixed-methods approach shown in Figure 2.1. Although these steps are numbered, the actual research was not linear and involved feedback between steps:

1. Characterize service personnel processes and identify common experiences by analyzing education, training, assignments, evaluation, and promotion processes.
2. Identify how service culture is reflected in service personnel processes.
3. Develop G/FO archetypes based on steps 1 and 2, using qualitative and quantitative analyses of professional experiences and other characteristics.
4. Test notional archetype profiles using the SLSE.

Using the results of these analyses and information gleaned from relevant literature, interviews, and the SLSE, we then developed conclusions about how experiences and service approaches might shape G/FOs' approaches to institutional leadership and management, and strategic-level advice. Figure 2.1 illustrates how methodology and data sources informed our analysis.

Figure 2.1. Methodology Steps and Use of Sources

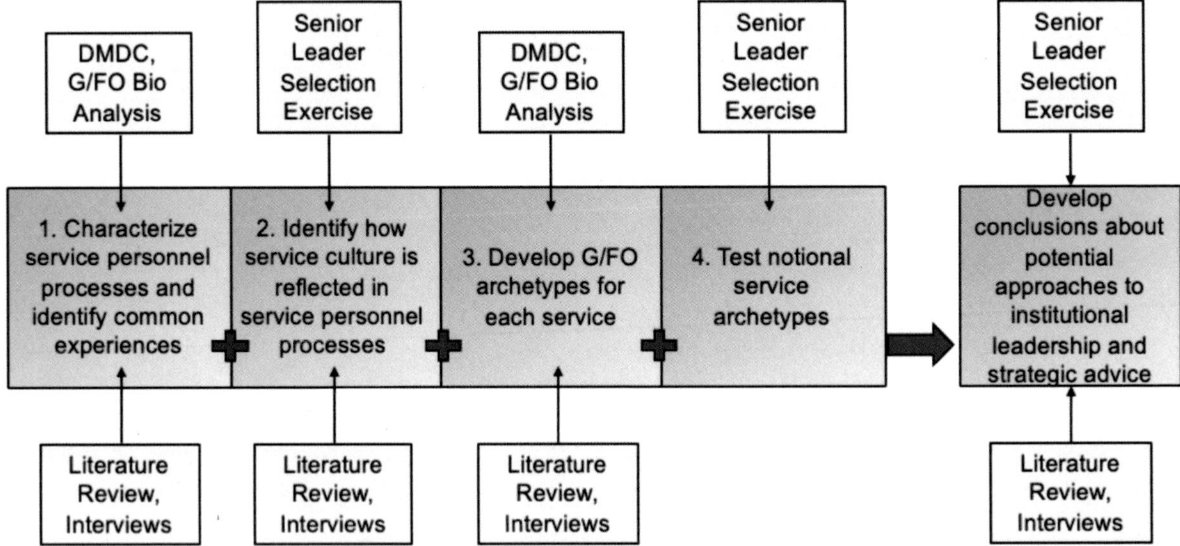

NOTE: DMDC = Defense Manpower Data Center.

Characterize Service Personnel Processes and Identify Common Career Experiences

We focused first on capturing the mechanics of service personnel processes by which officers in each service are developed and promoted to the grade of O-7. In Chapter 3, we provide general information on each of these processes as they relate to all services. These processes include

- commissioning source
- duty assignments
- education
- special training
- evaluations
- promotions.

Then, we conducted analyses of each service's *specific* personnel management processes and approach to developing senior officers. Through these analyses, we identified what professional experiences and other characteristics tend to be common among each service's G/FOs and how service personnel processes select for and develop those attributes. During this process, we also identified other factors that matter in service G/FO selection but whose effects are more difficult to measure (such as personality and networks), and we gained perspectives from literature, the SLSE, and interviewees on the impacts of these processes on service G/FOs. The professional experiences and other characteristics we analyzed by service include

- career field
- time in grade
- years in service
- commissioning source
- PME and civilian education
- special training
- duty assignments (including leadership experience, broadening and joint experience, deployment experience, and high-visibility assignments)
- other factors, such as additional certifications.

To understand these service personnel management processes and their possible impacts, we consulted service-specific regulations, DoD guidance and directives, active duty officers, and retired officers, publications written by civilian personnel experts, interviews with military and civilian subject-matter experts, and the SLSE to understand service preferences in senior leader selection. Further, we analyzed official service guidance on leadership and officer development and assessed each service's philosophical approach to officer development. We also augmented our qualitative findings by analyzing DMDC data to better understand certain factors, such as a service's tendency to promote officers early.

Each service analysis was led by one member of our team, and the entire team engaged regularly in collaborative discussions to share resources and insights that had implications for other service leads. For example, many interviewees from one service often noted their views of another, which service analysis leads shared with each other. The principal investigator routinely reviewed the progress of each service analysis to identify gaps or areas of additional research that all service leads could pursue. We then utilized findings and observations from the SLSE, as well as DMDC data analysis, to validate the information in the service-specific chapters.

Identify How Service Culture Is Reflected in Service Personnel Processes

As we characterized service personnel processes and identified common career experiences and other characteristics in each service, we also identified how aspects of service culture are reflected in, and often reinforced by, personnel management systems. Using the data sources described above, we identified key cultural attributes across each service and analyzed where those attributes were apparent in service personnel management processes. The most significant elements of culture we considered that informed our research were[29]

- major service defining characteristics
- competitive goals
- behavior in arenas of competition
- preferred arenas of competition
- preferred tactics of competition.

We included these reflections of service culture, along with characterizations of service personnel processes and common professional characteristics, in service-specific chapters (Chapters 4 through 7).

Develop G/FO Archetypes for Each Service

The integrated findings from steps 1 and 2 served as the basis for our second task. Using the common professional experiences and other characteristics identified through our service-specific analyses, including perspectives gained from a semistructured review of publicly available G/FO biographies, review of relevant literature, and interviewees, we developed G/FO "archetypes" at the grade of O-7 for each service that we further refined based on discussion and profile validation from the SLSE. Each archetype describes a notional profile composed of the most common characteristics for each service that we identified throughout the course of our research.

Although officers' career experiences and other characteristics—and how those experiences might influence an officer's leadership, management, and advising style—vary, these archetypes were useful to distill the information we had gained throughout our research into notional units of analysis by service.

---

[29] Our definition of "the most significant elements of culture" is largely based on our preceding work on this topic; see Zimmerman et al., 2019. Within the industrial/organizational psychology literature, culture can be defined as "what 'has worked' in the experience of a society that was worth transmitting to future generations" (Harry C. Triandis, "Individualism-Collectivism and Personality," *Journal of Personality*, Vol. 69, No. 6, 2001, p. 908).

The O-7 archetypes for each service, as well as our analysis of how they might influence institutional leadership and advice, are presented in Chapter 8.

Test Service Archetypes Using a Senior Leader Selection Exercise

As noted in the data sources section of this chapter, we developed the SLSE to socialize and validate the project's in-progress findings regarding how the services value certain professional experiences and other characteristics in O-7 promotion. Specifically, we used this exercise to determine whether SLSE participants (retired officers in the grades of O-6 to O-9 from each service) would make the same selection decisions that we would expect based on our research. We developed 50 notional senior O-6 candidate profiles per service, representing a wide range of realistic professional experiences and training based on our understanding of common career pathways and other characteristics. We then asked participants to rank profiles for "promotion" in three separate exercise stages. In Stage 1, individual participants ranked profiles from 1 to 50 without quotas or other constraints. In Stage 2, individual participants again selected profiles, but were limited to selecting only ten, under service-specific constraints akin to quotas. In the third stage, service-specific groups of participants selected ten notional profiles. The findings from these stages largely confirmed the characteristics and experiences we had identified in each of the service profiles.

As noted earlier in the "Data Sources" section, we also facilitated discussion between each stage of the SLSE to better understand the participants' choices. This feedback helped us to refine our archetype profiles and identify aspects of personnel processes we had not previously considered.

While this exercise was not intended to provide scientific validity to overall study findings or necessarily mimic true board proceedings, it also allowed us to refine our archetype profiles, compare how military services value different professional experiences and other characteristics of senior officers, and observe how unique cultural characteristics of the services factored into decisions. A more fulsome description of the structure of and findings from the SLSE is provided in Appendix E.

Develop Conclusions

Finally, using these archetypes built from our service-specific analysis, and also informed by our analysis of literature, interviews, and the SLSE, we developed our conclusions about how typical career experiences and other characteristics might shape the ways officers in each service could approach institutional leadership and management, and the type of advice they might provide to civilian decisionmakers, such as the Secretary of Defense or the service secretaries. We also assessed potential future changes to G/FOs by service based on emerging trends, and compare the importance of specific experiences and characteristics across the services.

Assumptions

To develop service archetypes, we relied on assumptions grounded in common themes within the literature, the data, our interviews, and the SLSE. Officers are accessed, educated, trained, evaluated, selected, and promoted within a closed system, which communicates each service's values through both expressed and implied means. We therefore assume that officers are shaped by their service's desired skills, traits, attributes, and experiences through explicit guidance *and* by observing the characteristics of those selected for promotion to G/FO. We assume that officers are provided with the necessary training and education to succeed within their service and career field, but that intangible factors (and the assignment to specific career fields themselves) influence officers' potential for selection to G/FO. Further, because future G/FOs are selected by current G/FOs, we assume that certain characteristics are likely to be replicated in those newly selected for G/FO; the analysis provided within this report is intended to identify which of those characteristics are consistently replicated among those selected for promotion to G/FO. Because some characteristics are consistently replicated within the services' G/FO corps, we assume that those consistently replicated characteristics provide information regarding the strengths (and potential weaknesses) that each services' archetypical G/FO may possess. Based on the literature, interviews, and SLSE, we assume that experience within an officer's service is more highly valued for promotion by the service than experience outside of the service, whether through broadening or joint assignments.

One of our key assumptions is that the way an officer is trained, educated, and gains experience through a service's personnel management system at more junior grades will likely be reflected in the ways the individual leads, manages, and advises as a senior officer. For example, we assume that a lack of training in and exposure to strategic analysis could mean that a G/FO's advice would not rely heavily on strategic analysis. We also assume that tactical training (and selection for promotion based on tactical performance) might lead to an officer being more likely to rely on tactical solutions, even beyond the tactical level. Third, few or no assignments in civilian environments and/or nonservice assignments might lead to officers who are either initially uncomfortable or underprepared when the officer arrives at an interagency, policy, and/or civilian organization.

Lastly, we caveat our assumptions by emphasizing that the archetypes are not intended to perfectly predict future trends. Rather, our research indicates that if status quo procedures remain in place, future G/FO skills, traits, and experiences are likely to strongly resemble current G/FOs, particularly because the G/FOs of the future are already being developed and selected today.

We do not claim that every G/FO in each service will advise, lead, and manage in the ways that we detail in Chapter 8; we instead highlight the potential characteristics of an officer who is exposed to the same experiences, processes, and culture as the service archetypes. The analysis relies directly on the development of the archetype profiles themselves, augmented with insight into the leadership approaches that might characterize the archetypical G/FO drawn from our data sources. Our conclusions about archetypical leadership and management approaches and advice to senior civilian leaders, while logically derived from the service profiles and these assumptions, are hypotheses that should be empirically verified in future research.

The Role of Organizational Culture in Service Approaches to Senior Leader Development

One of the premises of this report is that each service's culture is reflected and reinforced by the service's personnel processes. Thus, before delving into the discussions of officer characteristics within each service, we briefly explore the relationship between military culture and personnel policies.

What accounts for the differing paths to generalship among the military services? Certainly, the differing roles, missions, and sizes of the services necessitate unique approaches. But these factors do not appear to fully account for the observable differences in who becomes a G/FO and who does not. Rather, at least to some degree, these seem to be the result of different preferences and priorities of each of the military services linked to their organizational cultures. In this study, we treat organizational culture as a factor in the services' approaches to officer management that affects the way officers are developed and which officers are promoted. In turn, those who are developed and promoted have the ability to both uphold and amend (however slowly) the service culture from which they arose. This accounts both for the generally "sticky" nature of service preferences and for resilience to changes in response to external shocks. In this section, we explore the scholarly underpinnings of this view of the relationship between organizational culture and officer development and promotion.

The study of military organizational culture has a long academic history, both as a subject of inquiry in its own right and as an explanatory factor for other phenomena. In his landmark book *Bureaucracy*, James Q. Wilson described organizational culture as

> The situations they [employees] encounter, . . . their prior experiences and personal beliefs, the expectations of their peers, the array of interests in which their agency is embedded, and the impetus given to the organization by its founders. . . . These factors combine to produce an organizational culture—a distinctive way of viewing and reacting to the bureaucratic world—that shapes whatever discretionary authority . . . the operators may have.[30]

This description treats organizational culture as evolutionary—guiding the activities and preferences of individuals inside an organization, but not fixed in time. This is consistent with the work of Carl H. Builder, as well as recent RAND research on military culture, both of which

[30] James Wilson, *Bureaucracy: What Government Agencies Do and Why They Do It*, New York: Basic Books, 1989, p. 27.

find that services are powerful actors with a high degree of discretionary authority that is exercised according to preferences that are largely culturally determined.[31]

Often, service culture serves to fend off change. Since today's G/FOs control the promotion of future G/FOs, they can, as military sociologist Morris Janowitz observed, create "more or less clear-cut images of what constitutes the ideal career for the aspiring professional officer. More often than not, these images are firmly rooted in past experiences."[32] The continuity created by this dynamic, with subsequent generations selected for their similarity to previous cohorts, allows the military services to each maintain distinctive personalities that partly account for their ability to remain powerful independent actors inside the defense enterprise.

In the presence of changing external factors, however, personnel processes might become engines of slow change to service personalities. Shifts in institutional structure have the potential to affect service relationships and preferences, as seen in the strengthened role of OSD and the combatant commanders after the 1986 Goldwater-Nichols Department of Defense Reorganization Act (commonly known as Goldwater-Nichols),[33] which had follow-on effects in terms of the prestige of certain joint leadership positions.[34] And, as Erik Riker-Coleman demonstrated, the experience of Vietnam changed the G/FO corps, its preferences for the use of military power, and the type of advice it provided to policymakers, most evident when young Vietnam veterans rose to senior G/FO positions.[35] However, as Stephen P. Rosen notes, these changes must be accompanied by changes in the "structure of promotions" and occur "only as fast as the rate at which young officers rise to the top."[36]

Personality Traits, Experiences, and Abilities

The G/FO profiles that emerge from this research are rooted in observable characteristics largely composed of professional career experiences. However, in analyzing broad service approaches to generalship, we also discuss preferences for less measurable characteristics that were described in the SLSE, in interviews, and in literature.

---

[31] Carl Builder, *The Masks of War: American Military Styles in Strategy and Analysis,* Baltimore, Md.: Johns Hopkins University Press, 1989, p. 3; Zimmerman et al., 2019, p. 6.

[32] Morris Janowitz, *The Professional Soldier: A Social and Political Portrait*, New York: The Free Press, 1971, p. 148.

[33] Public Law 99–433, The Goldwater-Nichols Department of Defense Reorganization Act of 1986, October 1, 1986.

[34] Zimmerman et al., 2019, p. xii.

[35] Erik Blaine Riker-Coleman, *"Positions of Importance and Responsibility": U.S. Four-Star Military Leaders in a Changing World, 1968–2000*, dissertation, University of North Carolina, 2006, pp. 545–565.

[36] Stephen Peter Rosen, *Winning the Next War: Innovation and the Modern Military*, Ithaca, N.Y.: Cornell University Press, 1991, p. 105.

While each of the services approaches generalship differently, they nevertheless share the view that G/FOs should embody the best leadership qualities in their service. The desired traits of G/FOs are often described using intangible terms such as *trust*, *character*, and *integrity*. These traits are difficult to characterize and to measure, so it is challenging to determine definitively whether or not each service actually selects G/FOs with the traits that it says it wants. For example, each service prizes command (easily observable in an officer's assignment history), but some service processes rely more heavily than others on an officer's less observable personal connections, a concept David W. Moore and B. Thomas Trout call "visibility."[37]

In this section, we discuss the types of characteristics that form a full officer archetype and the degree to which these are discernable from service approaches to generalship. In this report, when we refer to G/FO archetypes or G/FO profiles, we are generally speaking about a constellation of common *personality traits*, *experiences*, and *abilities* possessed by a representative model service member. These terms, defined extensively in the psychology literature, are not interchangeable. Of note, throughout this report we use other, broader terms—*characteristics* and *attributes*—to refer to the collection of these traits, experiences, and abilities together.

Personality Traits

Personality traits are "an individual's characteristic patterns of thought, emotion, and behavior, together with the psychological mechanisms—hidden or not—behind those patterns."[38] Traits are stable over time.[39] Traits are the inherent qualities of the individual, such as those described by the so-called Big Five personality traits: extraversion, agreeableness, conscientiousness, neuroticism, and openness to experience.[40] Not all traits affect performance equally; for example, meta-analyses demonstrate that conscientiousness and emotional stability "predict performance outcomes in many, if not all, jobs," while agreeableness, extraversion, and openness to experience may be related to success in some (but not all) jobs.[41]

---

[37] David W. Moore and B. Thomas Trout, "Military Advancement: The Visibility Theory of Promotion," *American Political Science Review*, Vol. 72, No. 2, 1978, pp. 452–468.

[38] David C. Funder, *The Personality Puzzle*, 2nd edition, New York: Norton, 2001, p. 2.

[39] Gerald Saucier and Lewis R. Goldberg, "The Structure of Personality Attributes," in Murray R. Barrick and Ann Marie Ryan, eds., *Personality and Work: Reconsidering the Role of Personality in Organizations*, San Francisco, Calif.: Jossey-Bass, 2003, p. 2.

[40] Robert R. McCrae, Paul T. Costa, Jr., and Catherine M. Busch, "Evaluating Comprehensiveness in Personality Systems: The California Q-Set and the Five Factor Model," *Journal of Personality*, Vol. 54, No. 2, June 1986, pp. 431–446.

[41] Murray R. Barrick, Terence R. Mitchell, and Greg L. Stewart, "Situational and Motivational Influences on Trait-Behavior Relationships," in Murray R. Barrick and Anne Marie Ryan, eds., Personality and Work: Reconsidering the Role of Personality in Organizations, Vol. 20, John Wiley & Sons, 2004, p. 60; Leatta M. Hough and Adrian Furnham, "Use of Personality Variables in Work Settings," in Walter C. Borman, Daniel R. Ilgen, and Richard J. Klimoski, eds., *Handbook of Psychology*, Vol. 12: *Industrial and Organizational Psychology*, Hoboken, N.J.: John Wiley & Sons, 2003.

While the definition of *traits* above describes internal attributes, *traits* can also refer to external attributes. For example, personal attractiveness and "the reactions of others to the individual as a stimulus" may also be described as traits.[42] As we will later explore in this report, appearance and the perception of a person's ability to compel the behavior of subordinates, peers, and even superiors are important traits within the military services.

Extant literature addresses the possibility that organizations are "relatively homogeneous with respect to the personality characteristics of the people in them."[43] The research builds on previously tested hypotheses indicating that people within a given organization are "unique in that they are the ones attracted to, chosen by, and who choose to remain with an organization."[44] In relation to service cultures, it can therefore be presumed that individuals drawn to, selected by, and retained by each service share a certain number and type of values and traits. The literature further acknowledges two types of assessed traits within performance evaluation: maximal performance (what an individual is capable of) and typical performance (what an individual will do on a daily basis).[45] Maximal performance factors include such factors as math and verbal abilities, physical abilities, and specific experience, while typical performance factors relate more to the Big Five dimensions listed above and matters of "personality and integrity."[46] As will be explored in the following chapters, the dynamics regarding the importance of both maximal and typical performance factors matter to varying degrees across the services and among different ranks.

Some traits are easily correlated to service values; for example, as we will explore later in this report, the Navy values self-reliance consistent with its history of command at sea. However, while these personality traits might be important to job performance, they can be difficult to accurately represent in research, and even harder to reliably identify in the promotions process. For example, the Navy might believe it is selecting for self-reliance but not actually have a good method for evaluating and measuring it. Traits are believed to be largely innate and relatively static, but some research has shown that personality can change over time.[47]

By virtue of being largely unobservable, both to researchers and to those involved in the promotions process, personality traits are thus among the most difficult officer characteristics to incorporate into the analytic process. Where we have done so, it is in the narrative

---

[42] Saucier and Goldberg, 2003, p. 2.

[43] Benjamin Schneider, D. Brent Smith, Sylvester Taylor, and John Fleenor, "Personality and Organizations: A Test of the Homogeneity of Personality Hypothesis," *Journal of Applied Psychology*, Vol. 83, No. 3, 1998, p. 462.

[44] Benjamin Schneider, "The People Make the Place," *Personnel Psychology*, Vol. 40, No. 3, 1987, pp. 437–454.

[45] Neal Schmitt, Jose M. Cortina, Michael J. Ingerick, and Darin Wiechmann, "Personnel Selection and Employee Performance," in Walter C. Borman, Daniel R. Ilgen, and Richard J. Klimoski, eds., *Handbook of Psychology:* Vol. 12, *Industrial and Organizational Psychology*, Hoboken, N.J.: John Wiley & Sons, 2003, pp. 77–98.

[46] Schmitt et al., 2003, pp. 77–78; Anne Anastasi, "Evolving Trait Concepts," *American Psychologist*, Vol. 38, No. 2, 1983, pp. 175–184.

[47] See, for example, Romeo Vitelli, "Can You Change Your Personality?" *Psychology Today*, September 7, 2015.

characterizations of the services' approaches to promotion, based on the responses of interviewees about what their service appears to value.

Experiences

Experiences include the ways in which individuals "learn the methods and skills required for job performance over a period of time on the job."[48] In general, when we speak about professional experiences, we are speaking about career-relevant experiences, such as intermediate-level education (ILE), specific staff assignments, deployments, command positions, and so on. Professional experiences are much more easily observable, and therefore are able to form a larger part of our analysis. In some cases, we are able to provide nuance and qualification, such as an officer's performance in a particular assignment, but many experiences are treated as binary: boxes to be checked or unchecked. Depending on the service and career field, some experiences are essentially considered to be qualifying for promotion in and of themselves. Others have a circular relationship with promotion: For example, serving as executive officer to a four-star officer provides an opportunity to build a network of current G/FOs to support promotion, but, in addition, merely receiving such an appointment might signal that you are the type of officer worthy of, or expected for, promotion to higher grades. Using information drawn from interviews to augment data, we attempted to identify these experiential factors as much as possible.

Abilities

Our research considers the abilities of service members that are relevant to their promotion outcomes. Seven broad abilities are defined within the literature: "fluid intelligence [the ability to solve new problems], crystallized intelligence [the ability to rely upon experience], auditory perception, memory ability, retrieval ability, visual perception, and cognitive speediness."[49] Additionally, organizations such as the military services might also evaluate physical abilities, including "psychomotor" abilities, defined as "the combination of cognitive, sensory, and muscular activity."[50] Each of these abilities matter to varying degrees across the services and within grades, as will be explored in the following chapters.

These abilities do not form the majority of our analysis of promotion profiles, however, because they can be challenging to measure, and the assessment of abilities can be a largely subjective judgment that can vary within and among the services. Further, we did not have

---

[48] Frank L. Schmidt, John E. Hunter, and Alice N. Outerbridge, "Impact of Job Experience and Ability on Job Knowledge, Work Sample Performance, and Supervisory Ratings of Job Performance," *Journal of Applied Psychology*, Vol. 71, No. 3, 1986, pp. 432–429.

[49] Raymond Cattell, *Intelligence: Its Structure, Growth, and Action*, New York: Houghton Mifflin, 1971; Schmitt et al., 2003.

[50] Schmitt et al., 2003.

access to officer evaluation records, though their utility to examine differences in ability at the G/FO level would likely be limited. Current evaluation systems for all services rely heavily on two-page performance reviews with limited information, including the officer's performance relative to others being evaluated by the same senior rater. Those individuals seriously considered for promotion to G/FO tend to have similar performance evaluations, making it difficult to distinguish the difference between a strong candidate who is selected for G/FO and one who is not. Further, a key question is "ability to what?" As the following chapters will show, tactical-level leadership success is often equated with ability to lead at the strategic level, which might not be the case.

Similarly, job performance (the ability to complete the tasks required in an individual's line of work) serves as a discriminator between those who are considered for selection as G/FOs and those who are not. Superior job performance is a prerequisite for serious consideration for promotion to G/FO. However, because of this prerequisite, all candidates being considered for a given G/FO position possess evaluations demonstrating exceptional job performance.

Summary

In summary, we approached this research using a wide range of data sources, conducted both quantitative and qualitative analyses, and attempted to capture both the current processes of each service's approach to officer development and the ways those approaches shape how G/FOs lead, manage, and advise. Although we focus on the professional experiences that these processes tend to incentivize, we also acknowledge the role that less easily measurable characteristics, such as personality traits and abilities, play in officer development processes. In the next chapter, we provide an overview of the processes that each service employs to develop its officers, from accessions to promotions.

3. Key Processes in DoD Officer Career Management

Throughout this report, we refer to the specific personnel processes of each service. While certain parameters of these processes are governed by broader statutes and policies, many of the specific procedures, and emphasis placed on different attributes of G/FO candidates in each of these processes, vary among the Army, Navy, Air Force, and Marine Corps. In this section, we begin by summarizing the closely related factors of time in grade and years in service, because they vary across the services and have bearing on and reflect officer personnel management processes. Then, we provide a basic overview of each of these processes as context for the analysis of their potential impact on G/FO pathways in the subsequent service chapters. These personnel management processes include

- commissioning source
- career designation
- duty assignments
- education
- special training
- evaluations
- promotion.

Because joint qualification is part of both duty assignments and educational experiences, later in this chapter, we provide an overview of what constitutes joint experience, joint professional military education (JPME), and joint qualification. In Appendix B, we provide detail on select service personnel information, such as pay grade structure, end strength and the size of the officer corps, and the distribution of officers across the services. Also, readers should note that federal legislation, such as DOPMA, as well as formal G/FO management processes and legislative requirements, have substantial impact on these processes throughout the services. Additional detail on key legislation and DoD processes affecting officer personnel management, including G/FO management, can be found in Appendixes C and D.

Time in Grade and Years in Service

The concepts of time in grade and total years in service vary by service and, of course, by grade. Time in grade—the time in months or years an officer serves in a given grade—is a function both of DOPMA legislation and of each service's approach to developing officers. The DOPMA time-in-grade requirements are shown in Table 3.1. As shown in the table, an officer at the grade of O-1 must serve in that grade for 18 months before being eligible for promotion, whereas officers in the grades of O-6 and O-7 are eligible for promotion after serving only one year in grade.

Table 3.1. DOPMA Minimum Time-in-Grade Requirements

Grade	Minimum Time in Grade
O-1	18 months
O-2	2 years
O-3 through O-5	3 years
O-6 through O-7	1 year

SOURCE: 10 U.S. Code, Section 619, Eligibility for Consideration for Promotion: Time-in-Grade and Other Requirements.

In line with these requirements, officers in each of the services spend the most years in grades O-3 to O-6 (Figure 3.1). However, O-4s and O-5s in the Air Force and Army spend less time in grade than in the other services, reflecting earlier promotion than in the Navy and Marine Corps.

Figure 3.1. Time in Grade by Service for Rising Officers Promoted from That Grade in the Prior Year, Average, 2008–2018

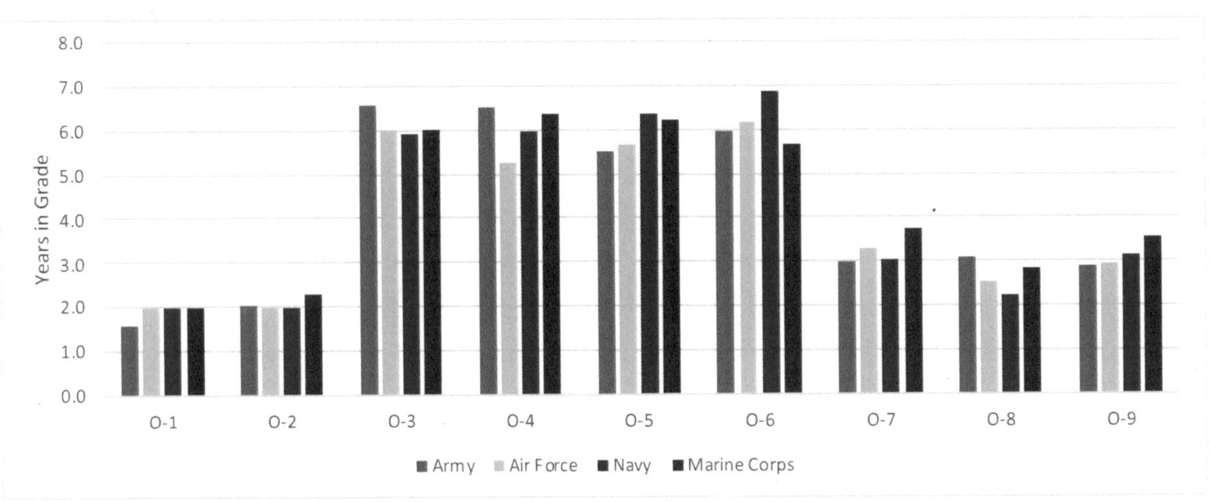

SOURCE: Authors' analysis of DMDC data.

The cumulative effect of these time-in-grade patterns is illustrated in Figure 3.2. As the figure shows, Air Force mid-grade officers and GOs have the least total years in service, compared with the other services. Part of this is due to the Air Force's use of early promotions, which will be discussed later in this report. Marine Corps and Navy officers spend six or more years on average in each of the mid-grades (O-4, O-5, and O-6), with the greatest time in grade exhibited by Navy O-6s (nearly seven years, on average). Army officers have more time in the grade of O-4 than any other service. Later in an officer's career, Marine Corps GOs spend more time in the grade than the other services, especially as O-7s and O-8s, which leads to Marine Corps GOs having the most total years in service, particularly at the highest ranks.

Figure 3.2. Average Years in Service by Grade for Rising Officers in All Services (Promoted in Prior Year), 2008–2018

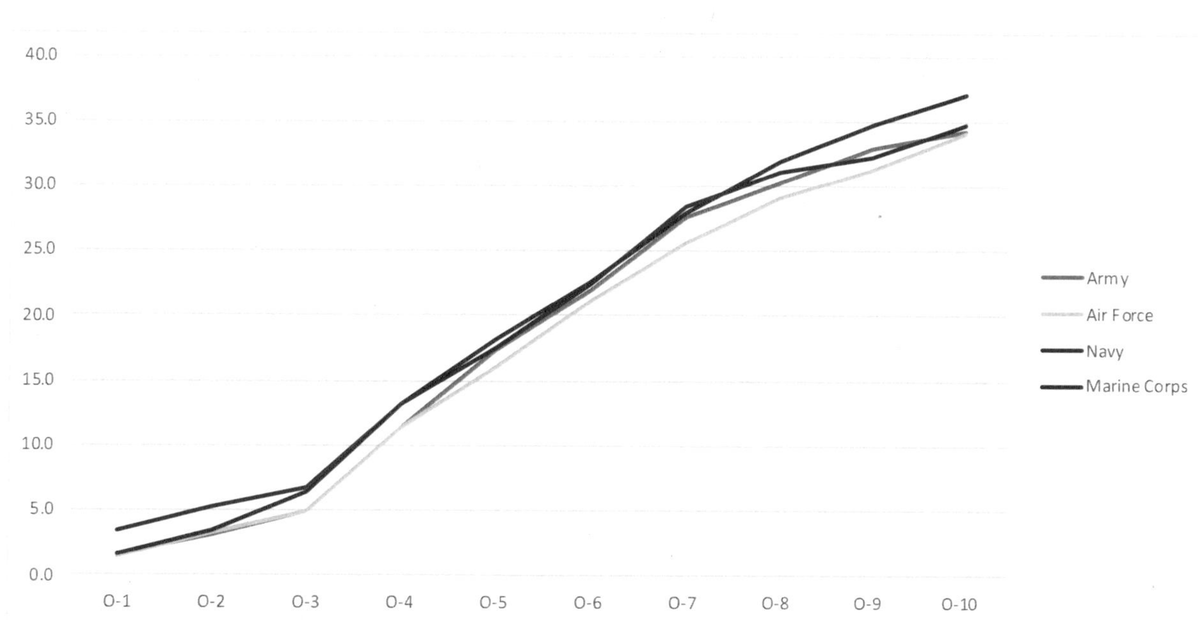

SOURCE: Authors' analysis of DMDC data.
NOTE: Years in service are calculated as of January each year, for officers promoted in the year prior.

Commissioning Source

The majority of officers are commissioned through one of three primary sources: Officer Candidate School (OCS), which is called Officer Training School (OTS) in the Air Force; Reserve Officer Training Corps (ROTC) programs at civilian colleges and universities; and the three service academies. While we focus on these three primary tracks in this report, additional pathways to commissioning include programs available to enlisted members to gain commissions, and "direct" commissioning programs that allow highly trained civilians, such as doctors, lawyers, or intelligence professionals, to earn a reserve commission directly into their related specialty through a condensed training pipeline.

Each of the primary commissioning, or accession, source pipelines offers notably different approaches to developing candidates for service. Officer candidates who commission through OCS/OTS enter with a bachelor's degree but generally have not participated in military training as college students. OCS/OTS participants undergo military training courses that vary in length depending on the service and incur a military service obligation upon completion. The Marine Corps runs a variation on the OCS program called the Platoon Leaders Course (PLC), where college students apply and attend military training during summer sessions and, upon completion of all requirements, attend OCS as the final step of their commissioning.

ROTC programs, offered at public and private universities throughout the United States, are another substantial producer of active duty commissions. ROTC participants attend a college or university while earning merit-based scholarships or stipends through ROTC programs. Upon college graduation and completion of other requirements, candidates receive commissions and incur a service obligation. Because the selectivity and rigor of ROTC programs and sponsoring universities vary by location, the ROTC-commissioned candidates' level of academic and military training is not uniform across all programs.[51]

Service academies, known for highly selective admissions policies and rigorous military and academic training throughout the four years of a candidate's attendance, are often viewed as producing officers with distinct advantages in preparation for and promotion to higher grades. Service academies include the Army's U.S. Military Academy (USMA), the Air Force's U.S. Air Force Academy (USAFA), and the U.S. Naval Academy (USNA), which prepares cadets for both the Navy and the Marine Corps.[52] We also note that, in the services in which service academy graduates comprise a high percentage of G/FOs, it might be difficult to parse which underlying factors drive higher representation. Such underlying factors might include higher aptitude, the signal or commitment to a military career, or access to highly connected networks, mentors, and advocates.[53]

The degree to which commissioning source matters to an officer's chances of becoming an O-7 depends on the service. In the Navy, for example, commissioning source appears to be a significant factor, with the majority of three- and four-star admirals hailing from the USNA, whereas in the other services G/FOs are pulled from the range of commissioning sources at different rates. In the subsequent chapters, we will examine specific trends in the relationship between commission source and promotion to G/FO for each of the services.

For comparison across services, Table 3.2 demonstrates that, among incoming O-7s over a ten-year period, military academy representation is highest compared with other commissioning sources in the Navy, and lowest in the Marine Corps.

---

[51] Hosek et al., 2001.

[52] The Marine Corps does not have its own service academy, but marines are commissioned from the USNA. The Coast Guard also has a service academy, but pathways of Coast Guard GOs are beyond the scope of this report.

[53] For example, Hardison et al. found that the United States Military Academy's "whole candidate score" for acceptance was "significantly associated with higher probability of promotion to O-5" (Chaitra Hardison, Susan Burkhauser, Lawrence M. Hanser, and Mustafa Oguz, *How Effective are Military Academy Admission Standards?* Santa Monica, Calif.: RAND Corporation, RB-9905-OSD, 2016).

Table 3.2. Commissioning Source of Incoming O-7s (Newly Promoted in Prior Year), by Service, 2008–2018 (%)

	Air Force	Army	Marine Corps	Navy
Academy	41	31	15	39
ROTC/NROTC	41	63	33	26
OCS/OTC	14	4	50	18
Direct appointment	3	2	0	9
Unknown/other	0	0	2	7
Total	100	100	100	100

SOURCE: Authors' analysis of DMDC data.
NOTE: NROTC = Naval Reserve Officers Training Corps.

Table 3.3 highlights interesting patterns at the O-9 and O-10 grades over the same time period. While the Marine Corps' share of academy graduates at those ranks remains comparatively low, likely due in part to that service's emphasis on its OCS program and lack of its own dedicated service academy, the percentage of G/FOs who attended a service academy markedly increases in the Army, Navy, and Air Force for these grades. This increase might be related to network effects and promotion boards favoring officers whose backgrounds look "similar to their own," factors that are explored later in this report in the individual service chapters.

Table 3.3. Commissioning Source of Incoming O-9s and O-10s (Newly Promoted in Prior Year), by Service, 2008–2018 (%)

	Air Force	Army	Marine Corps	Navy
Academy	52	52	14	60
ROTC/NROTC	37	44	17	19
OCS/OTC	9	3	68	8
Direct appointment	3	1	2	8
Unknown/other	0	0	0	5
Total	100	100	100	100

SOURCE: Authors' analysis of DMDC data.

Career Designations

Career field is another major factor in an officer's pathway to O-7. This is due in part to the experience required or traditionally desired in G/FO positions. Because the services are organizations whose fundamental mission is preparing for and executing warfighting responsibilities, operations-focused career fields tend to dominate their G/FO ranks. Figures 3.3 to 3.6 detail career field representation among each service's O-7s. In the Army, GOs with career fields in infantry and armor gain substantial ground between O-7 and O-10 (Figure 3.3). On the other hand, Navy aviation officers remain roughly equally represented from O-7 to O-10, but surface warfare officers (SWOs) and submariners gain proportionally as the grades increase, as do aviators but to a lesser extent (Figure 3.4). In the Air Force, fighter pilots, who already enter the O-7 grade at disproportionately high rates compared with their representation in the mid-grades, continue to grow in total share as officers approach O-10 (Figure 3.5). In the Marine Corps (Figure 3.6), infantry and aviation GOs each compose between 30 and 40 percent of GO O-9 positions, with GOs logistics and support career fields making up just over 20 percent. At the O-10 level, however, infantry officers compose over 80 percent of O-10 Marine Corps positions. Of course, at the O-10 level, percentages start to have less meaning than they do at the lower grades, given the small number of O-10s in each service, but the trends over a ten-year period are useful to note.

Figure 3.3. Percentage of Army General Officers by Type and Grade, Average, 2008–2018

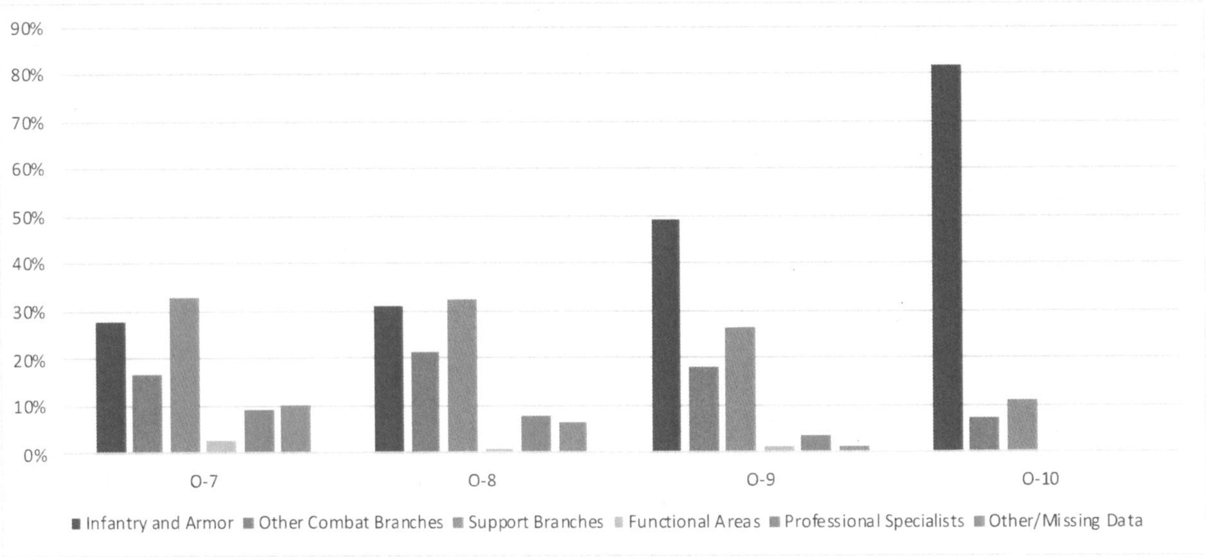

90%
80%
70%
60%
50%
40%
30%
20%
10%
0%

O-7 O-8 O-9 O-10

■ Infantry and Armor ■ Other Combat Branches ■ Support Branches ■ Functional Areas ■ Professional Specialists ■ Other/Missing Data

SOURCE: Authors' analysis of DMDC data.
NOTE: Officers are categorized by type using the primary service occupation codes assigned to each officer in any given year.

Figure 3.4. Percentage of Navy Flag Officers by Type and Grade, Average, 2008–2018

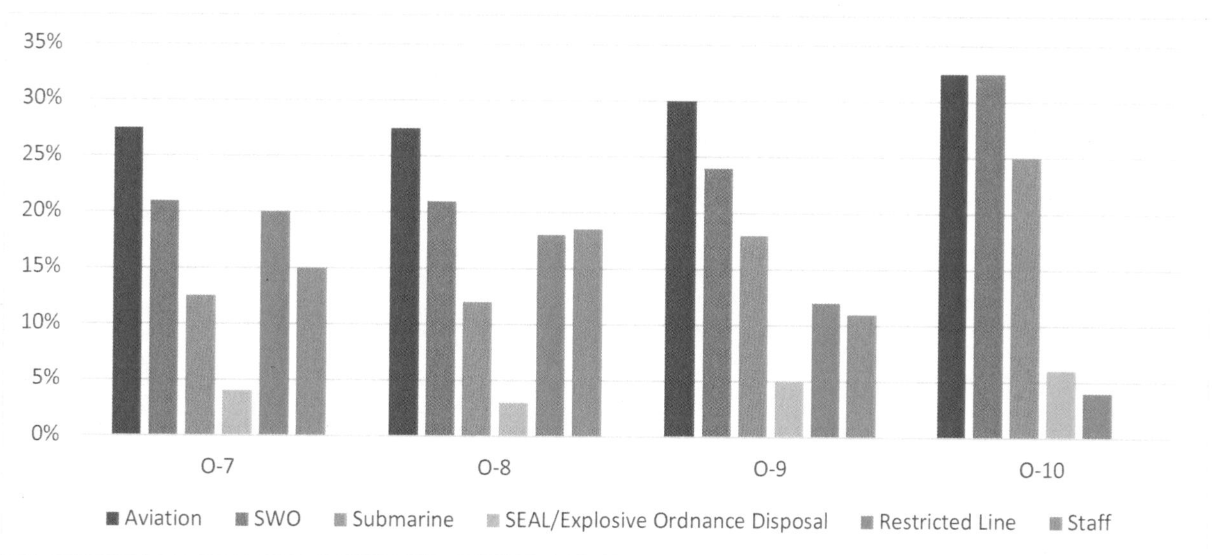

SOURCE: Authors' analysis of DMDC data.
NOTE: Officers are categorized by type using the primary service occupation codes assigned to each officer in any given year. SEAL = Sea, Air, Land.

Figure 3.5. Percentage of Air Force General Officers by Type and Grade, Average, 2008–2018

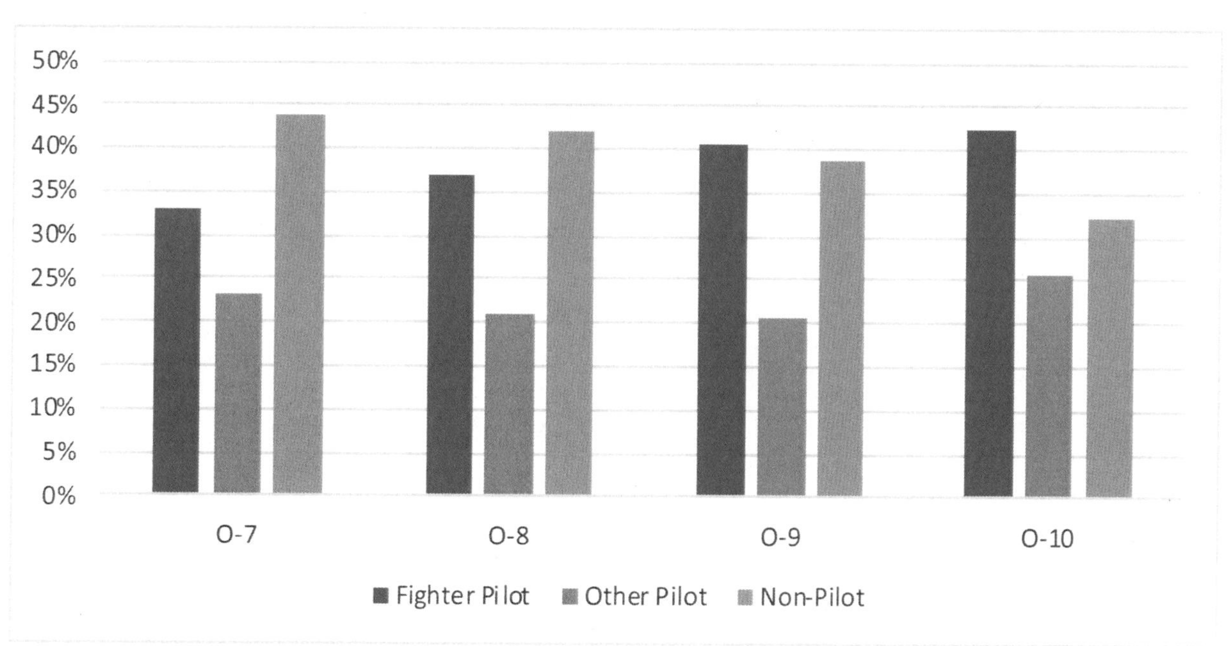

SOURCE: Authors' analysis of DMDC data.
NOTE: An officer is categorized as a "fighter pilot" if the officer has ever been assigned a fighter pilot primary, secondary, or duty service occupation code, whether currently or in a previous year. An officer is categorized as an "other pilot" if the officer has never been assigned a fighter pilot occupation code but has been assigned another pilot primary, secondary, or duty service occupation code, whether currently or in a previous year. All other Air Force officers are categorized as nonpilots.

Figure 3.6. Percentage of Marine Corps General Officers by Type and Grade, Average, 2008–2018

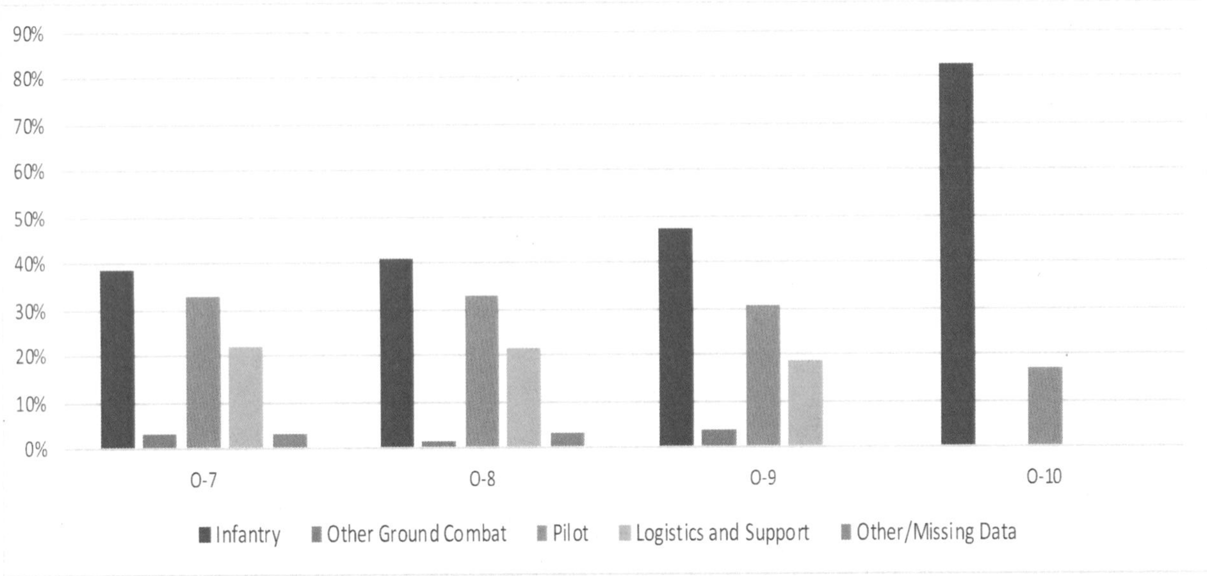

SOURCE: Authors' analysis of DMDC data.
NOTE: Officers are categorized by type using the primary service occupation codes assigned to each officer in any given year. When a Marine Corps officer is promoted to O-6, the officer is often assigned a generic senior officer primary occupation code. To correct for this, officers at the ranks of O-7 to O-10 are categorized by type using the primary service occupation code assigned to them as O-5s.

Duty Assignments

The military services are granted wide latitude in the management of the duty assignments process. By statute, each service secretary is empowered to "assign, detail, and prescribe the duties" of the military and civilian personnel in that service.[54] The type of assignment, performance in a given assignment, timing of specific assignments, and networks or contacts cultivated through assignments can all have substantial effects on an officer's career trajectory. Each service, and each career pathway within each service, values certain assignments differently and expects specific duty assignment requirements to be fulfilled in order to be eligible for selection to O-7. In each of the services, typical career paths to O-7 exist, which is generally reflective of the standardized training and milestone assignments many of these paths require, but also suggests that having the "right" assignments is of utmost importance to a board. As a 2001 RAND report noted, "Individuals with atypical assignment histories can have difficulty demonstrating career-field credibility."[55]

---

[54] This authority is granted to each of the secretaries of the military departments in three sections of United States Code: 10 U.S.C. 3013(g), 10 U.S.C. 8013(g), and 10 U.S.C. 9013(g). The Secretary of the Navy maintains these responsibilities for Marine Corps personnel.

[55] Hosek et al, 2001, p. 22.

Duty Assignment Processes and Joint Qualification

Regardless of service, officers generally move to new assignments every two to three years. Assignments are intended to be progressive, building on experiences and knowledge that are expected to be gained in earlier points of an officer's career. Most assignments must be filled by an officer of a particular grade or range of grades. Some assignments are required for advancement in each service, while others are strongly preferred.

Overall, force employment is governed by the Secretary of Defense–led Global Force Management (GFM) process, which balances force assignment, allocation, and apportionment to support the combatant commands (CCMDs).[56] More specifically, the process of determining individual assignments is centralized and structured in each service, as each assignment requires balance among legal requirements, the needs of the service, professional development and career timelines, and, in some cases, an officer's personal and family circumstances. In recent years, some services have focused attention on more deliberately matching officer backgrounds and preferences to available positions, but these tailored assignment-to-experience alignment efforts must support service and community needs.

The military services use both formal and informal mechanisms to manage assignments. Formally, each service uses a dedicated human resources or personnel organization to manage assignment decisions and processes, including command selection boards that have direct impact on subsequent assignments to those commands. Each service's career management organization is structured somewhat differently to reflect the needs and the culture of that service, but each features designated professionals that manage officers' assignments and career requirements. In the Army, for example, one individual manages officers' careers within a given career specialty, while in the Navy this management is conducted by a detailer, who focuses on the officer's career, and a community manager, who ensures that the needs of the career community are met.

Informally, assignments can be influenced by personal networks, requests from unit leadership, and an assignment officer's judgment. The extent to which these informal mechanisms affect assignments varies among the services and also among communities within each service. Further, once an officer is assigned to a particular unit, commanders are often allowed to align assigned officers to certain other positions within that command without changing the officer's formal assignment.

In general, the role of assignments is critical to an officer's career progression and the experience the officer will bring to future grades. As will be demonstrated in the individual service chapters, the services are quite different from each other in terms of the approaches they take to utilizing assignments: as a teaching tool, as a weeding mechanism, or as a mandatory requirement to be promoted to G/FO.

---

[56] For more information on the GFM process, see, for example, Joint Publication 3-35, *Deployment and Redeployment Operations*, Washington, D.C.: Joint Chiefs of Staff, January 10, 2018.

Types of Duty Assignments

Although each service categorizes assignments differently, several different types of assignments exist, and they are further refined by the specific requirements of an officer's branch or functional area. Broadly, we delineate professional assignments across the military services into the following three categories:

- *Core career field assignments* are those that are directly aligned with an officer's specific occupation and either develop or use the officer's tailored skills to execute the essential functions of that career field.
- *Supporting institutional assignments* are positions that are outside of an officer's specific career field but are considered to be supporting the service's primary central functions. These might include, for example, service staff, executive officers or aides to a same-service G/FO, personnel command detailers, or combat training instructors.
- *Broadening assignments* are those that are not directly related to an officer's career field but are intended to expose the officer to experiences and knowledge that can help expand the officer's understanding of the broader functions of the military and national security arena. These can include assignments at other agencies, executive officer or aide jobs with other-service G/FOs, combatant command staff, and civilian education opportunities.

Certain duty assignments carry more weight than others. As will be discussed in the service chapters, throughout all services, the greatest value is placed on core career field assignments, and command assignments in particular carry the highest value in each of the services. However, emphasis placed on—and time allowed for—supporting institutional assignments varies depending on the service. For example, in the Air Force, headquarters staff positions are viewed as a strategic investment in preparing today's officers to serve later in four-star positions. In other services, such as the Army and the Navy, staff work outside of one's core career field is generally viewed less favorably and as more of an interruption from operational assignments. The exception appears to be serving as an aide to a three- or four-star general or admiral, a trend that has remained true for decades. As explained by Janowitz in 1971,

> In the ideal definition of the prescribed career line, constant rotation back to service with troops or aboard ship is assumed to be essential. In actuality, the ranking military leaders displayed an early and persistent propensity for staff work. While the typical young officer who was destined to rise to the rank of Army colonel or naval captain was serving in the field, future members of the military elite were more often military aides.[57]

Broadening assignments, overall, appear to carry less value to the services, though the degree to which broadening is weighed in the formal promotion process varies. Because of service-centric cultures, as well as heavy deployment rotations to Iraq, Afghanistan, and other regions since 2001, enriching experiences, such as broadening assignments or civilian education, can be

[57] Janowitz, 1971, p. 166.

viewed as unnecessary trade-offs to critical operational or service-supporting assignments. This observation is further detailed in the service-specific chapters later in this report.

Joint Assignments and Joint Qualification

As noted previously, the military services have a large degree of flexibility in determining how to fill service positions with their officers. One major exception comes from changes driven by Title IV of Goldwater-Nichols, which set forth provisions intended to improve "jointness," or service integration, across the department.[58] This legislation sought to establish a cadre of "joint qualified" officers across the military departments, which would consist of officers trained in joint matters.[59] The definition of what constitutes *joint matters* has been refined by Congress over time, but is described today in Section 668(a) of Title 10 U.S.C. as

> The development or achievement of strategic objectives through the synchronization, coordination, and organization of integrated forces in operations conducted across domains, such as land, sea, or air, in space, or in the information environment, including matters relating to any of the following:
>
> - National military strategy.
> - Strategic planning and contingency planning.
> - Command and control, intelligence, fires, movement and maneuver, protection or sustainment of operations under unified command.
> - National security planning with other departments and agencies of the United States.
> - Combined operations with military forces of allied nations.

Although a full review of the joint qualification system is beyond the scope of this report, we can summarize some key aspects of the concept here.[60] Joint assignments can be broadening or core career field, but only in very rare cases would they be supporting institutional assignments, since those assignments are inherently service-oriented.

DoD Instruction 1300.19 provides policy guidance on joint qualification and states that "Attaining expertise in joint matters is a career-long accumulation of experiences that may be gained via various duties and assignments to joint organizations for extended periods or through the performance of temporary duties of shorter duration."[61] Broadly, joint qualification for active duty officers consists of a combination of assignments; education in the form of JPME, which

---

[58] Public Law 99–433, 1986.

[59] 10 U.S. Code, Section 661, Management Policies for Joint Qualified Officers; 10 U.S. Code, Section 668, Definitions.

[60] For additional information on joint qualification system, see Department of Defense Instruction (DoDI) 1300.19, *DoD Joint Officer Management (JOM) Program*, Washington, D.C.: U.S. Department of Defense, April 3, 2018; Harry J Thie, Margaret C. Harrell, Roland J. Yardley, Marian Oshiro, Holly Ann Potter, Peter Schirmer, and Nelson Lim, *Framing a Strategic Approach for Joint Officer Management*, Santa Monica, Calif.: RAND Corporation, MG-306-OSD, 2005.

[61] DoDI 1300.19, 2018.

will be explained in the next sections; and other qualifying experiences that determine one's eligibility to be a joint qualified officer (JQO). Only JQOs are eligible to promote to O-7, unless waived by the Under Secretary of Defense for Personnel and Readiness.[62] Despite this requirement, the extent to which jointness is embraced and rewarded in the promotions process is different from service to service, as we will show later in this report.

As part of joint "experience," joint assignments are managed by the Chairman of the Joint Chiefs of Staff (CJCS) through the Goldwater-Nichols-created Joint Duty Assignment List (JDAL), a centrally managed file of positions that are considered to provide an officer experience in joint matters. DoD allows officers to become joint qualified through a standard joint duty assignment (S-JDA); an experiential joint duty assignment (E-JDA), such as conducting joint operations, joint training, or exercises; or a combination of both. As a result, the type of joint experience that a G/FO has gained can vary substantially. We were unable to obtain data on specific joint assignments and time spent in joint assignments, but we believe additional analysis of how types of joint assignments, number of joint assignments, and time spent in those assignments affect G/FO experiences and perspectives is warranted.

Deployment Experience

Another specific type of duty assignment that merits additional discussion are deployments, which, like other duty assignments, can be core career field, supporting institutional, or broadening. In general, deployments, and often combat-related deployments, carry value throughout the services, though the nature and duration of those deployments vary greatly depending on the service and career field. It is challenging to measure the relationship between deployment time and promotion to O-7 because deployment time increased substantially after 2001, and the junior officers who deployed at that time have not yet been in service long enough to be promoted to the G/FO grades. While we have some indication from interviews and the SLSE about how the services view deployments in promotion decisions generally, future analysis of the relationship of deployments and O-7 promotion will be useful in further illuminating this relationship.

We found that what constitutes a deployment varies from service to service. In the Army, deployments tend to be longer and focused on combat or combat support. Deployments in the Marine Corps are similarly focused on combat or combat support, though deployments tend to be shorter than in the Army. In the Navy, time spent underway on a ship or a submarine is considered a deployment, even if that deployment is not directly connected to supporting combat operations. The Air Force also has a different approach to assigning value to deployments, given that personnel can be involved in critical missions while operating remotely piloted aircraft, for example.

---

[62] DoDI 1300.19, 2018.

Education

Education in the context of an officer's career usually means professional military education (PME) or joint professional military education (JPME). Often, PME and JPME are DoD-administered courses or programs, but certain civilian courses or degrees can also be counted. In addition, civilian schooling can be pursued on an officer's own time. These three facets of military education are discussed briefly in the following section.

Professional Military Education

PME refers to a wide range of activities intended to augment a service member's development. Draft CJCS guidance in late 2018 broadly defined the scope of education and emphasized its importance to military operations:

> Education is an essential aspect of agility and flexibility. In an unknowable future, tactical expertise untampered by education will handicap, if not defeat, the relevance of military actions to policy goals. Education, whether academic or training with industry, enables strategic adaptation to the unknowns that training cannot address, and helps to avoid drawing false comparisons with previous experience, enabling the Joint Force to react to unforeseen threats and prevail.[63]

In this subsection, we focus on the more defined, service-institutional education aspects of PME, including JPME. We categorize service-institutional PME as follows:

1. Basic-level PME, which is generally focused on developing core competencies, is the services' educational priority for O-1s to O-3s is training specific to one's career field.
2. ILE is typically assigned at O-4 and might or might not be completed in coordination with a master's degree.
3. Senior service college or senior service fellowships are assigned at the senior grades of O-5 or O-6. Master's degrees are conferred by all senior service colleges.

All services have a PME regimen that involves dedicated instruction at various points in an officer's career. Depending on the service, some PME is conducted in-residence, while other PME can be conducted via correspondence courses as distance learning. However, the services vary greatly in how much importance is placed on PME in practice and in promotion decisions, as we will explore later in this report.

The topic of PME has been debated recently in DoD, by Congress, and by the public, focusing on questions such as whether PME and JPME are sufficiently tailored to produce "strategic thinkers" and whether their curricula are poorly matched to national security realities.[64] The 2018 NDS provided DoD's current assessment and future vision of PME, stating:

---

[63] Jerome Lynes, Deputy Director Joint Staff, Joint Education and Doctrine, "Framing the Problem: Strategic Guidance and Vision," briefing, October 31, 2018.

[64] For example, see Thornhill, 2018.

> PME has stagnated, focused more on the accomplishment of mandatory credit at the expense of lethality and ingenuity. We will emphasize intellectual leadership and military professionalism in the art and science of warfighting, deepening our knowledge of history while embracing new technology and techniques to counter competitors. PME will emphasize independence of action in warfighting concepts to lessen the impact of degraded/lost communications in combat. PME is to be used as a strategic asset to build trust and interoperability across the Joint Forces and with allied and partner forces.[65]

Indeed, examinations of today's PME programs often reflect concerns about whether the services' senior-most leaders are adequately prepared by their curricula. As of 2019, all the services had various efforts underway to examine their approaches to PME, including, in some cases, the ways that PME is weighted in promotion decisions, and the timing of specific PME experiences in an officer's career, which might come later than is ideal for shaping an officer's thinking. Much of this discourse on reforming PME has focused on JPME, a subset of PME that is a critical element of joint qualification.

Joint Professional Military Education

JPME is a requirement for joint qualification, eligibility for certain positions, and promotions per Goldwater-Nichols, as described previously, and is focused on educating officers in joint matters. Specific JPME requirements exist in various sections of U.S. Code.[66] JPME requirements are fulfilled in a number of ways, depending on the service, but, as with PME, are generally completed at either service or joint institutions or through distance-learning online programs.

While *PME* and *JPME* are terms that are often used interchangeably, the distinction between them is important. Part of this confusion is because there is broad overlap between JPME and the services' institutional training between grades O-4 to O-6. CJCS Instruction (CJCSI) 1800.01E distinguishes the two while acknowledging their overlap:

> Services operate officer PME systems to develop officers with expertise and knowledge appropriate to their grade, branch, and occupational specialty. Incorporated throughout Service-specific PME, officers receive JPME from precommissioning to General/Flag Officer (GO/FO) level.[67]

The 1994 NDAA further defined the role of JPME:

> the primary mission of the joint professional military education schools is to provide military officers with expertise in the integrated employment of land,

---

[65] U.S. Department of Defense, 2018, p. 6.

[66] For additional information, see for example, Kristy N. Kamarck, *Goldwater-Nichols and the Evolution of Officer Joint Professional Military Education (JPME)*, Washington, D.C.: Congressional Research Service, January 13, 2016; Thie et al., 2005.

[67] Chairman of the Joint Chiefs of Staff Instruction 1800.01E, *Officer Professional Military Education Policy*, Washington, D.C.: U.S. Department of Defense, May 29, 2015, p. A-1.

> sea, and air forces, including matters relating to national security strategy, national military strategy, strategic planning and contingency planning, and command and control of combat operations under unified command.[68]

In the individual service chapters, we will discuss how varying degrees of importance placed on PME and JPME can affect the makeup of each service's G/FO corps. The services satisfy the requirements in ways that reflect their unique cultures, showing different preferences for the timing of a joint tour in a career, the importance of an S-JDA tour compared with an E-JDA tour, and the optimal length of schooling.

Civilian Education

Civilian education can also be pursued by military officers, though it is not always esteemed by the officer's service or career field, and certain tight career timelines might not readily allow for civilian education. Generally, when we refer to civilian education, we mean the pursuit of either a master's or a doctoral degree on a full-time basis. In some cases, the services have formal or habitual arrangements with civilian colleges and universities to send their officers for certain degrees as part of fellowships or career specialty requirements, and some types of officers, such as Army strategists, must obtain a master's degree as part of their training and often fulfill this requirement through a civilian program. Further, some officers are able to fulfill certain intermediate- or senior-level education requirements through civilian universities instead of traditional military institutions. The degree to which these civilian degrees are compared favorably with degrees conferred from a military school varies by service, as will be explored in later chapters.

One commonality throughout all the services is that, particularly when voluntary (such as through a fellowship that includes a master's program), the pursuit of civilian education can disrupt or even derail an officer's career timeline and prospects for promotion. For example, when appearing before a board, officers in the same year group and career field are expected to have completed certain assignments. If an officer pursued a civilian master's degree while their peers were completing these requisite or more common assignments, the officer's file might look comparatively weaker to the board.

This particular topic has received increased attention in Congress and at higher levels in DoD in recent years, as some policy efforts have focused on developing ways to allow service members to defer their promotion consideration so that they can pursue educational and other broadening assignments and still complete traditional assignments that they need in order to compete effectively.[69]

---

[68] Public Law 103-160, Section 921, National Defense Authorization Act for Fiscal Year 1994, November 30, 1993.

[69] See, for example, Navy Personnel Command, "Career Intermission Program," April 10, 2019b, and Sarah Sicard, "Air Force Expands Sabbatical Leave for up to 3 Years if Airmen Stay in," Task and Purpose, September 26, 2017.

Special Training

All career designators require some kind of training in order for an officer to establish and maintain proficiency in their field. Depending on the career field, this training can range from fairly basic to highly advanced and technical, but it is still grounded in specific requirements applicable to one's career field. Beyond this type of core training is what we refer to in this report as special training, or schools and other training programs that tend to be career-field-relevant but that are not usually required to maintain one's specialty. Though special training might not be required to meet basic requirements for one's career field and is often voluntary, it can serve as a badge of prestige and as a major indicator to peers, superiors, and promotion boards of one's skills, performance, and potential. For this reason, we include special training as a category of analysis where applicable.

In the service-specific chapters that follow, we highlight special training where we analyzed when attendance (and performance, in some cases) in the training programs was a common factor for many service G/FOs. Examples of special training include the Air Force's Weapons School, which teaches advanced weapons and tactics employment, and the Army's Ranger School, which administers a rigorous course focused on small-unit tactics and combat leadership skills.

Evaluations

The impact of evaluations on an officer's career is substantial, as they are the chief type of document used in board deliberations. Although each service has its own written evaluation forms and processes, some overall parameters apply across the services. A 2001 RAND study by Hosek et al. provides the following description of officer evaluations, which remains true today:

> [These] evaluations constitute the primary record of an officer's performance and are reviewed by selection boards (for augmentation, advanced education, promotion, and command) and those who make duty assignment selections. Generally, the evaluations are written by each officer's immediate supervisor and reviewed by a more senior rater. Although the specific format varies by service and has varied within the services over time, there are some common elements. The evaluation consists of brief written descriptions of the officer's job; his/her notable accomplishments during the period being evaluated (usually a year); his/her overall performance and potential; and recommendations for next career steps. In addition to the written comments, the officer's performance is rated on one or more scales.
>
> As officers progress through the ranks, their evaluations are given more or less weight depending on the job in which the officer is being rated and the identity of the senior rater. The more challenging the job, the more weight the performance evaluation carries; the same may be true for performance evaluations written by high-ranking officers.
>
> If an officer feels he or she has received an unfair or discriminatory performance evaluation, there is a formal appeals process. If the appeal is successful, the

evaluation form is removed from the officer's personnel record and a notice of the removal is included. Officers may write a letter to the promotion board that clarifies their record.[70]

More detailed information about each of the service's specific processes will be provided in the subsequent chapters, but some commonalities endure across the Army, Navy, Air Force, and Marine Corps. For example, Hosek et al. highlight that the identity and experience of the officer's raters, who perform the evaluation and sign the evaluation form, are important. Not only does that senior rater's reputation matter, but senior officers who are rating junior officers of the same service likely have more familiarity with that service's preferred language and writing style in performance evaluations, which interviewees across the services told us can affect a board's decisions. Further, if a senior rater is a civilian in OSD or the director of the National Security Council (NSC), for example, the senior rater might not know the right signaling words to use that set an officer apart from their peers on an evaluation form even if that officer performed superbly in a challenging position. A board also might not know the reputation or relative responsibilities and judgment of certain raters, military and civilian, outside of one's own service, which could also affect how the officer under consideration for promotion or selection is viewed by a board.[71]

Promotion

Promotions serve as the primary marker of whether the service has determined that an officer has adequately performed and shown aptitude for increased levels of leadership. Of course, promotions are also strongly tied to factors previously described in this chapter, such as education, assignment history, and evaluations. How the services incentivize and weight these factors in promotions, as well as how other factors affect which officers are selected for higher grades and which are not, can greatly differ, as we will see later in this report.

Promotion boards are at the center of promotions processes, but other boards critical to an officer's career path also exist—command selection boards, other milestone screening boards, and advanced education selection boards, as a few examples. However, we refer most to promotion boards because these other types of boards feed directly into promotion decisions. For example, being selected for command, and then performing well in that position, postures an officer for potential promotion.

The promotion process for officers in each service is complex, formal, and rooted in statute and DoD policy. However, readers should note that these processes are also starting to evolve as the services are taking a closer look at what experiences, skills, and other characteristics they

---

[70] Hosek et al., 2001, pp. 17–18.

[71] For additional information on performance evaluation scores and how evaluation scores can inflate over time, see Hosek et al., 2001, p. 18.

want to select for and foster in their personnel processes, so we anticipate continued changes after the publication of this report.

In the following subsection, we provide an overview across the services of officer promotion rates from O-1 to O-10 and of promotion boards and promotion zones for officers from O-1 to O-6. The unique processes governing G/FO selection, promotion, and management are covered in Appendix D.

Promotion Rates

Promotion rates at each grade vary considerably across grades and services, but the overall trajectory of officers' progression through the ranks is largely the same. In each service, promotions from O-1 to O-2 are considered noncompetitive and largely automatic, with very low rates of attrition. Although promotions from O-2 to O-3 are technically competitive, the promotion rate is so high that true competition only begins at grade O-4. Promotion rates then decline steadily through the mid-grades, before becoming very low (less than 10 percent) between O-6 and O-7, because of the small number of authorized O-7 slots and the sharp organizational and philosophical distinction between G/FO grades and other officers.

Once in the G/FO corps, promotion rates to O-8 jump back up to over 50 percent, then decline steadily again between O-8 and O-9 and between O-9 and O-10. Although there are some differences between the services—notably the Marine Corps, which appears to be a bit more selective up to O-6 and a bit less selective from O-7 to O-9—these differences are small relative to the overall similarity of the services' grade structure.

Figure 3.7, which shows the percentage of officers at each grade who are promoted to the next higher grade, highlights some of the differences among the services' promotion rates. These percentages are a function of the service's preferences, congressional authorizations for number of officers at each grade, and joint billet requirements that favor specific services at the higher levels. For example, we see that a smaller percentage of officers entering the Marine Corps reaches each of the grades between O-3 and O-6 compared with the other services. Of the services, Army and Air Force O-3s most frequently make O-4, Army O-4s most frequently make O-5, and Navy O-5s most frequently make O-6. At O-7, the Marine Corps then begins to catch up, with a greater percentage of Marine Corps officers progressing to the O-7, O-8, and O-9 grades. From O-9 to O-10, a greater percentage Air Force officers are promoted as compared with the other services.

Figure 3.7. Percentage of Officers Who Promote to the Next Grade, by Grade and Service, 2000–2010 Officer Cohorts

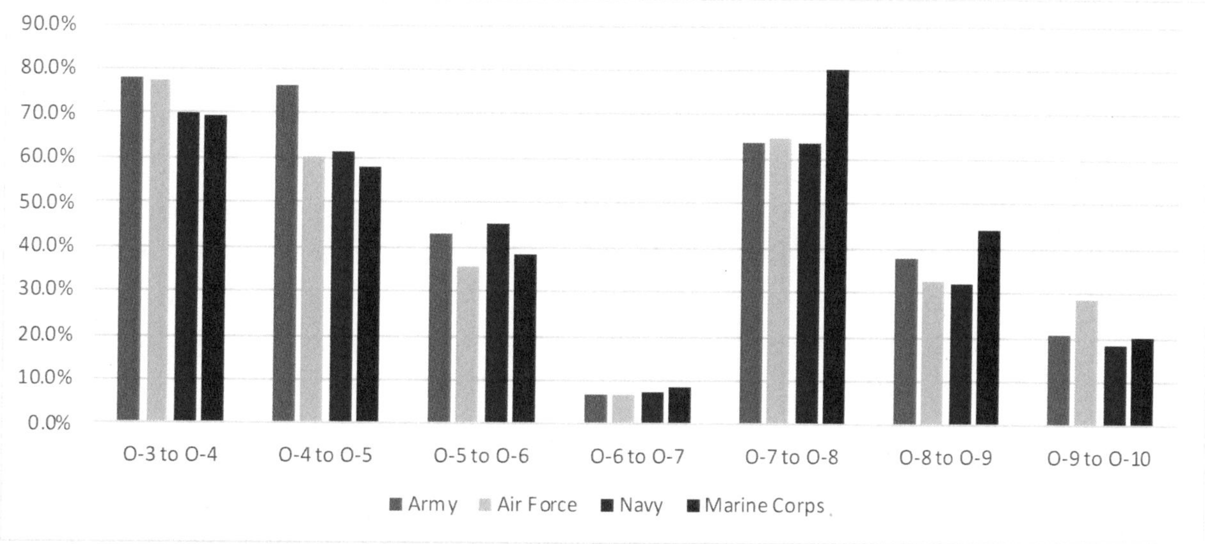

SOURCE: Authors' analysis of DMDC data.
NOTE: These numbers represent the average progression rate for the 11 (overlapping) cohorts of officers present in each grade at the beginning of each year from 2000 to 2010 and reflect these officers' observed rates of reaching the next higher grade at any point up to the beginning of 2018, the last year for which we have data. Multiple cohorts were used to soften out year-to-year variation. Post-2010 cohorts were not used in order to prevent censoring due to the dataset ending in 2018.

Promotion Boards and Promotion Zones (O-1 to O-6)

Promotion board proceedings vary from service to service, but some basic commonalities exist per DOPMA legislation and also in general practice. For example, as discussed earlier in this section, DOPMA provides specific guidelines that govern minimum time in grade and the composition of promotion boards in an effort to provide officers an equal opportunity to be assessed fairly by a board that understands the officer's qualifications.

In reviewing candidates for promotion, boards review elements of the components described earlier in this chapter: professional assignments, education, training and certifications, performance evaluations, and also adverse information, such as punishments or letters of reprimand. Some services' promotion boards also review the officer's current official photograph, while others do not. Depending on the service, board members also offer personal reflections on the officer if they are familiar with the candidate.

Service secretaries can also have influence on promotion selections through the use of precepts, which outline to the board certain specific characteristics the service needs in its officers. These precepts, or guidance, can take the form of quotas or broader language intended to relay the intent of the service secretary. The services vary in how precepts are utilized, but they represent a tool that can have significant bearing on who is selected for the next higher grade in a given year.

What boards are looking for depends on various factors: the needs of the service and career field, promotion board guidance, and, of course, service culture and the preferences of the board members. Of note, board proceedings are intended to be confidential, a charge taken seriously in each of the services that was also reflected in our interviews and the SLSE.

As described earlier, officers are divided into year groups based on their commissioning date, which drive the pool of peers against whom an officer competes for promotion and other selections. Officers can be promoted early, or prior to their primary period of promotion eligibility, which is referred to as "below the zone" (BZ) or "below-the promotion zone" (BPZ);[72] on time, or in line with DOPMA's career progression requirements, which is referred to as "in the zone"; or late, or after an officer's primary zone "look," which is referred to as "above the zone." The services vary substantially in how they utilize early promotions; the Air Force, for example, regularly promotes officers early, whereas the Marine Corps does not rely on early promotions at all—both trends that reflect service culture and philosophies of developing G/FOs, which will be explored in later chapters.

Figure 3.8 shows descriptive data on time in grade for all officers as compared with officers who eventually make O-7 or beyond. According to these data, early promotion to O-4 (as evidenced by times in grade at O-3) does not appear strongly connected to making G/FO for any of the services. Early promotion to O-5 and O-6 (shown by times in grade at O-4 and O-5) does appear to be related to the frequency in which an officer promotes to O-7 or higher. While this observation is true for all of the services to some extent, the relationship is strongest for Army officers who promote early to O-5, and for Air Force officers who promote early to O-6. This relationship between time in grade and promotion to G/FO is weakest in the Navy, for both promotions to O-5 and to O-6, though time in grade might be affected by several factors beyond just early promotion.

---

[72] The term *below-the-zone* (BZ) is used in the Army, Navy, and Marine Corps, and *below-the-promotion-zone* (BPZ) is used in the Air Force.

Figure 3.8. Years in Grade for All Officers, Compared with Officers Who Become General/Flag Officers, O-7-O-10, by Service and Grade, Average, 2008–2018

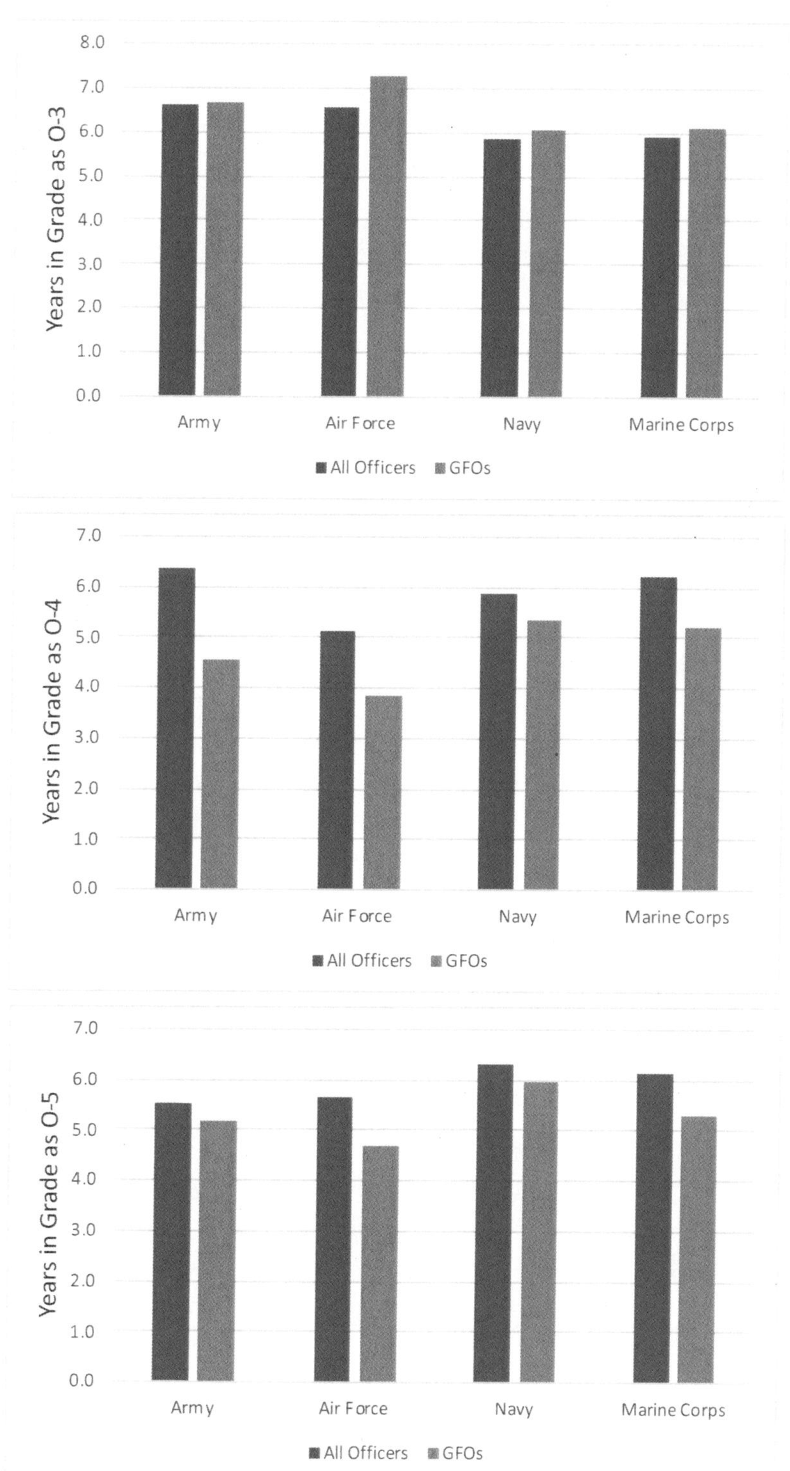

SOURCE: Authors' analysis of DMDC data.
NOTE: These data do not include an O-6 chart because it would not have meaning: Because we did not have data on O-6s who retired or separated before making O-7 and an officer needs to have completed the grade in order to be counted in the years in grade tabulation charts, an O-6 chart would show only an orange bar.

Summary

As the analysis throughout this chapter demonstrates, each of the services' G/FO cadres is notably different, reflecting varied organizational missions, goals, and valued career experiences that characterize service pathways to generalship. Of course, many aspects of personnel management are shared, largely driven by legislation and congressional oversight.

Overall, Air Force officers have the least time in service before reading GO grades and embrace early promotions as a method to move high-performing officers through the ranks quickly. Marine Corps GOs have the longest time in service overall, with longer time in grade at the GO grades than the other services. Accession source serves as a differentiator most in the Navy, and particularly at the highest grades, while the Marine Corps' reliance on its PLC program remains strong through O-10. One's career designator is of utmost importance on the pathway to G/FO for all the services, as it drives assignments and suitability for a number of senior field-grade and G/FO positions. Duty assignments are central drivers in all the services' pathways to generalship, as will be examined in the service-specific chapters later in this report, although whether the assignment itself or performance in the assignment matters most is dependent on the service. For the Army, Navy, Air Force, and Marine Corps alike, command positions are the most highly valued.

In terms of education, officers endeavor to meet their joint education requirements as specified by law and DoD policy, but the value of educational performance in the promotion process depends on the service. Special training also plays a role in distinguishing officers as top leaders, specifically in the Army and the Air Force—although, as we will see in later chapters, the role of certain training experiences might be less than is commonly believed. Across the services, even though processes and forms differ, securing stellar evaluations is crucial to promoting. Similarly, the language used on the form and the identity and style of the senior rater can affect promotion decisions across the services.

Each of the services approaches the promotions process and its promotion and selection boards differently. The Marine Corps, as well as the Navy to a lesser extent, tends to weed out officers early, promoting a smaller percentage of officers than the other services until the G/FO grades. The Air Force promotes the greatest percentage of officers to the O-4 level, the Army advances the greatest percentage to O-5, and the Navy to O-6.

Overall, G/FO processes differ substantially from those involved in the O-1 to O-6 grades, and G/FO requirements are carefully managed by DoD and overseen by Congress, as detailed in Appendix D. These processes and mechanisms are driven in large part by the supply of officers shaped by each of the service's approaches to developing G/FOs. The following service-specific chapters will explore the drivers and results of these unique pathways.

4. The Army's Approach to Generalship

As the largest service, the Army produces more GOs than the Navy, Air Force, or Marine Corps, and historically has filled key senior leadership roles across the joint force. As of January 2018, Army active duty end strength was 470,465, representing 36 percent of the active duty end strength for DoD.[73] The overall proportions of officers and of GOs in the Army closely mirror those of the U.S. military as a whole, with an average of 16.3 Army officers for every 100 uniformed personnel, and 6.7 Army GOs for every 10,000 uniform personnel. The total number of GOs in the Army is 316: 138 O-7s, 117 O-8s, 50 O-9s, and 11 O-10s.[74]

The Army's GOs, and the processes that shape them, reflect the culture of the organization in many ways, such as the premium placed on command experience and operational success. In recent years, debates internal and external to the service about the Army's approach to developing its leaders have led to several military personnel management initiatives intended to better align the Army's personnel development and retention goals with its practices.[75]

The following sections focus primarily on experiences and other characteristics held by the career fields most represented in the Army's GO corps: combat arms, combat support, and combat service support, which we will define later in this chapter. However, as we will explore below, the Army's standardized personnel management processes generally affect officers across the service, and the imprint of the Army's GOs often reflects the Army's culture and the values inherent to those processes, regardless of an officer's basic branch.

Army Culture

As the largest service, with a prominent National Guard component visible across the country, the Army is often synonymous with the military in the American public's eye.[76] The Army is inextricably linked to the nation's citizens, both in terms of its fundamental role in the creation of the United States and its historical role in the nation's wars. This idea of the Army's central role at the very heart of the formation and security of the United States helps to explain both the Army's belief that it understands war above all other services, and also—relatedly—its

---

[73] Defense Manpower Data Center, "Department of Defense, Active Duty Military Personnel by Rank/Grade, January 1, 2018," January 1, 2018.

[74] Officer and general officer numbers calculated by authors using DMDC data. For a comparison of these numbers to those for other services, see Table B.2.

[75] James C. McConville and Debra S. Wada, *U.S. Army Talent Management Strategy: Force 2025 and Beyond*, Washington, D.C.: Department of the Army, September 20, 2016.

[76] Zimmerman et al., 2019.

institutional resistance to turning down lead roles in missions.[77] In 1989, Builder described the Army's institutional link to the nation, an observation that remains true today:

> The Army has never seen itself as having an independent sense of mission or purpose apart from the country's. To repeat, the Army is the nation's most loyal and obedient servant. The Army, unlike the Air Force and Navy, has no vision of a war on its own terms. For the Army, war will always be on terms chosen by others—partly by the nation's enemies, partly by the nation's leadership—terms that are never satisfactory or welcome, but always to be met with a sense of duty, honor, and courage.[78]

Because of its size, the Army also is characterized in large part by its mass and diversity: The service has a greater ability than the other U.S. military services to operate globally, dominate joint organizations, and conduct a wide variety of missions. At its core, Army culture is defined in many ways by its domain: land. Although the service can operate across other domains, its land warfare capabilities shape both its organizational and force structure and resourcing arguments. The Army's central role in U.S. national security does not necessarily translate into leading the development of strategy, or even an emphasis on strategic thinking.[79] As Carl Builder observed, "the Army is more concerned about how well it can assimilate resources and employ them than it is about the assigned objectives and resources."[80] Further, as retired Lieutenant General Robert Scales has written, the Army's rhetorical devotion to strategy has not resulted in a system that pursues "strategic genius" in its personnel.[81]

Unlike other services, the Army is not seen as an institution in which one career specialty dominates the others. Rather, branches are grouped into combat arms, combat support, and combat service support, with the combat arms constituting the Army's "oligarchy."[82] This reflects both the Army's focus on combat as an organizing principle and, to some degree, its inherent egalitarianism.

It is often said that the Air Force and Navy man the equipment, while the Army equips the man. At the heart of the Army is the individual soldier, who must be prepared for battle. This concept is captured in a 2019 RAND report on service culture and interservice competition:

> [F]or the Army, the timeless pursuit of battlefield victory is an inherently human endeavor—every battle is won or lost by the accumulated successes of failures of

---

[77] Zimmerman et al, 2019, pp. 22, 27–28.

[78] Builder, 1989, p. 91.

[79] Sackett, Anna L., Angela Karrasch, William Weyhrauch, and Ellen Goldman, *Enhancing the Strategic Capability of the Army: An Investigation of Strategic Thinking Tasks, Skills, and Development*, Fort Belvoir, Va.: U.S. Army Research Institute for the Behavioral and Social Sciences, 2016.

[80] Builder, 1989, p. 86.

[81] Scales, 2016.

[82] Robert Allen Zirkle, *Communities Rule: Intra-Service Politics in the United States Army*, doctoral thesis, Cambridge: Massachusetts Institute of Technology, 2008, pp. 63–67.

> the individuals on the battlefield. Therefore, the Joes are the heart of the Army, and the true measure of an officer is in his or her ability to lead the troops.[83]

Often described as a "muddy boots" or "Spartan," the Army's dominant culture places value on those who are prepared to fight in war.[84] To many, there is no greater responsibility in the Army than the development of leaders capable of victory in battle.[85] This preference comparatively deemphasizes institutional leadership and staff positions.

Another aspect of the Army's culture is competition.[86] "Be all you can be," the Army's famed slogan, was intended to inspire recruitment, but it also speaks to Army officers' need to compete with their peers throughout all assignments. Several of our interviewees noted the need for officers to remain competitive by either avoiding positions that are out of step with favored pathways or receiving performance assessments that are less stellar than one's peers.

Finally, the Army's approach to instruction and operations is heavily doctrine-based. Its adherence to doctrine denotes the Army's empirical approach to mission accomplishment, though one interviewee said that it could lead to a "one-size-fits-all" approach to complex problems.[87] Despite being considered the experts on military planning among the other services, due in large part to its enormous body of doctrine (which often serves as the basis for other services' doctrine and joint doctrine), charges of anti-intellectualism have long the plagued the Army.[88]

Official Guidance on Army Officer Development

The Army's standard definition of a leader is an individual who "inspires and influences people to accomplish organizational goals," and its definition of leadership is "the process of influencing people by providing purpose, direction, and motivation to accomplish the mission and improve the organization."[89] This concept of leadership is not bounded by grade or commission: All soldiers are expected to be Army leaders, regardless of role and level of

---

[83] Zimmerman et al., 2019, p. 23.

[84] Charles D. Allen and George J. Wood, "Developing Army Enterprise Leaders," *Military Review*, July–August 2015, p. 44; A10, field-grade Army officer with personnel management experience, September 13, 2018; A30, Army civilian employee with personnel management experience, September 12, 2018; Susan Bryant and Heidi A. Urben, *Reconnecting Athens and Sparta: A Review of OPMS XXI at 20 Years*, Arlington, Va.: Institute of Land Warfare, No. 114, October 2017; A19, Army general officer, December 10, 2018.

[85] Zimmerman et al., 2019.

[86] James G. Pierce, *Is the Organizational Culture of the U.S. Army Congruent with the Professional Development of Its Senior Level Officer Corps? Carlisle Barracks?*, Carlisle Barracks, Pa.: U.S. Army War College Press, 2010, p. 101.

[87] A01, Army field-grade officer, August 9, 2019.

[88] Lloyd J. Matthews, "Anti-Intellectualism and the Army Profession," in Don M. Snider, project director, and Lloyd J. Matthews, ed., *The Future of the Army Profession*, 2nd edition, New York: McGraw Hill, 2005.

[89] Army Doctrinal Publication (ADP) 6-22, *Army Leadership*, Washington, D.C.: Department of the Army, 2012, p. 1.

responsibility, motivating others to accomplish the mission.[90] In line with the service's idea that leaders are shaped over time, the Army leverages a series of processes, such as training, education, assignments, self-development, and certification, in its formal leadership development process.[91] The idea that leadership is a skill that benefits from practice receives much support in Army doctrine, where leadership can be "learned, monitored, and improved."[92]

The Army describes its methodology for developing officers in Department of the Army Pamphlet 600-3, *Commissioned Officer Professional Development and Career Management*, which provides important insight into the Army's goals. The pamphlet describes "agile, innovative, and adaptive leaders of unimpeachable integrity, character, and competence who act to achieve decisive results and who understand and are able to exploit the full potential of current and future Army doctrine."[93] The same goals of agility and adaptiveness are reiterated in recent guidance for the O-7 promotion board, with the additional requirement that the selected officers be "capable of leading our forces in combat under conditions of uncertainty, leading joint, interagency, intergovernmental, and multinational organizations and of running the Army."[94]

Overall, officers across pay grades are evaluated and counseled on the following "leader attributes," which are considered fundamental to Army leadership:

- character (army values, empathy, warriors ethos/service ethos, and discipline)
- presence (military and professional bearing, fitness, confidence, resilience)
- intellect (mental agility, sound judgment, innovation, interpersonal tact, expertise)
- leads (leads others, builds trust, extends influence beyond the chain of command, leads by example, communicates)
- develops (creates a positive environment/fosters esprit de corps, prepares self, develops others, stewards the profession)
- achieves (gets results).[95]

One interviewee noted that the Army does not intentionally develop GOs, but rather senior leaders of the rank of O-6 and above.[96] By Army doctrine, O-6s, along with GOs, compose "the elite of the officer corps."[97] This is partly because the Army's approach to developing GOs

---

[90] ADP 6-22, 2012, p. 1.

[91] Department of the Army Pamphlet 600-3, *Commissioned Officer Professional Development and Career Management*, Washington, D.C.: Department of the Army, April 3, 2019, pp. 8–9.

[92] ADP 6-22, 2012, p. 1.

[93] Department of the Army Pamphlet 600-3, 2019, p. 5.

[94] Eric K. Fanning, Secretary of the Army, *Memorandum of Instruction—FY17 Brigadier General, Army Competitive Category, Promotion Selection Board—Change 1*, Washington, D.C.: U.S. Department of Defense, January 12, 2017.

[95] For more detail on the Army's leader attributes and core leader competencies, see ADP 6-22, 2012.

[96] A82, Army general officer, September 24, 2018.

[97] Department of the Army Pamphlet 600-3, 2019, p. 16.

includes narrowing the field-grade officer population down to its most successful brigade commanders and then choosing its O-7s from among them.

Some core tenets of the Army's approach to teaching leadership can be seen in its reliance on leadership development through repetition and increasing responsibility,[98] in its continuous emphasis that leadership is important in almost all circumstances,[99] and by requiring that senior officers demonstrate leadership capability as junior officers.[100] One interviewee noted that the Army's emphasis on leadership performance, and the de facto requirement that future promotions require previous leadership success in tactical assignments, narrows the field of potential GOs and eliminates some who might otherwise possess important and useful skills.[101] Even with that concern, one Army GO told us that the Army believes that it has a deep bench of talent among its senior leaders, from O-6 and above, in part because of the large pool of brigade commanders that can provide an ample supply of potential O-7s. According to the same interviewee, "if every one- and two-star GO in the Army keeled over dead today, the big machine would still be fine. It might blip, but it would be okay."[102]

Fundamental Elements of Army General Officer Pathways

The Army's approach to generalship, and the elements that define it, has a substantial impact on the professional characteristics that define many of its GOs. Several aspects of these pathways, such as some in personnel management processes, are written into law, but many others are driven by, and help to drive, Army culture. In the sections below, we describe how the Army's philosophical approach to generalship, competitive categories and typical pathways, career timelines, and personnel management processes help shape the Army's GO corps.

The Army's Philosophical Approach to the Officer Development Pipeline

The developmental path of most Army officers follows a framework that is designed around O-6-led combat brigades. Individual career fields manage their communities separately, but the similarities even among disparate career fields reflect cultural norms that transcend career field differences. At each rank, Army officers are expected to demonstrate strong performance relative to their peers, with performance in key command and staff roles of paramount importance. Across a wide variety of Army communities, one sees remarkable symmetry: a commanding officer role as an O-3/O-4, key staff responsibilities as an O-4, commanding officer

---

[98] Department of the Army Pamphlet 600-3, 2019, p. 11.

[99] ADP 6-22, 2012, p.1.

[100] A82, Army general officer, September 24, 2018; A52, Army general officer, December 7, 2018; A30, Army civilian employee with personnel management experience, September 12, 2018.

[101] A12, Army general officer, September 12, 2018.

[102] A82, Army general officer, September 24, 2018.

responsibilities as an O-5 and O-6, and a high visibility role following O-6 command are all positions named in interviews and the SLSE as essential to Army officer development. Our review of current Army GO bios also supported these observations.

At each of these defining positions, which the Army describes as a "key developmental" position within an officer's specific career field, the Army winnows its pool of promotable officers. For instance, the most qualified staff officers as O-4s will go on to O-5 command, and only a subset of O-5 commanding officers will go on to O-6 command. One must excel relative to peers to move on, and missing a key developmental step removes an officer from the funnel that eventually produces GOs for the Army.

Not all officers follow the same developmental model in an Army career, however. The Army divides its officer corps into two broad categories: basic branch officers and functional area officers.[103] Basic branch officers make up most officers in the Army; their career fields specialize in leading Army units. Functional area officers are technical specialists within the officer corps. Entering their career fields as O-3s or O-4s from a basic branch, functional area officers do not typically command an Army unit, instead focusing on key staff roles. While some functional area officer positions are in the tactical Army, many are in higher-echelon staffs, the institutional Army, or in the joint community, reflecting the strategic-level nature of certain functional area positions, such as strategists or foreign area officers.

The trust that the Army places in its officers to lead soldiers in combat yields an officer development model that selects and rewards those who are most adept at leading the Army's tactical units. This model is firmly grounded in Army culture, and it also reinforces the importance the Army naturally places on combat effectiveness. However, some of our interviewees questioned the Army's tendency to use success in small-unit leadership as a chief indicator of GO potential. As one GO noted, "What we are actually saying is tactical prowess is the key to strategic leadership—but that may not be the case."[104]

Competitive Categories

As in other services, the Army's career fields, or military occupational specialties (MOSs), are divided into competitive categories that guide the promotion process. The competitive categories are as follows:

- Operations—infantry, armor, field artillery, air defense artillery, aviation, Corps of Engineers, military police, chemical, Special Forces, civil affairs, and psychological operations
- Operations Support—military intelligence, Signal Corps, and several functional areas (strategic intelligence, space operations, public affairs, academy professor, foreign area

[103] Department of the Army Pamphlet 600-3, 2019, p. 11.

[104] A12, Army general officer, September 12, 2018.

officer, operations research and system analysis, force management, simulations, nuclear counterproliferation, strategist)

- Force Sustainment—logistics, adjutant general corps, finance corps, and acquisition
- Information Dominance—cyber and information operations
- Judge Advocate General's (JAG) Corps
- Chaplain Corps
- Army Medical Department (AMEDD), which includes five related competitive categories.[105]

Traditionally, the Army's branch distinctions are separated informally into three categories: combat arms (such as infantry, armor, field artillery), combat support (career fields that provide operational support to combat arms, such as signal corps, military police, and intelligence), and combat service support (career fields that provide administrative, medical, and other non-operational support to combat arms, such as nurses, the JAG corps, and finance officers).

While these competitive categories and informal categorizations were a useful starting point, we found that career development patterns emerged based on the type of command officers held at the O-5 and O-6 level, and the type of high-visibility role they filled when not in command.[106] Based on these patterns, we identified that the competitive category framework and the combat arms/support/service support framework are insufficient for understanding the pathways for GO rank. However, the construct of grouping similar career fields in specific categories provides useful insights. The pathways we identified are as follows:

- Infantry and armor (from the Operations competitive category)
- Other combat branches (field artillery, aviation, and special forces; from the Operations competitive category)
- Support branches (from the Operations, Operations Support, Force Sustainment, and Information Dominance competitive categories)
- Functional areas (from the Operations Support competitive category)
- Professional specialists (from the Operations Support, Force Sustainment, Judge Advocate, Chaplain, and AMEDD competitive categories).

Figure 3.1 shows how infantry and armor officers come to dominate the highest grades. When combined with other combat arms officers, infantry and armor officers initially account for almost 40 percent of all O-1s, or slightly less than the percentage of support branch officers. By O-6, the combat arms officers make up less than 25 percent of the O-6 population, while officers from the functional area or professional specialist communities account for nearly 50 percent. Several factors underlie this trend, including different attrition rates, officer transfers

---

[105] Army Directive 2017-08, *Competitive Categories for Commissioned Officers and Warrant Officers Serving on the Active Duty List and the Reserve Active Status List*, Washington, D.C.: Department of the Army, February 15, 2017.

[106] For instance, infantry and armor officers typically commanded brigade combat teams. Other combat arms officers rarely commanded brigade combat teams, but instead led units that corresponded to their specialty. Support branch officers led units within their specialty or served in a key staff role in lieu of command.

from combat arms to other communities (such as intelligence or operational research), and the arrival of some non–combat arms officers (such as doctors) straight to the O-3 or higher ranks via direct commissioning, among others. Promotion to O-7 starts a stark reversal of the trend, with infantry and armor officers promoted at higher rates than officers from other communities, resulting in their accounting for a growing percentage of GOs at each GO grade, while other pathways correspondingly shrink. This is especially evident in the highest grades, as the infantry and armor career fields provide nearly 30 percent of O-7s, then grow to over 80 percent of O-10s. One implication of this trend is that when a GO position does not directly align with a specific career field, GOs from the combat arms often fill those positions. Although a foreign area officer or strategist, for example, might have a suitable background to lead a major Army or joint organization, such as a CCMD, it is rarely the case that non–combat arms officers fill these types of positions.

Figure 4.1. Percentage of Army Officers, by Type and Grade, Average, 2008–2018

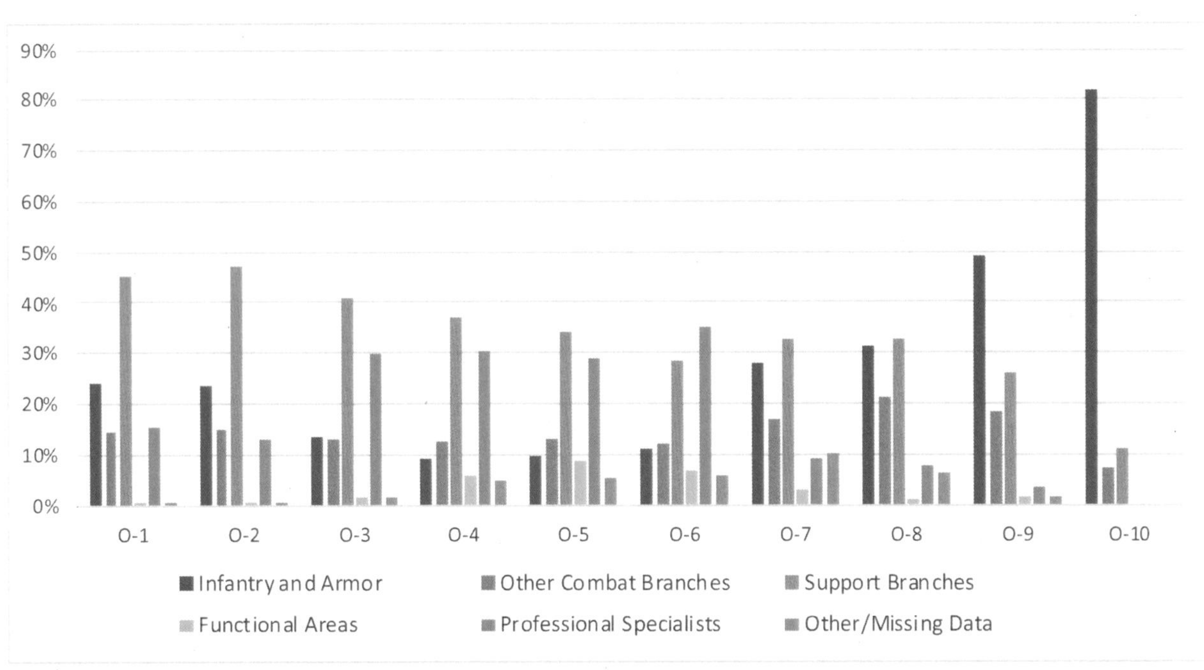

SOURCE: Authors' analysis of DMDC data. Officers are categorized by type using the primary service occupation codes assigned to each officer in any given year.
NOTES: The total number of Army officers analyzed by grade were as follows: O-1: 81,379; O-2: 134,626; O-3: 304,696; O-4: 178,425; O-5: 105,639; O-6: 47,141; O-7: 1,589; O-8: 1,226; O-9: 546; O-10: 125. The number of officers analyzed decreases between the lower grades and the higher grades. Because fewer officers are included in our analysis of higher grades, representation among the higher grades is more susceptible to fluctuations in year-over-year accession source differences.

Career Timelines

In the Army, career timelines are inextricably related to GO pathways. In this section, we provide an overview of career timelines and key milestones that apply broadly across the Army officer corps, and then describe specific pathways to GO.

Formally, the ideal career path for an Army officer is straightforward:

- Succeed in the proscribed positions at each rank.
- Attend formal PME in a resident status when selected.
- Become a joint qualified officer before the O-7 board.

The Army describes the ideal career path for each officer based on the officer's career field. Using the term "key developmental (KD) assignment," the Army directs that officers should serve in identified billets at each rank to develop the necessary skills and experience for future success in the career field.[107] The following is a generalized description of KD assignments by grade, but readers should note that the types of billets vary somewhat from career field to career field, and KD assignments lose some of their meaning when applied to functional area officers:[108]

- Captain/O-3: company commander
- Major/O-4: battalion/brigade operations officer or executive officer
- Lieutenant colonel/O-5: battalion commander or centralized selection list (CSL)–designated primary staff officer (some support branches)[109]
- Colonel/O-6: brigade commander or CSL-designated primary staff OFFICER (some support branches).

In general, to rise to O-5, Army officers must be successful in KD positions as O-3s and O-4s. In most communities, these positions include company command at O-3 and as key battalion staff officers at O-4. Those whose performance distinguishes them from their peers go on to serve as commanders at the O-5 level. For most career fields, we heard that the pathway generally does not truly start prior to the O-5 level, with the centralized selection for the first of two command positions. This observation is not new: As RAND's David Johnson noted in 2002, "Command is preeminent in the hierarchy of importance of assignments, evidenced by the centralized board selection process the Army uses to pick battalion and brigade commanders."[110]

---

[107] Department of the Army Pamphlet 600-3, 2019, p. 12.

[108] A functional area proponent may describe every billet coded for that specialty as key developmental. However, each functional area will internally identify the positions most important for promotion (A10, field-grade Army officer with personnel management experience, September 13, 2018).

[109] The Army uses a selection board known as the CSL board to select officers to fill command or key general staff billets. The CSL board selects officers at the O-5 and O-6 level. The positions are divided into four major categories: operations; strategic support; recruiting and training; and installation.

[110] David E. Johnson, *Preparing Potential Senior Army Leaders for the Future*, Santa Monica, Calif.: RAND Corporation, IP-224-A, 2002, p. 23.

The years before that point matter, as officers must demonstrate strong performance as O-3s and O-4s, especially in company-level command and battalion staff roles, to achieve selection for O-5 command. However, this performance is not enough to distinguish an officer to be on a path to GO. Some interviewees maintained that consideration for GO does not begin until following the completion of brigade command, a centrally selected command position at the O-6 grade.[111]

Along with KD assignments, officer career timelines overall include other broadening assignments, such as education and joint qualification assignments. Twice in a long career, officers will be centrally selected to attend PME: as senior O-3s for the Command and General Staff College (CGSC) and at O-5/O-6 for the Army War College.[112] Distance learning options are available for both programs, but successful officers—those competitive for future command positions—will generally attend in residence, although exceptions exist.[113] Army officers are also able to attend similarly favorable options beyond the Army-led courses, such as similar schools run by the Navy or Air Force.

Figure 4.2 shows Army GOs' average years in service at each grade, which climb fairly steadily, with larger jumps at O-4, O-5, and O-7. Figure 4.3 provides additional detail on this observation, highlighting that Army officers spend the most time in the O-3, O-4, and to a lesser extent, O-6 grades, which corresponds to these grades being intensive periods for KD and other required assignments.

---

[111] A20, Army field-grade officer with personnel management experience, September 4, 2018; A19, Army general officer, December 10, 2018; A30, Army civilian employee with personnel management experience, September 12, 2018; A82, Army general officer, September 24, 2018; A83, field-grade officer with personnel management experience, September 17, 2018.

[112] The Army has used two policies for intermediate-level education: centrally selecting officers and encouraging universal attendance. Regardless of the policy, competitive officers will typically attend in residence.

[113] Senior leader selection exercise notes, January 30, 2019, RAND Corporation, Arlington, Virginia.

Figure 4.2. Average Years in Service for Rising Army Officers, by Grade (Promoted in Prior Year), 2008–2018

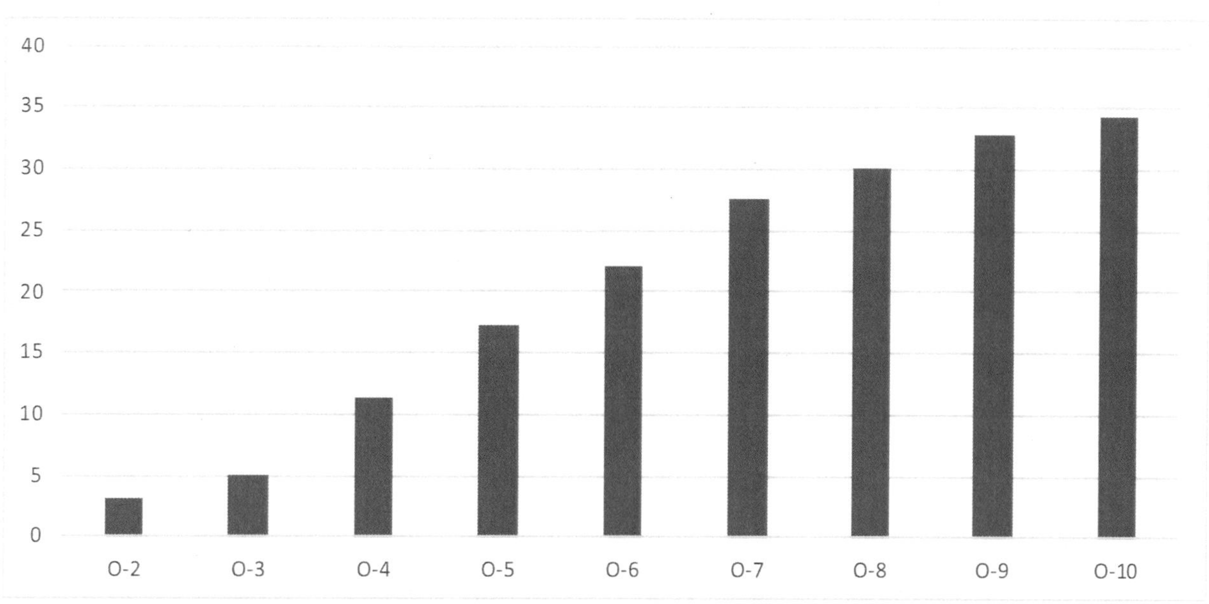

SOURCE: Authors' analysis of DMDC data. Years in service are calculated as of January each year, for officers promoted in the year before.

Figure 4.3. Time in Grade for Rising Army Officers Promoted from That Grade in the Prior Year, Average, 2008–2018

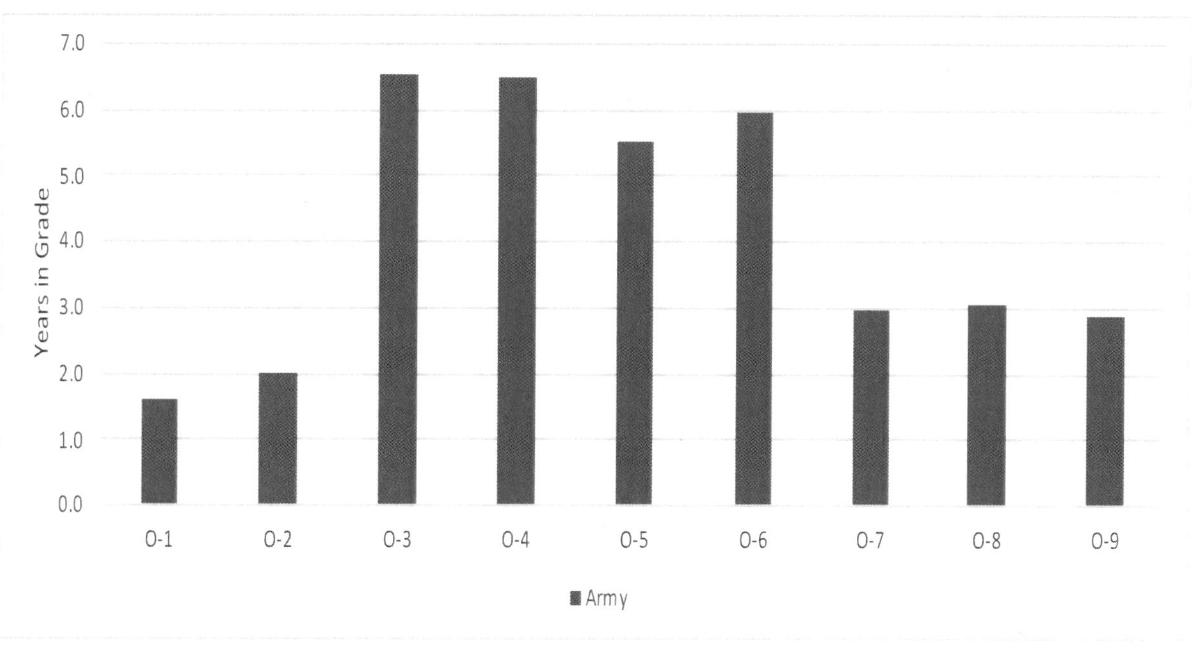

SOURCE: Authors' analysis of DMDC data.

An additional element contributing to overall career timelines is the role of BZ promotions. While BZ promotions do occur in the Army, they are still relatively rare compared with the Air Force and tend to be concentrated in the O-4, O-5, and O-6 grades. As several interviewees told us and discussion in the SLSE demonstrated, the Army uses BZ promotions selectively to identify and reward those who perform best among their peers. Interviewees emphasized, however, that BZ promotions only represent a snapshot in time; those selected BZ must continue to perform well to remain on track for future promotions.[114] Some interviewees questioned whether BZ promotions, which essentially eliminate potential years of experience, would adversely affect an officer's development by constraining the time in which an officer might receive broadening experience.[115]

Beyond these basic contours, the Army has several common pathways and associated career timelines to be promoted to GO starting around the O-5 level. We describe their timelines and typical professional assignments by pathway category in the following section.

Infantry and Armor Pathway

The infantry and armor pathways are clear and largely standardized. Key assignments start as early as O-3 in an infantry or armor officer's career. These officers must distinguish themselves in O-3 company command first and later as O-4 staff officers at the battalion level. Success in these positions can lead to other valuable assignments, such as an aide-de-camp to a senior officer. For example, among current O-7s, 19 of 24 infantry O-7s served as aides-de-camp or with the 75th Ranger Regiment, while eight of ten armor O-7s served as aides-de-camp, or at a combat training center.[116] However, while these experiences are critical, they are not necessarily sufficient to be on a GO track at this point in an officer's career: Many competitive officers will have similar experiences at the O-3 and O-4 grades, so the pool must be winnowed first.

As an O-5, tactical battalion command of an infantry or armor unit is essential: All current O-7s from the infantry and armor communities held this type of command. While other types of command are possible, such as an infantry training battalion, officers in this category served as commanders of infantry or combined arms battalions within brigade combat teams or commanded special mission unit squadrons. The average infantry or armor officer GO typically led a brigade combat team as an O-6, which is very rare for other combat arms officers who

---

[114] A30, Army civilian employee with personnel management experience, September 12, 2018; A82, Army general officer, September 24, 2018.

[115] A10, field-grade Army officer with personnel management experience, September 13, 2018; A82, Army general officer, September 24, 2018.

[116] These numbers reflect the experiences of officers prior to O-5 command. We selected this time period because officers in the Army tend to receive more personalized talent management attention after selection for O-5 command.

make O-7, who instead led functional units based on their career specialty.[117] Additionally, O-6 infantry officers generally command light brigades and armor officers command heavy brigades.[118] As an O-6, most served as a brigade combat team commander or special mission unit commander. After brigade command, O-7s from both infantry and armor typically serve in assignments designed to posture them for O-7 consideration, such as the high-visibility aide jobs described previously, compared with other combat arms officers.

Other Combat Branches Pathway

Officers from other combat arms communities also have a defined pathway to GO, which generally includes serving in command within their own communities at the O-5 and O-6 grades. An Army Special Forces O-6 will typically command a Special Forces group, and an aviation O-6 will typically command a combat aviation brigade. However, more flexibility exists in type of command than in the infantry or armor communities' pathway. For example, a field artillery officer might lead a battlefield coordination detachment rather than an artillery brigade.

Officers from the aviation, field artillery, and Special Forces career fields account for a more stable percentage of all officers than infantry and armor officers. Officers in this pathway account for between 10 percent and 20 percent of all officers for each grade between O-1 and O-9, before finally dropping below 10 percent at O-10.[119]

Support Branches Pathway

Officers from other basic branches cut across multiple Army competitive categories, but the officers tend to follow a pathway that is substantially different than the combat-centric branches. At the grade of O-5, these officers typically command a unit within their specialty or serve in a key billet within their specialty. Support branch officers who make O-7 have commanded a greater variety of units at O-6, including tactical brigades and strategic support brigades. In some career fields, such as Adjutant General Corps, Signal Corps, military intelligence, and finance, officers might serve in centrally selected key staff billets rather than battalion or brigade command.[120]

Officers from this pathway make up a large share of officers in the Army but a relatively small share of GOs. Initially, about 40 percent of O-1s and about 30 percent of O-6s are in the support branches. However, this pathway declines in percentage in the GO grades compared with officers from the combat arms career fields.

---

[117] David Johnson observed a similar trend, finding that "successful tactical brigade commanders are the officers most likely to be selected for brigadier general" (Johnson, 2002, p. 24).

[118] Author's analysis of Army GO biography data; A83, field-grade officer with personnel management experience, September 17, 2018.

[119] Authors' analysis of DMDC data.

[120] Department of the Army Pamphlet 600-3, 2019, p. 11.

Functional Area Officers Pathway

Functional area officers are those with a "technical specialty or skills . . . that usually require significant education, training, and experience."[121] These officers generally follow a separate career pathway that largely eschews command after O-3, and they rarely rise above the grade of O-7, as shown in Figure 3.1. From 2008 to 2018, the Army had an average of 298 O-6 functional area officers in any given year, but only four O-7, one O-8, and one O-9 functional area officer.[122] These officers do not typically serve in command roles, even those that become GOs, and are instead specialists in a narrow field.[123] Never constituting more than 10 percent of the officer corps, this pathway provides a very small share of officers in the GO ranks. Functional area officers often illustrate the primary nontraditional pathway to O-7, which will be discussed next. Their careers are built around different milestones, which do not tend to include the command of units. For example, functional area officers might rise to O-7 without having a command assignment at O-5 or O-6, a prerequisite in the traditional pathway to GO.[124]

Professional Specialists Pathway

Lastly, the professional specialists often compete for promotion up through O-7 in distinct competitive categories. Accounting for nearly 40 percent of officers at O-6, this pathway provides only 20 percent of O-7s and few officers above that rank. These officers come from the JAG, medical, chaplain, medical, acquisition, and military academy professor fields corps. Our definition of a professional branch is broader than that of the Army, which defines the professional branches only as JAG, medical, and chaplain. We also include the acquisition and military professor career fields with the other professional specialists because of pathway similarities.

Personnel Management Processes and Impact on Army General Officers

The Army's personnel management processes are rooted in both service culture and in statutory and DoD policy requirements. As we explain in the following section, the Army's personnel management processes, including commissioning, duty assignments, education and special training, evaluations, and promotion boards, have substantial impact on how Army GOs are developed and selected.

---

[121] Department of the Army Pamphlet 600-3, 2019, p. 11.

[122] Authors' analysis of DMDC data.

[123] One exception to this statement is Functional Area (FA)—40 Space Operations. FA-40 officers command Army space units such as the 1st Space Brigade; A52, Army general officer, December 7, 2018.

[124] Author's analysis of Army GO biography data; A52, Army general officer, December 7, 2018.

Commissioning Source

Four primary sources produce Army officers: USMA, ROTC, OCS, and direct commissions.[125] At the O-1 grade, ROTC graduates account for roughly half of officer commissions, while USMA and OCS graduates roughly split the other half. Less than 5 percent of O-1 commissions are sourced from direct commissions.

Commissioning source appears to play a role in which officers eventually rise to O-7, though the most marked change does not emerge until the top two grades of O-9 and O-10. Between O-1 and O-4, officers are promoted largely in proportion to initial commissioning rates. Many direct appointments, especially within the medical community, are commissioned into the O-3 and O-4 grades, which explains that category's increase at those grades, as shown in Figure 4.4. However, between O-5 and O-7, we see an increase in ROTC-commissioned officers promoted relative to their share of initial entry commissions. At the same time, OCS graduates are promoted at lower rates, and both ROTC and USMA officers begin to dominate the officer corps. Starting with promotion to O-7, USMA graduates start to surge in their share of officer positions, while the percentage of officers who commissioned through ROTC decreases slightly from O-7 to O-8. By O-9 and especially O-10, however, USMA graduates make up the vast majority of positions.

[125] USMA is also referred to as *West Point* due to its location in West Point, New York.

Figure 4.4. Accession Source of Rising Army Officers (Promoted in Prior Year), by Grade, Average, 2008–2018

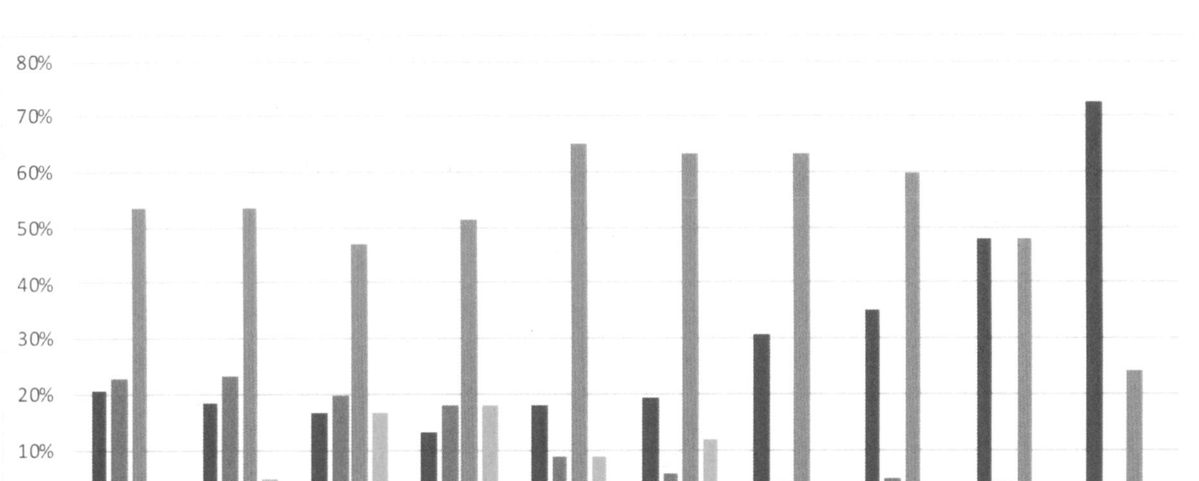

SOURCE: Authors' analysis of DMDC data.
NOTES: Because of the DMDC data structure, the total number of officers analyzed by MOS is different than the total number of officers analyzed by accession source. The total numbers of Army officers analyzed by grade were as follows: O-1: 54,550; O-2: 58,487; O-3: 55,306; O-4: 24,816; O-5: 16,782; O-6: 7,395; O-7: 474; O-8: 328; O-9: 151; O-10: 29. The number of officers analyzed decreases between the lower grades and the higher grades. Because fewer officers are included in our analysis of higher grades, representation among the higher grades is more susceptible to fluctuations in year-over-year accession source differences.

The disproportionality of USMA graduates in the Army GO ranks might result from the interaction of several factors. Network effects might be at play: USMA cadets are more likely to know each while in school, forging career-long acquaintances that ROTC programs, across multiple schools, do not replicate. SLSE participants and one interviewee did not acknowledge this difference between USMA and ROTC as a factor in career advancement, at least before the O-9 rank.[126] Alternatively, USMA graduates are more likely to serve in the combat arms, which traditionally provide more GOs than the support branches. In 2019, for example, 81 percent of USMA graduates commissioned into the combat arms, per Army leadership guidance.[127]

Prospective analysis indicates that, of all officers who served as O-4s between FY 1995 and FY 2018, 1.33 percent of USMA graduates attained the grade of O-7. By comparison, 0.13 percent of OCS graduates were promoted to O-7, and 0.72 percent of ROTC graduates were promoted to the grade of O-7. Academy graduates are promoted to O-7 at a rate of nearly ten times that of OCS, and 1.82 times ROTC graduates.

---

[126] A97, Army general officer, October 18, 2018; senior leader selection exercise notes, January 30, 2019, RAND Corporation, Arlington, Virginia.

[127] West Point Association of Graduates, "Branch Night 2018," website, undated.

Duty Assignments

Army assignments are highly focused on core career field skills and experiences, and Army needs drive supporting institutional assignments and true broadening assignments, if they occur. Army officers move from one assignment to another through a system that relies on both formal and informal elements. Formally, the Army Human Resources Command (HRC) manages the assignments and career development of officers, and thus maintains responsibility for moving an officer from one location to another. Another formal process, using centralized selection boards, identifies officers for intermediate and senior PME and O-5 and O-6 command positions. At the same time, unit commanders and senior staff officers also have responsibility within the assignment system, as those officers place subordinates into the actual job positions. While HRC will move an officer to a new posting, the local commander will determine what that officer does upon arrival and generally has authority to move the officer into a certain position in that command (though exceptions are noted below). This authority is considered critical; it has even been argued that, in extreme cases, the separation of talent acquisition from a commander's purview can create dysfunction for the Army.[128] Army GOs sometimes use by-name requests to circumvent normal assignment decisions, though their ability to do so is likely limited.

Each career field manages the assignment of its officers through HRC up through O-5, at which point the responsibility shifts to the Colonels Management Office (COMO) in the Army G-1. The assignment processes at HRC and COMO must balance two potentially contradictory mandates: (1) Meet the readiness requirements of the Arm, and (2) meet the professional development needs of its officers. Near-term readiness goals for the Army are important and sometimes outweigh longer-term professional development goals.

Centralized selection boards for PME and field-grade officer command positions are a unique variant on the assignment processes managed by HRC and COMO. With a centralized selection board for command, officers are slated for command of specific units; senior unit commanders cannot place their own candidates in the position.

Local senior commanders do play a large role in the assignment process, as they place officers in positions of responsibility that signal and prepare an officer for the command selection boards. One interviewee noted that the two most critical positions in determining career trajectories are the division commander and the brigade commander, who each select officers into assignments such as a brigade- or battalion-level operations or executive officer role. Who the commanders place into these key staff positions in effect largely shapes the next pool of battalion and brigade commanders. Other decisions, such as bypassing an officer for a key

---

[128] Anna Simons, *21st-Century Challenges of Command: A View from the Field*, Carlisle Barracks, Pa.: U.S. Army War College Press, 2017, p. 17.

position, can remove that officer from competition for future leadership positions. As one interviewee explained, "Those two positions have an outsized role in who our GOs will be."[129]

According to multiple interviews and observations from the SLSE, one particular type of core career field position that the Army values above all other assignments is command. The Army categorizes command into four bins:

- Operations: Units and key staff positions that are "expeditionary in nature and deployable worldwide"
- Strategic support: "(U)nits focused on providing support such as analysis, intelligence, communications, materials, medical, logistics, and technology to a theater"
- Recruiting and training: "Focused on generating Soldiers into conventional and SMUs of the U.S. Army and sister services"
- Installation: "Support tenant units or activities in a designated geographic area by organizing, directing, coordinating, and controlling installation support and service activities."[130]

Most officers who rise to O-7 will serve in command positions within the operations command category, which is especially true for those in combat arms.[131] Officers in the support branches will typically serve in command positions in the operations or strategic support command categories. Those who serve in the remaining two command categories are, in a sense, moving along a nontraditional path to O-7. Some officers who served in nontraditional O-6 command positions and later rose to the GO ranks followed their command position with a high-visibility role in the next assignment. One interviewee described such a role as "being rescued," in which a GO brought the nontraditional officer back into contention for O-7 through advocacy.[132]

Factors that are difficult to capture using available data could also explain why some officers succeed along a nontraditional pathway, at least regarding O-6 command positions. For example, officers can influence the type of positions in which they serve for O-6 command, submitting preferences that influence the type of command in which they serve. One interviewee told us that officers who score highly on the O-6 command board might be more likely to serve in their desired type of command, and, in general, most competitive officers prefer to serve in the most competitive command positions.[133] However, some officers might prefer to serve in a

---

[129] A division commander is an O-8 and senior rater for O-5 battalion commanders within the division. Between the O-5 battalion commanders and the division commander lie the O-6 brigade commanders; interview with A12, Army general officer, September 12, 2018.

[130] Department of the Army Pamphlet 600-3, 2019, pp. 11–12.

[131] A20, Army field-grade officer with personnel management experience, September 4, 2018; A82, Army general officer, September 24, 2018. This trend was also evident in our review or current GO biographies.

[132] A10, field-grade Army officer with personnel management experience, September 13, 2018.

[133] A83, field-grade officer with personnel management experience, September 17, 2018.

nontraditional command position. Those officers might have had performance records competitive with the top of their peers but decided to pursue a non-traditional command.

Supporting Institutional Assignments

Supporting institutional assignments in the Army are those that are not directly related to one's basic branch, but rather support the basic needs of the Army. Examples include serving as a training officer at a combat training center, which is generally viewed favorably for combat arms officers, or assignments at HRC or as an aide-de-camp to a GO. Particularly at junior levels, these assignments can serve as signaling tools to promotion boards that the officer has notable leadership potential, and/or these assignments can create support from senior officers. At the O-4 and O-5 grades, however, many officers feel pressure to stay close to their core career field and complete KD assignments in order to demonstrate tactical proficiency and secure high evaluation remarks from rating officers.

Service in institutional assignments requires unique skill sets. Previous RAND research into the knowledge, skills, and abilities (KSAs) required for different echelons summarized the issue: "The strategic, operational, tactical, and institutional echelons require distinctly different KSAs. That is, jobs at these different echelons differ in kind, not merely in degree."[134] The RAND study found that exposure was not sufficient, but rather that "developing expertise in any one of these domains requires focus and repetitive but varied experience."[135] To address these dynamics, some have recommended viewing expertise as existing in different functional forms, such as combat, political, institutional, and "anticipatory."[136] Others have argued that the Army should consider splitting the GO corps into warfighting and enterprise management tracks.[137]

Broadening and Joint Assignments

The Army defines broadening assignments as the "purposeful expansion of a leader's capabilities and understanding provided through opportunities internal and external to the Army."[138] Such a wide definition allows for a range of assignments to fall within the confines of broadening. The Army classifies broadening assignments into five categories: functional, tactical, or institutional; scholastic and civilian enterprise; joint or multinational; interagency or

---

[134] M. Wade Markel, Henry A. Leonard, Charlotte Lynch, Christina Panis, Peter Schirmer, and Carra S. Sims, *Developing U.S. Army Officers' Capabilities for Joint, Interagency, Intergovernmental, and Multinational Environments*, Santa Monica, Calif.: RAND Corporation, MG-990-A, 2011, p. 92.

[135] Markel et al., 2011, p. 92.

[136] Anticipatory genius is "the unique ability to think in time and imagine conceptually where the nature and character of war is headed" (Bob Scales, Major General, U.S. Army (retired), *Scales on War: The Future of America's Military at Risk*, Annapolis, Md.: Naval Institute Press, 2016, pp. 189–192).

[137] Barno et al., 2013, p. 12.

[138] Department of the Army Pamphlet 600-3, 2019, p. 12.

intergovernmental; and cross-component.[139] In line with our study's characterization of what constitutes a broadening assignment, we focus here on the latter four subsets.

Others recommend a more focused approach to broadening. Watson, Babcock-Lumish, and Urben recommend that a broadening assignment must accomplish two things: remove an officer from a comfort zone and improve critical thinking.[140] Assignments such as an exchange officer, serving in an initiatives group, or attending a civilian graduate school meet such a standard. Gerras and Wong recommend that "the best broadening experiences immerse an aspiring leader in an environment where the comfortable hierarchy of the Army is removed, frames of reference are questioned, and assumptions are tested."[141]

However, many Army O-7s do not have the opportunity to serve in those types of environments because of timeline constraints within a career and the need to focus on assignments more directly supportive of promotion.[142] Institutional pressures keep officers "on a narrow ridgeline of tactical, tactical, tactical."[143] Five other interviewees and SLSE participants stressed this same point that tactical assignments are highly prized by rising officers, but broadening assignments are pursued only when absolutely necessary.[144] When broadening does occur, the period before promotion to O-5 is preferred; one interviewee argued that the O-4 period should be focused on broadening for future senior leaders, rather than serving in key tactical staff positions.[145] For those officers who eventually rise to the GO ranks, highly selective broadening assignments, such as congressional fellowships or Commander's Initiatives Group positions, are more common.

As in all services, joint qualification is prerequisite for promotion to O-7. The timing of a joint tour can help or hinder individual officers' ability to become a GO. A competitive officer without joint experience will likely go to a joint assignment after O-6 command, but multiple interviewees cited this circumstance as undesirable.[146] At a time when the O-6 must become

---

[139] Department of the Army Pamphlet 600-3, 2019, p. 12.

[140] Zach N. Watson, Brian C. Babcock-Lumish, and Heidi A. Urben, "The Value of Broadening Assignments," *ARMY Magazine*, Vol. 66, No. 12, December 2016.

[141] Stephen J. Gerras and Leonard Wong, *Changing Minds in the Army: Why It Is So Difficult and What to Do About It*, Carlisle Barracks, Pa.: U.S. Army War College Press, 2013, p. 25.

[142] Johnson, 2002, p. 27.

[143] A83, field-grade officer with personnel management experience, September 17, 2018.

[144] Senior leader selection exercise notes, January 30, 2019, RAND Corporation, Arlington, Virginia; A10, field-grade Army officer with personnel management experience, September 13, 2018; A12, Army general officer, September 12, 2018; A19, Army general officer, December 10, 2018; A30, Army civilian employee with personnel management experience, September 12, 2018; A97, Army general officer, October 18, 2018.

[145] A52, Army general officer, December 7, 2018; A97, Army general officer, October 18, 2018.

[146] A12, Army general officer, September 12, 2018, A52; Army general officer, December 7, 2018; A82, Army general officer, September 24, 2018.

known to many GOs, a joint tour provides limited visibility. Earlier joint tours, such as immediately before O-5 command, present less risk to a career.[147]

As described in Chapter 3, the Army, like other services, satisfies the joint experience component of JQO attainment through both E-JDAs and S-JDAs. Approximately half of current Army O-7s completed their joint experience through an S-JDA tour. Many current Army O-7s received their joint duty credit through the E-JDA pathway, which is in a deployed environment. These officers, who became O-4s around the early 2000s, generally served their field-grade years in Iraq or Afghanistan, so this observation might not hold for future classes of GOs that are not subject to the same heavy deployment requirements. Many held prominent positions as unit commanders or operations officers, and these joint, multinational positions qualified them for E-JDA credit.[148] Because many of these positions would have been placed within Army-heavy, combat-focused organizations, the actual experience in broad "joint matters" could be limited.

Deployment Experience

Today's Army officers who reach O-7 usually have extensive operational experience: They have served in operational units and in combat zones. Unsurprisingly, given the deployment cycles of the past two decades, the vast majority of current O-7s from basic branches have served in command positions or the staff equivalent as O-5s and O-6s, and most have carefully followed the prescribed career path that put them into contention for O-5 command, O-6 command, and eventual selection to O-7. Since 2001, these command experiences frequently involved operational, combat-related deployments. This reflects the Army's cultural value of "muddy boots" and the importance—particularly for infantry and armor officers—of operational command. Participants in the SLSE stressed that in promotion decisions, deployments are not viewed as merely "checking the block," but instead present accumulated value from multiple deployments.[149]

However, the total time deployed might vary even with the combat arms fields, for a few reasons. First, many of the premier assignments in the other combat arms career fields tend to have shorter deployment times—some of the key aviation and Special Forces positions, for example, would not require the 12 to 15 months that are more commonly seen in infantry deployments. Second, the nature of critical assignments—and how combat-intensive they must be—between infantry and armor versus other combat arms career fields are somewhat different. In infantry and armor communities, effective combat leadership is the primary metric to demonstrate career field proficiency to promotion boards, but in some of the other combat arms

---

[147] A30, Army civilian employee with personnel management experience, September 12, 2018; A52, Army general officer, December 7, 2018, A97, Army general officer, October 18, 2018.

[148] Paul W. Mayberry, William H. Waggy II, and Anthony Lawrence, *Producing Joint Qualified Officers: FY 2008 to FY 2017 Trends*, Santa Monica, Calif.: RAND Corporation, RR-3105-OSD, 2019, pp. 63–66.

[149] Senior leader selection exercise notes, January 30, 2019, RAND Corporation, Arlington, Virginia.

specialties, a broader range of metrics, such as deploying on training missions and record of safety, are also important.

Combat-related deployments provide an additional benefit, beyond experience, that draws on a unique facet on the Army's evaluation system. A deployment can increase the quantity of Officer Evaluation Records (OERs) that a commander will receive. In a two-year command tour, a commander will typically receive two OERs. When deployed, the commander may receive up to four OERs: one before the deployment, one or two during the deployment, and one at the conclusion of the command tour. Additionally, the deployment will likely yield more OERs from a greater number of GOs. The accumulation of additional OERs during a deployment, reflecting the opinions of multiple GOs, gives the deployed O-6 commander a substantial advantage if the OERs are all very good.[150]

High-Visibility Assignments at the O-6 Level

O-6s that are seen as most competitive for promotion to O-7 will generally move to a high-visibility role after brigade command. These high-visibility roles are those positions with substantial interaction with G/FOs (and particularly Army GOs), such as prestigious aide or executive officer positions. As several interviewees mentioned, these high-visibility assignments are significant because, even with a very strong record of performance, only O-6s with a positive personal reputation with several board members have the greatest chance to advance to O-7. Discussion in the SLSE also validated this observation. Further, high-visibility roles, regardless of promotion pathway, provide Army GOs the opportunity to gain firsthand knowledge of the characteristics and potential of the top echelon of senior O-6s. Thus, the Army will assign those with the best likelihood of future O-7 promotion to positions that allow them the greatest visibility with future promotion board members. Nearly every interviewee stressed the importance of high-visibility roles for those who could potentially become Army O-7s.

In particular, an executive officer position for a four-star Army GO is considered very prestigious, because it says the GO chose that particular officer over any other officer in the Army.[151] The signaling value of the decision, combined with the likely exposure to many other GOs, provides an important boost to an officer's promotion potential.

The Army's emphasis on high-visibility, service-centric assignments at this career juncture has implications on timing of joint assignments. For example, one interviewee told us that a high-quality OER in a joint position will improve competitiveness, but the inability of sister service G/FOs to discuss their opinions during a promotion board limits the impact they can have.[152] Another interviewee agreed with this statement and added that, in most circumstances, only those officers still in need of joint experience move into a joint position after O-6 brigade

---

[150] The preceding paragraph is based on an interview with A52, Army general officer, December 7, 2018.

[151] Senior leader selection exercise notes, January 30, 2019, RAND Corporation, Arlington, Virginia.

[152] A10, field-grade Army officer with personnel management experience, September 13, 2018.

command.[153] RAND analysis from 2002, which found that one-third of O-7 and O-8 selectees did not complete a joint tour until after brigade command, underscores this point.[154] In the deployment-heavy 2000s, many officers were able to fulfill joint assignments at more junior levels in Iraq or Afghanistan. However, as deployments have retracted, it has become more challenging to place officers in joint billets earlier in their careers. It is possible that this shift could adversely affect officers who are not able to become joint qualified until after their O-6 commands. Alternatively, it could also affect how the Army approaches valuation of high-visibility assignments prior to O-7 promotion decisions.

Of note, what constitutes a high visibility position can change over time, as those positions only reflect current service expectations and preferences. For instance, several current Army O-7s served in the Office of the Chief Legislative Liaison (OCLL) as senior Army representatives to Congress when they were senior O-6s. The position exposes the officer to congressional deliberations and is viewed as building experience that will be of value to the Army. However, the current value placed on that assignment is a recent development.[155]

Education and Special Training

Overall, we found through multiple interviews and the SLSE that formal education in the Army is viewed as necessary, but not necessarily as a differentiating criterion in promotion decisions. For example, performance in education is not valued as highly as other experiences to promotion boards.[156] Army officers attend the CGSC or equivalent sister service schools as junior O-4s following a competitive selection board.[157] Those not selected for resident attendance complete their intermediate education through a mixture of resident and nonresident components or a completely nonresident program.[158] Officers not selected for resident attendance face steep odds for selection for O-5 command, if not O-5 selection.

Senior Service College

Army O-5s and O-6s can complete senior service college through two primary venues: a resident ten-month program or a ten-month fellowship at a university, think tank, or government agency. In our analysis of the bios of current O-7s, we did not identify an Army O-7 who completed a nonresident senior service program. The post–World War II Army adopted a

---

[153] A82, Army general officer, September 24, 2018.

[154] Johnson, 2002, pp. 27–28.

[155] Senior leader selection exercise notes, January 30, 2019, RAND Corporation, Arlington, Virginia.

[156] Senior leader selection exercise notes, January 30, 2019, RAND Corporation, Arlington, Virginia.

[157] Army Regulation 350-1, *Army Training and Leader Development*, Washington, D.C.: Department of the Army, 2017, pp. 53, 75–76.

[158] There are exceptions to this generalization. Some officers who participate in highly competitive broadening programs might achieve their intermediate education through the mixture of resident and nonresident CGSC. Likewise, some functional area career fields will primarily use the mixture of resident and nonresident CGSC.

"screening" approach to senior service college attendance, limiting attendance to selected officers and thus creating the impression that the war colleges "were good tickets to have when the selection boards had to decide which of the many officers available would receive the limited number of promotions."[159]

However, according to multiple interviews and observations from the SLSE, senior service college performance does not heavily influence future promotion potential. To that point, the FY 2017 O-7 promotion board instruction does not advise board members to consider academic performance while at the senior service college.

Graduate Education

Because the Army War College and other full-time senior service colleges award master's degrees, Army GOs typically have an educational degree beyond the baccalaureate. They do not, however, typically have a master's degree from a full-time civilian graduate program. Colarusso and Lyle found that the share of Army O-7s with a full-time civilian graduate degree declined from 54 percent in 1995 to 31 percent by 2010, which they ascribe to a steep decline in funded graduate school opportunities that occurred in the early 1990s.[160] Further, their analysis showed that O-5s and O-6s leaving the Army tended to have more civilian graduate education than the officers promoted to O-7. Colarusso and Lyle concluded that "(f)or almost 2 decades, however, the signal to the officer corps has been loud and clear: civilian graduate education is not critical to the Army profession. As a result, future senior officers possess less civilian education than their predecessors, a trend that is continuing."[161]

Some of the literature points to the advantage of graduate education for Army officers. Salmoni et al. observed that graduate education can play an important role in strategic education, and Gerras and Wong consider graduate education as an effective mechanism for broadening an Army officer's outlook.[162] Matthews expanded on this point, noting that graduate education can help the Army identify the "contemplative," or thoughtful and strategic, officer, if only as a signaling tool.[163] Colarusso and Lyle found that civilian graduate programs are "a proven way to develop mental agility and adaptability."[164]

The Army has taken recent steps to reemphasize graduate education, which might affect the trends that took root in recent decades. ROTC and USMA cadets can attend graduate school

---

[159] James H. Hayes, *The Evolution of Military Officer Personnel Management Policies: A Preliminary Study with Parallels from Industry*, Santa Monica, Calif.: RAND Corporation, R-2276-AF, August 1978, pp. 131–132.

[160] Michael J. Colarusso and David S. Lyle, *Senior Officer Talent Management: Fostering Institutional Adaptability*, Carlisle Barracks, Pa.: U.S. Army War College Press, 2014, pp. 109–110.

[161] Colarusso and Lyle, 2014, p. 111.

[162] Barak A. Salmoni, Jessica Hart, Renny McPherson, and Aidan Kirby Winn, "Growing Strategic Leaders for Future Conflict," *Parameters*, Vol. 77, Spring 2010, p. 77; Gerras and Wong, 2013, p. 25.

[163] Matthews, 2005, p. 66.

[164] Colarusso and Lyle, 2014, p. 111.

early in their careers through a retention program that the Army established in 2006.[165] It is unknown whether officers who make use of that opportunity will rise to the GO ranks, but the program will create a larger bench of officers with civilian graduate degrees.[166] More recently, the Army also started sending field-grade officers to doctoral programs through the Advanced Strategic Planning and Policy Program to prepare those officers for "key planning positions" in DoD, the NSC, other U.S. government agencies, Congress, and think tanks.[167]

Related to graduate education is teaching at an educational institution. Some have associated a USMA teaching tour with eventual promotion to high rank. Jaffe and Cloud, writing about the social science department at USMA, described two types of officers in the department: "generals-in-waiting and dissidents." They noted that in 2009, about 25 percent of Army O-10s had taught in the social science department at USMA.[168] Today, none have. The decline in USMA teaching as an important career accomplishment might be a function of the wars in Iraq and Afghanistan. We saw that future O-7s deployed frequently and often in important positions. For competitive officers, a USMA tour might have been less advantageous than pursuing opportunities in combat—a distinct difference from earlier generations of officers.

Instructors once enjoyed far greater importance in career models. Looking back at the Army from the vantage point of the late 1970s, Hayes notes that the post–World War II Army desired officers with "command, staff, student, and instructor" experience.[169] All Regular Army corps commanders in World War II had served as instructors in the prewar period.[170] No current Army O-7 has taught at the Army War College, which one interviewee observed is likely because a teaching tour at the Army War College lacks the high-visibility status required for promotion to O-7.[171] Some even argue that a late career teaching tour can effectively end a career.[172]

Special Training—Ranger School

One special training experience that many assume has an effect on whether an officer is likely to make O-7 is Ranger School attendance. Ranger School is a rigorous 63-day program for

---

[165] Colarusso and Lyle, 2014, p. 110.

[166] One interviewee questioned whether the "juice is worth the squeeze," as officers attending graduate school can fulfill a service obligation and depart the Army long before rising to senior officer levels (A97, Army general officer, October 18, 2018).

[167] Jim Tice, "Army Seeks Officers for Elite Military Studies Doctoral Program," *Army Times*, February 15, 2016.

[168] Greg Jaffe and David Cloud, *The Fourth Star: Four Generals and the Epic Struggle for the Future of the United States Army*, New York: Crown Publishers, 2009, p. 54.

[169] Hayes, 1978, p. 129.

[170] Douglas Orsi, "Professional Military Education and Broadening Assignments: A Model for the Future," *Joint Forces Quarterly*, Vol. 86, 3rd quarter 2017, p. 43. An Army corps oversees multiple Army divisions and would be commanded by an O-9.

[171] Author's analysis of Army GO biography data; A10, field-grade Army officer with personnel management experience, September 13, 2018.

[172] Orsi, 2017, p. 42.

both officers and enlisted members that focuses on developing functional combat skills. Many of our interviewees and SLSE participants noted that graduation from Ranger School is often considered a marker, especially in infantry and Special Forces (though not limited to those careers), of tactical proficiency, combat leadership, and physical and mental toughness. Ranger School attendance typically occurs during the earliest years of a career, although later exceptions certainly occur. Further, many Ranger school graduates started their career as infantry officers before switching to non-infantry career fields.

Analysis of DMDC data showed that in all career field categories except for functional area officers, those who attended Ranger School were promoted to O-7 more frequently than those who did not. We also learned from our interviews that there is a perception that Ranger School attendance plays a role in boards considerations for selection to GO, which could affect GO pathways by influencing officers to pursue Ranger School or senior officers to view Ranger School graduates as higher-caliber. Further, it might be the case that some of the most prominent senior positions (such as combatant commanders or Chief of Staff of the Army) are frequently held by Ranger School graduates, further contributing to this perception. The relationship of Ranger qualification and generalship also might strengthen as junior officers who attended Ranger School in the mid-2000s start to approach the O-7 threshold.

Figure 4.5. Percentage of Rising Army O-6s (Promoted in Prior Year) from 2000—2010 Who Are Later Promoted to O-7, by Ranger School Graduation and Career Type

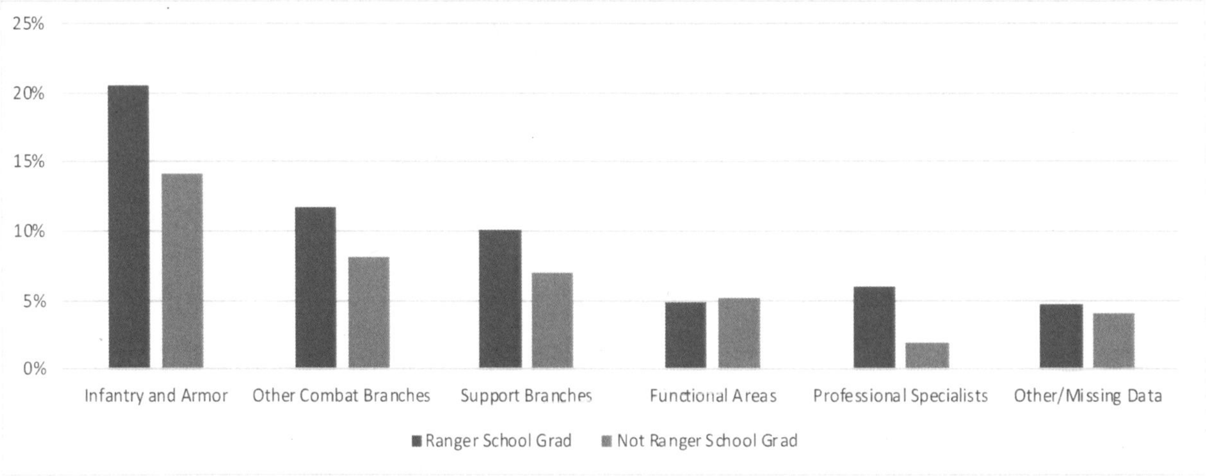

25%
20%
15%
10%
5%
0%
Infantry and Armor
Other Combat Branches
Support Branches
Functional Areas
Professional Specialists
Other/Missing Data
■ Ranger School Grad ■ Not Ranger School Grad

SOURCE: Authors' analysis of DMDC data.
NOTE: These numbers represent the progression rate for the 11 cohorts of Army O-6s who were recently promoted as of the beginning of each year from 2000 through 2010, and reflect these officers' observed rates of reaching O-7 at any point up to the beginning of 2018, the last year for which we have data. Percentages are broken out by type and by whether or not the recently promoted O-6 had or had not previously graduated from Ranger school.

Evaluations

The Army uses an evaluation system to identify those "who are best qualified for promotion and assignment to positions of greater responsibility."[173] For officers, the Army uses OERs, or performance evaluations, that are completed by raters (officers who directly supervise the evaluated officer) and senior raters (officers who oversee both the rater and of the evaluated officer). The OERs allow raters to evaluate an officer's performance and senior raters to evaluate an officer's potential. All officers in the grade of O-7 and below receive OERs, although the Army uses different forms for different grades. The evaluation system features several key characteristics that both reflect the culture and shape the type of GOs the service produces.

First, in most cases, a supervisor serves as an officer's rater, and the supervisor's supervisor serves as the senior rater. The relative standing in the organization determines the rating chain. We were unable to identify any formal training provided by the Army on how to conduct a performance or potential assessment, or how to assess the capability of an individual relative to any assessment skills.[174]

Army officers receive an OER on an annual basis at a minimum but may receive an evaluation that covers less than 12 months if the officer changes jobs, the rater changes, or the senior rater elects to provide an OER because the senior rater is departing.[175] The key feature, however, is that an OER covers only 12 months or less of job performance. In many jobs, 12 months might not provide enough hindsight to assess performance. For example, an officer in a policy position might be at a disadvantage when evaluated on a year-long time horizon. Many policy efforts are multiyear efforts, with the impact observed in subsequent years, so tying the officer's performance to achieved outcomes will not be possible when constrained by a 12-month evaluation cycle.

We have two observations about the limitations of the 12-month rating period. First, officers tend to be evaluated on how they perform in completing their work, rather than on the long-term goals that they achieve. This observation is consistent with Wilson's framework of the Army as a procedural organization—he notes that the output (or work) is the focus, as opposed to the outcome.[176] Second, and more consequentially, we find that the Army might not be positioned to understand which of its officers most successfully lead their organizations through periods of change.

The Army uses a forced distribution system in its evaluations, mathematically restricting senior raters to a cap on the highest level of ratings. For grades O-1 to O-5, the highest rating is a "Most Qualified" rating, limited to the top 49 percent of officers whom the senior rater has ever

---

[173] Army Regulation 623-3, *Evaluation Reporting System*, Washington, D.C.: Department of the Army, 2015, p. 3.

[174] In an interview on September 12, 2018, A12, Army general officer, also stated that this training does not formally exist.

[175] Army Regulation 623-3, 2015, pp. 66–70.

[176] Wilson, 1989.

evaluated in that grade.[177] For grades O-6 and O-7, the Army uses a modified system in which the top rating is "Multi-Star Potential" (top 24 percent), followed by "Promote to Brigadier General" (combined with Multi Star Potential, no more than top 49 percent). The forced distribution system prevents scenarios in which all officers receive the highest-quality evaluations. A senior rater maintains the same rating profile throughout a lifetime, even carrying the profile to positions as a senior government civilian employee. One interviewee noted that some raters choose to limit high ratings in order to maintain a reputation for discernment, saving their highest ratings for officers evaluated in future cycles, which can negatively affect an otherwise strong candidate in a promotion board.[178]

The forced distribution system also contains trade-offs between the senior rater's knowledge of subordinates and the senior rater's ability to provide high-quality OERs. Evans and Bae ran simulations using Army data to identify what they called "misidentifications," or instances where a high-quality officer did not receive a high-quality OER. They identified that challenges arise from two axes: The senior rater might not know officers well enough in a large pool but might not have much flexibility in a small pool. Their efforts focused on identifying the rating pool size that minimized the chance that an officer would be not selected for promotion.[179]

The typical Army OER contains assessments and administrative data and such information as the rating chain, the duty position, the duty description, the unit of assignment, and the period of the evaluation. The rating chain information allows one viewing an OER to recognize the authors of the report by name; an OER by a GO carries more weight in most circumstances that one authored by an O-6, according to an interviewee with experience sitting on promotion boards.[180] The duty title is often simplified to a key term, such as *battalion commander* or *brigade executive officer*, quickly allowing one viewing an OER to understand the scope of responsibility through preconceived notions of what particular duty titles mean.

The most influential portion of the OER is the senior rater comment and the senior rater's "block check" in the forced distribution system.[181] The Army asks for senior raters to assess potential using "performance-based assessments of rated officers' . . . ability to perform in positions of greater responsibility and/or higher grades compared to others of the same grade."[182] This regulatory requirement leads to what Army officers refer to as enumeration: Quality OERs will feature a statement from the senior rater numerically comparing the rated officer to peers.

---

177 Army Regulation 623-3, 2015, p. 39.

178 A52, Army general officer, December 7, 2018.

179 Lee Evans and Ki-Hwan Bae, "Simulation-Based Analysis of a Forced Distribution Performance Appraisal System," *Journal of Defense Analytics and Logistics*, Vol. 1, No. 2, 2017, pp. 120–136.

180 A52, Army general officer, December 7, 2018.

181 Senior leader selection exercise notes, January 30, 2019; A12, Army general officer, September 12, 2018.

182 Army Regulation 623-3, 2015, p. 5.

The importance of enumeration, combined with the forced distribution rating system and the significance of the duty position, creates a heuristic for assessing the quality of an evaluation. A quality evaluation will feature an influential duty position, a top rating in the forced distribution rating system, and exclusive enumeration.

Promotions

Like the other services, Army officers compete for promotion within a competitive category. Through O-7, officers of the medical, chaplain, and judge advocate communities exist within separate competitive categories. The remainder of active duty officers reside in a broad collection of competitive categories called the Active Competitive Categories (ACC).[183]

Through the O-3 promotion board, ACC officers compete against each other in one large promotion board. Beginning with the O-4 promotion board and continuing through the O-6 promotion board, the Army divides career fields into four large competitive categories: Operations, Operations Support, Force Sustainment, and Information Dominance. For the O-7 board, the four large competitive categories collapse back into the overarching ACC competitive category.

Army promotion board membership includes officers from each career field under consideration but also many officers from other career fields. All board members are senior to the officers under consideration by the board. The Secretary of the Army can influence the type of officer selected through promotion boards by choosing the membership of the promotion board; however, one interviewee with board experience told us that it is not clear whether such attention to board membership is frequently practiced.[184] However, it is well established that promotion boards tend to select officers in their own image,[185] or as one interviewee put it, "ducks pick ducks."[186] The Secretary of the Army also publishes guidance to the promotion board, although interviewees questioned the efficacy of such guidance outside of established the promotion quotas.[187]

Army promotion board quotas are established for career fields, and also for certain skills or experiences, such as a legislative liaison.[188] The promotion board instructions also provide a top-line number for the total number of officers to be selected to O-7, but quotas are not publicly released. The quota system does not account for every possible selection, and one interviewee

---

[183] Army Directive 2017-08, 2017.

[184] A97, Army general officer, October 18, 2018.

[185] Janowitz, 1971, p. 148.

[186] A97, Army general officer, October 18, 2018. Another interviewee said that boards will select in their own image (A10, field-grade Army officer with personnel management experience, September 13, 2018).

[187] A97, Army general officer, October 18, 2018; A19, Army general officer, December 10, 2018.

[188] Fanning, 2017.

told us that a small number of at-large selections will often be available.[189] The at-large selections allow the promotion board to select an officer even if the quota for that career field has been met.

Promotion board instructions also establish selection criteria on which the board should focus. As an example, the instructions for the FY 2017 O-7 promotion/selection board called on board members to select "agile and adaptive thinkers capable of leading our forces in combat under conditions of uncertainty, leading joint, interagency, intergovernmental and multinational organizations and of running the Army."[190] The board instructions provide generalized guidance regarding characteristics, but board members will interpret those characteristics through their own prism of experience. Further, guidance can highlight characteristics that are not readily discernible in an officer's file. Recent O-7 board instructions highlighted "conducting research (and) professional writing and publication of works about our profession" as noteworthy skills and accomplishments.[191] However, research results and writing samples are not part of an officer's performance record, leaving board members challenged to understand which officers possess those skills.

All Army promotion boards start with the board members reviewing the performance records of the considered officers. Each board member provides a numerical score for the considered officer, and the scores are then summed to an overall board score. The board will establish a cut-off point, or a point at which officers with a score below that point will not be promoted.[192] In promotion boards for O-6 and below, the board members base their decisions on the content of an officer's performance file.[193] Each board member arrives at a decision on an officer's promotion consideration independent of other board members.[194]

At the O-7 promotion board, board members first vote "yes" or "no" for each considered officer based on a review of the performance file. Then, the board introduces an additional process unique to GO boards: The board members will discuss the highest-rated files among themselves, methodically moving from one file to the next. When discussing prior knowledge of the candidate, board members may only use personal experience; they may not bring up secondhand information.[195]

Board members reach a decision on the candidates for promotion after extensive discussions. Interviewees mentioned the importance of having numerous individuals on the board who can

---

[189] A19, Army general officer, December 10, 2018.

[190] Fanning, 2017.

[191] Fanning, 2017.

[192] Department of the Army Memo 600-2, *Policies and Procedures for Active-Duty List Officer Selection Boards*, Washington, D.C.: Department of the Army, September 25, 2006, pp. 14–15.

[193] Department of the Army Memo 600-2, 2006, pp. 3–4.

[194] Department of the Army Memo 600-2, 2006, p. 4.

[195] Fanning, 2017.

discuss an officer's accomplishments and readiness to join the GO ranks. One GO learned, after the board, that he had personal interaction with 14 of the 18 board members prior to the board.[196] That officer had served in a position after O-6 command that featured frequent interaction with a variety of Army GOs and observed that, had he made a bad impression, such exposure would have been highly detrimental to his promotion prospects. Another interviewee described needing a threshold of four or five advocates for serious consideration for promotion to O-7.[197] Often, some of these advocates are gained during the high-visibility post-command O-6 roles discussed in the "Duty Assignments" section. All these factors together create a highly interactive discussion around prospective O-7s. One interviewee described the process of determining competitiveness as akin to a "stock market," with some officers' stock rising and others falling.[198]

Overall, Army promotion rates by grade, as depicted in Figure 4.6, show a steep drop-off from O-6 to O-7 (less than 10 percent of O-6s will promote to O-7 service-wide). Promotion rates recover significantly at the next level: Just over 60 percent of Army O-7s will eventually become O-8s.

Figure 4.6. Percentage of Army Officers Who Promote to the Next Grade, 2000–2010 Officer Cohorts

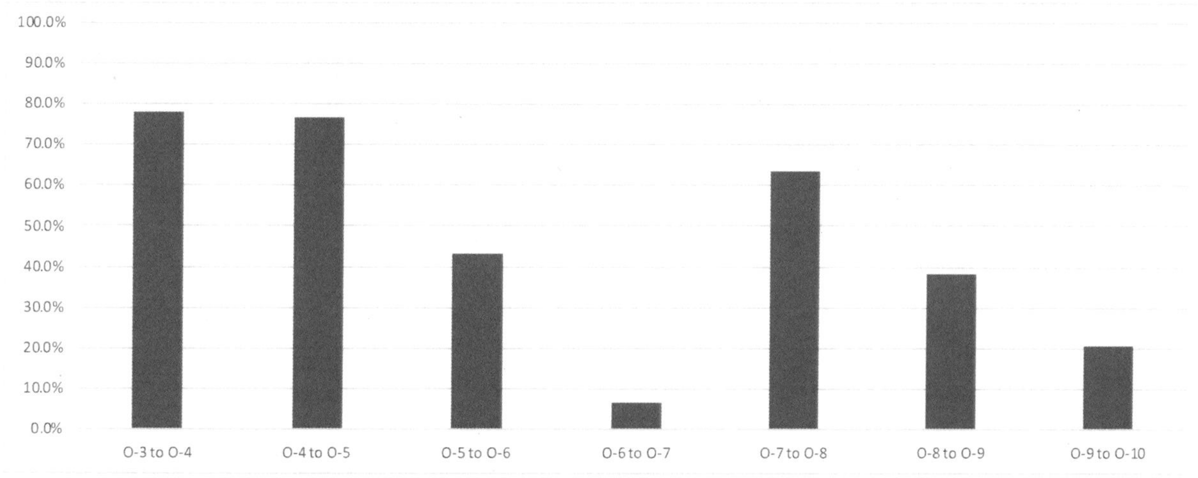

100.0%
90.0%
80.0%
70.0%
60.0%
50.0%
40.0%
30.0%
20.0%
10.0%
0.0%
O-3 to O-4
O-4 to O-5
O-5 to O-6
O-6 to O-7
O-7 to O-8
O-8 to O-9
O-9 to O-10

SOURCE: Authors' analysis of DMDC data.
NOTE: These numbers represent the average progression rate for the 11 (overlapping) cohorts of Army officers present in each grade at the beginning of each year from 2000 through 2010, and reflect these officers' observed rates of reaching the next higher grade at any point up to the beginning of 2018, the last year for which we have data.

---

196 A12, Army general officer, September 12, 2018.

197 A20, Army field-grade officer with personnel management experience, September 4, 2018.

198 A83, field-grade Army officer with personnel management experience, September 17, 2018.

Figure 4.7 shows a more granular depiction of promotion rate by career field grouping. While promotion rates stay fairly steady across career fields in promotions from O-3 up to O-6, combat arms officers compose the highest percentages in the O-6 to O-7 promotion category. Between 2000 and 2010, an average of 17 percent of infantry and armor O-6s go on to make O-7, a much higher proportion than in other Army career field groupings.

Figure 4.7. Percentage of Army Officers Who Promote to the Next Grade, by Grade and Career Type, 2000–2010 Officer Cohorts

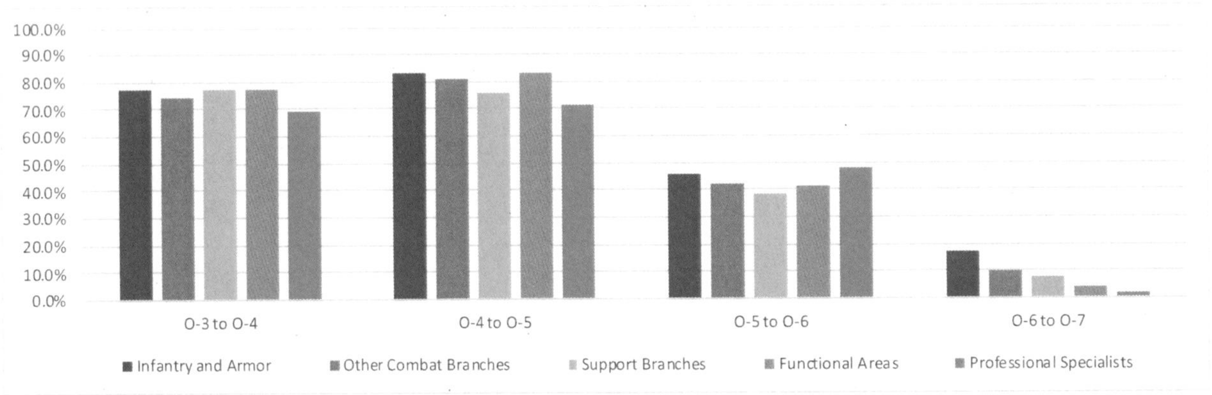

SOURCE: Authors' analysis of DMDC data.
NOTE: These numbers represent the average progression rate for the 11 (overlapping) cohorts of Army officers present in each grade at the beginning of each year from 2000 through 2010, and reflect these officers' observed rates of reaching the next higher grade at any point up to the beginning of 2018, the last year for which we have data.

Other Factors That Matter in Army General Officer Selection

Understanding the formal mechanics of an Army career, from accession source to the architecture of promotion boards, is necessary to understanding the typical characteristics of an Army O-7. But other factors, more difficult to define, also shape the mold of the typical Army GO. In the following section, we will explore other major factors that play an important role in the career progression of Army G/FOs, including connections and networks, personality, and factors in selecting out.

Connections and Networks

Although connections and networks are part of many of the factors that influence an officer's selection for GO, Army officers who reach O-7 appear to benefit directly from professional connections and important networks. One GO observed that a promotion system that relies on personal knowledge creates a professional need for strong social networks.[199] Sometimes, the specific unit to which an officer is assigned is a significant factor in career development. For

[199] A10, field-grade Army officer with personnel management experience, September 13, 2018.

example, as we noted previously, those who have served in the 75th Ranger Regiment appear to be disproportionately represented at the GO level. Decisions by the wider Army can also inadvertently undermine the role of certain units as incubators of future senior leaders. For example, as retired Lieutenant General Sean MacFarland noted in 2018, "For many years, armored cavalry regiments were the incubators of armor talent, much as the Ranger regiment is for infantry."[200] However, in 2011, the Army finished converting the armored cavalry regiments to infantry-dominated Stryker units.[201] As a result, armor officers no longer have armor-exclusive units to which to send its promising officers, and armor officers must share development opportunities with infantry officers. Armor officers are able to serve in key positions in certain infantry units, but they do not have an armor-specific elite unit in the same way that infantry officers have the 75th Ranger Regiment.[202]

Further, as described previously, early exposure to high-performing officers is probably important for future promotion potential. Lyle and Smith conducted a study on the effect of a high-performing mentor on an officer's career, using Army O-3s as the unit of study. Assuming that an O-3's unit of assignment is effectively random allowed them to compare the promotion outcomes of O-3s assigned to a high-performing mentor. They found that "exposure to a high-quality mentor increases early promotion," and that this effect is most pronounced among those with higher SAT scores.[203]

Personality

Attempts to generalize a broad topic such as personality can be challenging, but some common observations emerged in our analysis. Gerras and Wong, who conducted a study on openness as a personality factor, found that students at the Army War College scored lower on this dimension than the U.S. population in general. Their research further identified that the students who were selected for brigade command from that population scored lower than the average of their peers. Gerras and Wong highlight a tension: "The leaders recognized and selected by the Army to serve at strategic levels—where uncertainty and complexity are the greatest—tend to have lower levels of one of the attributes most related to success at strategic level."[204]

---

[200] Sean MacFarland, "It's Time to Invest in Armored Forces Again," *ARMY Magazine*, Vol. 68, No. 11, November 2018.

[201] Alan Vick, David Orletsky, Bruce Pirnie, and Seth Jones, *The Stryker Brigade Combat Team: Rethinking Strategic Responsiveness and Assessing Deployment Options,* Santa Monica, Calif.: RAND Corporation, MR-1606, 2002, p. 7; Heather Graham-Ashley, "3rd ACR Transitions to Strykers, Changes Name," U.S. Army, November 30, 2011.

[202] MacFarland, 2018; A12, Army general officer, September 12, 2018.

[203] David S. Lyle and John Z. Smith, "The Effect of High-Performing Mentors on Junior Officer Promotion in the US Army," *Journal of Labor Economics*, Vol. 32, No. 2, April 2014, p. 246.

[204] Gerras and Wong, 2013, p. 9.

The Army Research Institute, while researching the role of strategic thinking, highlighted common personality traits among Army officers: "a strong focus on tactical excellence (at the cost of long-term future-oriented thinking and reflection), uniformity (rather than diversity of capability and perspective), and chain of command (to the detriment of questioning and candor)."[205] Pierce, in a study on organizational culture, summarized attitudes as an "overarching desire for stability, control, formal rules and policies, coordination and efficiency, goal and results oriented, and hard-driving competitiveness."[206]

Factors in Selecting Out

As in the other services, officers also self-select out of the GO pipeline. This can be for a number of reasons, but the decision tends to center on family reasons (e.g., to support spouse employment or stay in one location to provide children stability), appeal of civilian career opportunities, desire for greater autonomy in career choices, or lack of interest in the jobs available at higher promotion levels. As described previously, the Army career can be intense and unforgiving, particularly with the numerous deployments and frequent moves that tend to characterize today's officer career paths. As one interviewee noted, many choose to leave because "I want to get off the treadmill."[207]

Summary

The Army's cultural values of loyal service, egalitarianism, and emphasis on conventional ground combat are seen throughout its personnel processes and approach to developing future GOs. Although an egalitarian, "muddy boots" organization, a natural hierarchy exists, with the combat arms, and specifically infantry, at the top. This is evident both in the combat arms' domination of GO ranks, particularly at the highest levels, and in the tendency to equate tactical proficiency with strategic leadership skills.

Because the Army is characterized by multiple large communities with GO requirements, several pathways to GO exist. While performance at the O-3 and O-4 levels is important, we found that the GO pathway across all career categories does not truly begin until O-5, where battalion-level command positions start to distinguish officers in many career fields, especially infantry and armor. The Army does utilize BZ promotions, but they are not necessarily required in order to become a GO. The importance of command, though, particularly in the combat arms, is essential to progressing toward O-7.

At commissioning, approximately half of Army officers come from ROTC and half from USMA and OCS. As officers promote through O-6, these proportions largely remain intact, with

---

[205] Sackett et al., 2013, p. 43.

[206] Pierce, 2010, p. 101.

[207] A52, Army general officer, December 7, 2018.

ROTC graduates gaining some ground. However, by the time officers reach O-10, the vast majority are USMA graduates, which could reflect network effects and/or the number of USMA graduates that commission into the combat arms.

The Army favors core career assignments, and some institutional assignments, if they are viewed as being related to one's career field and particularly enhancing to the Army's core missions. True broadening assignments are less valued—except for certain competitive broadening assignments, such as congressional fellowships—which reflects the Army's institutional valuation of tactical-level combat leadership over most other skills. Combat-related deployments and operational command assignments are also common in certain career fields. Other assignments that carry weight in an officer's trajectory include aide positions and other roles that increase exposure to GOs that can help influence promotion decisions, particularly at the O-6 level. Ranger school is a special training experience that many aspiring O-7s pursue, depending on their career field, and can serve as a signal of high potential to other officers. The importance of Ranger School in making O-7 might increase in the coming years, as those who attended as junior officers in the deployment-heavy 2000s become eligible for O-7.

As far as education, beyond formal requirements, the Army has not greatly valued additional education in the promotion process in the past few decades. However, the service does appear to be increasing the importance of graduate education by implementing a retention program to encourage junior officers to obtain master's degrees, and by investing in certain officers to develop strategic thinking skills through doctoral programs. However, the impact of this shift remains to be seen.

Evaluations play an important role in the Army personnel system. Both performance and potential are assessed through OERs, and signaling information, such as an officer's duty title, can be extremely significant, as it clearly relays the level of responsibility required by that officer's assignments. Additionally, the forced distribution system, which restricts the number of highest-level ratings a senior rater can provide, and the practice of enumerating officers overseen by a rater, creates a highly competitive and precise process for gaining top evaluations.

In addition to evaluations and career assignment histories, personal relationships have impact in promotion boards, particularly for O-7 promotions. Secondhand information is not allowed, and only firsthand impressions of candidates are considered. Quotas and board instructions are utilized, but the instructions frequently specify qualities that are not easy to discern in an officer's OER.

Other factors that appear to shape an Army officer's career development pathway include connections and networks, which many interviewees said were essential to eventually being chosen as an O-7. Certain elements of the Army's personnel processes are geared toward recognizing these factors, such as the practice of placing promising O-6s in high-visibility roles after their brigade-level command. Personality might also affect an officer's career path.

Taken together, these factors play key roles in shaping who eventually becomes an Army GO. In Chapter 8, we will explore the potential implications of these processes and cultural values on the perspectives and experiences of the Army's senior-most officers.

5. The Navy's Approach to Admiralship

Leadership in the Navy, first and foremost, means command at sea. Even though most FOs serve in headquarters positions rather than on a vessel at sea, they are brought up in a system that derives leadership values from those needed to command a ship, submarine, or aircraft squadron.[208] This focus on leadership at sea is embedded in Navy tradition, in officers' prescribed career paths, and in official service guidance on leadership development.

As of January 2018, active duty end strength in the Navy was 323,738, representing 25 percent of the total active duty end strength of the U.S. military.[209] The proportions of officers and of FOs in the Navy are very close to those for the U.S. military as a whole, with an average of 16.2 Navy officers for every 100 uniformed personnel, and 6.6 FOs for every 10,000 uniformed personnel. The total number of FOs in the Navy is 215: 102 O-7s, 66 O-8s, 38 O-9s, and 9 O-10s.[210]

This chapter discusses Navy leader development practices that apply across the entire officer corps, and it places particular emphasis on unrestricted line (URL) officers, or those qualified to command a combat unit or platform at sea, as these account for half of active duty Navy officers overall and the majority of active duty Navy FOs.[211] It furthermore focuses primarily on the main three URL communities—aviation, surface warfare, and submarine warfare—that are organized around the Navy's major platforms.[212] The Navy's senior-most leaders, as well as its overall culture and concept of leadership, come from these three communities and their experience of command at sea.

Navy Culture

Understanding Navy culture is central to understanding how the service approaches its development and selection of FOs. Particularly as it differs from the culture of other U.S.

---

[208] Lisa M. Harrington, Bart E. Bennett, Katharina Ley Best, David R. Frelinger, Paul W. Mayberry, Igor Mikolic-Torreira, Sebastian Joon Bae, Barbara Bicksler, Lisa Davis, Steven Deane-Shinbrot, Joslyn Fleming, Benjamin Goirigolzarri, Russell Hanson, Connor P. Jackson, Kimberly Jackson, Sean Mann, Geoffrey McGovern, Jenny Oberholtzer, Christina Panis, Alexander D. Rothenberg, Ricardo Sanchez, Matthew Sargent, Peter Schirmer, Hilary Reininger, and Mitch Tuller, *Realigning the Stars: A Methodology for Reviewing Active Component General and Flag Officer Requirements*, Santa Monica, Calif.: RAND Corporation, RR-2384-OSD, 2018, pp. 237–246.

[209] Defense Manpower Data Center, 2018.

[210] Officer and general officer numbers calculated by authors using DMDC data. For a comparison of these numbers to those for other services, see Table B.2.

[211] Authors' analysis of DMDC data, numbers are from the start of FY 2018.

[212] URL officers are those belonging to the following communities: surface warfare, aviation, nuclear (surface and subsurface), Naval Special Warfare, and Explosive Ordnance Disposal (EOD).

military services, Navy culture is shaped by the maritime domain in which the Navy operates. Further, its strong traditions and foundational role in the nation's inception contribute to the observation that "The Navy, more than any of the other services and over anything else, is an institution. That institution is marked by two strong senses of itself: its independence and its stature."[213]

Aspects of this culture are reflected in official leadership guidance, such as the ideal of leadership at sea, the absolute authority of command, and the importance placed on specialized technical expertise.[214] Other aspects of Navy culture are less fully incorporated into official guidance and might even exist in tension with this guidance. This includes the preeminence given to managing Navy platforms rather than teams of people, the isolation of individual Navy vessels and the commanding officers who guide them, the separation between Navy communities, and the lower priority placed on nontechnical education.[215]

The official guidance stressing the importance of accountability for Navy commanding officers, for example, coexists uneasily with the fact of Navy vessels' frequent isolation, and thus their distance from direct and regular oversight by their chain of command. Ship operations and readiness measurements are regularly reported to higher headquarters, but the specifics of the command climate on board ship are particularly opaque. The practical difficulties of enforcing oversight and accountability in this context likely contribute to the priority given to accountability in Navy leadership guidance. As one submarine officer argued, "toxic leaders continue to develop and progress. . . . Occasionally these leaders' effects don't stay hidden beneath the depths of the oceans but surface to the point that they are relieved of command."[216]

The main Navy officer communities each specialize in one of the three maritime domains, operating on the ocean's surface, its depths, or the air above it. They also specialize in operating the platforms specific to those domains. Navy culture derives partly from the central importance given to Navy platforms—ships, aircraft, and submarines—as they are the basis for mobility, operational impact, and support for personnel in the maritime environment.

The importance afforded to Navy platforms is also reflected in the fact that Navy force structure is measured in numbers of vessels, in contrast to the practice of other services, such as

---

[213] Builder, 1989, p. 31.

[214] Chief of Naval Operations, "Leadership Development Framework: Version 2.0," April 2018, p. 1.

[215] Roger W. Barnett, *Navy Strategic Culture: Why the Navy Thinks Differently*, Annapolis, Md.: Naval Institute Press, 2009, p. 74; Kelly L. Laing, *Leadership in Command Under the Sea*, Maxwell Air Force Base, Ala.: Air Command and Staff College, Air University, April, 2009, p. 13; Michael Mullen and Robert Natter, "We Can Fix the SWO Career Path," *U.S. Naval Institute Proceedings*, Vol. 144, No. 4, April 2018; Senior leader selection exercise notes, January 30, 2019, RAND Corporation, Arlington, Virginia.

[216] Laing, 2009, p. 13.

the Army, which measures force structure in personnel end strength.[217] This difference between the two services is reflected in the aphorism that "the Army equips the man, while the Navy mans the equipment."[218] On top of this, the complexity of managing technologies, such as carrier launch systems or submarine nuclear reactors, further enforces the need for officer specialization within distinct communities, as well as the prioritization of technical expertise over nontechnical soft skills.[219] While these aspects of Navy culture are largely incorporated into the Navy's official guidance rather than challenged by it, this guidance does push back against the overall notion that equipment is more important than people. The Navy Leadership Strategy, in particular, begins with the contention that "our people are our most valuable and important strategic asset. . . . There is no higher priority than to develop effective Navy leaders."[220]

Navy culture and leadership have also been shaped by the service's focus on continuously operating at sea, in times of conflict as well as peace. This fosters a view that the Navy "needs line officers more than it needs staff officers" perhaps to a greater extent than the other services.[221] The Navy, together with the Marine Corps, opposed the landmark Goldwater-Nichols legislation, in part because of the requirement that Navy URL officers complete joint education as well as joint assignments, which were often staff jobs.[222] The Navy communities continue to struggle to fit joint requirements into field-grade officer career paths that center on the need to develop platform-specific expertise during commands at sea.[223] One Navy officer stated that "The very technical nature of what we do at sea creates this conflict where we don't think we have time to do anything but learn our weapons systems" and that becoming a naval systems expert leaves very little time for joint assignments or education at the junior and mid-grade officer levels.[224] Emphasis on joint assignments changes after the O-7 promotion, where the Navy tends to fare relatively well in securing key joint positions at the FO ranks, as opposed to the field-grade level.

---

217 The Navy's equating force structure with ships is shown in the service's current overall goal of expanding to "a 355-ship fleet" released in 2016. See Ronald O'Rourke, *Navy Force Structure and Shipbuilding Plans*, Washington, D.C.: Congressional Research Service, October 19, 2018, p. 2. On Army force structure goals, see, for example, U.S. Army Public Affairs, "Department of the Army Announces Force Structure Decisions for Fiscal Year 2017," June 15, 2017.

218 Barnett, 2009, p. 74.

219 Mullen and Natter, 2018.

220 Chief of Naval Operations, "The Navy Leader Development Strategy," 2013, p. 3.

221 Norman Friedman, "The Navy Needs People Even More Than Ships," *U.S. Naval Institute Proceedings*, Vol. 144, No. 7, July 2018.

222 Kathleen J. McInnis, *Goldwater-Nichols at 30: Defense Reform and Issues for Congress*, Washington, D. C.: Congressional Research Service, June 2, 2016, p. 8; Friedman, 2018.

223 Mullen and Natter, 2018.

224 Senior leader selection exercise notes, January 30, 2019, RAND Corporation, Arlington, Virginia.

Although the Army, Air Force, and Marine Corps also tend to prioritize service needs over joint needs, the Navy appears to resist jointness more than others, in part because of the service's culture of command at sea and self-reliance within the maritime domain.[225] "Joint," in the Navy, is often construed to mean the Navy supporting others (in functions such as sealift), rather than receiving support from other services (given that the joint community has few resources to contribute to key missions, such as anti-submarine warfare, that are conducted independently by the Navy).[226] The Navy also sees itself as inherently "joint" to begin with, because of its execution of multidomain operations simultaneously above, below, and on the surface of the ocean; its synchronization of operations, logistics, maintenance and other functions on a ship; and its departmental relationship with the Marine Corps' ground forces operating on land.[227] Even so, aversion to cross-service jointness is a facet of Navy culture observed throughout DoD. As Colin Roberts noted in 2009, "In addition to bolstering the Navy's uncooperative ('defiant') image, this reluctance toward jointness also engendered perceptions of the Navy as tradition bound and overly unresponsive to change."[228]

While Navy culture focuses on constant sea-based deployment and operations, it is also shaped by the fact that the United States has not fought a major maritime battle for decades. Furthermore, the Navy has been less involved than the other services in the recent wars in Iraq and Afghanistan, with the exception of some communities such as Navy Sea, Air, Land (SEALs). This is not to say that the Navy has not held substantial combat leadership positions in that time, however: Navy admirals are still selected to lead combat-centric joint task forces, including Odyssey Dawn, the 2011 Air Force–heavy operation in Libya.

One final aspect of Navy culture is the importance of traditions that differentiate the Navy from other services. Unlike the other three services, which share a common set of rank names for each of the officer grades, the Navy has its own names for each rank. Similarly, the Navy calls its senior military leaders *flag officers* (a term reflecting the Royal Navy tradition of an admiral flying a distinguishing flag to mark his position in a fleet), rather than *general officers*. Navy officers are also kept more separate from the enlisted ranks as compared with other services. This separation is maintained by officers and enlisted wearing different uniforms, living and eating in different quarters, and following customs such as a commanding officer's presence being announced by bells when arriving or departing a vessel.[229] Some aspects of this separation, such as officers eating together in a separate wardroom, can lead to additional opportunities for

---

[225] Colin Roberts, "The Navy," in Zimmerman et al., 2019.

[226] Barnett, 2009, pp. 95–96, 107.

[227] Barnett, 2009, pp. 106–108.

[228] Roberts, 2009, p. 74.

[229] Roberts, 2019, p. 44.

fostering officer cohesion, even as they limit opportunities for officers to socialize with enlisted sailors.[230]

Official Guidance on Navy Officer Development

The Navy shares many of the same leadership ideals as the other services, though it places particular importance on values of independence, self-reliance, and technical competence, arising from the traditional isolation and self-containment of maritime vessels. The Navy's Leader Development Strategy states:

> Leadership in the naval profession of arms demands self-reliance and independence, humility and integrity, discipline and resourcefulness, and trust and confidence.[231]

The most detailed statement of Navy leadership is found in the Navy's Charge of Command, which was published in 2011 by Chief of Naval Operations (CNO) Admiral Jonathan Greenert and republished again with slight modifications in 2018 by CNO Admiral John M. Richardson. Although it is a relatively recent document, it draws heavily from established Navy regulations and foundational statements on leadership. The Charge of Command asserts:[232]

> Command is the foundation upon which our Navy rests. Authority, responsibility, accountability, and expertise are four essential principles at the heart of command. . . .
>
> The responsibility of the Commanding Officer for his or her command is absolute. . . . The authority of the Commanding Officer is commensurate with his or her responsibility. . . . delegation of authority shall in no way relieve the commanding officer of continued responsibility for the safety, well-being and efficiency of the entire command. . . .
>
> There are two standards to measure officers in command. The first is the standard for criminal behavior, which should be well known to you. The second—and higher standard—is trust and confidence, both with the American people we are sworn to protect and across all levels of the chain-of-command.
>
> A commander's competence and character lead to trust and confidence. . . . Trust and confidence are the two coins of the realm that enable decentralized command and operations at sea; they are the key to our effectiveness as a force.

The Charge of Command is accompanied by two enclosures. The first is the Commander-in-Chief, U.S. Atlantic Fleet, Serial 053 of January 21, 1941, from Admiral Ernest King, which stresses the importance of delegating authority to subordinates and refraining from micromanagement. The first paragraph of this serial had also featured prominently in earlier

---

[230] "Command Excellence and the Wardroom," Navy Leadership and Ethics Center, Naval War College, undated, p. 10.

[231] Chief of Naval Operations, 2013, p. 3.

[232] Chief of Naval Operations, 2018, p. 1.

Navy doctrine, including on the title page of Naval Doctrine Publication 6, *Naval Command and Control*:[233]

> I have been concerned for many years over the increasing tendency—now grown almost to "standard practice"—of flag officers and other group commanders to issue orders and instructions in which their subordinates are told "how" as well as "what" to do to such an extent and in such detail that the "Custom of the service" has virtually become the antithesis of that essential element of command—"initiative of the subordinate."

The second enclosure is a 1952 editorial on the sinking of the USS *Hobson* following a collision during a U.S. Navy exercise. The editorial states:

> On the sea there is a tradition older even than the traditions of the country itself . . . it is the tradition that with responsibility goes authority and with them goes accountability . . . the choice is [between accountability] or an end to responsibility and finally, as the cruel sea has taught, an end to the confidence and trust in the men who lead, for men will not long trust leaders who feel themselves beyond accountability for what they do.[234]

Taken together, the Charge of Command and its accompanying documents reflect a leadership ideal that emphasizes Navy officers' personal initiative, expertise, and independent authority at sea. They also place atop this ideal, to balance out its potential shortfalls, the need for effective delegation to subordinates and the need for officers' absolute accountability to standards for criminal behavior and to the trust placed in them by their country, their superiors, and their crew.

Unlike the other services, the Navy did not possess official guidance on leadership development until 2013. Historically, the Navy did provide some doctrinal guidance on how an officer should lead, as well as inspirational examples of Navy leadership in historical campaigns.[235] Yet official guidance on how the Navy should best produce good leaders was missing.[236] In its place, the Navy looked to less formal modes of leadership development rooted in tradition and centered on tours at sea, which featured both on-the-job learning and an expectation of "transference" of leadership skills from commanding officers to subordinates via exposure.[237] This was supplemented by a modest set of mandated leadership training

---

[233] Naval Doctrine Publication (NDP) 6, *Naval Command and Control*, Washington D.C.: Department of the Navy, May 19, 1995.

[234] "Hobson's Choice," *Wall Street Journal*, May 14, 1952.

[235] See, for example, NDP-6, 1995.

[236] Walter E. Carter, Jr., "President's Forum," in "Winter 2014 Review," *Naval War College Review*, Vol. 67, No. 1, 2014, pp. 18–19.

[237] Edward Brennan, *Leading Airmen: Taking Leadership Development Seriously*, Maxwell Air Force Base, Ala.: School of Advanced Air and Space Studies, Air University, June 2012; James Kelly, "Strengthening our Naval Profession Through a Culture of Leader Development," *Naval War College Review*, Vol. 67, No. 1, Winter 2014, p. 13.

requirements tracing back to the 1960s, though many observers saw these as patched together rather than forming a systematic or cohesive approach to leadership development.[238]

In 2013, the Naval Leadership Development Strategy was published as part of a push by Greenert to prioritize and formalize leadership development as a continuous focus throughout a Navy officer's career.[239] This built on an initial effort by CNO Admiral Michael Mullen to establish a "leadership development continuum," announced in 2006.[240] It was also followed in 2017 by the publication of the Naval Leadership Development Framework under CNO Admiral John Richardson.[241] Senior Navy leaders and some outside observers have characterized these publications as part of an important effort to formalize and prioritize continuous leadership development, spanning officers and sailors' entire careers, with effects that will be seen most fully in the coming generations of Navy leaders.[242]

This focus on leadership development has continued under multiple CNOs and been rendered official in several guiding documents, including the 2011 Charge of Command, the 2013 Leadership Development Strategy, and the 2017 Leadership Development Framework. It has also been at least partially institutionalized, with the establishment of the Leader Development Continuum Council and the Naval Leadership and Ethics Center at the Naval War College.[243] Furthermore, since 2017, each of the Navy community leads has been required to brief the CNO or vice chief of naval operations (VCNO) on leadership development implementation on a semiannual basis.[244] At the same time, the recent criminal investigations of Navy officers involved in the Glenn Defense Marine Asia ("Fat Leonard") contracting scandal, in addition to two ship collision incidents in 2017, have increased scrutiny on safety, ethics, accountability, and overall leadership in the U.S. Navy.[245] One interviewee observed that these incidents have lent additional impetus to this effort.[246]

---

238 Brennan, 2012, pp 98–99.

239 Carter, 2014, p. 18.

240 Brennan, 2012, p. 101.

241 Chief of Naval Operations, "Navy Leader Development Framework: Version 1.0," January 2017.

242 Kelly, 2014, p. 16; Also see Michael J. Mazarr, *Developing Senior Leaders for the Reserve Components*, Santa Monica, Calif.: RAND Corporation, PE-194-OSD, 2017, p. 5.

243 Chief of Naval Operations, 2013; Carter, 2014, p. 19.

244 Chief of Naval Personnel Public Affairs, "Leader Development Framework Implementation Plan Announced," March 10, 2017; Chief of Naval Operations, Naval Administration Message (NAVADMIN) 060/17, *Navy Leader Development Framework Implementation Plan*, Washington, D.C.: Department of the Navy, March 9, 2017.

245 The Fat Leonard contracting scandal was a highly publicized corruption case that involved Naval personnel trading classified information to a federal contractor in exchange for money and gifts as far back as 2006. It resulted in several FOs being frozen in their positions pending completion of Navy investigations; Eric Schmitt, Thomas Gibbons-Neff, and Helene Cooper, "Navy Collisions That Killed 17 Sailors Were 'Avoidable,' Official Inquiry Says," *New York Times*, November 1, 2017.

246 N8, active duty Navy flag officer, October 12, 2018.

Leadership development in the Navy has long relied on officers learning on the job in a series of successively more important leadership assignments. These assignments occur on a narrowly prescribed path that is set forth by each Navy officer community, with particular focus on milestone assignments that feature leadership at sea.[247] Leadership development on this path was "assumed to be a naturally occurring process" that "just happens," via what Admiral James Stavridis described as "transference . . . [the idea that you should] just do what I do and you will be a good leader."[248]

New official guidance has since set forth a systematic leadership development continuum for the Navy. The Navy's Leadership Development Framework describes two lanes of this effort—competence and character—and three methods to progress in both these lanes: education, on-the-job training, and self-guided learning.[249] The framework also highlights the importance of mentorship and formally encourages mentors to advocate for their proteges when professional opportunities arise.[250]

The extent to which this new and formal approach to leader development will mark a departure from existing practice remains unclear. One FO we interviewed described the leader development continuum as "potentially the greatest enhancement of our Navy's professional development since John Paul Jones helped to establish it during the American Revolution."[251] Yet while the new guidance does place additional and explicit emphasis on leader development throughout an officer's career, it does not yet appear to have brought actual change in officer career paths or in assignment and promotion practices. Some changes are indeed underway in education, such as establishing competitive boards to select applicants for in-residence graduate education and adding this as a prerequisite for assuming O-6 major command.[252] Other aspects of the Navy's new leadership development guidance, such as senior leaders mentoring and advocating for officers under their command, have long been widely practiced, though official guidance might make this more universal.

The Navy's official guidance on FO leadership characteristics is not especially different than that for officers in the mid-grades, which will be discussed later in this chapter. One partial exception is the Navy's published Standards of Conduct for Flag Officers.[253] These standards primarily focus on avoiding misuse of resources (such as government-provided vehicles) and are

---

[247] See, for example, the career paths laid out in: Navy Personnel Command, "FY-18 Active Line Officer Community Brief," undated a.

[248] Kelly, 2014, p. 13; Carter, 2014, p. 19.

[249] Chief of Naval Operations, 2017, p. 6.

[250] Chief of Naval Operations, 2017, p. 8.

[251] Carter, 2014, p. 18.

[252] NAVADMIN 263/18, *Update to Navy Graduate Education Program*, Washington, D.C.: Chief of Naval Operations, October 25, 2018.

[253] Vice Chief of Naval Operations, "Memorandum for All Flag Officers: Standards of Conduct," August 12, 2008.

presented as a reaction to recent cases of FO misconduct. Moreover, these standards are presented as the same ones that apply to all Navy officers, just reissued with additional emphasis for FOs, given their prominence.[254] The Leadership Development Strategy also provides some guidance on what is expected of an FO, such as being a "Guardian of Navy Core Values." These are presented as a continuation of the expectations of Navy officers at lower ranks, however, with the main difference being that FO leadership specifically can have strategic, Navy-wide impact.[255]

As this report was written in 2019, the Navy was beginning to undertake a series of new officer career management initiatives. Starting in 2018, the Navy took steps to start implementing alternatives to "up or out" career pathways so that certain officers, such as aviators, can remain in their preferred jobs longer, and promotion board deferrals so that officers can pursue educational and fellowship opportunities without penalty. Another significant change that the Navy is pursuing is enabling earlier promotions for high performers. Starting in 2019, the order in which certain mid-grade promotions occurred is based on merit rather than commissioning date.[256] Several of these changes were prompted by changes in the FY 2019 NDAA and its reforms to DOPMA. It is unknown what the impact of the Navy's efforts will be on pathways to admiralship, but the initiatives could represent a cultural shift.

Fundamental Elements of Navy Flag Officer Career Pathways

Several processes and bureaucratic structures compose the Navy's overall approach to developing and selecting FOs. While each of these elements is, at its base, mechanical and procedural by nature, service culture and the Navy's priorities are evident throughout the entire system. As we detail below, philosophical approach, competitive categories and typical pathways, career timelines, and personnel processes outline these fundamental levers that shape the professional characteristics that tend to define Navy leadership.

The Navy's Philosophical Approach to the Officer Development Pipeline

The Navy's approach to officer development up through and including O-7 is managed primarily by the individual Navy communities. While the specifics might differ between these communities, the overall process is largely the same. Expectations of officers at each grade are explicitly laid out in annual briefings and center on one or more community-specific milestone assignments at each grade. To progress through the ranks, an officer must be selected for a milestone assignment and then again be selected for promotion. Each of these steps is

---

[254] Vice Chief of Naval Operations, "Raising Our Standards," *Navy Live*, April 12, 2018.

[255] Chief of Naval Operations, 2013, p. 11.

[256] Mark D. Faram, "Here's How the Navy Is Revolutionizing Officer Career Paths," *Navy Times*, February 28, 2019.

characterized by heavy competition, particularly at the mid-grades, and each step sees the pool of eligible candidates for progression narrow. One's prospects for FO selection become most apparent only after promoting to O-6, after which point an officer must select for major command, then perform better than one's peers at major command, and finally be selected for a high-visibility post-command assignment.[257]

This process has been described as the most "laissez-faire" or "Darwinian" approach to senior leader development of the services, resembling a funnel that narrows down successively at each step of selection, with multiple such winnowing steps at each individual grade.[258] While officers start accruing qualifications and building a network useful for selection to flag grade as early as O-4, they compete on a fairly level playing field at each step, with the primary criterion for promotion being how their performance during their milestone command compares with that of their immediate peers.[259] The Navy's evaluation system is detailed later in this chapter.

Competitive Categories

Navy officers are divided into three categories: URL officers, restricted line (RL) officers, and Staff Corps officers. These categories are, in turn, divided into a combined total of 27 communities, each with their own specific career path.

The URL officers are "not restricted in their performance of duty" and are able to command ships and other Navy warfighting platforms, in contrast to RL officers.[260] URL officers are those most directly involved in warfighting and are at the top of the Navy hierarchy. As noted previously, the five URL officer communities are surface warfare, aviation, submarine warfare, Naval Special Warfare, and Explosive Ordnance Disposal (EOD). URL is the largest category of Navy officers and make up the great majority of FOs, as shown in Figure 5.1. These first three communities are the largest communities in the entire Navy; combined, they account for 48 percent of the Navy's total active duty officer corps and 66 percent of its FOs. By contrast, the Navy Special Warfare and EOD officer communities are much smaller, representing 2 percent and 1 percent of the Navy's total active duty officer corps, respectively.[261]

---

[257] N1, retired Navy mid-grade officer, September 28, 2018; N8, active duty Navy flag officer, October 12, 2018; N12, retired Navy senior civilian leader, October 16, 2018.

[258] Roberts, 2019, p. 58; N23, active duty Navy mid-grade officer, November 26, 2018.

[259] N1, retired Navy mid-grade officer, September 28, 2018; N20, active duty Navy mid-grade officer, November 15, 2018; N23, active duty Navy mid-grade officer, November 26, 2018.

[260] Navy Personnel Command, *Manual of Navy Officer Manpower and Personnel Classifications*, Vol. 1, Part A: *Billet and Officer Designator Codes*, January 2019, p. A-2.

[261] Authors' analysis of DMDC data.

Figure 5.1. Percentage of Navy Officers by Type and Grade, Average, 2008–2018

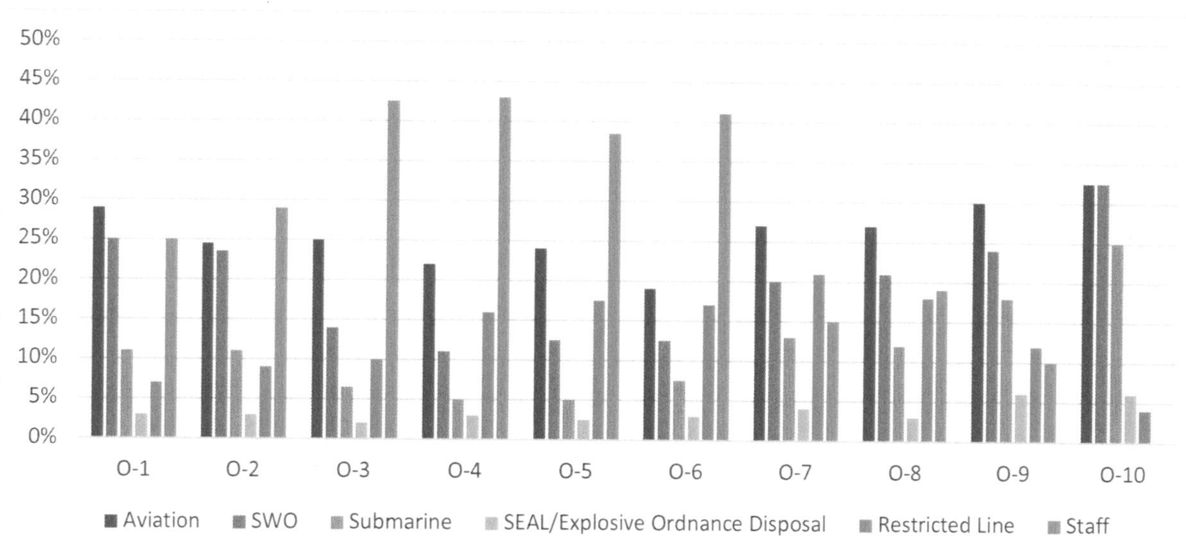

SOURCE: Authors' analysis of DMDC data. Officers are categorized by type using the primary service occupation codes assigned to each officer in any given year.
NOTES: The total numbers of Navy officers analyzed by grade were as follows: O-1: 73,402; O-2: 70,257; O-3: 193,173; O-4: 114,386; O-5: 73,898; O-6: 35,372; O-7: 1,126; O-8: 737; O-9: 412; O-10: 113. The number of officers analyzed decreases between the lower grades and the higher grades. Because fewer officers are included in our analysis of higher grades, representation among the higher grades is more susceptible to fluctuations in year-over-year accession source differences.

The greater representation of Navy URL officers in the FO corps is similar to the prominence of tactical warfighting occupations found in the GO corps of the other three services. This is particularly true at the highest flag ranks. From 2008 to 2018, for example, an average of 90 percent of Navy O-10s were from the surface warfare, aviation, and submarine warfare URL communities, as Figure 5.1 also shows.[262] Since the end of World War II, the CNO has always come from the surface, aviator, or submariner communities, with roughly equal numbers of CNOs coming from each community.[263] Submariners have been particularly well represented, given that they have produced a similar number of CNOs as the surface and aviation communities despite being smaller in size. This provides credence to Carl Builder's assertion in 1989 that "The submariners (or more generally, the nuclear power community) are rising relative to the aviators and surface warfare officers in the Navy."[264]

Yet this disproportionate prominence of warfighters in senior service leadership, as compared with the overall officer corps, is actually lower overall in the Navy than in some of the other services, given that URL officers also make up a large portion of Navy officers at the junior and

---

262 Authors' analysis of DMDC data.

263 Naval History and Heritage Command, "Chiefs of Naval Operations," undated.

264 Builder, 1989, p. 88.

mid-grades.[265] At these levels, the Navy is predominantly organized around supporting the platforms led by the URL communities, particularly the surface, aviation, and submarine officers.

RL officers are "restricted in the performance of duty" to their designated specialty.[266] There are 13 separate RL officer communities, the largest being intelligence, cryptologic warfare, and information professional. Together, the RL represents 13 percent of the Navy's total active duty officer corps and 19 percent of the Navy's FOs. There are also nine separate communities within the staff corps, including various medical officer communities, judge advocates general, civil engineers, chaplains, and supply officers. The staff corps makes up 37 percent of the Navy's total active duty officer corps, including large numbers of medical officers at the mid-grades, but only 13 percent of the Navy's FOs.[267] URL officers with two or more years of service can apply for "lateral transfer" to join a staff corps, or more commonly, an RL community, bringing additional experience at sea to the non-URL officer corps. Surface warfare officers (SWOs) are the largest source of transfers, which occur most often at the O-3 grade.[268]

Each of the RL and staff officer communities constitutes its own competitive category for promotion. This leaves the Navy with the most competitive categories of any service, and ensures that a minimum number of officers progress through the grades in each of the community specialties. One interviewee observed that this avoids problems that might occur in other services—for example, officers in a specialty of growing importance, such as cyber warfare, failing to promote against their peers.[269]

In contrast, all URL officers are considered for promotion in the same competitive category, which some have criticized as allowing for imbalances between the URL communities and shortages in some specialties.[270] In practice, however, this is somewhat mitigated by promotion board guidance on minimum selection numbers for URL specialties to meet specific service needs.[271] The importance of competing against URL officers from other communities is also mitigated by the fact that one of the most important factors for promotion is selection for milestone assignments, for which officers compete solely against others in their community. Moreover, one interviewee with experience in Navy personnel management told us that the personnel managers that provide guidance on what proportion of officers to promote at the mid-

---

265 Military Leadership Diversity Commission, *Issue Paper #23: Military Occupations and Implications for Racial/Ethnic and Gender Diversity*, March 2010, p. 1.

266 Navy Personnel Command, 2019, p. A-2.

267 Authors' analysis of DMDC data; numbers are from January 2018.

268 Ryan T. Dailey, *Leading Factors Determining Lateral Transfer Success*, Monterey, Calif.: Naval Postgraduate School, March 2013, pp. 29–30.

269 N23, active duty Navy mid-grade officer, November 26, 2018.

270 Robert Tortora, "Unrestricted Line Officer Promotions: Best and Fully Qualified?" July 2014.

271 See, for example, the minimum selection numbers provided in Secretary of the Navy, 2016c.

grades design their calculations deliberately to provide sufficient promotion slots for all those who were selected for and then successfully completed their milestone assignments.[272] The career field managers for the RL must be very careful in managing their career pyramids to avoid assignment bottlenecks in any grade.

Career Timelines

As previously mentioned, each community has its own prescribed career path, centered on milestone assignments at each grade. For the three main URL communities, as well as many of the others, these milestone assignments are at sea and culminate in a succession of command assignments with increasing levels of responsibility. An SWO, for example, first serves onboard a ship as a division officer; then as a department head while an O-4; then in an O-5 command, such as destroyer commanding officer; then a major (O-6) command, such as command of a cruiser or a destroyer squadron.[273] Community and joint schooling, Navy assignments ashore, and joint assignments all fit into the space in between these milestone assignments, which means that timelines are very tight given the number of requirements.

The Navy has traditionally promoted very few officers below the zone, and even more rarely promotes an officer early multiple times, unlike the Army or especially the Air Force.[274] This reflects the Navy's laissez-faire approach to identifying FOs, as discussed above, as well as the need to allow officers sufficient time to meet their communities' requirements for each grade along their prescribed career path. This also leads to Navy O-7s having more years in service than their counterparts in some of the other services. The average Navy officer promoted to O-7 between FY 2013 and FY 2018 had 29.0 years in service (Figure 5.2), compared with a military-wide average of 27.4 years in service.[275] Within the Navy, aviators have an average of 29.0 years in service by the time they make O-7, and submarine officers have slightly more years in service, at 29.3 years. This likely reflects the Navy's philosophy of leader development and the extensive training requirements in those communities.[276] As Figure 5.3 shows, Navy officers, on average, spend the most time at O-6 (nearly seven years), followed by O-5 (just under 6.5 years) and O-3 and O-4 (six years in each).

---

[272] N23, active duty Navy mid-grade officer, November 26, 2018.

[273] Navy Personnel Command, "FY-20 Active Line Officer Community Brief," undated b.

[274] Ronald R. Shaw, Jr., "Now Hear This—Let Talented Officers Opt-In for Early Promotion," *U.S. Naval Institute Proceedings*, Vol. 142, No. 3, March 2016; Guy Snodgrass and Ben Kohlmann, *2014 Navy Retention Study*, September 1, 2014, p. 35.

[275] Authors' analysis of DMDC data.

[276] See aviation and submarine officer timelines in Navy Personnel Command, undated b.

Figure 5.2. Average Years in Service for Rising Navy Officers, by Grade (Promoted in Prior Year), 2008–2018

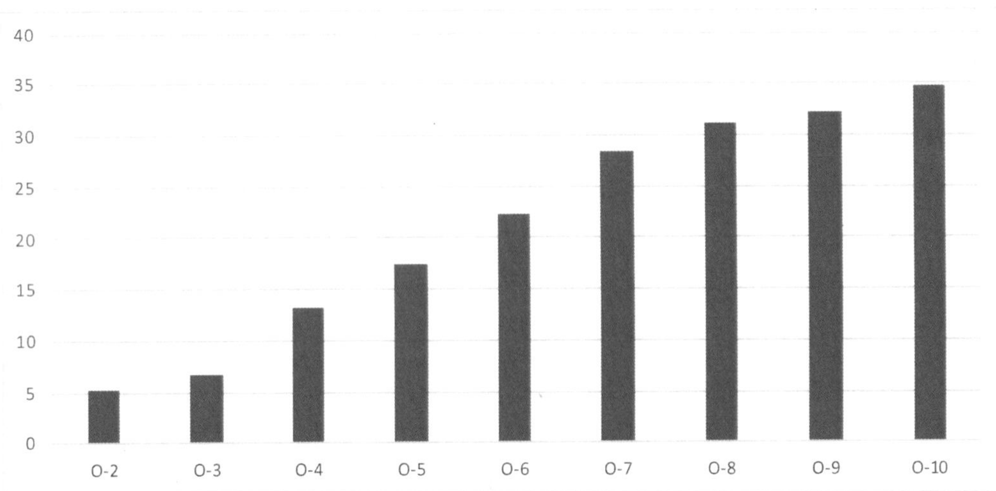

SOURCE: Authors' analysis of DMDC data.
NOTE: Years in service are calculated as of January each year, for officers promoted in the year before.

Figure 5.3. Time in Grade for Rising Navy Officers Promoted from That Grade in the Prior Year, Average, 2008–2018

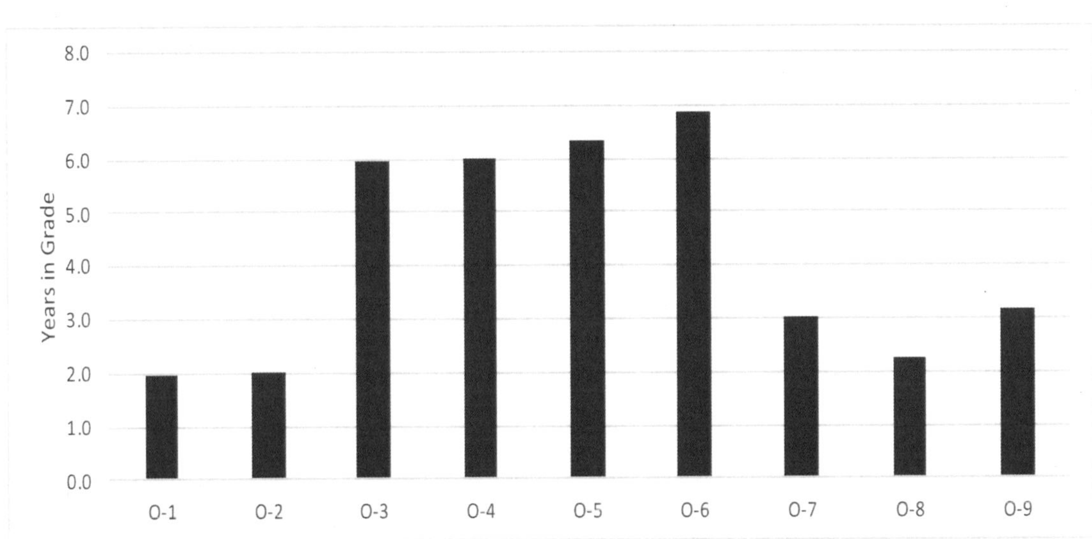

SOURCE: Authors' analysis of DMDC data.

Personnel Management Processes and Impact on Navy Flag Officers

As in all the services, an officer's career is governed by the personnel processes that are defined by statute, service policy, and practice. The sections below outline the personnel management processes, including commissioning, administrative screening boards, duty assignments, education and special training, evaluations, and promotion boards, that have substantial bearing on Navy FO development and selection.

Commissioning Source

The vast majority of Navy officers earn their commissions through OCS, Naval Reserve Officers Training Corps (NROTC), or their service academy, the USNA. How initial entry assignments are specifically determined varies by commissioning source but generally reflects a combination of needs of the service, an individual's preference, and the individual's demonstrated performance. Some of the most highly sought commissions include those in the URL and also in the Marine Corps: approximately 25 percent of the USNA's class of 2019 commissioned as marines.[277]

USNA graduates have a built-in network of officers with shared undergraduate experience that lasts throughout the entirety of their Navy careers. This is much less the case for officers commissioning through NROTC or even OCS. One interviewee estimated that out of a total of 400 fellow OCS graduates, only ten made it to O-6, and only one served 30 years in the Navy.[278] This phenomena is borne out in our analysis of personnel data, as shown by the shrinking proportion of OCS officers at the higher grades in Figure 5.4. The built-in network for NROTC graduates is even smaller, as there might be just a dozen officers entering the Navy from even a relatively large university, only one of which might make O-6.[279] In contrast, a USNA graduate enters the Navy with more than 780 fellow academy alumni, of which an average of 110 will make O-6 and 13 will make O-7.[280] The size of this network, and the strength of personal connections made prior to commissioning, might contribute to the overrepresentation of academy graduates in the FO corps, particularly at the highest ranks of O-9 and O-10 (see Figure 5.4).

---

[277] U.S. Naval Academy News Center, "Class of 2019 Receives Service Assignments," November 19, 2018.

[278] N1, retired Navy mid-grade officer, September 28, 2018.

[279] Senior leader selection exercise notes, January 30, 2019, RAND Corporation, Arlington, Virginia.

[280] Authors' analysis of DMDC data from 2008 to 2018. On number of USNA graduates commissioning into the Navy, also see U.S. Naval Academy, "Class of 2018 Statistics," May 25, 2018.

Figure 5.4. Accession Source of Rising Navy Officers (Promoted in Prior Year), by Grade, Average, 2008–2018

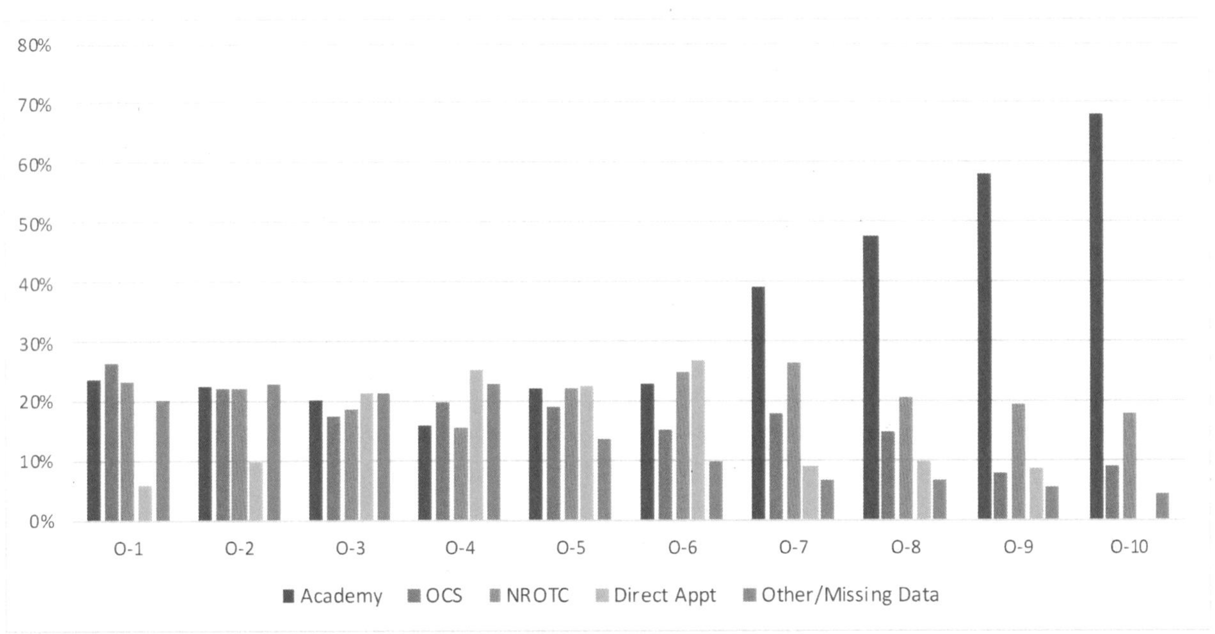

SOURCE: Authors' analysis of DMDC data.
NOTES: Because of the DMDC data structure, the total number of officers analyzed by MOS is different than the total number of officers analyzed by accession source. The total numbers of Navy officers analyzed by grade were as follows: O-1: 36,298; O-2: 35,850; O-3: 38,136; O-4: 20,501; O-5: 11,418; O-6: 5,291; O-7: 371; O-8: 252; O-9: 124; O-10: 22. The number of officers analyzed decreases between the lower grades and the higher grades. Because fewer officers are included in our analysis at higher grades, representation among the higher grades is more susceptible to fluctuations in year-over-year differences in accession sources.

Prospective analysis indicates that, of all officers who served as O-4s between FY 1995 and FY 2018, 1.02 percent of USNA graduates attained the grade of O-7. By comparison, 0.53 percent of OCS graduates and 0.81 percent of NROTC graduates were promoted to the grade of O-7.

Administrative Screening Boards

The most important step for selection for mid-grade promotion does not occur at the promotion board itself, but rather at each communities' administrative screening boards, which select officers for milestone command assignments.[281] Screening for milestone command assignments occurs at O-4, O-5, and O-6. Just like promotion boards, which will be explained later in this chapter, these screening boards are convened annually and evaluate officers on the basis of their Fitness Reports (FITREPs) and official record.[282] Officers generally receive two or three separate "looks," or opportunities, to be selected for command, thereby reducing the effect

---

[281] Erik Slavin, "Navy's Promotion System Struggling to Root Out Unfit Commanders," *Stars and Stripes*, May 16, 2010.

[282] Slavin, 2010.

that any one board and its particular set of members' biases can have.[283] Screening rates are higher for O-4 department head than for the O-5 or O-6 command assignments. In one year in the late 2010s in the aviation community, for example, 66 percent of eligible officers were selected for department head, while 22 percent were selected for O-5 command and 23 percent for O-6 command.[284]

Numeric selection targets for different types of commands are provided to ensure that there are sufficient officers to fill required billets, and special consideration is given to officers in that community's acquisition corps.[285] Crucially, these screening boards are made up of senior members of an officer's specific community. Because command selections are so tightly linked to promotions, this effectively allows aviators to control aviator promotions, SWOs to control SWO promotions, and so on, further enforcing community control over officer advancement. Several interviewees referred to the communities as each comprising their own "fiefdom" or "tribe," reflecting their high degree of importance, autonomy, and control over officer careers.[286]

Duty Assignments

Officers who are selected for command are given a specific assignment by a detailer, who is typically a fellow officer from within their community working at the Navy Personnel Command in Millington, Tennessee. Detailers are expected to consider officers' career progress when making decisions on assignments, though this is balanced against their responsibility to fill billets to meet their community's requirements.[287] Having a well-informed, proactive, and sympathetic detailer is especially crucial for officers who find themselves on a nonstandard career path or who face time constraints in fulfilling their next set of command selection or promotion requirements, according to one FO.[288] Another interviewee told us that the communities place a high priority on having respected and competent detailers and that they frequently select their head detailers from among the senior O-6s who have been effective in major command and are seen as most likely to be promoted to FO.[289]

Detailers pay particular attention to fitting officer assignments into the prescribed career timeline for their specific community, though the ultimate responsibility for managing one's

---

[283] See, for example, Deputy Chief of Naval Personnel, "Order Convening the FY-20 Surface Commander Command Screen Board," November 28, 2018, pp. 3–4.

[284] These figures are from a recent (as of late 2019), but undated, briefing (Navy Personnel Command, undated b, slide 12).

[285] Deputy Chief of Naval Personnel, 2018.

[286] N1, retired Navy mid-grade officer, September 28, 2018; N12, retired Navy senior civilian leader, October 16, 2018; Senior leader selection exercise notes, January 30, 2019, RAND Corporation, Arlington, Virginia.

[287] Navy Personnel Command, "Officer Community Management and Detailing: Officer," undated c.

[288] N8, active duty Navy flag officer, October 12, 2018.

[289] N1, retired Navy mid-grade officer, September 28, 2018.

career to fit in milestone assignments falls to individual officers. As the SWO detailers' official website states:[290]

> Make no mistake about it, PERFORMANCE gets you promoted/screened, but TIMING into your next job (i.e. Department Head) is important in this business and delaying your arrival in an important afloat job has a cascading effect from which it may be difficult to recover.

This leaves officers with only a small, highly prescribed amount of time available for education and for assignments outside of one's core career path, with supporting institutional assignments that support Navy operations usually prioritized. The exact mix of institutional Navy, joint, and educational assignments in an officer's career matters less for promotions up through the mid-grades, as long as these assignments do not prevent an officer from completing milestone commands. An officer's broader career history does, however, become an important discriminating factor in selection to O-7. In particular, O-7 level carrier strike group (CSG) command positions appear to carry particular weight in later promotion decisions. Of current Navy O-9s and O-10s, four out of nine (44 percent) O-10s were CSG commanders, and 12 out of 42 (29 percent) O-9s were CSG commanders, demonstrating the value placed on multidomain, large-scale operational experience.[291] Certain other types of duty assignments and their ultimate bearing on a Navy officer's career trajectory are explained below.

Supporting Institutional Assignments

The degree to which supporting institutional assignments are valued by promotion boards depends highly on the position. Community-specific institutional experience is generally viewed as the most important, followed by experience in Navy-wide institutions.[292] Post-command assignments as head community detailer, as chief of staff to the community senior leader (or type commander), or as commanding officer of the community school (such as the Naval Surface Warfare Officer School), are all viewed as "varsity-level" positions looked upon favorably by O-7 selection boards, according to one active duty FO.[293] Serving as the O-6 executive officer to the senior-most leaders in the Navy, especially the CNO or VCNO but also other O-10s and key O-9 leaders. such as Deputy Chief of Naval Operations for Integration of Capabilities and Resources, is also considered highly valuable.[294] Experience in the most important shore

---

[290] Navy Personnel Command, "Let's Talk Timing," undated d.

[291] Authors' analysis of all official Navy biographies for current flag officers; U.S. Navy, "United States Navy Biographies," webpage, undated (accessed July 25, 2018).

[292] Senior leader selection exercise notes, January 30, 2019, RAND Corporation, Arlington, Virginia.

[293] N8, active duty Navy flag officer, October 12, 2018.

[294] Senior leader selection exercise notes, January 30, 2019, RAND Corporation, Arlington, Virginia; N8, active duty Navy flag officer, October 12, 2018; N12, retired Navy senior civilian leader, October 16, 2018.

commands, such as naval bases in Pearl Harbor, Norfolk, and San Diego, is also looked upon favorably.[295]

Broadening and Joint Assignments

Broadening experiences, such as assignments to interagency organizations or North Atlantic Treaty Organization (NATO) staff, are considered to be of limited value for promotion, and can even be "career-killers" if they take the place of a standard assignment along the expected community career path.[296] In general, time spent in the Navy, and specifically in assignments directly related to one's own career field, are most prized, and broadening assignments are viewed as unnecessary distractions.

Relatedly, joint experience and experience in interagency and multinational organizations in particular are usually valued less in promotion selection.[297] Joint assignments are generally viewed as simply a "box to check" in order to meet the statutory joint qualification requirements for FOs, rather than as an important broadening experience in its own right.[298] There are a few exceptions to this, however. Serving in a joint environment under a high-profile Navy admiral, such as in U.S. Indo-Pacific Command (USINDOPACOM), is viewed favorably for officers in all communities. Outside of the main three URL communities, some officers are also expected to serve in high-profile joint assignments, such as SEALs in certain USSOCOM headquarters billets or Navy intelligence officers on CCMD staffs.[299]

Deployment Experience

While command at sea is treated as both an operational and deployed naval experience, it does not usually include direct combat experience, given the absence of any significant maritime battles in recent decades. This contributes to an observation that Navy judgments on officer performance are based on "how well people do at meetings, how smart the ship looks, and all those kinds of subsidiary factors," in the absence of demonstrated leadership in naval combat.[300] As another interviewee put it bluntly, "the Navy missed the war . . . and you need a good war sometimes to sort out who your administrative bandits are versus your good wartime leaders."[301]

There are some exceptions to this relative lack of deployment time. One interviewee mentioned that aviation officers, including those stationed on carriers, have often been involved

---

[295] Senior leader selection exercise notes, January 30, 2019, RAND Corporation, Arlington, Virginia.

[296] Senior leader selection exercise notes, January 30, 2019, RAND Corporation, Arlington, Virginia.

[297] Senior leader selection exercise notes, January 30, 2019, RAND Corporation, Arlington, Virginia.

[298] Senior leader selection exercise notes, January 30, 2019, RAND Corporation, Arlington, Virginia; N3, retired Navy mid-grade officer, October 23, 2018.

[299] Senior leader selection exercise notes, January 30, 2019, RAND Corporation, Arlington, Virginia.

[300] N1, retired Navy mid-grade officer, September 28, 2018.

[301] N20, active duty Navy mid-grade officer, November 15, 2018.

in wartime missions in Iraq and Afghanistan, and having a reputation as a "preeminent warfighter" can be key to standing out, and being selected for O-7, in this community.[302] This is even more true of Navy EOD and SEAL officers, whose command tours often include land combat operations, including in Iraq and Afghanistan. Even SWOs and submarine officers have served in Iraq and Afghanistan, though usually as individual augmentees for positions such as Provincial Reconstruction Team leaders. While promotion guidance directs that such augmentee assignments are to be looked upon favorably, they take crucial time away from an officer's standard career track and ability to complete milestone commands at sea, which is also prioritized in official guidance.[303]

Education and Special Training

As with on-the-job experience discussed above, not all education and training is created equally when it comes to Navy officer development and selection to O-7. Community-specific education and training, such as at the Naval Surface Warfare Officer School, Naval Submarine School, or one of the Naval Aviation Schools, is mandatory for officer progression, and performance at these schools can matter for promotion.[304] This also includes the technically demanding Naval Nuclear Power School, which is required for submarine officers and, while only mandatory for certain high-profile aviation and SWO nuclear commands, is valued highly in those communities as well. Having education and training in specialties that are statutorily preferred or in particularly high demand, such as acquisition or financial management, can also be a distinguishing factor for selection to O-7.[305]

In the Navy, PME has traditionally been viewed as "pro forma" and a "box to check"—just another statutory requirement for selection to FO, similar to joint assignments.[306] Intermediate-level PME is given especially short shrift, with many Navy officers completing this requirement via nonresident correspondence courses taken concurrently with a standard career path assignment, often while at sea. The submarine officer community brief explicitly states that graduate education is valued equally "regardless of source or method of achievement," including, specifically, "distance learning."[307] As one Navy officer stated, it's viewed as "good to not send someone for 12 months to go to a war college somewhere, getting unobserved FITREPs, just

---

[302] N12, retired Navy senior civilian leader, October 16, 2018.

[303] Secretary of the Navy, "Order Convening the FY-18 Promotion Selection Boards to Consider Officers in the Line and Staff Corps on the Active-Duty List of the Navy for Permanent Promotion to the Grade of Rear Admiral (Lower Half)," October 11, 2016b; interview with active duty Navy flag officer, October 12, 2018.

[304] N13, retired Navy mid-grade officer, October 11, 2018; N8, active duty Navy flag officer, October 12, 2018.

[305] N8, active duty Navy flag officer, October 12, 2018; Senior leader selection exercise notes, January 30, 2019, RAND Corporation, Arlington, Virginia.

[306] N12, retired Navy senior civilian leader, October 16, 2018; Senior leader selection exercise notes, January 30, 2019, RAND Corporation, Arlington, Virginia.

[307] Secretary of the Navy, 2016b.

studying. . . . Instead it's better to send them to operational staff or out to sea, and get Navy work out of them." Traditionally, the officer continued, "It has been kind of a wink and a nod that doing [PME] online is perfectly fine, and if you do it during a command tour, then that is great."[308]

Historically, Navy officers who do choose to attend in-residence intermediate PME are perceived as deviating from the standard path and in danger of missing the opportunity for milestone assignments.[309] Unlike intermediate-level PME, senior service school education is required to be in-residence, but also has generally been viewed as a box to check. Which school an officer attends, and how an officer performs in that school, is not valued in the Navy.[310] In 2014, one professor at the Naval War College highlighted "the irony . . . that the Navy itself has over the past forty years made every effort to avoid sending its best officers to [the Naval War College at] Newport, or to any other PME institution, despite the fact that the Naval War College has provided far and away the most intellectually challenging education in strategy" of all the senior service schools.[311]

This is likely to change in the future, at least partially, with new official requirements for selective admission to senior service schools and for strategic-level graduate education becoming a prerequisite for assuming O-6 major command.[312] Additionally, the Navy announced an overhaul to its education system in early 2019, centralizing its PME schools in an effort to address ongoing resourcing and utilization issues.[313] However, the current Navy FO corps has been brought up in the traditional system lamented by Rear Admiral James Kelly, dean at the Naval War College in 2014:[314]

> We must acknowledge that as a Navy we tend to undervalue the contribution of education in developing our Sailors as leaders. We limit the time Sailors are given to attend schoolhouses, or we seek to waive the requirement altogether. We mandate the shortest possible course lengths, while structuring career paths designed to maximize operational experiences. This has created a culture where going to the schoolhouse or attending war college is considered "time off"—rather than an uncompromising investment in our people and in our profession.

---

[308] N8, active duty Navy flag officer, October 12, 2018.

[309] Senior leader selection exercise notes, January 30, 2019, RAND Corporation, Arlington, Virginia; Craig R. Olson, "Naval Leadership: Developing Operational Leaders for the 21st Century," Naval War College, May 4, 2009.

[310] Senior leader selection exercise notes, January 30, 2019, RAND Corporation, Arlington, Virginia.; N1, retired Navy mid-grade officer, September 28, 2018; N8, active duty Navy flag officer, October 12, 2018.

[311] Williamson Murray, "Is Professional Military Education Necessary," *Naval War College Review*, Vol. 67, No. 1, Winter 2014, p. 154.

[312] NAVADMIN 263/18, 2018.

[313] David Thornton, "Navy Education Overhaul Creates New CLO," Federal News Network, February 15, 2019.

[314] Kelly, 2014, p. 16.

Other graduate education outside of the PME system has been viewed through this same lens. As one interviewee described, "I arrived in the Navy with a Ph.D., one of a very small number of officers who had that [level of education], but most people didn't know that I had it."[315] Another officer saw his pursuit of a Ph.D. while a mid-grade officer perceived as a negative factor by a promotion board, which assumed wrongly that it meant he had spent years outside his standard career path.[316] Graduate education that has specific relevance to a particular community is valued, however, such as a master's degree in business or engineering for engineering duty officers, or a master's in computer science or another technical field for cryptologic warfare officers.[317]

Evaluations

Navy officers are evaluated by their reporting senior officer in annual FITREPs, which follow a standard template. An officer's performance is graded from 1 to 5 on several performance "traits," and this then forms the basis for a "member trait average" score for that officer.[318] A score of 1 is intended to signify "disappointing performance" and 5 reflects "superstar performance," but the absolute number matters less than how an officer's score compares with those of other officers evaluated by the same reporting senior.[319] Table 5.1 depicts Navy FITREP evaluation traits.

---

[315] N1, retired Navy mid-grade officer, September 28, 2018.

[316] Senior leader selection exercise notes, January 30, 2019, RAND Corporation, Arlington, Virginia.

[317] Navy Personnel Command, undated a.

[318] Bureau of Naval Personnel Instruction (BUPERSINST) 1610.10D, Change Transmittal 1, *Navy Performance Evaluation System*, Washington, D.C.: Chief of Naval Personnel, February 25, 2016, pp. 1-15–1-16.

[319] BUPERSINST 1610.10D, 2016.

Table 5.1. Traits Evaluated in Navy Fitness Reports

Measures of Performance, Junior and Mid-Grade FITREPs	Measures of Performance, O-7 and O-8 FITREPs	Measures of Potential, O-7 and O-8 FITREPs
Tactical performance		
Command or organizational climate/equal opportunity		
Teamwork		
Professional expertise	Operational professional competence	
Mission accomplishment and initiative	Mission accomplishment	
Military bearing/character	Military bearing	
Leadership	Leadership judgment	
	Communication skills	
	Geopolitical fluency	
	Vision/strategic thinking	Strategic thinking
	Fiscal planning/organizational skills	Fiscal planning/organizational skills
	Leading change	Potential leading change
		Personal growth
		Professional growth (fostering subordinates' growth as leaders)

SOURCE: Mark F. Light, "The Navy's Moral Compass," *Naval War College Review*, Vol. 65, No. 3, Summer 2012, p. 149; BUPERSINST 1610.10D, 2016, pp. 1-15–1-16, 19-5–19-10.
NOTE: For definitions of each of these characteristics, see BUPERSINST 1610.10D, 2016.

Navy junior and mid-grade officers are evaluated on a somewhat different set of traits than Navy O-7 and O-8 FOs, as shown in Table 5.1, though there is some overlap. Navy O-7s and O-8s are evaluated on both performance and potential, and in some cases on both performance and potential of the same "traits" (e.g., strategic thinking).

The overall member trait average score for an officer is calculated as the average grade received on all seven traits (for junior and mid-grade officers) or 14 traits (for FOs).[320] This, in effect, gives each of seven traits used to evaluate junior and mid-grade officers equal weight. The 14 FO traits are also given equal weight, but because three traits are included twice in the list—as a measure of performance and separately as a measure of potential—they are essentially weighted double. These three traits are those focused on strategic thinking, financial planning/organizational skills, and leading change, and we note that although these skills are given extra weight in evaluations of FO job performance, they are not present at all in the O-6 evaluations that are used to select FOs in the first place. This suggests that there is likely a steep learning curve in an officer's first flag-level assignment, which could have substantial effects on performance depending on the assignment and the individual filling that role. Further, this indicates that an officer is selected based on one set of criteria but rated according to a different set, which could create situations where an officer whose file looks promising to a promotion board performs poorly in O-7 positions. Likewise, this could mean that officers who perform

[320] BUPERSINST 1610.10D, 2016, pp. 1–16, 19–10.

well as O-7s could be passed over by the board for promotion to higher grades if they are weighing other nonperformance criteria more heavily.

An officer's evaluation scores are compared with the officer's immediate peers in the same competitive category and same grade serving under a particular reporting senior officer; these peers are officially termed a *summary group*.[321] An officer's scores are also compared against all other officers whom that reporting senior officer has overseen over the course of their career, as captured by a lifetime average of the evaluation scores the reporting senior officer has imparted.[322] These comparisons are generally made among other officers within the same community. The most important aspect of an evaluation is how an officer "breaks out" when compared against their peers during milestone command tours at sea.[323]

The importance of relative evaluation scores leads reporting seniors to carefully manage their annual and lifetime averages in order to have their performance assessments have the most impact. One common practice is to rank officers somewhat lower in their earlier years in any given grade or assignment, then to rank them higher in their final evaluations, closer to when they are eligible for promotion or screenings for milestone commands. One interviewee said that this allows a reporting senior to maintain a lower overall career average while providing higher scores to subordinates at the times that matter most.[324] The same interviewee contended that another practice is to allow for modest inflation in one's lifetime average by providing somewhat lower scores to subordinates at the beginning of one's career, then slowly increasing scores over time.[325] As a lifetime average increases, it retroactively lowers the relative value of evaluation scores given in previous years, but at a point when those early scores matter less in an officer's career.

These practices are derided at times as unfairly gaming the system and can result in resentment among officers who feel they are being unfairly penalized simply because they are newer in their grade or assignment. As one officer argued, "How you are ranked against your peers at a particular command—of the paramount importance to promotion—is based more on seniority than performance."[326] Yet the Navy's rigid numerical approach to comparing member trait averages provides limited room for manipulation. Furthermore, the general practice of not promoting officers early, together with the disproportionate emphasis on one's final evaluation in

---

[321] BUPERSINST 1610.10D, 2016, p. 8.

[322] BUPERSINST 1610.10D, 2016, p. 5.

[323] N1, retired Navy mid-grade officer, September 28, 2018; N12, retired Navy senior civilian leader, October 16, 2018.

[324] N20, active duty Navy mid-grade officer, November 15, 2018.

[325] N20, active duty Navy mid-grade officer, November 15, 2018.

[326] Anna Granville, "4 Reasons I Am Resigning My Commission as a Naval Officer," Task and Purpose, April 13, 2015.

command compared with one's immediate peers, limits the impact of individual trait averages being influenced by one's years in grade or years in assignment.

Missing a final evaluation in an assignment or being evaluated by a reporting senior who does not fully understand the system can be detrimental. One interviewee related the story of a top-performing Navy lieutenant who was transferred to a higher-responsibility billet shortly before he would have had the opportunity to be evaluated as number one of ten lieutenants in his old assignment. The effect was that "His commander gave him a kill shot for promotion just because he didn't know how to best manage his subordinates and didn't know the consequences."[327]

Whether an officer pursues the standard, competitive career path in their own community can also affect FITREP evaluation scores. High-performing officers who are seen as taking themselves off of the standard career track—by pursuing a nonstandard assignment or deciding to retire from service, for example—also might receive poor FITREP trait grades, as their reporting senior will often choose to save higher grades for others who are still perceived to be competitive for future promotions.[328] The extent to which this occurs in any given peer group can affect both its members' absolute and relative evaluation scores.[329]

FITREPs also include an overall promotion recommendation designating an officer as "Early Promote," "Must Promote," "Promotable," "Progressing," or "Significant Problems." Reporting senior officers are limited in the number of Early Promote and Must Promote recommendations they can give subordinates. For all grades, Early Promote recommendations are limited to 20 percent of the total number of officers being evaluated in any given summary group. Limits on Must Promotes vary by grade and are counted together with Early Promotes. For O-3s, there is a combined limit of 60 percent of officers who can receive one of these two recommendations, and this limit goes down to 50 percent for O-4s, and 40 percent for O-5s and O-6s.[330]

The FITREPs, importantly, are visible to the officers being reviewed, as well as to promotion and command screening boards. This provides the officer the opportunity to contest or provide additional information in response to a negative FITREP, and it also allows for the use of FITREPs as potentially useful feedback during required performance counseling sessions.[331] At the same time, however, it makes FITREPs less likely to contain fully honest appraisals of less-than-stellar performers.[332] As one officer contended, "There is a wide reluctance to give lackluster officers poor performance reviews, and instead it's much easier to wait for mediocre

---

[327] N20, active duty Navy mid-grade officer, November 15, 2018.

[328] Senior leader selection exercise notes, January 30, 2019, RAND Corporation, Arlington, Virginia.

[329] Senior leader selection exercise notes, January 30, 2019, RAND Corporation, Arlington, Virginia.

[330] BUPERSINST 1610.10D, 2016, p. 1–20.

[331] BUPERSINST 1610.10D, 2016, pp. 3–4, 8–9.

[332] Slavin, 2010.

officers to transfer out of the command and become someone else's problem."[333] Some have argued that this should be changed so that only promotion and command screening boards have access to FITREPs, and not the reviewed officers themselves, to encourage more-candid evaluations.[334]

Promotion Boards

The Navy's promotion process works hand-in-hand with its administrative screening board process for specific milestone assignments in an officer's career. Both are critical to understanding the Navy's approach to officer development. In this section, we focus on Navy promotion processes to the grades of O-4 through O-8. Promotions to the junior grades of O-2 and O-3 do not involve selective promotion boards; instead, officers are automatically promoted to these grades if they complete statutory time in grade requirements and receive promotable evaluations in their FITREP.[335] On the other end of the spectrum, FOs are promoted to O-9 or O-10 as a consequence of assignment decisions by Navy and DoD leadership together with approval by the President and confirmation by the U.S. Senate.

The most direct and consequential guidance on what the Navy looks for in its FOs is found in instructions given to the promotion boards that select O-7 FOs from the pool of eligible O-6s. The overall leadership characteristics sought at the O-7 rank are generally the same as those sought at the mid-grades.[336] At both levels, emphasis is placed on "proven and sustained superior performance in command" and adherence to the values of integrity, accountability, initiative, and toughness. The main differences unique to the O-7 promotion guidelines are those relating to statutory requirements, such as joint qualification and preferential consideration for acquisition professionals, as well as the Navy's specific billet-filling needs at the O-7 rank in the upcoming year.[337]

Navy promotion boards are convened annually for each of the grades between O-4 and O-8, with separate promotion boards established for each of the competitive categories. URL officers from all communities are considered for promotion by a single selection board, which is made up of officers from each of the URL communities in proportions reflecting their relative size. URL boards are required to include at least five aviation officers, four SWOs, three submarine officers, one EOD officer, and one SEAL officer, with at least one of the group also being an

---

[333] Granville, 2015.

[334] Slavin, 2010.

[335] Navy Personnel Command, "Active Duty O3 Line," undated e.

[336] Secretary of the Navy, "FY-18 Active-Duty and Reserve Navy Flag Officer Promotion Selection Board Precept," September 19, 2016a; Secretary of the Navy, "FY-18 Active-Duty and Reserve Navy Officer and Chief Warrant Officer Promotion Selection Board Precept," December 12, 2016c.

[337] See, for example, Secretary of the Navy, "Order Convening the FY-18 Promotion Selection Boards to Consider Officers in the Line on the Active-Duty List of the Navy for Permanent Promotion to the Grade of Commander," February 13, 2017b; Secretary of the Navy, 2016b.

acquisition professional.[338] Separate boards are also established for each of the RL and staff officer communities, with each typically including five or more officers from that community.[339] Together with the community-centric administrative screening boards described previously, this allows the communities substantial control over the career pathways of their own officers and likely contributes to officers selecting those who most closely resemble their own experiences and pathways.

The communities only begin to lose this control once an officer is eligible for O-7, as promotion boards, which for URL officers are composed of officers from across the URL communities, become an important step for selection to this grade. Promotion rates to O-7 are in the low single digits, by far the lowest faced by any officer over the course of a career, even given the fact that officers receive up to six looks for promotion, according to one FO.[340] Another interviewee observed that eligibility is still shaped by community screening board decisions on whether an O-6 serves in a major command, which winnows out approximately half of O-6s, and community detailer decisions that determine where an O-6 is assigned following major command also matter.[341] But the decision of which small number of O-6s to promote out of the larger pool of those eligible finally comes down to the promotion board. Navy O-6 officers have multiple opportunities for consideration at the annual O-7 selection board. It is highly unlikely for someone to be selected for O-7 in their final look, but one interviewee noted that this has happened in rare cases.[342] The communities cede even more control at the higher FO ranks, as once an officer becomes an O-7, decisionmakers from the broader Navy, rather than simply from within the URL community, have greater sway on officer assignments and promotions.[343]

Boards are predominantly composed of officers two or more ranks above the officers being considered. In FY 2018, for example, URL selection boards for O-4 were made up entirely of O-6s, the O-5 selection board was made up of O-6s and a few rear admirals, and the O-6 selection board was made up of mostly rear admirals.[344] The president of the selection board for each of the grades is an FO, including a vice admiral presiding over the O-6 selection board.[345] O-7 and O-8 promotion selection boards are composed entirely of FOs, and their presidents are O-10

---

[338] Secretary of the Navy, Instruction (SECNAVINST) 1401.3A, *Selection Board Membership*, Washington, D.C.: Department of the Air Force, December 20, 2005.

[339] SECNAVINST 1401.3A, 2005. Also, see selection board memberships published by Navy Personnel Command, for example: Navy Personnel Command, undated f.

[340] N8, active duty Navy flag officer, October 12, 2018.

[341] N1, retired Navy mid-grade officer, September 28, 2018.

[342] N8, active duty Navy flag officer, October 12, 2018.

[343] N12, retired Navy senior civilian leader, October 16, 2018; N3, retired Navy mid-grade officer, October 23, 2018.

[344] Navy Personnel Command, "Board Membership, FY-18 Active-Duty Navy Captain Line Promotion Selection Boards," undated g.

[345] SECNAVINST 1401.3A, 2005.

admirals.[346] While the composition of the board can affect who is selected, with the president holding particular sway, these effects should even out over time, as board composition varies from year to year and any given Navy officer is considered for promotion multiple times under different boards.[347]

O-4, O-5, and O-6 promotion boards for each competitive category are provided with an authorized selection percentage designed to ensure that the board does not promote more officers than needed to the next grade. This percentage varies by competitive category, though they all fall within a fairly narrow range.[348] Navy selection rates decrease fairly steadily with each higher grade, with nearly automatic selection to O-2 and O-3 decreasing to selection rates around 50 percent for promotion to O-6, at least in most officer categories.

Yet, in practice, the Navy mid-grade promotion boards are less selective than these rates would suggest. Navy mid-grade selection rates are actually calculated to allow "100 percent opportunity" for officers who successfully completed their milestone assignments to promote to the next grade, said one interviewee.[349] As a result, selection for and successful completion of milestone assignments is a more important step in the mid-grade promotion process than the promotion board itself. As one interviewee stated, "In the unrestricted line, anybody that successfully completed their O-5 command is automatically selected for O-6."[350] Officers can have multiple promotion selection opportunities (below, in, or above the zone), but are generally not even considered for promotion prior to completing the milestone assignments for each grade, with some exceptions made for officers who served in Iraq or Afghanistan and thus outside of their "traditional community career path."[351] This factor also limits the number of early promotions in the Navy, because while it is possible to be below the zone and have completed milestone tours, it is hard and relatively rare.[352]

Figure 5.5 shows the percentage of Navy officers overall who are promoted to the next highest grade, reflecting the highly competitive selection from O-6 to O-7. In Figure 5.6, these promotion rates are broken down by type of officer career category. One interesting observation

---

[346] SECNAVINST 1401.3A, 2005.

[347] Senior leader selection exercise notes, January 30, 2019, RAND Corporation, Arlington, Virginia.

[348] Secretary of the Navy, "Order Convening the FY-18 Promotion Selection Boards to Consider Officers in the Line on the Active-Duty List of the Navy for Permanent Promotion to the Grade of Captain," January 5, 2017a, 2017b; Secretary of the Navy, "Order Convening the FY-18 Promotion Selection Boards to Consider Officers in the Line on the Active-Duty List of the Navy for Permanent Promotion to the Grade of Lieutenant Commander," May 2, 2017c.

[349] N23, active duty Navy mid-grade officer, November 26, 2018.

[350] N1, retired Navy mid-grade officer, September 28, 2018.

[351] Secretary of the Navy, January 5, 2017a; Secretary of the Navy, 2016c, pp. 8–9. For more on promotion eligibility below, in, and above the zone, see SECNAVINST 1420.1B, *Promotion, Special Selection, Selective Early Retirement, And Selective Early Removal Boards for Commissioned Officers of the Navy and Marine Corps*, Washington, D.C.: Department of the Air Force, March 28, 2006.

[352] Authors' analysis of DMDC data; N23, active duty Navy mid-grade officer, November 26, 2018.

is that SEALs and EOD officers promote from O-5 to O-6 at higher rates than other officers, which might be due to the increased demand for those tailored skills in the combat-heavy 2000–2010 time frame.

Figure 5.5. Percentage of Navy Officers Who Promote to the Next Grade, 2000–2010 Officer Cohorts

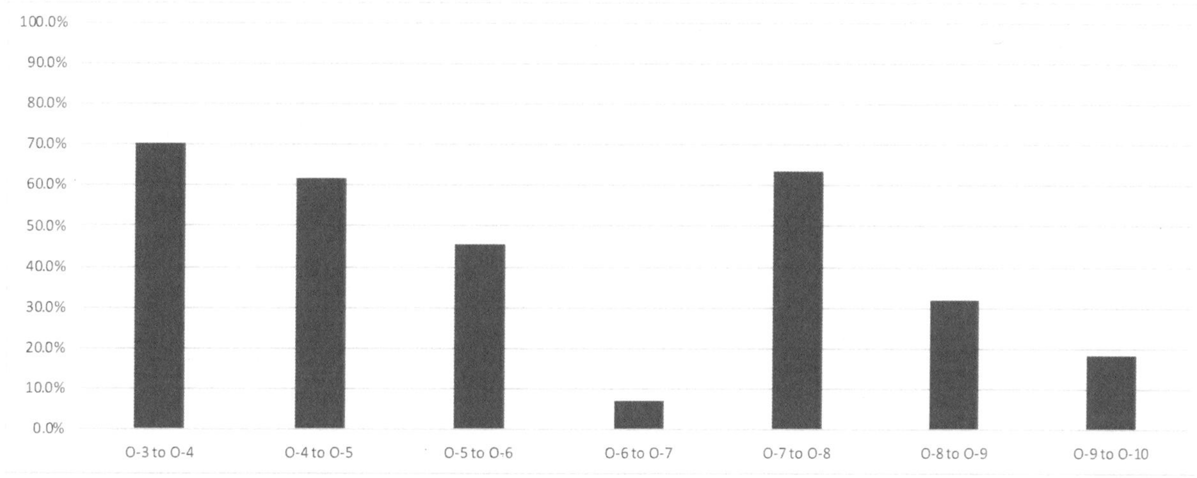

SOURCE: Authors' analysis of DMDC data.
NOTE: These numbers represent the average progression rate for the 11 (overlapping) cohorts of Navy officers present in each grade at the beginning of each year from 2000 through 2010, and reflect these officers' observed rates of reaching the next higher grade at any point up to the beginning of 2018, the last year for which we have data.

Figure 5.6. Percentage of Navy Officers Who Promote to the Next Grade, by Grade and Career Type, 2000–2010 Officer Cohorts

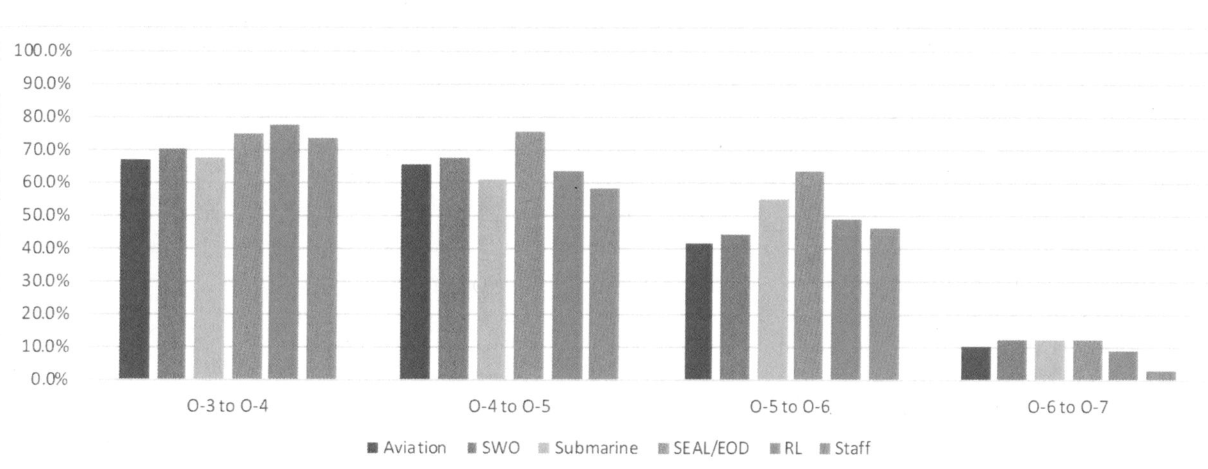

SOURCE: Authors' analysis of DMDC data.
NOTE: These numbers represent the average progression rate for the 11 (overlapping) cohorts of Navy officers present in each grade at the beginning of each year from 2000 to 2010, and reflect these officers' observed rates of reaching the next higher grade at any point up to the beginning of 2018, the last year for which we have data.

Command as a Promotion Factor

The importance of commanding Navy platforms at sea is firmly embedded in Navy culture and official guidance. At each of the mid-grades, being selected for the community standard milestone command at sea is competitive, and successfully completing command at sea is the single most important factor in promoting to the next grade. For selection to O-7, given the very small number of promotion slots available, it is not sufficient to have successfully completed command at sea. One interviewee said that it is also necessary to have "broken out" against one's peers, with FITREP rankings as the number one officer in a peer group.[353]

The type of command at sea also often matters, with certain communities often giving preference in promotions to certain platforms over others. The hierarchy of platforms for each community often reflects platform size, technical complexity, command prerequisites, or merely the centrality of a particular platform in that community's culture. For Navy aviation officers, command of a nuclear-powered aircraft carrier is often viewed as the most prestigious O-6 assignment, with carrier air group command next-most prestigious.[354] Officers who select for and successfully complete these commands are among those most likely to make O-7. Conversely, fewer aviation officers with experience in certain other platforms (such as rotary wing aircraft) are chosen for O-7. In the surface warfare community, one SWO with amphibious command experience is usually chosen for O-7 each year, but more SWOs with experience commanding cruisers or destroyer squadrons are chosen.[355]

Other Factors That Matter in Navy Flag Officer Selection

The personnel processes that define Navy career paths discussed thus far in this chapter matter immensely in determining who becomes a FO. However, they do not tell the entire story. Some aspects of an officer's career matter more than others, and promotion board members often use informal criteria when judging FO candidates, in addition to official guidance.[356] Other factors have such importance that they permeate multiple personnel processes that affect FO selection, and we discuss these in the following sections. These factors include the role of luck and timing, personal connections, personality characteristics, and an officer's individual priorities, and they can have an outsize importance in the competition for promotion to O-7, given the large pool of high-performing candidates competing for a very small number of available slots, with board decisions sometimes hinging on small distinctions. As one

[353] N1, retired Navy mid-grade officer, September 28, 2018.

[354] Senior leader selection exercise notes, January 30, 2019, RAND Corporation, Arlington, Virginia.

[355] Senior leader selection exercise notes, January 30, 2019, RAND Corporation, Arlington, Virginia.

[356] N1, retired Navy mid-grade officer, September 28, 2018; senior leader selection exercise notes, January 30, 2019, RAND Corporation, Arlington, Virginia.

interviewee argued, "Performance counts up until you make O-6—after that there is a whole other set of things that count, and performance isn't the biggest one of them."[357]

Pacific Experience

There is a marked regional tilt to the Navy's senior officers who are promoted to FO, with officers having Pacific experience better represented in the FO corps than those with Atlantic experience. This is perhaps not surprising, given the central importance that the Navy places on leading USINDOPACOM.[358] Official biographies of 150 out of the 275 current Navy FOs mentioned Pacific experience; 94 mentioned experience in the Atlantic. Looking at the fleets specifically, 28 bios mentioned experience with the "Atlantic Fleet," compared with 69 bios with experience in the "Pacific Fleet." This regional tilt still exists at the highest flag ranks, though slightly less pronounced, as eight O-9 and O-10 biographies mention Atlantic Fleet experience compared with 12 with Pacific Fleet experience.[359] Part of this regional concentration might be simply attributed to more positions being available in the Pacific than in the Atlantic, given that the Pacific is larger, has its own geographic combatant command (GCC), and directly borders more potential adversaries. However, regardless of why more positions exist in the Pacific, the absence of Pacific experience might be a detractor in certain promotion decisions.

This focus on Pacific experience is also reflected in the hierarchy of certain community type commanders. For example, the overall Commander of Naval Surface Forces (the surface warfare "type commander") and the Commander of Naval Surface Force Pacific are the same person; the Deputy Commander of Naval Surface Forces position goes to the lower-ranking Commander of Naval Surface Force Atlantic. This same regional hierarchy also holds in the aviation type command.

Timing

Given that FITREP evaluations are relative, the exact composition of one's peer group can be a deciding factor in achieving the coveted number one evaluation during milestone command assignments. Who writes an officer's FITREP also can matter, with evaluations from a higher-ranking or better-known officer carrying more weight with a promotion board.[360] Being asked to take a Navy assignment at an inconvenient time in one's career can derail an officer's prospects

---

[357] N13, retired Navy mid-grade officer, October 11, 2018.

[358] Roberts, 2019, p. 52.

[359] Authors' analysis of all official Navy bios for current flag officers. See U.S. Navy, "United States Navy Biographies," webpage, undated (accessed July 25, 2018).

[360] N13, retired Navy mid-grade officer, October 11, 2018; senior leader selection exercise notes, January 30, 2019, RAND Corporation, Arlington, Virginia.

for promotion.[361] One Navy O-6 officer relayed that the CNO personally asked him to fill a Navy staff position deemed critical, rather than assuming a major command assignment. The officer noted that the CNO was in effect telling him he had to take the staff job for the sake of the Navy, even though "we know it won't take you anywhere," since declining major command would make him ineligible for O-7 selection. The officer continued: "This happens quite a bit, this type of nonstandard path. I'm not an exceptional case. At least once a year, once a cycle, there are people in my situation. And they have to make a hard choice—do what serves their career, or what they are called to do."[362]

The Navy's demand for FOs from particular communities, or with particular subspecialties, also often changes from year to year. This can make the difference in being selected for promotion to FO,[363] particularly for the most senior flag ranks. In recent years, for example, the Fat Leonard scandal resulted in several FOs being frozen in their positions pending completion of Navy investigations. Other Navy officers missed the opportunity to promote and fill these billets because they did not open up until a couple years later.[364] At the same time, this bottleneck later opened, providing greater opportunities to officers who were eligible for promotion at that time.

Personal Networks

Maintaining a robust and supportive network of personal connections also matters for selection to O-7 and the higher FO ranks. While these networks are often generated from attendance at USNA or other specific schools, personality appears to play a major role in growing and effectively leveraging those networks throughout an officer's career.

Perhaps not surprisingly, being an outgoing person who is easily "able to move inside the community and make people feel comfortable with you" matters.[365] Having a reputation as an effective officer who successfully takes initiative and acts independently also helps, as does being known for taking care of subordinates and looking out for fellow officers.[366] Some of these

---

[361] N8, active duty Navy flag officer, October 12, 2018; N13, retired Navy mid-grade officer, October 11, 2018; N20, active duty Navy mid-grade officer, November 15, 2018.

[362] N13, retired Navy mid-grade officer, October 11, 2018; senior leader selection exercise notes, January 30, 2019, RAND Corporation, Arlington, Virginia.

[363] N1, retired Navy mid-grade officer, September 28, 2018; senior leader selection exercise notes, January 30, 2019, RAND Corporation, Arlington, Virginia; authors' analysis of promotion board convening orders for FYs 17, 18, and 19.

[364] N1, retired Navy mid-grade officer, September 28, 2018; N8, active duty Navy flag officer, October 12, 2018; N12, retired Navy senior civilian leader, October 16, 2018.

[365] N1, retired Navy mid-grade officer, September 28, 2018. Also see N12, retired Navy senior civilian leader, October 16, 2018.

[366] N20, active duty Navy mid-grade officer, November 15, 2018; N23, active duty Navy mid-grade officer, November 26, 2018.

characteristics are also recognized in high-profile awards, such as the Vice Admiral James Bond Stockdale Award for Inspirational Leadership, which requires nomination from multiple peers.[367]

Ambition is another related factor. Officers are even officially encouraged to self-select for some of the higher-profile assignments. For example, officers are encouraged to reach out directly to community detailers, and provide a current official photo, if they are interested in serving as an FO aide.[368] Fitting in, particularly within one's specific community, is also important. As one interviewee stated:

> It is definitely a "ducks pick ducks" thing. If a person really wants to make flag, the smart thing to do is to cultivate the community leadership so they all know who you are, and take high visibility billets, and do well in major command, of course.[369]

Factors in Selecting Out

Of course, some Navy officers do not actively seek to become an FO. By the time they are considered for promotion to O-7, they are eligible for retirement, and one interviewee observed that they might negatively view the prospect of moving their family multiple times from post to post to accommodate FO rotations.[370] O-5 and O-6 assignments ashore are sometimes seen as filled with "drudgery work," which can make the prospect of continued service as an FO less attractive, especially because most FO positions are "desk jobs" rather than deployed sea assignments.[371] According to one interviewee, this can lead officers to retire early after accomplishing their milestone commands at sea, which are often viewed as the pinnacle of a Navy career.[372] It can also lead to officers pursuing assignments that are more personally fulfilling, or more compatible with their family's preferences, rather than the assignments most valued by their community, effectively taking them out of the running for FO selection. It is unclear how prevalent these different types of career decisions are in the Navy, but in a 2014 survey, 52.4 percent of more than 3,000 officer respondents answered "no" to the question "Do you want your boss's job?"[373] Because this was a web-based poll with a less than 2 percent response rate, however, it is hard to know how broadly representative this finding is of views

---

[367] Chief of Naval Personnel Public Affairs, "Navy Announces 2018 Stockdale Award Recipients," September 4, 2018. The Stockdale Award is awarded to two officers annually, and awardees are selected based on their demonstrated ability to act as a moralist, jurist, teacher, steward and philosopher. For more information, see Chief of Naval Personnel Public Affairs, "Navy Announces 2018 Stockdale Award Recipients," U.S. Navy, NNS180904-22, September 4, 2018.

[368] Navy Personnel Command, "Flag Aide," undated h.

[369] N1, retired Navy mid-grade officer, September 28, 2018.

[370] N8, active duty Navy flag officer, October 12, 2018.

[371] N8, active duty Navy flag officer, October 2018; N12, retired Navy senior civilian leader, October 18, 2018.

[372] N8, active duty Navy flag officer, October 12, 2018.

[373] Snodgrass and Kohlmann, 2014, pp. 10, 22.

within the Navy officer corps as a whole, or among those who could be O-7 contenders in particular.

Summary

Navy culture greatly informs the personnel processes that develop and select Navy officers to O-7 and beyond. The Navy's mission orientation as a service toward peer adversaries and maritime operations is firmly embedded in its approach to leadership development and its FOs' career paths, and some of the service's chief cultural characteristics, such as high valuation of traditions, operational independence, and technical expertise, can also be observed in its approaches to developing future admirals.

Although the Navy's warfare communities each have distinct traditions and even cultural attributes, a personnel hierarchy exists, with URL officers at the top. Most commonly, the typical Navy FO comes from the URL's aviation warfare, surface warfare, or submarine warfare communities. Submarine warfare officers are particularly overrepresented at the higher FO ranks. In terms of commissioning source, USNA graduates dominate the FO ranks, especially at the highest levels—more so than equivalent academy graduates from other services. Several interviewees noted that promotion boards tend to favor officers whose backgrounds look most similar to their own, which might suggest some uniformity of experience and perspective in those selected for FO. Yet the high degree of community-specific culture and control over officer careers up through O-7 selection also counterbalances this, to an extent.

Beginning as O-3s, officers continually compete for assignments and promotions, with the main criteria being performance in command at sea and adherence to a detailed and technically focused community career path. This, in turn, creates an officer corps that is self-reliant, technically competent, and specialized in a particular platform and operational domain. Given the inherent ground-based nature of the United States' most recent campaigns, most of the Navy's future senior leaders will not have seen major combat. They will, however, have extensive operational experience at sea, especially in the Pacific.

Mid-grade duty assignments for URL officers tend to often involve multidomain operations, particularly at sea. This relates to value placed on ability to operate and, later, command at ships in multidomain environment: Many Navy FOs, particularly those who go on to become O-9s or O-10s, have commanded carrier strike groups. The Navy's emphasis on operating at sea also means that Navy officers generally have limited joint and business management experience prior to making O-7, due to packed mid-level career schedules that leave little space for joint or educational opportunities. Further, joint assignments are not widely considered as valuable developmental tools, but rather necessary requirements to be fulfilled.

The Navy tends to emphasize service- and community-specific educational opportunities, which is reflective of the Navy's cultural emphasis on independent operation. As a result, some believe that this detracts from Navy officers' training in strategic thinking and analysis, which requires more "learning by doing" at the O-7 and O-8 grades. Overall, despite the quality of the Navy's intermediate and senior service schools, educational performance is not highly valued in promotion decisions. This might change as the Navy looks to reform its education system and several officer career management practices.

The typical Navy FO likely possesses extensive technical expertise in their naval platforms, grounded in on-the-job experience as well as training and education in a science, technology, engineering, and math (STEM) field. Some possess expertise in a particular high-demand subspecialty, such as financial management.

Interviewees and SLSE participants noted that Navy FOs tend to be outgoing, ambitious, and able to fit in easily with other Navy officers, particularly within their own community, where they have built a strong personal network through high-visibility assignments. As they move up the FO ranks, their ability to stand out and build strong networks eventually matters more than their standing in their specific community.

What these typical pathways, and the experiences they tend to cultivate, might mean for senior Navy officers in the future will be explored in Chapter 8.

6. The Air Force's Approach to Generalship

The Air Force's current personnel system has created a pool of GOs who have largely promoted quickly through its grades, serving in key positions that are required within what is often described as a tight time frame. The Air Force has *rated* and *nonrated* career fields: Rated officers are those who work in flying specialties (such as pilots, combat systems officers, air battle managers, and remotely piloted aircraft pilots), and nonrated officers are those who specialize in nonflying careers (such as space, intelligence, logistics, and personnel management). For rated career fields, officers aspiring to O-7 are expected to undertake a standard, rigorous series of requirements throughout their careers that include PME, three levels of command, and staff and joint duty experience. The specific requirements can differ for nonrated personnel, but there are also fewer GOs in these disciplines, which has focused the conversation about the Air Force's promotion system more narrowly on the rated world.

The Air Force's GO corps is proportionally larger than those of the other services. As of January 2018, Air Force active duty end strength was 317,200, making up 25 percent of the active duty end strength for DoD.[374] In fact, the Air Force includes a higher proportion of officers overall than any other service, with an average of 19.1 officers for every 100 service members and 8.8 GOs for every 10,000 service members. The total number of GOs in the Air Force is 279: 145 O-7s, 85 O-8s, 36 O-9s, and 13 O-10s.[375]

Officer development in the Air Force was the subject of both public and internal debate throughout the research period of this study. Active duty officers, including some under pseudonym, have publicly expressed their concerns about a promotion system that rewards early performers with career-long opportunities at the expense of those who peak later in their careers, a topic that will be discussed later in this chapter.[376] These criticisms—though not shared by all Air Force officers—have captured the attention of the Air Force's current chief of staff, David L. Goldfein, who has openly discussed the need to shift traditional personnel processes within the service. However, implementing lasting change in the Air Force's personnel management system will require top-down guidance to shift service culture and its long-held notions of what incentives ought to look like in the service.

---

[374] Defense Manpower Data Center, 2018.

[375] Officer and general officer numbers calculated by authors using DMDC data for January 2018. For a comparison of these numbers to those for other services, see Table B.2.

[376] For example, see Colonel Ned Stark's 2018 commentaries in *War on the Rocks* (Ned Stark, list of commentaries, undated).

Air Force Culture

Air Force culture is defined by its focus on technology and technological innovation, strategic analysis, and personnel development.[377] These attributes, understandably, center around airpower, which Builder described in 1989 as fundamental to Air Force identity:

> Who is the Air Force? It is the keeper and wielder of the decisive instruments of war—the technological marvels of flight that have been adapted to war. What is it about? It is about ensuring the independence of those who fly and launch these machines to have and use them for what they are—the ultimate means for both the freedom of flight and the destruction of war.[378]

Bombers reigned supreme at the service's inception, but they were soon surpassed by fighter pilots, who remain the most prominent personnel and symbols of the Air Force today.[379] This pilot-centric culture aligns with the Air Force's organizational mission. It is the fighter pilots being at the center of the service, as reflected in the composition of today's Air Force GO pool, that is notable. Indeed, the service has never had a nonpilot chief of staff.[380] However, the Air Force has cyber, space, nuclear, and other mission areas that are not always directly connected to its primary—and storied—flying missions. Within the Air Force, this diversity of missions prevents the service from espousing one unified culture.[381] Even so, the dominance of pilots throughout the service's senior leadership positions is culturally defining across the service's mission areas.

One result of this cultural hierarchy that directly impacts personnel management is that pilots are frequently tapped to fill positions whose duties many other nonpilots could theoretically perform. According to an active duty field-grade officer we interviewed, "Pilot wings were called a 'universal management badge' because you could put a pilot in charge of anything but you couldn't put just anyone in charge of a pilot."[382] This same idea was captured in a 2019 RAND report on service culture, which quoted an interviewee as saying, "There is a school of thought in the Air Force that pilots are in the best position to run the service because their situational awareness and multitasking skills translate to leadership, but it's not clear if they do."[383] Some of this has to do with the premier command opportunities that have tended to

---

[377] Natasha Lander, "The Air Force," in Zimmerman et al., 2019, pp. 77–78; William H. Burks, *Blue Moon Rising? Air Force Institutional Challenges to Producing Senior Joint Leaders*, Fort Leavenworth, Kan: U.S. Army Command and General Staff College School of Advanced Military Studies, 2010, p. 9-15.

[378] Builder, 1989, p. 32.

[379] Mike Worden, *Rise of the Fighter Generals: The Problem of Air Force Leadership 1945–1982*, Maxwell Air Force Base, Ala.: Air University Press, 1998, pp. 223–224.

[380] Colin Clark, "Hyten Likely Air Force Chief of Staff Nominee; Carlisle Next," *Breaking Defense*, March 2, 2016.

[381] Lander, 2019, p. 81.

[382] AF12, active duty field-grade officer, September 26, 2018.

[383] Quoted in Lander, 2019, p. 83, quoting AF65, a RAND analyst with a research specialty in Air Force culture, November 18, 2016.

garner the most attention, many of which have historically only been available to rated officers. As some have noted, this tendency could prove problematic to Air Force manning overall as the pilot shortage continues.[384] Captain David Geaney noted in 2017 that

> The problem, and many pilots will privately agree, is that we have "Golden Calfed" our operators, making them out to be super humans that must not only fly the most advanced aircraft in the world, but lead swathes of people from all backgrounds, and serve on staffs or deploy in positions that don't require operators.[385]

The Air Force's core values ("integrity first," "service before self," and "excellence in all we do"), its ethos ("fly, fight, and win"), and the concepts of "global strike, global reach, and global vision" are all embedded in its culture. Each pertains to a type of operational excellence that the Air Force asserts that only airmen can achieve. This underscores another element of Air Force culture, which is that the service seeks to reinforce that it can provide a leading role in the nation's wars, rather than simply one that enables the other services to operate.[386]

These principles are also embodied in the service's core missions: air and space superiority; intelligence, surveillance, and reconnaissance (ISR); rapid global mobility; global strike; and command and control. Prior RAND research indicates that air superiority is viewed as chief among these missions, while the others serve to support it.[387] That attitude contributes to the notion that the service advances a pilot-centric culture over a common culture.

These principles have also shaped how the Air Force views opportunities that enhance officers' contributions to the service over those that enable greater joint experience, even at the joint task force and geographic combatant command levels. Opportunities for advancement to GO tend to emphasize institutional knowledge of the Air Force, such as serving on the staff of a three- or four-star general in an Air Staff position. Joint experience is also valued, at least more than in the other services, as it provides an opportunity to enhance an Air Force officer's professional network, understand how to compete with the other services in arenas such as strategic planning and resource management, and observe how senior leaders in other services lead. Ultimately, however, assignments that enhance an officer's understanding of and contributions to the service have historically made an officer more competitive than one who has spent that time in joint roles.

Given the complex systems pilots must master to fly their aircraft, technical mastery is of utmost importance to the Air Force. In a culture that rewards technical excellence, those who demonstrate potential early in their careers are often afforded prized opportunities. Accordingly,

---

[384] Scott Maucione, "New Study Shows Grim Outlook for Future of Air Force Pilot Shortage," Federal News Network, April 15, 2019.

[385] Capt. David Geaney, "We Ask Too Much of Our Air Force Pilots," *Foreign Policy*, June 1, 2017.

[386] Lander, 2019.

[387] Lander, 2019, p. 82.

educational opportunities are traditionally held in high esteem in the Air Force, though their inclusion in officer history during promotion board has changed over time. Later in this chapter, we discuss two particularly notable educational experiences—the tactically focused Weapons School and the School of Advanced Air and Space Studies (SAASS), the Air Force's strategy school—in which high performance is consistently cited as critical to an officer's ability to become a GO.

Pilots' focus on mastering their weapon systems early does not always include broad leadership opportunities akin to those in the Army or Marine Corps. This contributes to the perception that pilots are more individualistic than their peers in these services. The Air Force has been viewed by other services as being overly attendant to its technology at the expense of caring for its personnel, though airmen's mastery of their aircraft is fundamental to their career development and success.[388] Further, as we will discuss throughout this chapter, there are multiple education, command, and other requirements that an Air Force officer must achieve prior to GO selection. The focus on demonstrating early aptitude could mean that those who take longer to progress and show their capabilities later in their careers might have already missed the narrow selection window for opportunities (such as below-the-zone promotions) that have proven critical to becoming a GO.

Official Guidance on Air Force Officer Development

Leadership is defined in the Air Force as "the art and science of motivating, influencing, and directing airmen to understand and accomplish the Air Force mission in joint warfare."[389] This definition has evolved since the Air Force grew out of the Army Air Corps. Since its formation as a separate service, the Air Force has emphasized two key elements in its concept of leadership: people and mission. Today's doctrine is deeply rooted in the Air Force's history, with quotations from famed Air Force generals and other legendary former leaders found throughout published doctrine. To achieve an effective balance between the people who make up the service and missions they are charged to employ, leadership in the Air Force has become defined by its core values: "integrity first," "service before self," and "excellence in all we do."[390] Figure 6.1 demonstrates how these values have evolved over time from attributes a leader must possess, to traits, and finally core values. "Excellence in all we do" has become a broad way to encompass leadership characteristics such as humaneness, emotional stability, energy, and decisiveness, which were considered individually in prior iterations of Air Force leadership doctrine.

---

[388] Lander, 2019, p. 78; Air Force Doctrine Document (AFDD) 1-1, *Leadership and Force Development*, Maxwell Air Force Base, Ala.: Lemay Center for Doctrine, 2011, p. v.

[389] AFDD 1-1, 2011, p. 22.

[390] AFDD 1-1, 2011, pp. 23–32.

Leaders in the Air Force must hone their expertise at the tactical level within their career field. They must also demonstrate operational competence, which can require intense training to master the many highly technical jobs airmen often occupy. At higher ranks, strategic vision is necessary to marry the leadership of airmen with vision for the service. Air Force Doctrine Document (AFDD) 1-1, *Leadership and Force Development*, explores what leadership means at each of these levels (tactical, operational, and strategic).[391] These dimensions are depicted in Figure 6.1, and categorized by Air Force Manual (AFM), Air Force Pamphlet (AFP), and AFDD. Some concrete examples exist, such as when training or other educational opportunities should occur, but concepts such as strategic vision, relationship building, and looking out for other airmen are considered more broadly.

Figure 6.1. Evolution of Air Force Leadership Dimensions

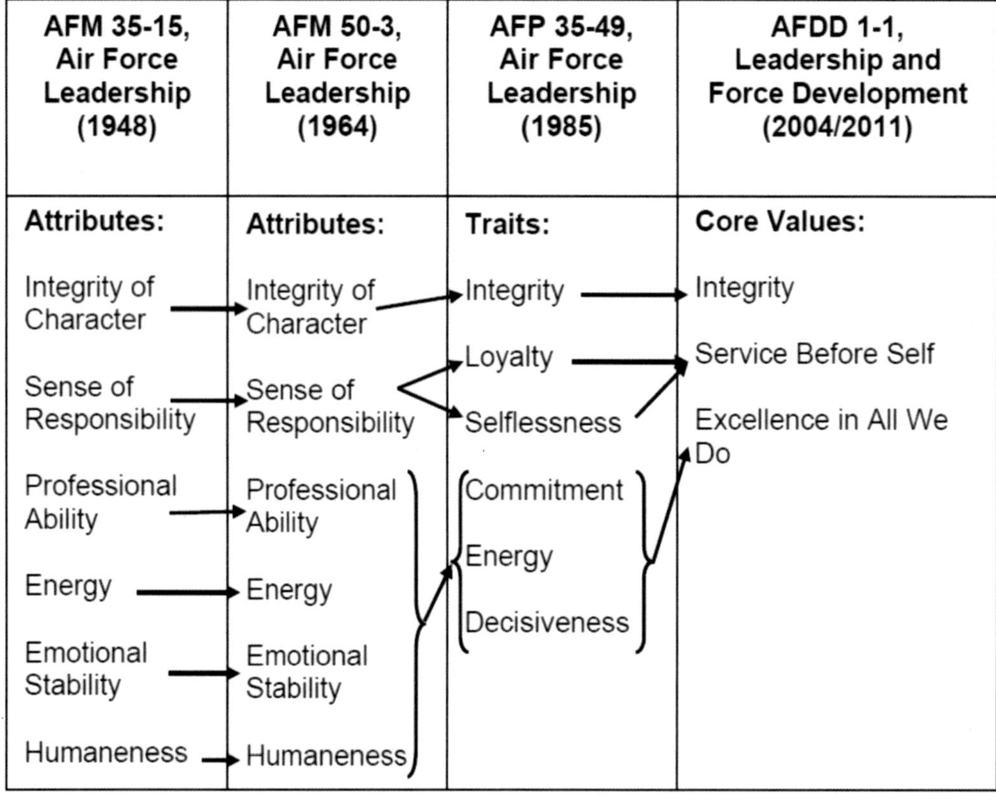

SOURCE: U.S. Air Force, *Air Force Core Doctrine*, Vol. II: *Leadership*, Maxwell Air Force Base, Ala.: Curtis E. Lemay Center for Doctrine Development and Education, 2015, p. 33.

Air Force leadership doctrine also states that leadership is inherent in all airmen: "Leadership does not equal command, but all commanders should be leaders."[392] For the Air Force,

---

[391] AFDD 1-1, *Leadership and Force Development*, Washington, D.C.: Department of the Air Force, 2011.

[392] U.S. Air Force, 2015, p. 27.

leadership involves two primary components: (1) institutional competencies, which differ based on whether an officer has tactical, operational, or strategic command—where the ability to "conceptualize and integrate" becomes more important—and (2) leadership actions, which are summarized as *influence*, *improve*, and *accomplish*.[393] Figure 6.2 depicts how the importance of competencies shifts as an officer ascends the ranks. Those at the strategic level by definition have greater organizational responsibilities. The Air Force appears not to focus as heavily on personal competencies later in an officer's career, which might reflect lack of focus on individual learning and growth at higher grades, perhaps in recognition that an officer would not continue to promote without demonstrating aptitude in these individual dimensions at more junior grades.

Figure 6.2. Air Force Leadership Levels and Institutional Competencies

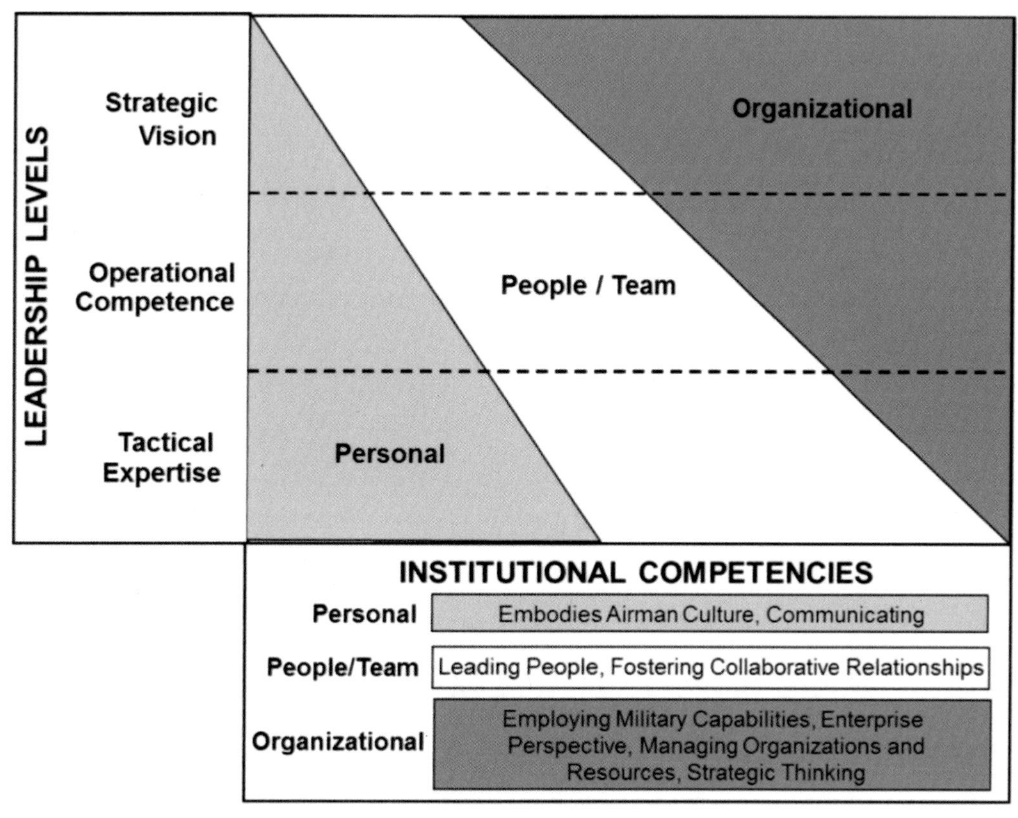

SOURCE: U.S. Air Force, 2015, p. 34.

Whereas previous iterations of AFDD 1-1 had been critiqued for a lack of specificity regarding the Air Force's leadership competencies and how to achieve them,[394] the 2011 update

---

[393] U.S. Air Force, 2015, pp. 42–43.

[394] See Robert G. Steele, Kelly E. Fletcher, William F. Nadolski, Emily Ann Buckman, and Stephen W. Oliver, Jr., *Competency-Based Assignment and Promotion to Meet Air Force Senior Leader Requirements*, Maxwell Air Force Base, Ala.: Air University, 2006, p. 29.

to AFDD 1-1 provides greater detail. Personal competencies focus on developing relationships to promote cohesive units. These are bestowed on junior officers; as the officers progress, they require additional competencies to meet the demands of their more robust jobs. People and team competencies build on personal competencies to continue growing relationships that will enable mission success. Organizational competencies are more complex and require a blend of technical skill, joint and multinational experience, and the ability to create and implement strategic visions.[395]

As they ascend the ranks, Air Force leaders are expected to perform at more-strategic levels. According to doctrine, that means marrying tactical competencies with institutional knowledge and the ability to motivate and lead teams. It also requires an appreciation and understanding of the Air Force's role in the joint, interagency, and multinational environment. Programmatic and managerial responsibilities often expand at higher levels of leadership as well, though some positions do also require highly technical proficiency. Development through educational and training opportunities is intended to enhance Air Force officers' experience as they move through their careers.[396]

When asked about the personality characteristics needed to become a GO, participants we interviewed noted two in particular: rule-abiding and risk-aversion. An active duty field-grade officer we interviewed described this risk-aversion as the "absence of controversy—not so much what they do, but what they avoid doing."[397] Risk-aversion pertains especially to pilots and operators, who have been described as having a "checklist mentality." Their technical competency requires them to master complex systems and follow strict guidelines, because, according to one GO we interviewed for this study, "We operate nuclear weapons, multibillion-dollar satellite systems, and advanced weapons systems that are capable of killing many."[398] One interviewee summarized this by saying the gravity of these responsibilities necessitates adherence to rules and guidelines and can also drive Air Force officers to continue the practice of seeking guidance and oversight as they advance in their careers.[399]

Fundamental Elements of Air Force General Officer Pathways

Professional experiences and other characteristics of Air Force GOs are substantially shaped by the pathways that promote and develop them throughout the officer ranks. Tailored to the needs and the values of the Air Force, these pathways are reflective of and influenced by Air Force culture. The sections below provide an overview of the Air Force's philosophical approach

---

395 AFDD 1-1, 2011, pp. 34–35, 40–41.

396 AFDD 1-1, 2011, pp. 3–33.

397 AF12, active duty field-grade officer, September 26, 2018.

398 AF75, active duty general officer, November 30, 2018.

399 AF75, active duty general officer, November 30, 2018.

to generalship, competitive categories and typical pathways, career timelines, and personnel processes that work together to help shape the Air Force's GO corps.[400]

The Air Force's Philosophical Approach to the Officer Development Pipeline

The Air Force's approach to developing its GOs looks both like a funnel, in which officers are selected out at progressive stages, and a pipeline, in which talented officers are identified early and assisted in gaining the experiences and networks needed to continue to thrive. Strict timelines for meeting key career milestones keep rated officers on path to push them through the pipeline, which favors early performers. Those who demonstrate aptitude later in their careers can be funneled out of consideration. According to a retired GO we spoke to, "The Air Force approach is to look for early technical competency discriminators to shrink the pool of potential GOs early and put them on a specialized path to make sure they have what are considered the minimum requirements to qualify them to be a general."[401]

An active duty field-grade officer we interviewed called this system flawed, saying that instead of a system that truly develops its officers, the Air Force uses a "weeding-out process to find that one person who is going to be CSAF."[402] This sentiment was shared by another active duty field-grade officer we interviewed, who believed the Air Force's approach to producing GOs was not about producing just any general; rather, the focus is on producing four-star generals.[403]

Interviewees and SLSE participants noted that backing up the timeline to account for all of the requirements officers must fulfill by the time they are considered for GO means that officers need to be preparing for generalship while they O-3s, or, "regardless of the true value of the experiences, you have to have these checks in the box[es]."[404] This means that some officers, particularly "late bloomers," might be out of contention for GO before many even realize the process had begun.

Some study interviewees also pointed to a disconnect between what the Air Force says it values in leaders and the types of leaders the service actually produces. Air Force leadership doctrine states the importance of personnel leadership beginning at the earliest stages of one's career, but in practice this is dwarfed by the need to master the technical competencies required for operational success. For rated officers, the early portion of the career, spent learning tactical

---

[400] Formal guidance on Air Force officer development can be found in AFDD 1-1, 2011; Air Force Policy Directive 36-26, *Total Force Development and Management*, Washington, D.C.: Department of the Air Force, March 18, 2019; Air Force Instruction (AFI) 36-2640, *Executing Total Force Development and Management*, Washington, D.C.: Department of the Air Force, August 30, 2018; and AFI 36-2611, *Officer Professional Development*, Washington, D.C.: Department of the Air Force, July 26, 2018.

[401] AF92, retired general officer, October 12, 2018.

[402] AF12, active duty field-grade officer, September 26, 2018.

[403] AF19, active duty field-grade officer, September 28, 2018.

[404] AF19, active duty field-grade officer, September 28, 2018.

leadership, focuses on mastering their major weapon system, which can subsume the first decade of their career.[405] While this seeming disconnect might be described as a progression over an officer's career of the types of experiences the service values, two active duty field-grade officers we interviewed offered the following perspectives on the Air Force's leadership philosophy in practice:

> The Air Force is still obsessed with technology, and we want one-size-fits-all approaches. As a service, we have some really good leaders, but they are not intentionally created. Our system and our culture does not intentionally mold leaders. If given the choice, we will always favor the technology over the person.[406]
>
> Early on, we become masters of leading people who look and talk just like you, and taking care of a $225 million asset, and maybe the formation of those aircrafts. [Marines divide] into four-man strike teams that lead hundreds of marines. We've become very good at taking something very expensive or munitions that don't belong to us and employing them. We probably struggle where marines and soldiers excel at leading large teams and developing individuals.[407]

This is also consistent with the Air Force's cultural preference for technology: Air Force officers might be leaders of fellow service members by definition, but, particularly at the early stages of their career, they are consumed by being leaders of technology on account of being trained rigorously to fly their aircraft in junior grades. This is a contrast from early leadership opportunities in the Army or Marine Corps, where O-3s and O-4s could lead companies of more than 100 fellow soldiers or marines. Opportunities to lead that many people in the Air Force do not exist until squadron command, at the O-5 grade at earliest.

This is particularly true of those in the rated world. One interviewee we spoke to described the highly individualistic nature of being an Air Force officer in the first few years of one's career. In the interviewee's experience,

> I never had to evaluate and build teams until I was a squadron commander and that was 14-15 years in. Being a leader within an organization, running a section, is not only being responsible for the legal aspects of the squadron, but the ability to take care of them personally and professionally.[408]

This officer, a USAFA graduate, said that they learned the principles of leading personnel from the GOs they most admired, not from formal training received to that point in their career.

---

[405] Russell L. Mack, *Creating Joint Leaders Today for a Successful Air Force Tomorrow*, Maxwell Air Force Base, Ala.: Air Force Research Institute, 2010, p. 34.

[406] AF12, active duty field-grade officer, September 26, 2018.

[407] AF62, active duty field-grade officer, December 7, 2018.

[408] AF19, active duty field-grade officer, September 28, 2018.

Competitive Categories

Air Force Specialty Codes (AFSCs) are divided into competitive categories that drive how officers are compared against one another in promotion decisions. As noted previously, there are two primary designations of officers in the Air Force: rated and nonrated. Further, the Air Force has eight competitive categories of occupational specialty:[409]

- Line of the Air Force (LAF)
- JAG
- Medical Corps
- Dental Corps
- Chaplains
- Medical Service Corps
- Biomedical Sciences Corps
- Nurse Corps.

The dominant competitive category in the Air Force is LAF. LAF was created by early Air Force leaders who, after separating from the Army, wanted to avoid what they considered stove-piping between separate Army branches.[410] LAF encompasses the Air Force's combat arms career fields, as well as intelligence, logistics, and others. The result is a system that seeks to evaluate an individual holistically, but with so many disparate careers included in one category, important nuances might be lost when examining these officers alongside one another. Pilots, intelligence specialists, and numerous other types of officers of varying disciplines are all held to similar developmental standards, which has led to criticism that the LAF category is too broad to ensure equal development for all of the jobs included in it.[411] The Air Force is working to delineate between these varied disciplines by creating competitive categories more specific to the milestones inherent in other disciplines. According to an active duty GO familiar with these plans, the new promotion system could enable the service to promote for the different career paths as they "should be" rather than how the Air Force has traditionally managed them.[412]

This dominance of the LAF, and specifically of fighter pilots, is well documented and can be traced historically. *Rise of the Fighter Generals*, a seminal book by Colonel Michael Worden, describes how fighter pilots began to dominate Air Force G/FO ranks in the late 20th century over their bomber brethren. As a major, Wm. Bruce Danskine wrote *Fall of the Fighter Generals*, which seeks to uncover whether another such shift is coming. Danskine's work includes a comparison of the backgrounds of Air Force senior leaders from 1960 to 2000, broken

---

[409] RAND Corporation, "RAND DOPMA/ROPMA Policy Reference Tool: Promotion Timing, Zones, and Opportunity," webpage, undated, "Competitive Categories" section.

[410] Steele et al., 2006, p. 46.

[411] Dave Blair, "Seven Stories for Seven Tribes," *Over the Horizon: Multidomain Operations and Strategy*, April 9, 2018.

[412] AF75, active duty general officer, November 30, 2018.

down by Air Staff and commanders. In both categories, over this 40-year span, the number of nonrated GOs was far lower than the number of GOs who were bomber and fighter pilots.[413] More recently, from 2008 to 2018, more than a third of Air Force GOs have been former fighter pilots.[414]

This finding might seem unsurprising, since flying is the core mission of the Air Force. Fighter pilots also claim a greater connection with the Army and Marine Corps in their ground-based operations through the provision of close air support—a critical function the Air Force has provided in the ground wars in Iraq and Afghanistan. However, according to Danskine, even in 2001 "Only 5.3 percent of all officers in the USAF are fighter pilots, yet they occupy 67 percent of the four-star GO positions and command 63 percent of all major commands."[415] The heavy representation of fighter pilots in GO positions, particularly at the highest grades, is also evident in our analysis of DMDC data (Figure 6.3).

Although the LAF is one competitive category, we found it more useful to delineate officer career fields into three broad categories when analyzing pathways to generalship in the Air Force. While there are other career pathways, some of which lead to generalship, the most useful distinctions are observed along these categories:

- Fighter pilot (if an officer has ever been assigned a fighter pilot primary, secondary, or duty service occupation code, whether currently or previously)
- Other pilot (if an officer has never been assigned a fighter pilot occupation code, but has been assigned another pilot primary, secondary, or duty service occupation code, whether currently or previously)
- Nonpilot (includes both LAF and non-LAF competitive categories).

Figure 6.3 shows the breakdown of Air Force officers across career category and grade, which highlights the disproportionate representation of fighter pilots in the GO grades.

---

[413] Wm. Bruce Danskine, *Fall of the Fighter Generals: The Future of USAF Leadership*, Maxwell Air Force Base, Ala.: School of Advanced Air Power Studies, Air University, June 2001, pp. 130–136. Several other authors have reached similar conclusions: See Travis D. Rex, *Speed Trap: The USAF 24-Year Pole to General Officer*, Carlisle Barracks, Pa.: U.S. Army War College, April 2015; Brian J. Collins, *The United States Air Force and Profession: Why Sixty Percent of Air Force General Officers Are Still Pilots When Pilots Comprise Just Twenty Percent of the Officer Corps*, doctoral thesis, Georgetown University, August 2006, pp. 7–8.

[414] Authors' analysis of DMDC data. See Figure 6.3 for exact percentages by grade.

[415] Danskine, 2001, p. 1.

Figure 6.3. Percentage of Air Force Officers, by Type and Grade, Average, 2008–2018

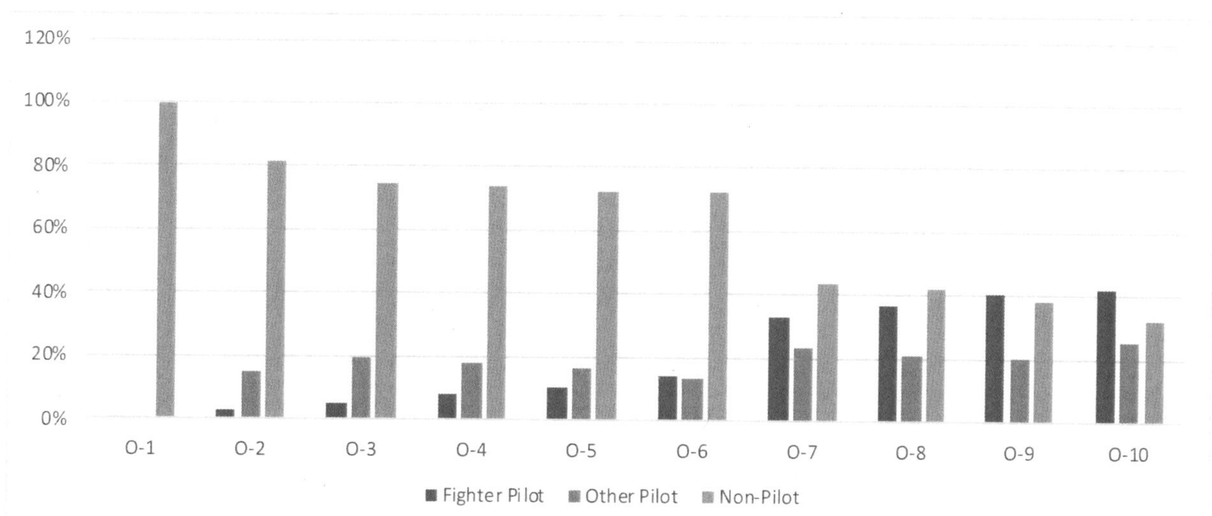

SOURCE: Authors' analysis of DMDC data.
NOTES: The total numbers of Air Force Officers analyzed by grade were as follows: O-1: 68,312; O-2: 78,905 ; O-3: 235,845; O-4: 152,636; O-5: 107,713; O-6: 38,045; O-7: 1,580; O-8: 993; O-9: 437; O-10: 137. The number of officers analyzed decreases between the lower grades and the higher grades. Because fewer officers are included in our analysis in higher grades, representation among the higher grades is more susceptible to fluctuations in year-over-year differences in accession sources.

Consistent with Air Force culture, rated officers, and particularly fighter pilots, claim many of the most highly influential positions in the Air Force, creating a sense of predominance that can be viewed negatively by peers in nonrated career fields. As other missions, such as space and cyber, continue to grow, the sustained emphasis on advancing the careers of rated officers could mean a mismatch in the skills of the Air Force's most senior leaders with these other missions that are such critical parts of modern warfare. Further, if the number of pilots continues to decrease, a promotion system that favors pilots could have fewer candidates from which to draw. Alternatively, it is possible that the reduction in the rated force can provide new opportunities for officers in other career fields to promote.

Career Timelines

Career timelines in the Air Force tend to be tightly managed, and a key characteristic of many typical Air Force GO career pathways and their requisite timelines is early promotion. In this section, we discuss the Air Force's formal career milestones and associated grades, typical professional experiences, and the role of early, or BPZ, promotions in continuing along the development pipeline.

Our interviewees all described a similar pathway to becoming a typical, rated GO in the Air Force, which includes squadron, group, and wing command; a joint tour; and at least two levels of in-residence PME at the intermediate and senior developmental levels. According to a retired GO we interviewed, "Those are the key steps, and everybody knows if you aren't a squadron commander, you won't be competitive for group command, and then you aren't on track for the highly coveted experience that gets you to wing command."[416] The Air Force's force development doctrine describes the various milestones and opportunities officers are supposed to reach at every grade through O-6, including positions such as executive officer, Air Staff, joint positions, and multiple command assignments. Nonrated officers can follow similar developmental milestones toward becoming GOs, but the variety of roles and missions they perform can sometimes make side-by-side comparisons challenging.

For rated officers, multiple interviewees acknowledged that there are some exceptions to the pathway described above, but, for most officers, very few opportunities to promote to GO exist outside of this pathway. Air Force officers spend the early years of their careers honing their tactical mastery. As O-4s and O-5s, they transition to the more operational portion of their careers, where command opportunity becomes an important milestone. According to one interviewee, "Your O-4 leadership opportunity is the point to distinguish yourself. Once you're a major, if you aren't competitive for BPZ to lieutenant colonel, you're really not on the path to becoming a GO."[417] Even among those who have deviated from this pathway, there is typically a recognition that they are doing so and that they might have advocates to get them into key positions to ensure they stay on course. This perception appears consistent with much of the literature and public debate we reviewed.[418] Intermediate developmental education (IDE), particularly in-residence opportunities that hone strategic thinking skills, is also crucial to complete at this stage. These experiences prepare officers for the strategic-level leadership at the O-6 grade. However, the most important element is command. Throughout these stages are also opportunities to gain exposure to the strategic environment, such as working on an air or joint staff at the Pentagon. Prior analysis of Air Force promotion pathways yields six prerequisites for becoming a GO, which are also consistent with our analysis: "command, a joint duty tour, in-residence PME, operational credibility, a Pentagon or Washington, D.C. tour, and probably the most important prerequisite, BPZ promotion."[419]

Below-the-Promotion-Zone Promotions

The role of BPZ promotions is a particularly important topic for the Air Force. First, they are used as a signaling tool, as officers who are promoted below the zone early in their careers indicate future potential. Second, BPZ promotions are also a fundamental aspect of the typical rated GO pathway in the Air Force: To achieve the number of requirements that are expected of them in their tightly managed career, rated Air Force officers generally must be promoted below the zone at least once, and twice is very common. This abbreviated timeline means less time

---

[416] AF92, retired general officer, October 12, 2018.

[417] AF12, active duty field-grade officer, September 26, 2018.

[418] For more analysis on this topic, see, for example, Rex, 2015.

[419] Mack, 2016, p. 42.

overall—perhaps by two years, the length of some full assignments—in the development pipeline prior to O-7, as compared with their peers in the Navy, Marine Corps, and, to a lesser extent, the Army.

Air Force Instruction (AFI) 36-2501 provides guidance on Air Force officer promotion policies. According to this instruction, O-1s must complete 24 months in grade to be eligible for promotion to O-2; O-2s can be considered for subsequent IPZ (in-the-promotion-zone) promotion after serving 24 months, and O-3s, O-4s, and O-5s must serve at least three years in their current grade before becoming eligible for promotion.[420] However, BPZ promotions, which are highly valued within the service, are common in typical Air Force pathways to GO.

An active duty GO noted on the role of BPZ promotions:

> We have to be able to trust that our promotion system values the best individual, irrespective of the promotion zone. The statistics will always indicate that [BPZ] promotions will ascend to the general officer ranks, and I think they should be. It meant they were high performers against their peers, and if they got promoted again below the zone, then they outperformed that year group and were selected below the zone. We look at the mark and forget to look at the record. . . . There are always going to be cases where someone without the pedigree can advance if they exhibit the qualities that BZs exhibit. I do believe that people mature at different rates and our boards have been to be able to account for that. I think we do a pretty good job at that.[421]

There is a perception that because of the heavily scheduled, BPZ-reliant pathway, GOs are essentially selected when they are still very junior officers, before they have had a chance to demonstrate the character and leadership qualities expected of a senior military leader.[422]

One SLSE participant likened the promotion pathway for junior officers to a surfer who catches a wave early, noting "If you stay on the surfboard and stay up, you're good. If you didn't, and you missed the wave, you're off."[423] This participant highlighted a common theme throughout our interviews and the exercise: that late bloomers in the Air Force have a much harder time becoming GOs because they might have missed key assignments in the concentrated pipeline. This can create a "halo effect" whereby an officer that was identified as a high performer early and has received assignments as a result might continue to be viewed as a top officer even if their later performance does not warrant it.[424]

---

420 AFI 36-2501, *Officer Promotions and Selective Continuation*, Washington, D.C.: Department of the Air Force, July 16, 2004.

421 AF75, active duty field-grade officer, November 30, 2018.

422 Senior leader selection exercise notes, January 30, 2019, RAND Corporation, Arlington, Virginia.

423 Senior leader selection exercise notes, January 30, 2019, RAND Corporation, Arlington, Virginia.

424 Senior leader selection exercise notes, January 30, 2019, RAND Corporation, Arlington, Virginia.

Promotion opportunities decrease for Air Force officers as they progress from O-3 to O-6, while BPZ promotions increase steadily from O-4 to O-6.[425] Officers do not generally promote early to O-3, and the Air Force has also stopped promoting officers BPZ to O-4. Figure 6.4 shows the average number of years that Air Force officers have already served at the time they are promoted to a particular grade. The shorter time in grade, associated with the Air Force's use of early promotions, is highest when compared with the other services and contributes to the relatively lower average age and years of service of Air Force officers. Figure 6.5 provides additional detail on how many years an officer typically spends in each grade before promotion to the next higher grade. The result of these shorter times in grade is that Air Force GOs tend to be younger, on average, than their counterparts in other services, as shown in Chapter 3. While some believe that this relative youth might translate to a disadvantage in the joint arena because of the perception of having less experience, it is possible that concern is overstated. Nevertheless, it is a factor that cannot be ignored. As an active duty field-grade officer with experience on the Joint Staff observed the following during his joint tour:

> I had an opportunity to witness the interaction between [forward-deployed] GOs and the Chairman while they tirelessly prepared briefs for the next day's meetings. At the end of the day, I didn't perceive any difference in the quality of work between an Army and Air Force two-stars. There may be a latent bias from the other services, not to mention different cultures that exist. I don't think the quality of work was hurt. But there is probably an extra step an Air Force GO has to take based on not having walked the earth as long as their peers have. . . . No one is putting in any more time than anyone else at that level. Just by the fact that we promote our individuals so quickly forces us to learn on the run.[426]

---

[425] Authors' analysis of DMDC data; promotion opportunities are all officers of a particular grade selected for promotion, regardless of zone.

[426] AF62, active duty field-grade officer, December 7, 2018.

Figure 6.4. Average Years in Service for Rising Air Force Officers, by Grade (Promoted in Prior Year), 2008–2018

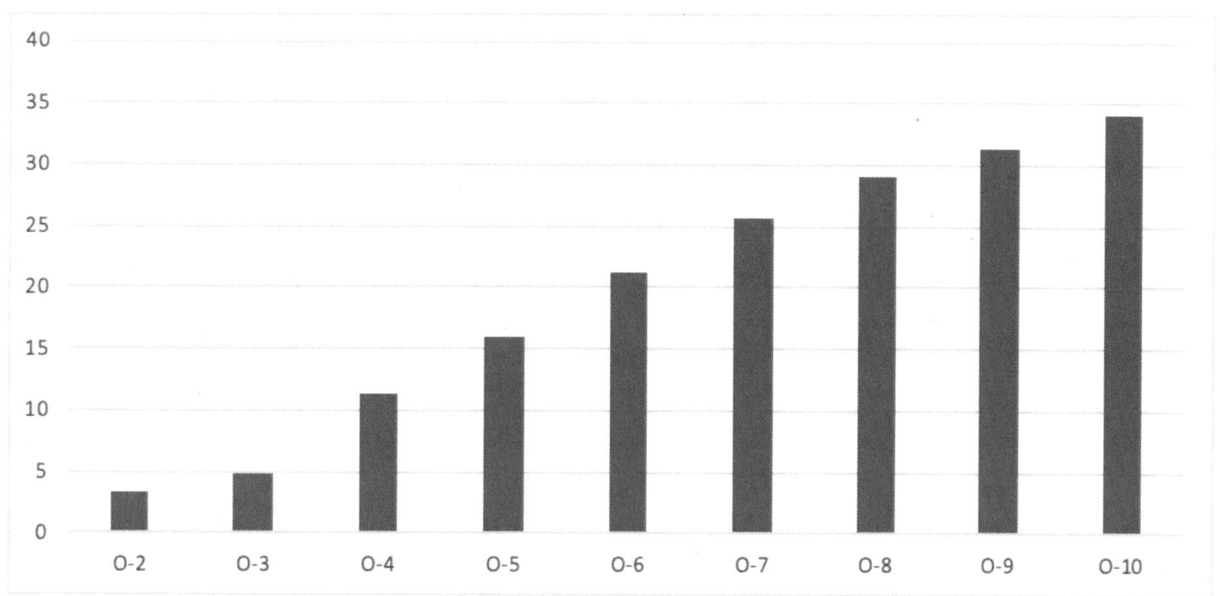

SOURCE: Authors' analysis of DMDC data.

Figure 6.5. Time in Grade for Rising Air Force Officers Promoted from That Grade in the Prior Year, Average, 2008–2018

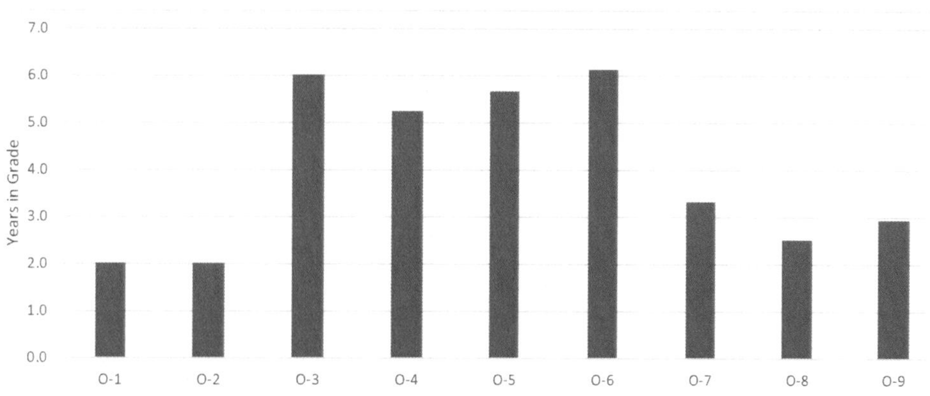

SOURCE: Authors' analysis of DMDC data.

These timelines have been analyzed in prior research of Air Force leadership development, and their results are consistent with what our study team found—particularly the importance of BPZ promotions. The following excerpt from one such study, regarding the compressed timelines within which Air Force officers need to achieve key milestones if they seek to become a GO, remains true. It states that the GO pathway

> can be divided into three sections: the first 10 years, a period of technical skills acquisition and mastery; the next 12, for career broadening, leadership

opportunities, and career growth leading to promotion to colonel; and the final two years, where wing command is the recognized crucible for increased leadership and promotion consideration. For the successful general officer candidates, promotion to colonel will occur considerably earlier than 22 years due to below-the-zone promotions.[427]

Personnel Management Processes and Impact on Air Force General Officers

The Air Force's personnel management processes are guided by federal statute, DoD and Air Force policies, and, significantly, Air Force culture and values. In the following section, we detail how the Air Force's personnel management processes, including commissioning source, duty assignments, education and special training, evaluations, and promotion boards, shape the development and selection of its senior officers.

Commissioning Source

Overall, DMDC data indicate that, on average from 2008 to 2018, 22.2 percent of all Air Force officers were commissioned through the USAFA, while 42.7 percent were commissioned through ROTC programs, 18.3 percent through OTS, and 16.7 percent through direct commissioning.[428] Several interviewees we spoke to said that commissioning source did not play a major role in an officer's career development, which appears consistent with DMDC data analysis results up to the O-6 grade. However, as shown in Figure 6.6, at O-7 and above, USAFA graduates make up an increasing proportion of GOs, while direct commission officers and OTS graduates lose relative share. ROTC graduates' makeup of O-7 through O-10 grades decreases as well, particularly at O-8 and O-9, but remains roughly proportional to initial commissioning rates at the O-10 rank.

One possible explanation for this increase in USAFA graduates' domination of GO grades could be network effects, a phenomenon observed in the Army and the Navy as well. However, we heard through our interviews and the SLSE that, while there might be some camaraderie among USAFA graduates, what young officers do early in their career—not how they were commissioned—determines how far they will go.[429]

---

[427] Karen Currie, John Conway, Scott Johnson, Brian Landry, and Adam Lowther, *Air Force Leadership Study: The Need for Deliberate Development*, Maxwell Air Force Base, Ala.: Air University Press, Air Force Research Institute, 2012, p. 21.

[428] Authors' analysis of DMDC data.

[429] Senior leader selection exercise notes, January 30, 2019, RAND Corporation, Arlington, Virginia; AF92, retired general officer, October 12, 2018.

Figure 6.6. Accession Source of Rising Air Force Officers (Promoted in Prior Year), by Grade, Average, 2008–2018

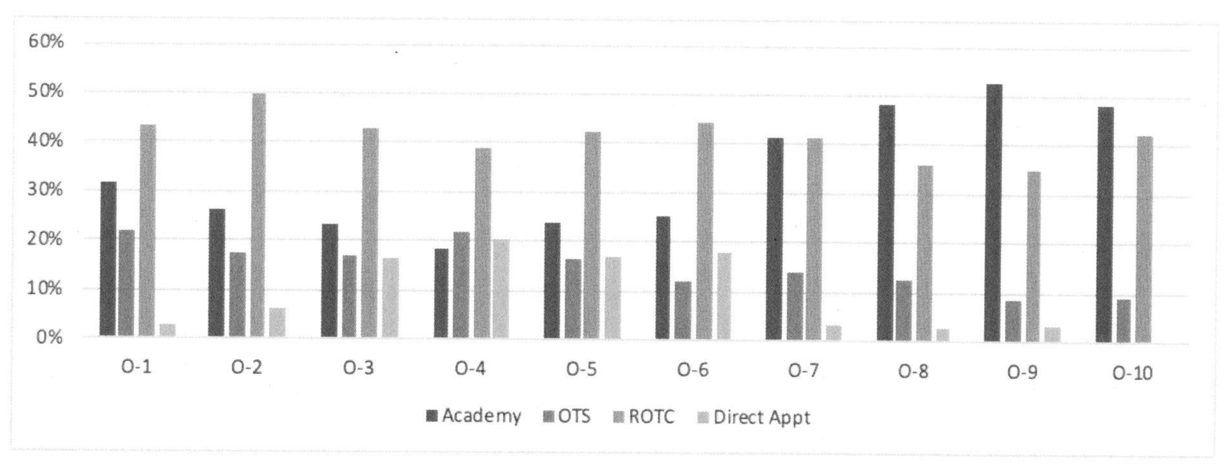

SOURCE: Authors' analysis of DMDC data.
NOTES: Because of the DMDC data structure, the total number of officers analyzed by MOS is different than the total number of officers analyzed by accession source. The total numbers of Air Force Officers analyzed by grade were as follows: O-1: 68,331; O-2: 78,946 ; O-3: 235,816; O-4: 152,596; O-5: 107,695; O-6: 38,060; O-7: 1,580; O-8: 993; O-9: 437; O-10: 137. The number of officers analyzed decreases between the lower grades and the higher grades. Because fewer officers are included in our analysis in higher grades, representation among the higher grades is more susceptible to fluctuations in year-over-year differences in accession sources.

Prospective analysis indicates that, of all officers who served as O-4s between FY 1995 and FY 2018, 1.216 percent of USAFA graduates attained the grade of O-7. By comparison, 0.37 percent of OCS graduates were promoted to O-7, and 0.597 percent of ROTC graduates were promoted to the grade of O-7.

Duty Assignments

In most cases, the Air Force matches its personnel to available billets based on skills and qualifications. A Special Experience Identifier (SEI) can be used to aid assignments that require personnel with particular skills, experiences, or certifications, or when it is necessary to "rapidly identify personnel to meet unique circumstances, contingency requirements, or other critical needs."[430] If there are volunteers for specific positions among a group of qualified personnel, those individuals are selected first. In the absence of volunteers, qualified candidates are prioritized by factors such as time on station. Exceptions can occur for various reasons, including medical and family issues, an officer is pursuing educational opportunities, or an officer's spouse being an active duty service member, since attempts are made to keep spouses together.[431]

Assignments in the Air Force are monitored by the Air Force Personnel Center, but there have been changes in recent years to how GOs are managed in the service. Until recently, the

---

430 AFI 36-2110, *Assignments*, Washington, D.C.: Department of the Air Force, June 8, 2012, p. 30.

431 AFI 36-2110, *Total Force Assignments*, Washington, D.C.: Headquarters, Department of the Air Force, October 5, 2018; Rod Powers, "Air Force Assignment System," The Balance Careers, December 17, 2018.

General Officer Management Office (called briefly the Air Force Executive Talent Management Office) reported directly to the Vice Chief of the Air Force, but as this report was being written in 2019 it moved back under AF/A-1, the Air Force's personnel directorate. Prior to this change, efforts were undertaken to broaden the expertise of GOs, whom former CSAF Michael Ryan believed to be overly specialized. RAND analysis in support of this initiative found that GOs should have a secondary specialty that would broaden their experience.[432] This requirement was expanded to O-6s, at least for a time, starting in 2002.[433]

The Air Force might assign more generalist roles to rated officers who have demonstrated that they are on the path to generalship, whereas officers working in human resources, logistics, or intelligence are likely to become more specialized. The idea is that if someone is judged to have the potential to go beyond O-7 or O-8, they will need a broader understanding of the service and of principles of strategic analysis that are so important to the Air Force. Staff jobs in AF/A3 (operations, plans, and requirements), and AF/A5/8 (strategic plans and programs) or certain other staff positions might help get them these types of experiences.[434]

In addition to the critical squadron, group, and wing command positions mentioned previously, other highly coveted experience comes from staff opportunities, which are essential for building joint experience. Premier staff jobs include those on the Air Staff (AF/A3, AF/A5/8), OSD, or Joint Staff. As previously discussed, PME is also required at two levels—IDE and senior developmental education (SDE). Some believe the highest-potential officers are frequently selected to attend Weapons School and/or the SAASS at O-4, further emphasizing the early designation of officers on the pathway to generalship.

The unit to which an officer is assigned also conveys their high potential status. Positions that command greater attention are commands with named or famous units, such as the 1st and 4th Fighter Wings, or wing commander at Joint Base Lewis-McChord. When it comes to joint experience, time on the Joint Staff or on an OSD staff are the premier opportunities. These provide the most exposure to a wide range of personnel outside the service and can greatly enhance an officer's networking opportunities, according to one interviewee.[435] One active duty field-grade officer we interviewed observed, based on their experience in the Air Force and the joint environment, that "Senior captains and young majors fight for being an [executive officer] or aide to someone. Those [jobs] are seen as a quick path to being [promoted below the zone].

---

432 Albert Robbert, Steve Drezner, John E. Boon, Jr., Lawrence M. Hanser, Craig Moore, Lynn Scott, and Herb Shukiar, *Integrated Planning for the Air Force Senior Leader Workforce: Background and Methods*, Santa Monica, Calif.: RAND Corporation, TR-175-AF, 2004, p. xiii.

433 Steele et al., 2012, pp. 26–27.

434 Senior leader selection exercise notes, January 30, 2019, RAND Corporation, Arlington, Virginia; AF89, retired field-grade officer, October 26, 2018.

435 AF12, active duty field-grade officer, September 26, 2018.

When you say 'below the zone' in the Air Force, you mean general officer. They are inextricably linked."[436]

Other prestigious high-visibility assignments include being an executive officer or aide to a three- or four-star general or their civilian equivalent or serving as the director of operations for a unit. According to a retired GO we interviewed, "The biggest advantages of working for a four-star is the view of the bureaucracy that you get."[437]

Supporting Institutional Assignments

Institutional assignments, and specifically staff assignments, within the Air Force are viewed in the promotions process as extremely important. In theory, Air Staff roles enable an officer to learn about how the service runs from an enterprise perspective, but these roles also create opportunities to think more critically about tactical and operational issues. Overall, supporting institutional assignments appear to be valued more than joint experience, which is reflective of the Air Force's culture, which has traditionally prized GO positions within the service over those in the joint environment. Typically, a GO who has served an important joint assignment, such as on the Joint Staff, might look to become commander of Air Combat Command (ACC), an Air Staff section such as A/5 or A/3, or even CSAF. While the Air Force as an institution would like to see more of its officers in joint billets with strategic significance, such as U.S. Central Command (USCENTCOM) or U.S. European Command (USEUCOM), individual Air Force officers are still more inclined to view senior positions within their service as the opportunities for which to aim.[438] Some of this mindset could start to change under CSAF Goldfein's leadership, but the long-term effects on this perspective remain to be seen.

Broadening and Joint Assignments

Because of the typical tightly managed career timeline, Air Force officers are not afforded ample opportunity to pursue broadening assignments. This creates an inherent tension between career timeline requirements and the Air Force's emphasis on developing strategic-thinking, well-rounded leaders. In theory, the skills an officer might gain in additional joint and/or broadening assignments should be valued, but not at the expense of forgoing career field-specific assignments necessary to staying on a typical promotion pathway. Therefore, AFSC- and Air Force–specific assignments carry greatest value in the promotions process, even though the Air Force does tend to assign value to joint positions beyond fulfilling Goldwater-Nichols mandates.[439] Part of this might be due to the inherent support role that the Air Force has played

---

[436] AF19, active duty field-grade officer, September 28, 2018.

[437] AF06, retired general officer, November 15, 2018.

[438] Caitlin Lee, Bart E. Bennett, Lisa M. Harrington, and Darrell D. Jones, *Rare Birds: Understanding and Addressing Air Force Underrepresentation in Senior Joint Positions in the Post–Goldwater-Nichols Era*, Santa Monica, Calif.: RAND Corporation, 2017, RR-2089-AF, p. 36.

[439] Senior leader selection exercise notes, January 30, 2019, RAND Corporation, Arlington, Virginia.

in the ground combat–heavy wars in Iraq and Afghanistan since 2001: Many of the most consequential combat-specific positions an Air Force officer could hold in that time would have been joint in nature. This attitude extends to joint staff positions. For example, because the other services tend to be assigned the powerful J-3 (operations) and J-5 (strategic plans and policy) positions at joint commands, the Air Force focuses on securing resource management, or J-8, positions in these commands. While the J-3 and J-5 positions are still highly prized by the Air Force, these J-8 positions are considered critical to the Air Force, as they allow its officers to have greater control over resourcing decisions in organizations that might not be Air Force–specific but certainly affect Air Force missions and personnel substantially.[440]

While educational broadening assignments can be considered a deviation from the prescribed pathway, strategic education overall appears to be valued in the Air Force. For example, in the SLSE, we observed that Air Force participants gave more positive consideration to participants who received advanced degrees from top-tier schools than those who might have completed an advanced degree via correspondence through an online program. We also observed that academic fellowships are well regarded but that doing one in place of attending the Weapons School, for example, might not be as beneficial for promotion consideration.

Indeed, the value of jointness and strategic thought was described at the SLSE by several participants. One participant noted that key questions for promotion include,

> Can he or she lead their tribe, going from operation to strategic, can they think strategically and adapt strategically? Then, will they succeed in the joint environment? Not because we are trying to be the big joint service we are told we are. . . . We don't care about being contributors to the joint fight, we care about the fight. You represent the Air Force in whatever fight is in front of you. Likely, it will be a joint fight.[441]

Others in the same exercise noted that the need for joint perspective is not critical for some officers, such as nuclear officers, but certainly is for the officers such as fighter pilots whose jobs frequently support joint operations. One retired GO noted that most Air Force generals do not have the luxury of focusing exclusively on service-specific opportunities, because, at least currently, "Wars are fought on land."[442] How these mandates between service and joint assignments are balanced given the stringent career timeline requirements appears to consistently challenge many Air Force officers.

Deployment Experience

Deployments can indicate commitment to the service and a connection to the operational Air Force, according to participants in the SLSE. As one participant, a retired Air Force GO, stated:

---

[440] Lander, 2019.

[441] Senior leader selection exercise notes, January 30, 2019, RAND Corporation, Arlington, Virginia.

[442] Senior leader selection exercise notes, January 30, 2019, RAND Corporation, Arlington, Virginia.

"At the GO ranks, if you don't have deployment credibility after a 20-year war, you can't get a meaningful joint job. You can't employ force without deploying."[443] This mentality, if shared broadly throughout service, could perpetuate the reverence of fighter pilots, since these are often the officers with the greatest number of opportunities to deploy. Some career fields, such as space and cyber, do not have the same deployment opportunities that pilots do. This imbalance of opportunity can create scenarios in which contracting officers or maintainers, for example, seek deployments as a "box-checking exercise," when their expertise could be better used domestically.

As noted above, given the nature of the United States' most recent major combat operations in Iraq and Afghanistan, the Air Force is largely familiar with supporting joint operations. However, this relative comfort with jointness—especially compared with the Navy, for example—is in tension with the Air Force's competitive goal to "reinforce an identity that does more than enable."[444]

Perhaps unlike some other services, operational experience in the Air Force need not necessarily translate to war zone deployments. According to Caitlin Lee, a RAND researcher who specializes in Air Force personnel issues, in the Air Force,

> You can easily have great command opportunities that don't require a deployment, like being a wing commander in the U.S. Part of being an airman is using instruments of war that allow you to operate at a greater distance with speed, reach, and flexibility. It is more intuitive to an airman that you wouldn't be deployed with your weapons system. For example, remotely piloted aircraft pilots can deploy to launch and recovery elements downrange, but they can also conduct wartime operations from ground control stations in the continental United States.[445]

Promotion boards highly value deployment experience, according to participants in the SLSE and an active duty GO with promotion board experience whom we interviewed. The Air Force is still a warfighting organization, even if combat operators are defined differently for the air domain. Remote piloting and ISR are different approaches to combat operations, and it is harder to build relationships the same way as boots on the ground, according to one GO.[446] However, given the Air Force's highly technical nature, the value they provide often comes from these types of missions and their ability to enhance other services' operational capabilities.

---

[443] Senior leader selection exercise notes, January 30, 2019, RAND Corporation, Arlington, Virginia.

[444] Lander, 2019, p. 83.

[445] Caitlin Lee, political Scientist, RAND Corporation, interview with authors, Arlington, Virginia, October 25, 2018.

[446] AF75, active duty general officer, November 30, 2018.

Education and Special Training

PME has been described as an essential part of an Air Force officer's career development. For both intermediate-level and senior-level PME, in-residence programs are generally viewed as more prestigious, as they present an opportunity to achieve "distinguished graduate" status, another essential indicator in promotion boards for those with GO aspirations.[447] PME in the Air Force is also marked by a greater focus on strategic analysis than in the other services, a defining characteristic that is also stressed in Air Force training and duty assignments.

One of the most coveted PME opportunities in the service is the U.S. Air Force Weapons School, the Air Force's premier training opportunity for ensuring tactical excellence and producing weapon instructors. Attending Weapons School has been important for some time: Even in 2001, for example, Danskine's research indicated that attendance there is an indicator of elite potential. Completing the six-month course earns the participant a shoulder patch, which Danskine describes as the "patch effect," or a visible symbol on an officer's uniform that they have completed this elite program, which tends to be rewarded in determining promotions or assignments.[448] Weapons School slots are highly competitive, and although some officers do turn them down in favor of fellowships or other opportunities, Weapons School attendance has traditionally carried more weight.

Subsequent analysis of the effects of Weapons School attendance on promotion shows that the patch effect tends to favor fighter pilots disproportionately, though most SLSE attendees could trace either direct or indirect effects of attendance on their career advancement.[449] Further, as demonstrated in Figure 6.7, our analysis of DMDC data on Weapons School attendees who became GOs demonstrated that pilots who attend Weapons School make O-7 far more frequently than pilots who do not. In fact, among the fighter pilot community, officers who attended Weapons School are represented at nearly four times the rate of those who did not attend. This is also true of operations officers, though they promote to O-7 at a lower rate overall than pilots. Substantial evidence exists in other analyses that this relationship is strong, and, importantly, interviewees expressed that there is a widespread perception that Weapons School attendance is an indicator of future consideration for GO, which could influence officers' career choices and desire to attend Weapons School and also board decisions.[450] As an example, a retired GO we interviewed who both sat on and chaired promotion boards believed that establishing early

---

[447] Danskine, 2001, p. 91.

[448] Danskine, 2001, p. 94.

[449] Ryan Middleton and William Wagstaff, "Promoting What We Value: Weapons School and Talent Management in the Air Force," *War on the Rocks*, December 5, 2018.

[450] Authors' analysis of DMDC data; AF12, active duty field-grade officer, September 26, 2018; AF19, active duty field-grade officer, September 28, 2018; AF62, active duty field-grade officer, December 7, 2018.

discriminators that make a candidate more attractive to promotion to O-5 is critical, and Weapons School is definitely one of those discriminators.[451]

Interviewees we spoke to also indicated the strong effect of attending SAASS on promotion because it is the Air Force's "strategy school," where those who demonstrate potential are sent to hone their strategic thinking skills, but were unable to analyze DMDC data to test these assertions.[452]

Figure 6.7. Percentage of Rising Air Force O-6s (Promoted in Prior Year) from 2000–2010 Who Are Later Promoted to O-7, by Weapons School Graduation and Career Type

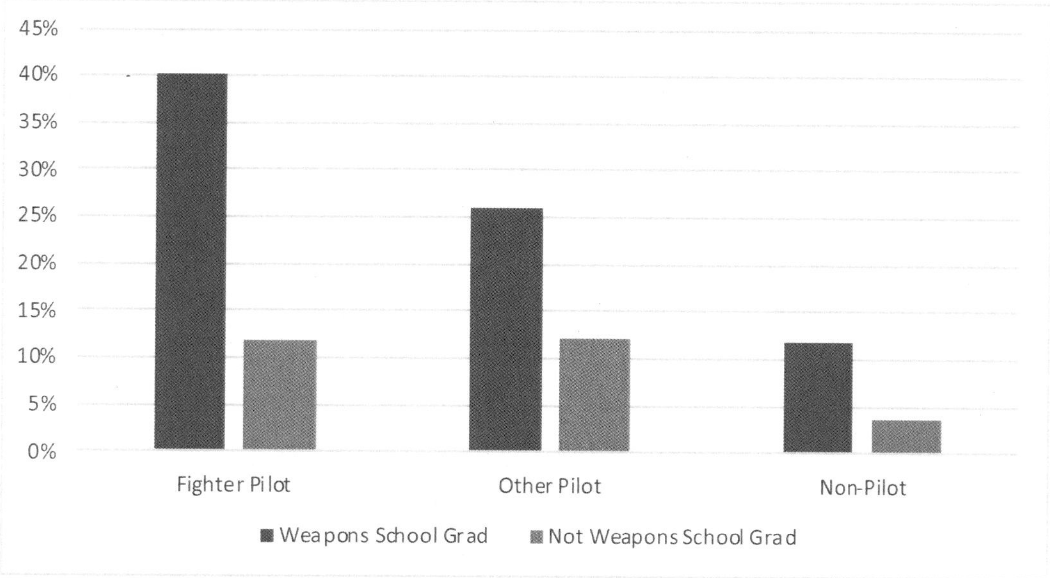

SOURCE: Authors' analysis of DMDC data.
NOTE: These numbers represent the progression rate for the 11 cohorts of Air Force O-6s who were recently promoted as of the beginning of each year from 2000 through 2010, and reflect these officers' observed rates of reaching O-7 at any point up to the beginning of 2018, the last year for which we have data. Percentages are broken out by type and by whether the recently promoted O-6 had previously graduated from Weapons school.

Until recently, O-4 promotion boards proved highly critical not just for promotions, but also for identification of the 15 percent of officers who would attend IDE in-residence. This designation was used as an early indicator that the officer would later attend the prestigious Air Command and Staff College or a similar school later in their career, an important experience for a prospective GO. In effect, this created "an early two-track promotion system of haves (IDE selects) and have-nots, with extremely limited opportunities for those not selected."[453] However, starting in 2017, commanders started nominating officers for IDE, rather than promotion boards.

---

[451] AF92, retired general officer, October 12, 2018.

[452] AF12, active duty field-grade officer, September 26, 2018; AF19, active duty field-grade officer, September 28, 2018; AF92, retired general officer, October 12, 2018.

[453] Rex, 2015, pp. 7–8.

These nominations are intended to place more decisionmaking authority with commanders, who are presumed to be in a better position to assess an officer's performance and aptitude for IDE placement.[454] However, it is too early to determine the impact of this change on the makeup of the Air Force's GO corps.

The Air Force also encourages O-3s, O-4s, and O-5s to go to schools outside the Air Force, such as the National War College or the Eisenhower School for National Security and Resource Strategy at the National Defense University, or apply for fellowships, such those at Harvard, Yale, MIT, Stanford, and RAND. Regardless of the esteem afforded to these opportunities, they still appear to pale in comparison to prestigious opportunities such as Weapons School and SAASS. According to one active duty officer we interviewed, "The opportunities that have fewer seats are seen as more competitive and career-enhancing."[455]

Not all PME opportunities provide equal benefits throughout the Air Force. As mentioned earlier, in-residence programs are often viewed more favorably than correspondence programs, particularly for rated officers. Additionally, according to a retired field-grade officer we interviewed, doubt exists over whether there is enough rigor at certain PME institutions to warrant an advanced degree. In certain career fields, such as logistics or acquisitions, a master's degree from PME and a master's degree in supply chain management or finance provide very different qualifications to their respective recipients. For these nonrated officers, there exists a tension between learning the profession of arms and becoming a well-educated professional within one's specialty.[456]

The Air Force's focus on PME can also have effects on command positions that ostensibly offer greater leadership opportunities. Officers can be pulled from operational commands early if selected for opportunities such as Weapons School or SAASS. Two active duty field-grade officers we interviewed do not believe this is healthy for the service:

> I don't leave a good party because someone tells me there's a better party down the street. Every command opportunity is an opportunity to learn so much about people and yourself. . . . I'm sure [leaving command early] benefits someone but I don't think that is a good idea at all.[457]
>
> One of the more disturbing elements I've seen in how we treat our O-4s is that [PME] can be seen as a block-checking exercise to get them to school. We will pull people from leadership positions one year into a two-year command to go to school because school is seen as more important than leading airmen. . . . Some of this is because school is one of the few opportunities where you can take people from every AFSC and compete them against each other. School is one of the few opportunities to grade them against each other, but what does that

---

[454] Stephen Losey, "Air Force: Commanders, Not Promotion Boards, Now Pick Officers for Developmental Education," *Air Force Times*, July 13, 2017.

[455] AF12, active duty field-grade officer, September 26, 2018.

[456] AF89, retired field-grade officer, October 26, 2018.

[457] AF19, active duty field-grade officer, September 28, 2018.

> competition mean? Who are we looking for? [Who] do we want to be our strategists and commanders?[458]

Evaluations

The Air Force's Officer and Enlisted Evaluation Systems have three primary purposes:

> - To establish performance standards and expectations for ratees, meaningful feedback on how well the ratee is meeting those expectations, and direction on how better to meet those established standards and expectations;
> - To provide a reliable, long-term, cumulative record of performance and promotion potential based on that performance;
> - To provide officer Central Selection Boards (CSBs) . . . and other personnel managers with sound information to assist in identifying the best qualified officers and enlisted personnel for promotion, as well as other personnel management decisions.[459]

Evaluations are performed for Air Force officers through Officer Performance Reports (OPRs) and Promotion Recommendation Forms (PRFs). OPRs document an officer's performance in their role, and PRFs are used to communicate an officer's promotability up their chain of command. In May 2019, the Air Force announced modifications to the PRF, including providing clearer guidance to senior raters tasked with completing them. According to Lieutenant General Brian Kelly, the Air Force's deputy chief of staff for manpower, personnel and services, these changes to the PRF are intended to "restore the PRF to its original intent of providing a way for senior raters to communicate an officer's potential to serve in the next higher grade directly with promotion boards."[460]

The following performance factors are included on OPR forms:

- job knowledge: whether the officer has the knowledge to carry out their current duties, and whether they work to further that knowledge
- leadership skills: the officer's ability to lead and motivate others, promote the health of their organization, demonstrate initiative and confidence, and earn the respect and confidence of others
- professional qualities: includes exhibiting "loyalty, discipline, dedication, integrity, honesty, and officership," in addition to upholding personal appearance and fitness standards, maintaining objectivity, and accepting responsibility for their actions
- organizational skills: includes the effective use of resources, timeliness, and problem-solving

---

[458] AF12, active duty field-grade officer, September 26, 2018.

[459] AFI 36-2406, *Officer and Enlisted Evaluation Systems*, Washington, D.C.: Department of the Air Force, November 8, 2016, p. 10.

[460] Secretary of the Air Force, Public Affairs, "Air Force Simplifies Promotion Recommendation Forms for Officers," U.S. Air Force, May 8, 2019.

- judgment and decisions: an officer's ability to make appropriate decisions accurately, logically, and while under stress, and whether the officer recognizes and seizes opportunities
- communication skills: refers to both oral and written skills.[461]

OPRs are required of all officers O-6 and below, except for O-6s who have already been selected for O-7, and OPRs are completed annually, when the rater changes, or if the officer has to make a permanent change of station (PCS) to attend school or separates from the Air Force.[462] According to the AFI for Officer and Enlisted Evaluation Systems, "The reviewer is the highest level endorser in the ratee's rating chain. The senior rater must be in the grade of at least a colonel or civilian equivalent (General Schedule [GS]-15), or higher, serving as a wing commander or equivalent and designated by the Management Level."[463]

PRFs can be marked with "Do Not Promote This Board" (DNP), "Promote" (P), or "Definitely Promote" (DP). DPs are limited by specific quotas in each grade, competitive category, and year, and Ps are also monitored to ensure the number provided is reasonable. DPs are highly prized, because being marked a P will not help an officer advance. This potentially creates a bloated field of DPs, because raters might mark up average officers for fear of tainting them with a "scarlet P," according to one interviewee.[464] However, a rating of DP is not guaranteed to lead to promotion on its own if an officer is in a competitive environment, such as a Pentagon assignment. According to those familiar with Air Force performance evaluations, an officer in such a position would require something more on their evaluation to separate them from their peers. One interviewee and SLSE participants told us that recommendations in an evaluation from a commander who can speak to an officer's character and expertise are also important signaling mechanisms for the individual's performance at the unit level.[465]

In practice, evaluations heavily consider performance, which is considered an indicator of future potential and the officer's ability to effectively interact with other airmen. Performance assessment is communicated in large part through stratification and "push" lines, which are essential parts of an officer's evaluation. *Stratification* refers to the rank an officer is given by their rater relative to their peers. For example, being named number one of 12 majors by a major command (MAJCOM) commander is extremely significant, but it is potentially less so if the officer is ranked as number one of two majors at a lower-level command. The same concept is true at the O-5 and O-6 grades. One interviewee noted that previous OPRs speak to what an officer has accomplished earlier in the officer's career, while the promotion to GO is more about

---

[461] Bulleted list adapted from Air Force Form 707, *Officer Performance Report*, version 1, July 31, 2015.

[462] AFI 36-2406, 2016, p. 109.

[463] AFI 36-2406, 2016, p. 88.

[464] AF12, active duty field-grade officer, September 26, 2018.

[465] AF89, retired field-grade officer, October 26, 2018; Senior leader selection exercise notes, RAND Corporation, Arlington, Virginia, January 30, 2019.

potential.[466] Push lines are the last line of the PRF, where the rater will indicate their recommendation regarding whether the evaluated officer is a PD, P, or DNP. Stratification becomes essential as a one- and two-star general.[467] Officers at the O-7 and O-8 grades must complete the AF-78, the "Air Force General Officer Promotion Recommendation" form, once per year. The form becomes optional for O-8s who are either promoted to O-9 or announce their retirement.[468]

Promotion Boards

The structure of Air Force promotion boards is outlined in AFI 36-2501, *Officer Promotions and Selective Continuation.*[469] As with the other services, board proceedings themselves are not public, though the results of promotion boards, of course, are. The Air Force does not publish board instructions publicly, nor are there publicly available records of past boards, though additional guidance is available and promotion board statistics are maintained internally. The Air Force Personnel Center (AFPC) does publish the following criteria that determine in which sequence officers already selected for promotion will promote:

- current grade date of rank
- previous grade date of rank, if applicable
- total active federal commissioned service
- total federal commissioned service
- regular officers will precede Reserve officers. Regular officers will rank among themselves based on date of Presidential nomination for appointment as a Regular officer
- regular Air Force acceptance date; based on the date of the Air Force Form 133, Oath of Office
- graduates of service academies, appointed as regular officers and assigned the same date of rank, on the active duty list in order of their graduation class standing
- date of birth, with the earliest date taking precedence
- reverse social security number, with the lowest number taking precedence.[470]

In general, promotion rates are based on available vacancies and within the numbers that maintain the end strength of the service. Attempts are made to provide "reasonable progression" for officers who are qualified and motivated to ascend the ranks, while remaining within the

---

[466] AF89, retired field-grade officer, October 26, 2018.

[467] Since three- and four-star positions are nominative, those officers are not evaluated under the same system.

[468] AFI 36-2406, *Officer and Enlisted Evaluation Systems*, Washington, D.C.: Department of the Air Force, May 10, 2019, pp. 213–214, 217.

[469] AFI 36-2501, *Officer Promotions and Selective Continuation,*Washington, D.C.: Department of the Air Force, July 16, 2004.

[470] U.S. Air Force, Air Force Personnel Center, "Officer Promotions," undated.

constraints imposed by DOPMA guidelines for how long officers should remain in a grade before they can be promoted.[471]

At the GO promotion board level, retired Air Force Lieutenant General Richard Newton stressed that the secrecy is largely to limit outside influence on proceedings, and that board composition is largely reflective of certain characteristics of the pool of candidates being considered for promotion. He continued, "The Air Force, at the direction of the Secretary of the Air Force, endeavors to ensure the GO promotion process is as level a playing field as possible. Much of the process is underscored by law and Air Force policy, hence it's less smoke and mirrors as one would think."[472]

In our interviews, we heard that the Air Force tries to select a broad range of GOs to serve on its GO promotion boards in order to promote diversity of career field, professional experiences, gender, race, ethnicity, and other characteristics overall and in the panel of officers that adjudicates candidate choices. Newton stressed that "Diversity means [diversity of] experience as well as these other factors," and noted that it directly relates to operational readiness. Commenting on the need to embrace diversity of career field experiences in the Air Force, he remarked,

> The Air Force roles and missions are evolving. We fly and fight in cyber, air, space, the joint arena, and the coalition arena. A C-17 tail showing up in Kenya or Nigeria can be nearly as effective as a B-2 putting 24 [Joint Direct Attack Munitions] on a runway in Libya. . . . We need to engage the American people to ensure they know we're not only essential to maintain air power supremacy but for other domains as well such as space and cyber, which is vital to the U.S. Air Force, and the nation. Therefore, it is key for us to continue to recruit and retain high quality people in a very competitive race for talent for a wide variety of highly skilled, technical Air Force jobs in air, space, and cyber.[473]

The single LAF category for combat arms does make mission diversity more challenging, but, as noted previously, the Air Force is considering changes to its system that would create competitive categories more like those of the other services. In congressional testimony provided in February 2019, Lieutenant General Brian Kelly noted

> Our officer evaluation system has not seen significant changes since 1988 and our current Line of the Air Force promotion competitive category structure has not changed since the founding of our Air Force in 1947. We are currently working to make adjustments to the Line of the Air Force competitive category structure, including holding a recent mock board to explore options. This restructure, coupled with the increased flexibilities provided by Congress give us the ability to create more agile development paths and better match the officer

---

[471] RAND Corporation, undated.

[472] Interview with retired lieutenant general Richard Newton, February 21, 2019.

[473] Interview with retired lieutenant general Richard Newton, February 21, 2019.

inventory to actual requirements which is vital to increasing readiness and lethality.[474]

Selection to O-7 is highly competitive across the services, including the Air Force, because of the dramatic difference between eligible O-6s and available O-7 positions. As seen in Figure 6.8, promotion rates from O-7 to O-8 increase sharply because of greater ratio of eligible O-7s to available O-8 positions, then drops again, reflecting the limited number of O-9 and O-10 positions across DoD. The dominance of officers with fighter pilot experience starts to be reflected in the relatively higher promotion rate for fighter pilots, as well as other types of pilots, from O-6 to O-7, as shown in Figure 6.9, but increases with grade.

Figure 6.8. Percentage of Air Force Officers Who Promote to the Next Grade, 2000–2010 Officer Cohorts

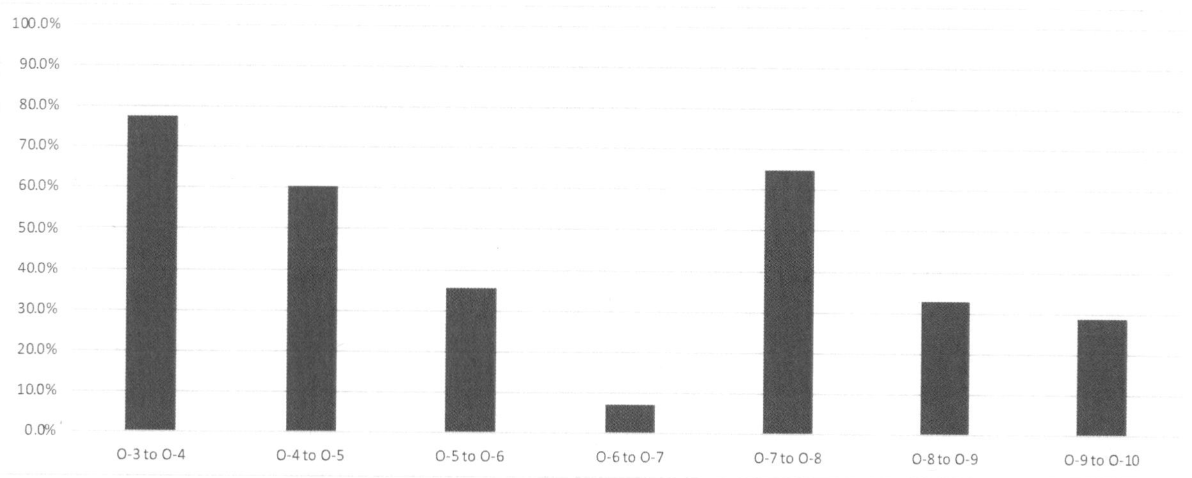

SOURCE: Authors' analysis of DMDC data.
NOTE: These numbers represent the average progression rate for the 11 (overlapping) cohorts of Air Force officers present in each grade at the beginning of each year from 2000 to 2010, and reflect these officers' observed rates of reaching the next higher grade at any point up to the beginning of 2018, the last year for which we have data.

[474] Lieutenant General Brian T. Kelly, *FY20 Posture Statement*, Department of the Air Force Presentation to the Subcommittee on Personnel Committee on Armed Services, Senate Armed Services Committee, Washington, D.C., February 27, 2019, p.12.

Figure 6.9. Percentage of Air Force Officers Who Promote to the Next Grade, by Grade and Career Type, 2000–2010 Officer Cohorts

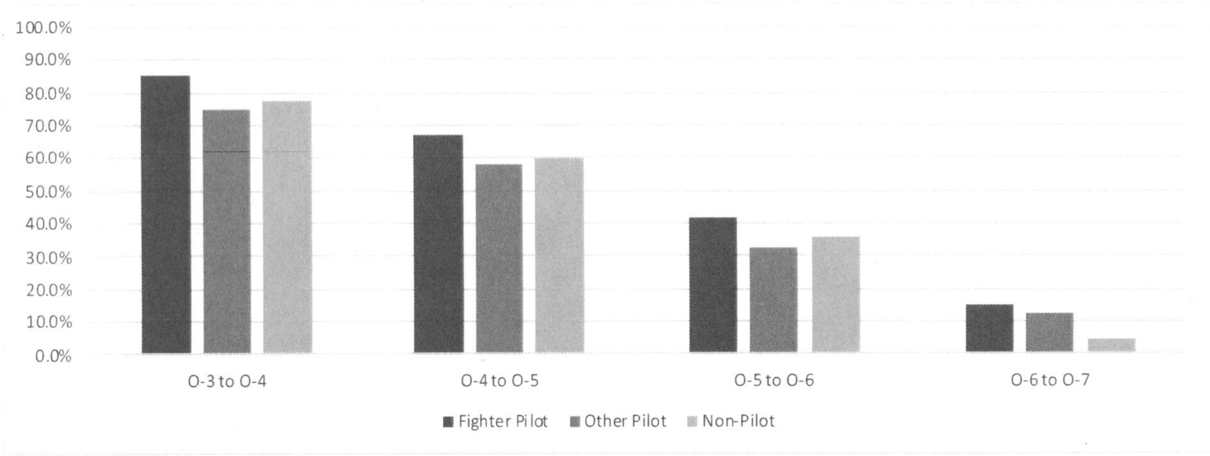

100.0%
90.0%
80.0%
70.0%
60.0%
50.0%
40.0%
30.0%
20.0%
10.0%
0.0%

O-3 to O-4 O-4 to O-5 O-5 to O-6 O-6 to O-7

■ Fighter Pilot ■ Other Pilot ■ Non-Pilot

SOURCE: Authors' analysis of DMDC data.
NOTE: These numbers represent the average progression rate for the 11 (overlapping) cohorts of Air Force officers present in each grade at the beginning of each year from 2000 to 2010, and reflect these officers' observed rates of reaching the next higher grade at any point up to the beginning of 2018, the last year for which we have data. An officer is categorized as a fighter pilot if they have ever been assigned a fighter pilot primary, secondary, or duty service occupation code, whether currently or in a previous year.

Other Factors That Matter in Air Force General Officer Selection

In addition to the process-related factors we describe above that affect an Air Force officer's likelihood to be selected as a GO, we also identified others that, while difficult to quantify, might have substantial bearing on promotion opportunities.

Personality

Our analysis identified that Air Force GOs possess technical ability, less hands-on personnel leadership experience than management experience, and a more service-specific focus than a joint focus (despite greater valuation of joint experience in the Air Force than in other services). A recurrent theme in our research was that Air Force GOs should exhibit command presence, which they might demonstrate through exceptional briefing skills—an asset at both junior and senior levels, particularly when interfacing with senior military and civilian decisionmakers.[475] These attributes are underpinned by being highly motivated to succeed and exhibiting the discipline and self-control required to enable such success. Further, we also heard that intangible, human-centered leadership skills also play a large role in promotion to GO. As Newton told us,

> As officers are considered for more senior positions, first and foremost, it's how well Mary or Bob have succeeded in command and/or other leadership

---

[475] AF31, Air Force personnel expert, October 25, 2018, for example. See also Lander, 2019, p. 77–78; Burks, 2010.

> opportunities that came their way. . . . Secondly, people skills are very important—how well you get along with others (peers and subordinates), how effective you are at communicating, do you understand what it means to be a servant leader, and so forth? Regarding servant leadership, that connotes strength, not weakness. That all said, if you're a below average one-star or two-star or you don't have the requisite focus or concern for others, you're going to stick out like a sore thumb.[476]

Indeed, GOs are highly scrutinized and in the public eye. As such, part of an Air Force GO's polish should reflect the GO's character, which relates to the need to avoid scandal. One such example was Major General James Post, former vice commander of ACC, who said to an audience that included A-10 pilots at Nellis Air Force Base that anyone who supports keeping the A-10 is guilty of treason. He was thought to be on the fast track to O-10, but these remarks arguably derailed his career.[477] In the opinion of a retired GO we interviewed, a strong moral compass can make an officer successful throughout their career, including as a GO. In this view, being a GO is about taking care of one's people while carrying out the mission that has been entrusted to them, which can prove to be conflicting objectives at times. It can also expose a person to greater ethical challenges, which one retired GO noted means that success can be viewed as navigating these challenges appropriately.[478]

Personal Networks

Networks with peers and/or more senior officers are essential to becoming a GO in the Air Force. Although determining the impact of networks on an officers' trajectory to generalship is nearly impossible to measure, we heard consistently that networks do make a difference. These networks range from relationships developed early with officers of similar grade to seeking out the mentorship and support from a senior officer within one's "tribe." The informal relationships forged early in an officer's career can be influential later on. Even something as casual as playing cards at the Officer's Club on a Friday night can build bonds with fellow officers who may follow them to future assignments. These opportunities may be more significant at remote bases, but the bonds fostered over time can create broader networks throughout an officer's career, said one interviewee.[479] More formally, fostering good relationships with commanders can extend one's network as these commanders progress through their own careers. An active duty field-grade officer we spoke to offered the following example to illustrate this point:

> I shot a note to an old squadron commander of mine and said, I don't know what I'm supposed to be doing. I was at SAASS at the time and everyone else was working their own job even though the Air Force tells you not to. . . . He said,

---

[476] AF23, retired lieutenant general Richard Newton, February 21, 2019.

[477] Jeff Schogol, "Two-Star Fired for 'Treason' Rant Against A-10 Supporters," *Air Force Times*, April 10, 2015.

[478] AF06, retired general officer, November 15, 2018.

[479] AF31, Air Force personnel expert, October 25, 2018.

> you can trust the Air Force to put you somewhere that will take advantage of [your time at] Weapons School and SAASS, and then he asked if I had any interest in going to the Joint Staff. A month later, he said he was pulling me up to the Joint Staff. We as an Air Force do that but we're tribal. . . . The maintainers I've worked for are guys I've worked with on the line but I have to fight to maintain that relationship. A guy I've flown with, I've got a relationship with him that's lasted 20 years. We have pockets where we break those down to good effect. The Weapons School does a great job of that. It forces all tribes to live in the same building.[480]

As discussed earlier in this section, developing these networks is one of most important parts of Air Staff or joint assignments. According to one active duty GO we interviewed, it should not be the position that gets an officer promoted, but the experience gained from that position and how it affects one's performance that should influence promotion. This interviewee noted, "My concern sometimes is we focus on the network in terms of enabling you to get promoted and advance, versus the value of the network to help you do your job better. That should be the primary role of the network."[481]

Serving in a joint billet can broaden and expand an officer's network, which can lead to knowledge or opportunities they might not have known about otherwise. An active duty field-grade officer provided the following personal anecdote to illustrate how critical their networks were to achieving eligibility for prime positions:

> Working on the Air Staff, there were 49 majors in that directorate. How I got there was tied directly to my performance at [operational unit] and the Coalition of the Believing that I could go do a job like that and represent [my] community not only as a worker but as a person. Once there, the interactions I had with the [General Schedule] GS-15 civilians [were] essential. The reason I was ranked so quickly to number one was the input of the GS-15 who had more interaction with me than the commander. . . . Where the network truly came into play was: I had no business interviewing for [a high-level position], but [another officer] was there I worked with in my first squadron [that] I stayed in touch with over four years. We reconvened in the Pentagon and went to lunch one day four/five months into my time in the Pentagon and he said he could get me an interview for his job. He asked the hardest questions of anyone on the panel and I got the job. . . . None of that would have happened without the network I built up over time.[482]

Finally, one factor raised multiple times that is related to network effects was nepotism. Interviewees we spoke to offered anecdotally that, in their views, having a parent or parent-in-

---

[480] AF19, active duty field-grade officer, September 28, 2018.

[481] AF75, active duty general officer, November 30, 2018.

[482] AF62, active duty field-grade officer, December 7, 2018.

law who has served as a GO increases an officer's ability to also rise to that level.[483] It was beyond the scope of this analysis to verify whether this perception is founded in data.

Factors in Selecting Out

Interviewees cited decisions pertaining to one's personal life as reasons for selecting out before O-7. Being a GO is a demanding position that often puts pressure on officers' personal lives.

Officers with young families, elderly parents, or other situations that do not easily lend themselves to moving every few years can have a strong disincentive for staying in the service. One retired GO characterized it as "losing control of your life," given the all-consuming nature of GO jobs.[484] Another interviewee elaborated on this point:

> Success needs to be a much more individualized and personalized answer. If you allow the institution to define success for you, you will be disappointed. Eventually the institution will not need you anymore. Whether it's not making your next star or your next position. What do you want to do, your family, what are your passions? What does success look like for you?. . . . I can't tell you how to be a GO because I am not one [and would be wary of anyone who could]. Find a GO to tell you what their path looked like. If it's a path that sounds good, then go down it.[485]

Summary

In summary, we found that Air Force career development processes are informed by Air Force culture, which tends to be largely focused on technology and strategic analysis. Although the Air Force prizes innovation conceptually, its approach to officer development, which is characterized by highly standardized, technical training that incentivizes rule-following, appears to be more conducive to developing risk-aversion. Also, given the Air Force's support role in the majority of DoD's major campaigns in the past 20 years, we found that Air Force officers tend to serve in both leadership and support positions, and that, as a service, the Air Force has learned to seek out influential positions in joint commands outside the coveted operations and planning positions, such as resource management.

In line with its flying history and culture, we found that the most common Air Force pathway to GO is for rated officers, and specifically pilots. Fighter pilots, in particular, dominate the culture of the Air Force. Further, the typical pathway is largely formulaic in terms of career

---

[483] AF12, active duty field-grade officer, September 26, 2018; AF19, active duty field-grade officer, September 28, 2018.

[484] AF06, retired general officer, November 15, 2018. These issues are not unique to the Air Force, and they are receiving greater attention. See Tom Barron, "To Retain Today's Talent, the DoD Must Support Dual-Professional Couples," Center for a New American Security, January 7, 2019.

[485] AF62, active duty field-grade officer, December 7, 2018.

experiences and educational performance, and in most cases is conducted on a tight development and promotion timeline reliant on early promotions that leaves little room for broadening experiences. This packed, service-focused timeline is in perpetual tension with one of the Air Force's key goals for its senior leaders: the ability to think strategically and be well-rounded. Potential candidates for GO are identified early—as early as O-3, in some cases—and some worry that tactical proficiency as a junior officer might not be a sufficient predictor for future strategic leadership. Some leadership opportunities exist at junior levels, but in general this type of experience is more focused on technical mastery and is gained later than in the Army or Marine Corps.

Air Force officers tend to share common professional experiences. Assignments are used as signaling tools that an officer is potential GO material, so both performance and position have weight in promotion decisions. Command positions—specifically of squadrons, groups, and wings—are highly prized in promotion decisions. Training experiences at Weapons School and SAASS also appear to be common among top GO candidates and tend to be valued more in promotion decisions than other competing opportunities, including broadening assignments.

Outside of an officer's core career field, certain Air Staff and Joint Staff positions are prized, as are aide positions that can lead to powerful mentors and networks. While both Air Force doctrine and our interviewees told us that joint service and strategic-level experience is important for future GOs, service-specific experience is still incentivized over other opportunities. Reflecting its culture of strategic analysis, the Air Force seems to value educational performance in its promotion decisions at the intermediate and senior PME levels far more than any other service. Deployments play a role in GO pathways, but deployments in active combat zones and less dangerous deployments to large bases, such as Al Udeid in Qatar, appear to be regarded similarly by promotion boards.

While much is unknown about Air Force promotion board processes, we do know that stellar OPRs throughout one's career are essential and that "people skills' carry weight in board decisions, particular at the O-7 threshold. Finally, we heard through the SLSE and our interviews that the impact of mentoring and influential networks on an officer's career is substantial. We discuss our analysis of the possible impact of these cultural values, Air Force goals, and other factors influencing common personnel pathways to GO in the Air Force in Chapter 8.

7. The Marine Corps' Approach to Generalship

The Marine Corps, which falls under the Department of the Navy, has deep roots in amphibious warfare that are reflected in its officer corps. Structurally, the Marine Corps is organized into Marine Air-Ground Task Forces (MAGTFs) of varying sizes, including ground, aviation, logistics, and command elements, which drives a culture that values combined arms. The Marine Corps' forward-based missions provide most officers with significant time overseas, whether on Marine Corps bases in Japan, time afloat, or, in the post-9/11 era, deployments to Iraq and Afghanistan. Marine Corps culture values its rich heritage and history of participation in every U.S. conflict since the founding of the nation.[486]

Marine Corps personnel management and GO development is influenced by its small size relative to the other services. As of January 2018, Marine Corps active duty end strength was 183,036, making up 14 percent of the active duty end strength for DoD.[487] The Marine Corps contains a smaller proportion of officers, including GOs, than any other service, with an average of 10.4 officers for every 100 marines, and 4.6 GOs for every 10,000 marines. The total number of GOs in the Marine Corps is 85: 37 O-7s, 26 O-8s, 18 O-9s, and 4 O-10s.[488]

The small size of the Marine Corps GO corps requires a high degree of selectivity at each promotion point in an officer's career. Thus, the Marine Corps personnel management system yields cohorts of O-6s who are highly competitive for promotion to GO. Because the number of Marine Corps GOs selected annually is so small and the competition is so strong, marines generally share a sense that many of those not selected for promotion to O-7 are just as competitive as those who are promoted, both reflecting and impacting the Marine Corps' egalitarian culture.

Additionally, the Marine Corps personnel management system promotes officers to the GO grades later than other services—28 years for promotion to O-7 (as compared with the service-wide average of 27.2 years), and 37.1 years to the grade of O-10 (as compared with the service-wide average of 34.5 years).[489] Marine Corps GOs therefore, tend to have more years of experience than their counterparts in the other services.

---

486 Dan Madden, "The Marine Corps," in Zimmerman et. al., 2019, pp. 81–87.

487 Defense Manpower Data Center, 2018.

488 Officer and general officer numbers calculated by authors using DMDC data. For a comparison of these numbers to those for other services, see Table B.2.

489 Authors' analysis of DMDC data.

Marine Corps Culture

The deeply rooted Marine Corps culture, predicated in large part on the weight it places on its traditions and heritage, plays a significant role in shaping its personnel management systems and preferences.[490] Much of Marine Corps culture is predicated on what the service defines as "enduring Marine Corps principles":[491]

- Every Marine is a rifleman.
- The Marine Corps is an expeditionary naval force.
- The Marine Corps is a combined arms organization.
- Marines will be ready and forward deployed.
- Marines are agile and adaptable.
- Marines take care of their own.

Marine Corps Warfighting Publication (MCWP) 6-11, *Leading Marines*, captures several components of Marine Corps culture. Of note, Marine Corps culture and Marine Corps leadership are often described as being inextricably linked, both in *Leading Marines* and in broader publications by and about the Marine Corps. For example,

> Being a Marine is being part of something larger than oneself. There is a spirit—an *esprit*—that defines our Corps. To understand what it means to be a Marine, you must understand how we make Marines by instilling and abiding by the core values of honor, courage, and commitment. As a Marine leader, you must also understand our naval character and expeditionary mindset, our philosophy that every Marine is a rifleman, and our commitment to selfless service, all of which are in keeping with Marine tradition.[492]

The Marine Corps aphorism "every Marine a rifleman" captures multiple facets of Marine Corps culture. First, it stresses the Marine Corps' regard for egalitarianism and equal value being placed on all its members, regardless of rank, career field, or any other distinguishing factor. Second, it communicates the centrality of infantry operations to the Marine Corps culture.[493]

Marine Corps culture can further be characterized by a number of values, including tradition, servant leadership, and discipline. The Marine Corps emphasis on tradition is clearly displayed in its ceremonial aspects, such as the storied history of Marine Corps dress uniforms. Servant leadership, while displayed in myriad ways, is perhaps best captured by the way marines are served "chow" (food): Officers eat last. Discipline, underlying all aspects of Marine Corps training and operating, is evidenced through a range of expression—ranging from the marine dedication to physical fitness and personal presentation to the movements of the silent drill team.

---

[490] Madden, 2019, pp. 81–87.

[491] Marine Corps Doctrinal Publication 1, *Marine Corps Operations*, Washington, D.C.: Headquarters Marine Corps, 2011, pp. 1-4–1-5.

[492] MCWP 6-11, *Leading Marines*, Washington, D.C.: Headquarters Marine Corps, August 1, 2014.

[493] Madden, 2019.

Leading Marines describes the value placed on discipline in the service, particularly what is considered the most evolved version: self-discipline.

> Marine leaders strive to develop self-discipline in their Marines. Self-disciplined Marines are those who exercise self-control and take personal responsibility. They subordinate personal considerations such as convenience and comfort to do the right thing. Self-disciplined Marines do the right thing when no one is looking and they maintain their discipline because their fellow Marines are counting on them.[494]

The Marine Corps places substantial value on being an elite institution, one that is not suitable for everyone and that requires characteristics and dedication that few possess. As referenced in *Leading Marines*, "We ask, "Do you have what it takes to be a Marine?' not, 'What can the Marine Corps do for you?'"[495] Marine Corps recruitment literature highlights the exclusive nature of the Corps; the quintessential example being the Marine Corps recruitment ad campaign summoning "The Few, the Proud, the Marines." The ethos presented through such campaigns serves as a type of threshold test, appealing to a smaller subset of the larger population who may feel a propensity to serve in the Armed Forces.

Marine Corps culture is also driven by organizational structure. The MAGTF serves as the principal organizational structure for Marine Corps units. Each MAGTF is made up of a command element, a ground combat element, an aviation combat element, and a logistics combat element. Every Marine Corps organization—ranging from a 2,600-member Marine Expeditionary Unit (MEU) to a 20,000-member Marine Expeditionary Brigade (MEB) through a Marine Expeditionary Force (MEF) (up to 90,000 marines)—is organized as a MAGTF.[496] Accordingly, the Marine Corps personnel management system values all MOSs and provides a path to attaining the rank of O-7 across each career field. Additional information on the Marine Corps' approach to the RL and URL will follow later in this chapter.

Finally, Marine Corps culture is strongly defined by the notion of pride—of service, of self (or more specifically, selflessness), and of belonging to an elite organization. As noted in a 2019 RAND Corporation study on service culture,

> Indeed, Marine pride in its unique characteristics is a marker of Marine culture itself. While the other services have strong branch identities, Marines identify most closely with the corps level over branch distinctions. The Marine Corps reinforces this institutional pride by frequently invoking the word "pride" in its recruitment and other branding efforts. Even *Semper fidelis*, meaning "always faithful," the Marine Corps' motto since 1883, deeply underscores the unwavering dedication to other Marines, the mission, and the nation.[497]

---

494 MCWP 6-11, 2014, pp. 2–15.

495 MCWP 6-11, 2014, pp. 1–4.

496 U.S. Marine Corps Concepts and Programs, "Types of MAGTFs," U.S. Marine Corps, undated.

497 Madden, 2019, p. 100.

Official Guidance on Marine Corps Officer Development

The Marine Corps fundamentally operates as a people-centric service, and its concept of leadership development stems directly from that principle. As the smallest service with the smallest budget, the Marine Corps is less focused on the acquisition of technology and more on developing its main asset: marines. Directly reflective of this idea is how closely the Marine Corps links leadership development to its maneuver warfighting ethos. As stated in Marine Corps Order 1500.61, *Marine Leader Development*,

> Our commitment to developing Marines is closely linked to our warfighting philosophy. . . . Maneuver warfare places a high priority on decentralized execution and exploiting opportunities in the absence of explicit orders. This method of warfighting demands leaders of high moral character and professional competence who are not just technically and tactically proficient but who earn and breed trust among subordinates. These leaders in turn form the foundation of effective warfighting units characterized by mutual understanding, implicit communication, and esprit de corps.[498]

This emphasis on the mutual, and critical, development of tactical competence alongside less tangible moral and ethical attributes is repeated throughout Marine Corps doctrine and official publications.[499] Several key doctrinal publications include guidance on Marine Corps officer development and ethical leadership, such as Marine Corps Doctrinal Publication (MCDP) 1: *Warfighting*, MCDP 6: *Command and Control*, Marine Corps Tactical Publication (MCTP) 6-10A: *Sustaining the Transformation*, and MCTP 6-10B: *Marine Corps Values: A User's Guide for Discussion Leaders*.[500] Each of these publications highlights and institutionalizes specific aspects of the characteristics valued in Marine Corps leaders. *Leading Marines* is one of the core doctrinal documents in understanding the Marine Corps approach to developing leaders.[501] In it, the service defines its ethos, foundations of leadership, and means and importance of overcoming challenges. Reflective of Marine Corps culture, *Leading Marines* quotes heavily from marines of all ranks and reinforces throughout its text the importance of selflessness, courage, and morality to true leadership.

The Marine Corps further identifies six "functional areas of leadership development" in official guidance that are intended to frame the holistic, multifaceted definition the service uses for leadership:

---

[498] Marine Corps Order 1500.61, *Marine Leader Development*, Washington, D.C.: Headquarters Marine Corps, July 28, 2017.

[499] See, for example, MCWP 6-11, 2014; Marine Corps Order 1500.61, 2017; Marine Corps Tactical Publication (MCTP) 6-10B: *Marine Corps Values: A User's Guide for Discussion Leaders*, Washington, D.C.: Headquarters Marine Corps, May 2, 2016.

[500] MCDP 1, *Warfighting*, Washington, D.C.: Headquarters Marine Corps, April 4, 2018; MCDP 6, *Command and Control*, Washington, D.C.: Headquarters, U.S. Marine Corps, October 4, 1996; MCTP 6-10A, *Sustaining the Transformation*, Washington, D.C.: Headquarters Marine Corps, May 2, 2016; MCTP 6-10B, 2016.

[501] MCWP 6-11, 2014.

- Fidelity. Faithfulness to one another, our Corps, and the Nation. It is expressed through our motto, "Semper Fidelis," meaning "Always Faithful," as well as our core values, leadership traits and principles, heritage, and high standards of ethical conduct.
- Fighter. The cumulative skill-sets and knowledge that make Marines well-rounded warriors. This addresses Professional Military Education (PME), as well as the classifications of duties, such as Military Occupational Specialty (MOS)/Navy Enlisted Code (NEC)/Navy Officer Billet Classification (NOBC), and corresponding standards of performance, interpersonal communication skills, and on and off-duty education. This area also helps focus training of both individuals and the team.
- Fitness. Physical, mental, spiritual, and social health and well-being. Ensuring holistic well-being boosts morale, cohesiveness, and resiliency—enabling Marines to execute the toughest challenges and recuperate in shorter time.
- Family. The bedrock, fundamental social relationships from which Marines draw strength, and cumulatively make a stronger Corps. The challenges of military life require families to be resilient like the Marines they support.
- Finances. The disciplined practice of personal financial responsibility. Marines and Sailors who are financially responsible mitigate stress and are better prepared for deployments, family changes, big financial decisions (e.g., buying a home or vehicle), and transition to civilian life.
- Future. The practice of setting and accomplishing goals in all of the other five functional areas of leader development. Goal-setting maximizes the likelihood of personal and professional success, which carries through to civilian life.[502]

Leadership development is considered continuous throughout one's Marine Corps career, and is fostered beginning at the junior and small-unit levels, because exemplification of leadership, particularly along moral and ethical dimensions, is considered essential at every rank.[503] To that point, in order for a Marine to continue to promote, the Marine has to perform well at every echelon—there are few "kingmaker" positions that signal that an officer is favored for future promotion over another. The typical future Marine Corps GO starts competing with their cohort shortly after commissioning. This begins with The Basic School (TBS), which trains newly commissioned officers from the same year group in the "high standards of professional knowledge, esprit-de-corps, and leadership to prepare them as company grade officers in the operating forces."[504] This standardized training at the basic level helps to form the foundation of Marine Corps officer development, and it reinforces the Marine Corps ideal of team over self and

[502] Marine Corps Order 1500.61, 2017.

[503] Daniel C. Rhodes, "Moral and Ethical Leadership: The Challenges of Implementing the Appropriate Training," *Marine Corps Gazette*, Vol. 93, No. 5, May 2009, pp. 54–56.

[504] U.S. Marine Corps Training Command, "The Basic School," website, undated b.

adherence to the notion that effective, principled leadership of fellow marines is of utmost importance in an officer's path.

Marine Corps doctrine and official literature places a strong emphasis on desired leadership characteristics and principles, which are nested with the Marine Corps' formal core values of honor, courage, and commitment. The Marine Corps' formal leadership "traits" include the following: justice, judgment, dependability, initiative, decisiveness, tact, integrity, enthusiasm, bearing, unselfishness, courage, knowledge, loyalty, and endurance.[505]

The leadership principles differ slightly from leadership traits, serving as maxims Marine Corps officers pursue:

- Be technically and tactically proficient.
- Know yourself and seek self-improvement.
- Know your marines and look out for their welfare.
- Keep your marines informed.
- Set the example.
- Ensure the task is understood, supervised, and accomplished.
- Train your marines as a team.
- Make sound and timely decisions.
- Develop a sense of responsibility among your subordinates.
- Employ your unit in accordance with its capabilities.
- Seek responsibility and take responsibility for your actions.[506]

Both the leadership traits and leadership principles encapsulate and operationalize elements of Marine Corps culture and further influence the way Marine Corps leaders are developed and selected by the personnel system. Traits such as loyalty, dependability, and judgment correlate with the Marine Corps sense of tradition; decisiveness, initiative, enthusiasm, bearing, courage, and endurance reflect the Marine Corps sense of discipline. Many of the leadership principles emphasize the Marine Corps focus on developing, leading, and investing directly in subordinates. As such, marine behavior inculcates the value system on successive generations of marines, and the Marine Corps personnel system values and promotes those who embody the Marine Corps leadership ethos. Indeed, many of these qualities cannot be measured, a reality the Marine Corps readily acknowledges. As Marine Corps commandant C. B. Cates is quoted in official Marine Corps leadership training documents:

> Leadership is intangible, hard to measure, and difficult to describe. It's quality would seem to stem from many factors. But certainly they must include a measure of inherent ability to control and direct, self-confidence based on expert knowledge, initiative, loyalty, pride and sense of responsibility. Inherent ability cannot be instilled, but that which is latent or dormant can be developed. Other

[505] U.S. Marine Corps Training and Education Command, "RP 0103-Principles of Marine Corps Leadership," undated. The Navy and the Marine Corps share the same formal core values and leadership traits.

[506] MCWP 6-11, 2014.

ingredients can be acquired. They are not easily learned. But leaders can be and are made.[507]

Fundamental Elements of Marine Corps General Officer Pathways

The Marine Corps' GOs are shaped by several factors, many of which are inherent in the Marine Corps' personnel processes and other elements of its GO pathways. While some of these elements are structured according to DoD policy or federal statute, they all are tailored to Marine Corps purposes and accordingly reflect many aspects of Marine Corps culture. The following sections detail the philosophical approach, competitive categories and typical pathways, career timelines, and personnel processes that help to define key characteristics of Marine Corps GOs.

The Marine Corps' Philosophical Approach to the Officer Development Pipeline

The Marine Corps approach to developing GOs operates largely as a funnel: At every echelon, Marine Corps officers are tested on their performance within their given assignments. Unlike other services, such as the Air Force, where specific assignments might signal that an officer has been initiated into a pipeline toward a GO billet, Marine Corps officers are largely evaluated and promoted at each grade based on their performance within their assignments since their last promotion. Moreover, the Marine Corps places equal weight on both operational tours and institutional tours (or "B" billets), requiring and incentivizing the participation of all Marine Corps officers, from recruiting depots, basic training units, and active duty assignments to reserve units. This practice is distinctive to the Marine Corps, as other services might be more likely to place their less competitive officers in similar roles in order to free up operational billets for high performers. Further, the centrally managed Marine Corps personnel system provides marines with clear assignment paths and communicates the career path and specific options at each step in an officer's career through the marines' career monitors. These paths and options generally do not include much flexibility for officers to pursue broadening assignments. Some of this central management can be attributed to the relatively small size of the Marine Corps, since promotion boards select from far fewer officers in each grade compared with the other services. However, the Marine Corps could select a variety of ways to manage its officers, so the service's use of this model is also partially a design choice.

The Marine Corps evaluation and promotion system, both formally and informally, does not mark certain individuals as "GO potential" early on through personnel practices such as BZ promotions or high-visibility billets, although certain billets might exist that enable a Marine Corps officer to demonstrate their potential or broaden their network more effectively than in other billets. Instead, the Marine Corps culls less competitive officers beginning early in their careers through the career designation board (CDB), which is explored in detail below, leaving a

[507] U.S. Marine Corps Training and Education Command, undated.

pool of increasingly more competitive officers at each successive rank beginning at the O-4 grade. The competitive process ensures a robust pool of candidates competing for future GO billets. Given the small number of Marine Corps officers promoted to GO in a year—approximately 35 individuals—this process also ensures that the Marine Corps is led by a strong cadre of O-6s who will never be promoted to O-7 because of the relatively small number of O-7 billets. In the Marine Corps, officers are likely to be identified as having the potential for GO later in their careers, at the O-5 and O-6 grades, particularly in command billets in each echelon.

While the Marine Corps maintains formal definitions of leadership, the service philosophy on leadership is more comprehensive. The Marine Corps leadership philosophy centers around discipline in many facets. Successful marines are those who follow instruction from their superiors and from the service. They are unlikely to question orders, and they value adherence to existing doctrine, concepts, and policies. Successful marines "from the Commandant down [are] followers. The good followers, those who may be depended on to carry out their instructions precisely, are the substance of the Corps."[508] The Marine Corps philosophy on leadership includes intuitive aspects, such as the ability to compel subordinates to action, but it puts equal emphasis on "following" as a central tenet of the Marine Corps leadership philosophy.

Within the Marine Corps, officers are both formally and informally assessed on "command presence" and "bearing." In some respects, both command presence and bearing exhibit the core value of discipline. Physical prowess and appearance are valued as an expression of discipline. Significantly, Marine Corps promotion boards place a high premium on the role of the Official Military Personnel File (OPMF) photo. Board preparation guidance notes that "Photographs provide a visual representation of the Marine to selection boards." If a marine exceeds weight standards, they are required to include their body fat percentage along with their photo. However, marines may exempt themselves from including their body fat percentage if they scored above a 285 (out of 300) on their last Marine Corps Physical Fitness Test.[509]

Competitive Categories

Although the quintessential image of a Marine Corps GO is an infantryman ("every Marine a rifleman"), the MAGTF construct leads to fairly equitable promotion pathways, with roughly equal rates of promotion to O-7 for infantry, aviation, and combat service support (including logistics and intelligence). Each career field has a viable path to promotion to O-7 and O-8, but infantry officers in the Marine Corps achieve the grades of O-9 and O-10 much more often.

---

[508] MCWP 6-11, 2014, pp. 2–19.

[509] Marine Administrative Message (MARADMIN) 548/16, *Official Military Personnel File (OMPF) Photograph Guidance*, Washington, D.C.: Headquarters Marine Corps, October 17, 2016.

Furthermore, the commandants of the Marine Corps have traditionally been infantrymen.[510] Figure 7.1 depicts the heavy emphasis on infantry officers in the GO grades.

The equity among promotion paths to O-7 across ground, aviation, and logistics/combat service support begins early in officer career assignments. Whereas the other services submit their list of desired career fields shortly before commissioning, Marine Corps officers do not submit their career field preference lists until the end of TBS—at which point they have competed against all other Marine Corps officers in their cohort. The Marine Corps then assigns officers to the three major career fields by ensuring that each career field receives an equal distribution of the top, middle, and bottom thirds of the overall Order of Merit list (OML).[511] The OML is based on performance along academic, tactical, and leadership dimensions, although only academic grades received at TBS are considered.[512] This practice reflects both the egalitarian nature of the Marine Corps and the service reliance on each MAGTF element, ensuring that one element does not monopolize the most competitive talent but rather that talent is distributed across all MOSs.

---

[510] General Leonard Chapman, an artillery officer, served as commandant from 1968 to 1971, and James F. Amos was the only aviator to fill the role, from 2010 to 2014.

[511] Hosek et al., 2001, p. 13.

[512] Hosek et al., 2001.

Figure 7.1. Percentage of Marine Corps Officers, by Type and Grade, Average, 2008–2018

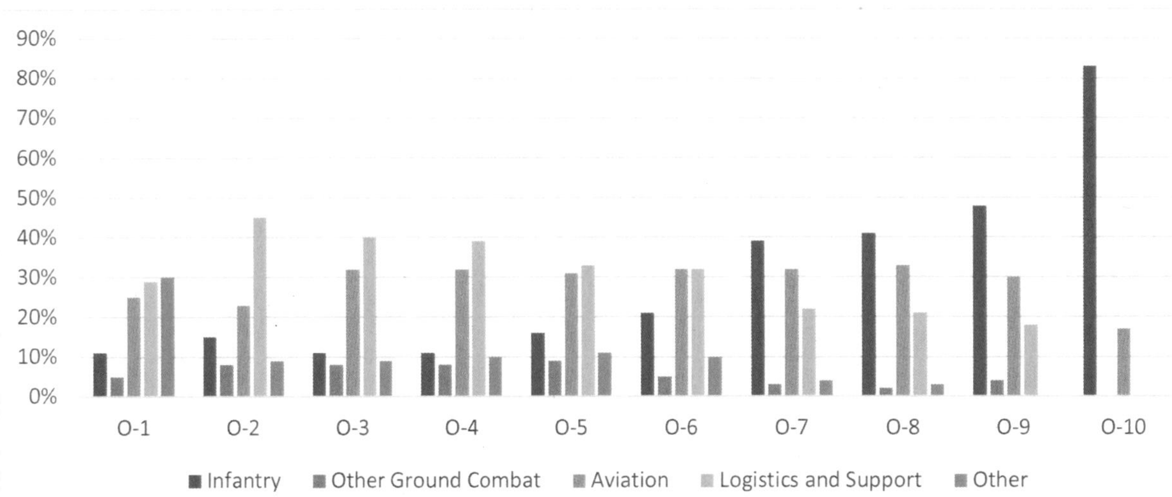

SOURCE: Authors' analysis of DMDC data.
NOTE: Officers are categorized by type using the primary service occupation codes assigned to each officer in any given year. When a Marine Corps officer is promoted to O-6, they are often assigned a generic senior officer primary occupation code. To correct for this, officers at the ranks of O-6 to O-10 are categorized by type using the last meaningful, nongeneric, primary service occupation code assigned to them as O-5s. The total numbers of Marine Corps officers analyzed by grade were as follows: O-1: 31,750; O-2: 36,709; O-3: 69,939; O-4: 41,770; O-5: 20,804; O-6: 7,055; O-7: 400; O-8: 291; O-9: 186; O-10: 45. The number of officers analyzed decreases between the lower grades and the higher grades. Because fewer officers are included in our analysis at higher grades, representation among the higher grades is more susceptible to fluctuations in year-over-year differences in accession sources.

The list of officer MOSs is narrower than other military services. The Marine Corps does not have organic specialty fields, such as medical and chaplains; instead, the Marine Corps draws on Navy corpsmen to fulfill those functions. The MOSs in the Marine Corps, grouped into broader occupational categories useful for our analysis of pathways to generalship, are as follows:

- Infantry (infantry officers)
- Other Ground Combat (field artillery, amphibious assault vehicle, and tank officers)
- Pilot (flight officers, fixed-wing, and rotary/tilt rotor pilots)
- Logistics/Support (communications, combat engineer, logistics, intelligence, aviation maintenance, aviation supply, aviation command and control, ground supply, and military police officers)[513]
- Other (financial management, JAG, public affairs, and adjutant officer).

Although MOSs differentiate Marine Corps officers into career specialties, Marine Corps officers are more likely to affiliate as a marine rather than by their MOS. Culturally, this affiliation is symbolized in the insignia on Marine Corps dress blues. Whereas other services distinguish between MOSs on dress uniforms through means such as coding lapel colors and

---

[513] Additionally, four intelligence MOSs exist (ground, human source, signals intelligence/ground electronic warfare, and air intelligence), as do four aviation command and control MOSs (low altitude air defense, air support control, air defense control, and air traffic control). Navy Marine Corps (NAVMC) 1200.1C, *Military Occupational Specialties Manual*, Washington, D.C.: Headquarters, U.S. Marine Corps, April 17, 2017.

including branch insignia pins until achieving the rank of G/FO, marines do not distinguish their MOS on their dress uniforms. Instead, all Marine Corps officers bear the insignia of the Eagle, Globe, and Anchor.

The Marine Corps maintains two competitive categories for promotion: the URL (all MOSs but one) and financial management officers, who make up their own separate competitive category. Therefore, Marine Corps officers from the remainder of MOSs compete against one another for promotion. In practice, this means that caps on promotion rates, as outlined in DOPMA and by DoD promotion policy, apply to the entirety of the Marine Corps officer corps without necessarily ensuring that the same percentage of officers are promoted within each MOS. For example, the promotion rate from O-4 to O-5 is 70 percent. But there is no guarantee that, for example, 70 percent of tank officers or ground supply officers will be promoted to O-5, only a guideline that 70 percent of all MOSs combined in each competitive category will promote to O-5. As a result, if officers from one MOS (particularly infantry) are overrepresented, it comes at the expense of promotion rates for officers in another MOS. An inherent tension can exist between the egalitarianism across MOSs and the "every marine a rifleman" culture valued across the Marine Corps, which emphasizes the value placed on infantry skills. Board precepts that highlight critical skill set shortages (as opposed to establishing quotas) attempt to mitigate potential imbalances in selection for promotion, but they rarely yield equal promotion rates across MOSs.

In the Marine Corps, nontraditional pathways to GO rarely exist. The limited number of MOSs among officers guides this structurally, as the Marine Corps does not maintain organic specialty fields (such as a medical corps or chaplain corps). The Marine Corps does have JAG officers, but the pool is small, and thus the number of GOs who rise from that community is also very limited.

Career Timelines

Marine Corps GOs tend to be older than their counterparts in other services because of the length of time they spend as O-3s and O-4s. The average Marine Corps officer promotes to the grade of O-4 at 13.1 years of service (nearly two years after their Air Force and Army counterparts). Marine Corps officers are promoted to O-7 at an average 28 years of service, two years later than their Air Force counterparts.[514] At the most senior ranks, recently promoted Marine Corps O-10s have an average of 37.1 years of service—nearly three more years than O-10s in all other services.[515] Figure 7.2 depicts the steadily increasing average years in service for Marine Corps officers at each grade, and Figure 7.3 highlights that the grades in which these officers spend the greatest number of years are O-3, O-4, and O-5, followed by slightly less time at O-6.

---

[514] Authors' analysis of DMDC data.

[515] Years in service comparisons for each grade and military service are illustrated in Chapter 3.

Figure 7.2. Average Years in Service for Rising Marine Corps Officers, by Grade (Promoted in Prior Year), 2008–2018

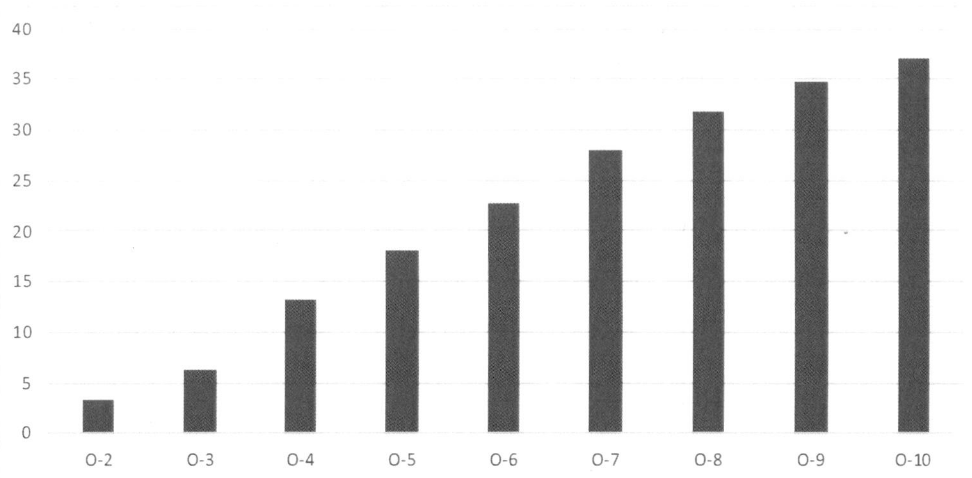

SOURCE: Authors' analysis of DMDC data. Years in service are calculated as of January each year, for officers promoted in the year before.

Figure 7.3. Time in Grade for Rising Marine Corps Officers Promoted from That Grade in the Prior Year, Average, 2008–2018

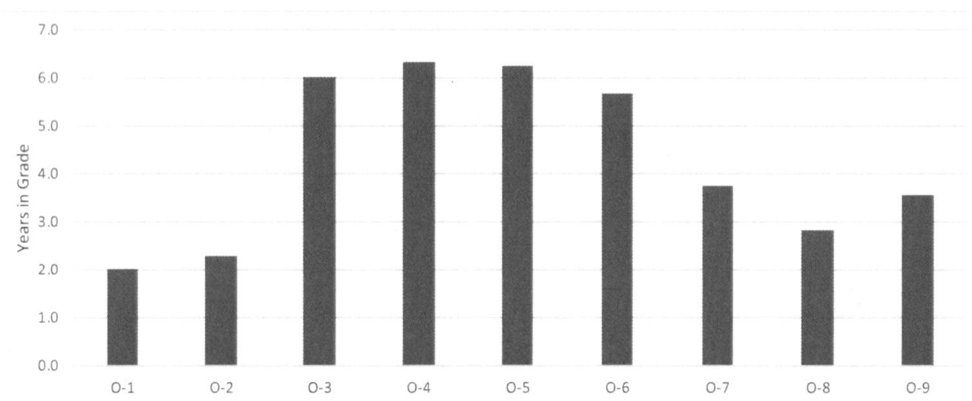

SOURCE: Authors' analysis of DMDC data.

Additionally, the Marine Corps has the same ability as the other services to utilize authorities for BZ promotions (up to 10 percent of promotion selectees for any given promotion board), but the egalitarian nature of the Marine Corps officer personnel management system eschews the use of the authority. Many in the Marine Corps cite the necessity to pursue egalitarian promotion policies as the positive reason for dissuading the use of BZ promotions, but some critique that the aversion to BZ promotions is tied to the Marine Corps aversion to change.[516]

---

[516] Aaron Marx, *Rethinking Marine Corps Officer Promotion and Retention*, Washington, D.C.: Brookings Institution, 2014, p. 16.

In general, Marine Corps officers follow the same cycle of PME, operational tours, and supporting institutional tours outside of their MOSs (B-billets), including recruiting commands and basic training units. Marine Corps officers attend TBS upon commissioning, followed by their MOS-specific school. As lieutenants, marines are assigned to the operational force (otherwise known as the "fleet"). Marine Corps officers are then selected by the CDB, which we explore later in this chapter. Once promoted to captain (at roughly five years of service), Marine Corps officers tend to cycle into a supporting institutional tour, including recruiting and basic training commands. Marine Corps officers then typically attend their career-level PME around their eighth year of service before returning to the operating force for their O-3 command tour. Marine Corps officers are promoted to O-4 during their tenth or eleventh years of service, at which point they fulfill intermediate-level PME and a second supporting institutional tour. As a senior O-4, most Marine Corps officers cycle into key operational billets, serving as battalion executive officers or operations officers at roughly 14 years of service. Marine Corps officers typically attain the grade of O-5 between 16 and 17 years of service, then cycle through command in the operating force and a key staff position. Marine Corps officers generally promote to O-6 between 22 and 23 years of service, then either assume command or serve in a key staff role.[517] As will be discussed later in this chapter, the experience of command is valued most highly in Marine Corps promotions deliberations.

Personnel Management Processes and Impact on Marine Corps General Officers

Marine Corps officers' career pathways are guided by personnel management processes that reflect both statutory and DoD policy requirements, and also service culture. Below, we analyze how the Marine Corps' personnel management processes—including commissioning, duty assignments, education and special training, evaluations, and promotion boards—influence Marine Corps GO development and selection.

Commissioning Source

The dominant commissioning source in the Marine Corps is OCS. The Marine Corps offers two distinct forms of OCS: the traditional Marine Corps Officer Candidate School (OCS) and the Platoon Leaders Course (PLC). The PLC is offered in two different ways: two six-week courses (either freshman summer of college and junior summer of college, or sophomore summer of college and junior summer of college) or one ten-week course the junior summer of college. The PLC offers the same training as OCS, which is offered to those who have just graduated college or later (before 28 years old).[518] Those who complete PLC are not obligated to commission—and the Marine Corps is not obligated to offer a commission to an individual who has completed the program. The program therefore offers a chance for individuals to test whether they are

---

[517] 9th Marine Corps District, "Staying Marine: Example Career Progression—Officer," website, June 2009.

[518] U.S. Marine Corps, "Becoming a Marine: Marine Corps Officer: Officer Eligibility," webpage, undated.

committed to a career in the Marine Corps and allows the Marine Corps to thoroughly assess individuals before they commission. This might account for the high retention rates of PLC and OCS graduates in the Marine Corps. The repeat nature of PLC serves as a threshold test for those individuals who wish to return and go on to commission, weeding out those who might leave during their first year.

The Marine Corps does not have its own dedicated service academy or ROTC programs. Instead, the Marine Corps commissions its officers in part through NROTC and the USNA. Marines represent the minority of USNA graduates; Marine Corps commissions represented 24.5 and 22.6 percent of USNA commissions in the classes of 2017 and 2018, respectively.[519]

Unlike the other services, the Marine Corps has the lowest rate of academy-commissioned officers promoted to GO. As shown in Figure 7.4, 15 percent of Marine Corps O-7s and 14 percent of Marine Corps O-9s and O-10s are USNA graduates. By comparison, 50 percent of Marine Corps O-7s and 69 percent of Marine Corps O-9s and O-10s commission through OCS. The distribution in commissioning source representation indicates that all commissioning sources have the potential for GO development, and—unlike the other services, where service academy graduates are highly represented at the most senior ranks—OCS graduates compose the majority of Marine Corps GOs overall.

Prospective analysis indicates that, of all Marine Corps officers who served as O-4s between FY 1995 and FY 2018, 0.8 percent of USNA graduates attained the grade of O-7. By comparison, 0.4 percent of OCS graduates were promoted to O-7, and 1.5 percent of NROTC graduates were promoted to the grade of O-7.

---

[519] U.S. Naval Academy, 2018; U.S. Naval Academy, "Class of 2017 Statistics," May 30, 2017.

Figure 7.4. Accession Source of Rising Marine Corps Officers (Promoted in Prior Year), by Grade, Average, 2008–2018

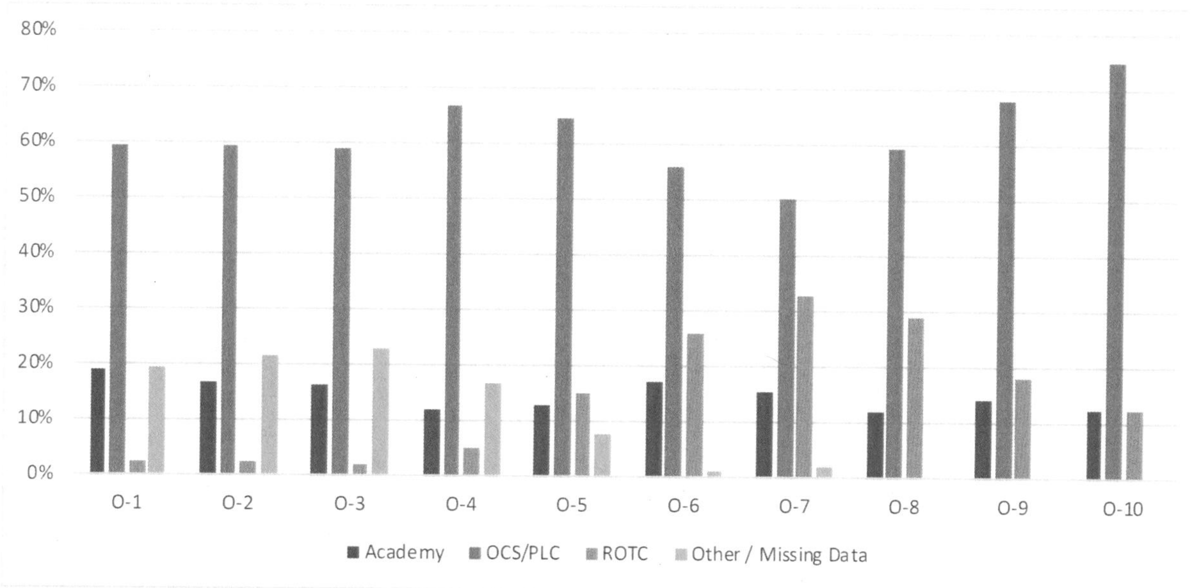

SOURCE: Authors' analysis of DMDC data.
NOTES: Because of the DMDC data structure, the total number of officers analyzed by MOS are different than the total number of officers analyzed by accession source. The total number of Marine Corps officers analyzed by grade were: O-1: 15,088; O-2: 16,185; O-3: 13,578; O-4: 6,907; O-5: 3,497; O-6: 1,136; O-7: 104; O-8: 93; O-9: 50; O-10: 8. The number of officers analyzed decreases between the lower grades and the higher grades. Because fewer officers are included in our analysis at higher grades, representation among the higher grades is more susceptible to fluctuations in year-over-year differences in accession sources.

Duty Assignments

Throughout a Marine Corps officer's career, individuals are managed by career monitors from their MOS. Monitors are assigned to Headquarters Marine Corps, Personnel Management Division of the Manpower Department. The monitor is charged with satisfying three goals: "the needs of the Marine Corps, the career needs of the individual, and the personal desires of the individual."[520] Career monitors travel to marines at their base to conduct brief interviews, and serve the function of an assignments officer and a career counselor.[521]

Officers must perform well in operational force tours and supporting institutional assignments alike.[522] The Marine Corps officer personnel management system maintains a high degree of control over officer career paths in order to ensure that all officers are aware of and aligned with the required billets at the right time in their career. As noted previously, each new assignment provides officers the opportunity to prove their performance in the position, which is

---

[520] "Meet the Monitors," *Marine Corps Gazette*, Vol. 70, No. 1, January 1986.

[521] MARADMINS 308/18, *FY19 Manpower Management Officer Assignments (MMOA) Command Visit*, Washington, D.C.: Headquarters Marine Corps, June 4, 2018.

[522] Senior leader selection exercise notes, January 30, 2019, RAND Corporation, Arlington, Virginia.

particularly important in the Marine Corps, as there are few specific "kingmaker" positions or "glide paths" to GO that exist more strongly in other services.

The requirements-driven, centrally managed assignment process yields a tightly controlled pathway for promotion to GO. The Marine Corps personnel system therefore limits joint and broadening assignments, beyond Goldwater-Nichols requirements, yielding GOs with little time and experience outside the Marine Corps, according to one active-duty interviewee.[523] The system further produces Marine Corps officers with fairly similar assignment and training histories, creating a degree of uniformity in experience and reducing the number of assignments seen as particularly competitive or career-ending. Thus, promotion boards rely heavily on performance in a given assignment as the discriminating factor when selecting officers for promotion.[524]

Marine Corps officers are able to turn down assignments offered to them, but the practice is widely looked down upon. Turning down an assignment—particularly an overseas assignment, and especially if the overseas assignment is a command—is viewed as a lack of commitment to the Marine Corps. Moreover, in the event that an officer turns down an overseas assignment, another officer must take their place. As expressed by a retired Marine Corps GO, "It's all or nothing. If you turn down a command, everyone knows who you are, and knows that you forced someone to take your place."[525]

High-visibility roles are less emphasized in the Marine Corps than other services. All post-command O-5 and O-6 officers complete a key institutional support role at the staff level, typically within Headquarters Marine Corps or OSD, or at Marine Corps Base Quantico in Virginia. In these roles, marines might serve as military advisers to civilian leadership across a range of functionalities. These positions can increase their visibility within the Marine Corps. However, because all Marine Corps officers cycle through these billets in due course, assignments to high-visibility roles do not necessarily distinguish one officer's record from another.

Within the Marine Corps, few "career-ending" assignments exist. In part, the lack of such assignments can be attributed to universal supporting institutional assignments, or B-billets, thus raising the value of assignments that might be considered detrimental in other services.[526] For example, officers assigned to a Marine Corps recruitment depot tend to exemplify Marine Corps values, including bearing and fitness, whereas such an assignment might be considered detrimental to an officer in the Army. Additionally, the requirements-based nature of Marine Corps assignments—communicated both informally and formally (through board precepts) leads

---

[523] M7, active duty marine O-6, September 5, 2018.

[524] Senior leader selection exercise notes, January 30, 2019, RAND Corporation, Arlington, Virginia.

[525] Senior leader selection exercise notes, January 30, 2019, RAND Corporation, Arlington, Virginia.

[526] Positions considered B-billets are recruiting commands, basic training commands, and reserve component commands.

to a widespread understanding that marines are assigned to billets because the service needs to meet a requirement, and that marines do not maintain a high degree of control over where they are assigned. In the Marine Corps, a career is much more likely to be cut short because of failure to perform within a given billet than because the officer was assigned to a less-desirable billet.

Supporting Institutional Assignments

The use of B-billets in a typical officer's career path provides the basis for supporting institutional experiences within the Marine Corps. The B-billet provides officers the opportunity to demonstrate their ability to excel in assignments where they might not be the subject-matter expert and increase their exposure to a broader set of marines. B-billet assignments are understood by promotion boards to require different leadership skills than an operational assignment within an officer's core MOS.[527] Beyond recruiting depots and basic training units, some active duty Marine Corps officers are assigned to lead reserve units for a B-billet assignment. These assignments enable the Marine Corps Reserve to benefit from active duty officer leadership and experience and increase exposure between the two components. Because active duty officers assigned to reserve units are considered within the B-billet category, the active duty officers assigned to those billets are not adversely affected by the assignment when considered for promotion.

As with operational assignments, there are no specific B-billets that predetermine an officer's pathway to GO. However, all Marine Corps officers promoted to GO are expected to have demonstrated consistent, competitive performance in B-billets and MOS-specific tours alike. While no one type of B-billet is seen as "better" than another, recruiting commands do enable officers to demonstrate their ability to meet specific targets on a monthly basis for the entirety of the two- to three-year command. As one retired Marine Corps GO noted, a recruiting battalion command can be viewed as "36 individual one-month deployments."[528] We identified one exception to this observation that B-billets are largely perceived as equal: Officers in certain MOSs (particularly those without a specific command path, such as adjutants) have reported the need to be strategic about B-billet assignments in order to present themselves as a well-rounded MAGTF officer.[529]

Broadening and Joint Assignments

Because of the Marine Corps GO's standardized, service-focused career pathway, broadening experience outside of the Marine Corps is not always valued in the service. Structurally, the assignment system limits marines from pursuing broadening experiences that might harm their

---

527 Katherine Keleher, "B-Billets Boost Marines' Careers," U.S. Marine Corps Training and Education Command, February 6, 2009.

528 Senior leader selection exercise notes, January 30, 2019, RAND Corporation, Arlington, Virginia.

529 Nicole V. Bastian, "The Problem with Becoming an Irreplaceable Marine Officer," Task and Purpose, December 9, 2015.

promotion potential or career path. However, some marines are passed over for promotion after pursuing compelling broadening experiences. Those who deviate from the standard career path and endeavor to pursue most broadening assignments generally have to work against the recommendation of their career monitor to do so. One interviewee and multiple SLSE participants noted that while individuals are given the opportunity to pursue such opportunities, they do so at the potential risk of being passed over at the next promotion board.[530] In these instances, particularly where the broadening assignment is not a joint requirement, Marine Corps officers are essentially opting out of future service while still on active duty.

When an individual is placed in a broadening billet, which is frequently joint, that the marine did not pursue specifically, it is only to meet specific needs of the Marine Corps. Therefore, the precepts specifically address this type of career pattern, and state that "the boards' evaluation of officers whose careers may have been affected by assignment policies and practices made in the best interests of the Marine Corps must afford them fair and equitable consideration."[531]

One example of a particularly valuable, nontraditional broadening assignment that the Marine Corps does prize is its congressional assignments. The Marine Corps Congressional Fellowship Program enables officers to obtain a master's degree in public policy, serve as a personal staff member on Capitol Hill for one year, and follow their congressional experience with an operational tour upon completion of the fellowship.[532] While the other services offer similar programs, the Marine Corps places a higher value on congressional assignment than other services, as reflected in their follow-on assignments and promotion potential. Marines who serve as congressional fellows as O-6s tend to follow this assignment with a prestigious regimental command, and the Marine Corps GO ranks include a number of officers who served as Congressional fellows.[533] The value the Marine Corps places on congressional fellowships underscores the importance the Marine Corps places on the ability to advocate for their priorities in Congress. While none of our interviewees identified this as a "kingmaker" position, it is the closest that we could identify to a signaling assignment for GO in the Marine Corps—but performance in that position is still of tantamount importance.

Further guidance is provided on the value of joint duty assignments in promotion board precepts. The Goldwater-Nichols Act imposed structural changes and attempted to drive cultural changes among the service to recognize the value of joint assignments, and the precept language acknowledges that Marine Corps culture may gravitate away from valuing joint service and

---

[530] M1, active duty marine O-6, July 15, 2018; senior leader selection exercise notes, January 30, 2019, RAND Corporation, Arlington, Virginia.

[531] Assistant Secretary of the Navy (Manpower and Reserve Affairs), memo to Brigadier General Kevin M. Iiams, U.S. Marine Corps (AVN), "Precept Convening the Fiscal Year 2019 U.S. Marine Corps Selection Board," August 11, 2017b, p. 5.

[532] U.S. Marine Corps, Office of Legislative Affairs, "Congressional Fellowship Program," webpage, undated.

[533] Madden, 2019, p. 120.

therefore must explicitly highlight the value of joint service in the precepts. The Marine Corps acknowledges in the precepts that the

> ability to operate effectively with the other Services is vital to our warfighting capability. . . . These assignments [are] critical for the future success of the Marine Corps, [and] may have resulted in a career pattern different from officers who have served exclusively in their primary military operational specialty (MOS).[534]

The precepts further guide that joint assignments should have the same value as similar assignments within the Marine Corps and defines their relative equivalents: Joint Staff is equal to Headquarters; U.S. Marine Corps and Combatant Commander Staff is equal to Marine Force Staff.

The Marine Corps provides MOS-specific schooling to nearly all MOSs, but three MOSs—field artillery, air defense artillery, and armor—are trained by Army schools because of resourcing constraints within the Marine Corps. Structurally, this leads to more joint training experience within those MOSs. However, joint experience in these MOSs tends to be at the training and education level, rather than the utilization or assignment level.

The typical Marine Corps GO appears to be less averse to jointness than some other services might be, which might be reinforced by the fact that joint experience, especially for senior O-6s, is viewed as a "marker of breadth."[535] Further, because marines are required to serve in B-billets that increase their exposure to marines across the service, some say that marines are more comfortable with working alongside others with different skill sets—an asset in a joint environment. Further, we also heard that, because there are so few Marine Corps GOs, the service is not opposed to filling joint positions, it just often does not have extra GOs to spare.[536]

Deployment Experience

The Marine Corps has been heavily deployed in the past two decades, and particularly between 2005 and 2010, a factor that has had notable impact on current pathways to generalship. Assignments that offer operational experience are tantamount to the Marine Corps officer career path. In the post-9/11 era, deployment experience in Iraq and particularly in Afghanistan, where the Marine Corps played a major role, provided a significant theater for operational experience. However, even before the wars in Iraq and Afghanistan, the Marine Corps had long valued overseas rotations and time "afloat" in selecting and promoting officers. The Marine Corps footprint in Okinawa, Japan, has offered opportunities for overseas experience even in eras of relative peace. Further, Marine Corps participation in embassy security has long offered opportunities for overseas experience in support of the Marine Corps mission. Combat

---

[534] Assistant Secretary of the Navy (Manpower and Reserve Affairs), 2017b, p. 4.

[535] Senior leader selection exercise notes, January 30, 2019, RAND Corporation, Arlington, Virginia.

[536] M8, official familiar with general officer management, June 25, 2019.

experience appears to be so fundamental to officer career pathways that, in some ways, it loses its distinguishability, according to observations from multiple interviews and the SLSE conducted by RAND. This might be because all infantry marines are generally deployed in roughly equal amounts, a further reflection of Marine Corps egalitarian culture and valuation of common experience.

Special Training and Education

The Marine Corps' concept of training and education is firmly rooted in its egalitarian principles, which is illustrated in the way every Marine Corps officer gains foundational knowledge through the same experience: TBS. MOS-specific and other advanced training that follows TBS later in an officer's career still reflects in the principles taught in TBS, and Marine Corps PME follows from the same core tenets as well. TBS's equalizing experience can be viewed in the Marine Corps' approach to higher education, where we observe that individual performance in intermediate- and senior-level PME do not serve as a distinguishing criterion in promotion, highlighting again the Marine Corps' prioritization of team and service above self.

The Basic School

In all other services, officers commission and generally attend their relevant career field officer basic training with only the individuals within their given MOS. Upon commissioning as O-1s, or second lieutenants, marines attend TBS. TBS is generally offered three times per year group. The TBS experience tests all marines within a given cohort against one another and generates a lineal precedence number to each graduate. The number assigned to an officer remains with them for the rest of their career, establishing seniority for promotion to each successive grade. Officer performance is compared across the three classes within a given year group, so that the top performer of each of the TBS classes is guaranteed to be in the top three of their year group (and so on).[537] Officer performance in TBS determines MOS assignments; after TBS, Marine Corps officers are then tested once again upon attendance at the appropriate school(s) for their MOS.

TBS provides a few frames of reference that stick with marines throughout their careers. First, it feeds into the ethos of "every marine a rifleman," as TBS emphasizes small group tactics. It therefore fuels a combined arms training lens for all marines; those who stay in the ground forces/infantry, and those who separate out to aviation and logistics. Additionally, it adds to the egalitarian nature across career fields. Every Marine Corps officer started on an equal footing with their counterparts in the other MOSs.

---

[537] Michael S. Holt, *Evolution of the Marine Corps Officer Promotion System: A Re-Evaluation of the Current Marine Corps Officer Promotion System*, Quantico, Va.: Marine Corps University, 2005.

Professional Military Education

In general, PME is largely viewed as a requirement, not a differentiator. Expeditionary Warfare School (EWS), previously referred to as Amphibious Warfare School, is the Marine Corps' PME for company-grade Marine Corps officers. Officers typically attend EWS as senior O-3s. EWS focuses on six core courses: Profession of Arms, Warfighting, MAGTF Operations Ashore, MAGTF Operations Afloat, Future Operating Environment, and Occupational Field Expansion Course.[538] In-residence students spend 41 weeks at Quantico. The program is also offered via distance; distance students are allowed up to three years to complete the program.[539] The Marine Corps offers weekday, weekend, online, and blended seminars in order to facilitate completion.

While an officer must complete EWS for promotion and future assignments, the Marine Corps places less emphasis on the distinction between in-residence and distance education for the purposes of promotions and assignments.[540] Moreover, boards examine whether a Marine Corps officer completes their mandatory PME at the appointed time in their career, but boards place little emphasis on performance rankings within a given course. Individual profile selections in the SLSE reflected that the policy aligns with cultural preferences: Of the top ten profiles selected, five represented Marine Corps officers who completed EWS in residence, and five profiles represented Marine Corps officers who attended EWS via distance education.[541] Of note, the top performer is recorded as a distinguished graduate, but that designation is not a major factor in board decisions.

As senior O-4s, Marine Corps officers attend the Marine Command and Staff College (CSC). During CSC, Marine Corps officers prepare for joint operations, focusing on the theory and nature of war, national and international security studies, operational art, joint warfighting, small wars, MAGTF expeditionary operations, amphibious operations, and operations planning.[542] The in-residence program takes place over the course of ten months at Quantico. Twenty percent of each O-4 cohort attends CSC in-residence.[543] Because of operational demands and the small number of individuals who attend CSC in-residence, the Marine Corps developed a robust distance education program in order to meet the JPME requirements. The distance program takes place over the course of a year, providing two resident seminar periods (five weeks and six weeks, respectively) at the beginning and end of the program and three nine- to 11-week online

---

538 Marine Corps University, "Expeditionary Warfare School," webpage, undated.

539 Marine Corps University, "Expeditionary Warfare School Distance Education Program," webpage, undated.

540 Marine Corps Order 1553.4B, *Professional Military Education*, Washington, D.C.: Headquarters Marine Corps, January 25, 2008, p. 3.

541 Senior leader selection exercise notes, January 30, 2019, RAND Corporation, Arlington, Virginia.

542 Gina Douthit, "Command and Staff College Distance Education Program," *DISAM Journal*, September 2008, p. 9.

543 Douthit, 2008, p. 1.

seminars in between. Similar to EWS, both Marine Corps policy and culture do not make a distinction between officers who attend CSC in-residence or via distance, and completion of the course—rather than an individual officer's ranking within the course—matters most in promotion board considerations. CSC provides class rankings and further designates up to 20 percent of a graduating class as "distinguished graduates," a designation reported on an officer's Fitness Report (FitRep).[544] While promotion boards consider the distinction is as a positive attribute, a "distinguished graduate" designation does not carry as much weight as performance in command when boards consider candidates for GO.[545]

Senior Service College

Senior service college matters to marines, who have their own Marine Corps War College at Marine Corps Base Quantico. Each year, a small number also attend senior service college at the Army, Naval, and Air War colleges. While senior service college does matter, it does not necessarily launch a Marine Corps officer's career trajectory toward GO; instead, it fulfills a requirement. It is a necessary but not sufficient indicator of future leadership. While some services may value senior service college fellowships at think tanks or within government departments (equivalent to war college attendance), the Marine Corps views these opportunities as just another way to fulfill the senior PME requirement. Attendance at a sister service PME program appears to afford the same weight as the Marine Corps War College.

In 2006, a Marine Corps University study sought to elevate the role of PME, including senior service college, in an officer's candidate file.[546] The study requested that the Commandant issue a formal statement to "elevate the importance of PME within the institution and place it on an equal or higher plane with other priorities such as physical conditioning."[547] The study further advocated a change in the culture of placement in in-residence programs, assigning the most competitive officers to in-residence programs and training manpower managers to select competitive individuals rather than those who are "easiest to move" or "need breaks."[548] In the intervening years, the weight of in-residence senior service college attendance has seemed to increase when evaluating an officer's competitiveness in promotion to O-7.

---

[544] Marine Corps University, *Student Handbook*, Quantico, Va., February 7, 2017, p. 26; Interview M8, June 25, 2019.

[545] Interview M8, June 25, 2019; senior leader selection exercise notes, January 30, 2019, RAND Corporation, Arlington, Virginia.

[546] Charles E. Wilhelm, Wallace C. Gregson, Jr., Bruce B. Knutson, Jr., Paul K. Van Riper, Andrew F. Krepinevich, and Williamson Murray, *U.S. Marine Corps Officer Professional Military Education 2006 Study and Findings*, Quantico, Va.: Marine Corps University, PCN 50100121000, 2006, p. 3.

[547] Wilhelm et al., 2006, p. 3.

[548] Wilhelm et al., 2006, p. 16.

Graduate Education

As a result of the requirements-driven assignments process, graduate school must be tied to a specific job requirement within the Marine Corps, and few assignments require one. Therefore, marines—less than members in any other service—rarely pursue a graduate degree for any sort of broadening experience.

A graduate degree attained on an officer's own time (nights and weekends) is acknowledged in their promotion file but does not afford the officer an advantage during a promotion board. As noted by one retired marine, "General Mattis never received a graduate degree," referring to retired Marine Corps Commandant and former Secretary of Defense James Mattis and implying that success in the Marine Corps does not rely on advanced education.[549] Marines who do achieve graduate degrees through full-time programs might even be penalized in a promotion board, as the pursuit indicates time out of the fleet and away from the task that matters most: leading marines.

The rote career path provides stability and a sense of promotion predictability for those willing to stay on the career path but leaves less ability for individuals to pursue skill sets that might help the Marine Corps in the long run. Indeed, the inability to pursue graduate education until late in a typical Marine Corps officer's career might harm retention.

Evaluations

As discussed previously, the Marine Corps' formal evaluation system begins early in an officer's career, whether in the competitive Marine Corps commissioning process from USNA, NROTC, OCS, or PLC. After commissioning, Marine Corps officers are then evaluated against one another during TBS, where they are assigned a ranking in the OML relative to all other marines in their year group. The competitive nature of the evaluation system persists throughout a marine's career, which must be balanced with the Marine Corps values that place service and team above self.

At each grade, Marine Corps officers are formally evaluated annually in their FitReps. FitReps enable promotion boards to evaluate the best-qualified individuals for future promotions. The reports are intended to capture "performance of assigned duties and responsibilities against an understood set of requirements, individual capacity, and professional character."[550] The key concepts guiding FitRep completion include fairness, focus, measurement, ethics, "avoiding zero defects," and counseling.[551] The emphasis on "avoiding zero defects" admonishes reporting officials to consider that "Marines develop by having the latitude to make mistakes," and reflects a certain cultural attitude toward encouraging "initiative, aggressiveness, creativity, courage, and

---

[549] Senior leader selection exercise notes, January 30, 2019, RAND Corporation, Arlington, Virginia.

[550] Marine Corps Order 1610.7, *Performance Evaluation System*, Washington, D.C.: Headquarters Marine Corps, February 13, 2015.

[551] Marine Corps Order 1610.7, 2015.

development of warfighting skills."[552] The words within a FitRep matter, though the Marine Corps "does not value 'Shakespeares'"; a strong file provides succinct evidence of superior performance.[553]

The FitRep form itself (USMC Fitness Report 1610/NAVMC 10835) is a five-page document. Among other administrative data collected on the first page is a subsection for special information, including weight, body fat, and performance on the physical fitness test, indicating the significance given to physical fitness and appearance. The Marine Corps officer is rated on their performance on mission accomplishment, individual character (including courage, effectiveness under stress, and initiative), leadership (defined by ability to lead and develop subordinates, set an example as a model marine, ensure the well-being of subordinates, and communication skills), and intellect and wisdom (defined by performance in PME, decisionmaking ability, and judgment).[554] Each metric is evaluated on a seven-point scale ranging from A to G, where "A" is the lowest, "G" is the highest, and "H" is reserved for no observation.[555]

Officers are evaluated by a reporting senior (RS), the boss of the marine reported on, and a reviewing officer, who is the reporting senior's boss. FitReps are maintained and tracked within the Headquarters Marine Corps Personnel Management Support Branch, who generates a relative value (RV) for each RS. The RV provides an average of all FitReps completed by the RS for marines of the same grade (in that year, and over time), providing context to evaluate how tough the reporting senior grades their subordinates.[556] The weighting system is intended to balance out inconsistent patterns between evaluators and aims to ensure equitable comparisons based on merit across all marines of the same rank.

Promotion Boards

In the Marine Corps, promotions are used to signal accomplishment in the key billet required of the previous grade. As referenced previously, key command billets at the O-3, O-5, and O-6 grades play a key role in promotion consideration, in addition to a key staff assignment (primarily a battalion executive officer or operations officer) at the O-4 grade. However, as noted earlier, the specific assignment does not necessarily serve as a discriminator, given that O-4s serve as either a battalion executive officer or operations officer as a developmental assignment

---

[552] Marine Corps Order 1610.7, 2015.

[553] Senior leader selection exercise notes, January 30, 2019, RAND Corporation, Arlington, Virginia.

[554] While the FitRep specifically lists "performance in PME" as a metric by which Marine Corps officers are evaluated, exercise participants indicate that completion of mandatory PME at the appointed time in an officers' career path is what matters for promotion. Senior leader selection exercise notes, January 30, 2019, RAND Corporation, Arlington, Virginia.

[555] U.S. Marine Corps Fitness Report (1610), "Commandant's Guidance," NAVMC 10385, revised July 2011.

[556] U.S. Marine Corps Training Command, "Fitness Reports I," in *Fitness Reports B3K3738 Student Handout*, Basic Officer Course student handout, Camp Barrett, Va., undated, p. 6.

and thus have very similar assignment histories. Performance in B-billets is also taken into consideration, particularly as these assignments demonstrate leadership ability when officers are out of their subject-matter expertise and comfort zone. These positions, including assignments in recruitment depots or basic training units, rely less on an officer's specific operational area of expertise and more on their ability to develop, compel, mentor, and lead subordinates within the Marine Corps. Other requirements, particularly PME, are viewed more as a "box to check" rather than a key performance consideration within a promotion package.[557] Ratings related to PME are included in officer evaluations, but SLSE participants noted that this is largely to record the data, rather than influence promotion decisions.

Because the Marine Corps evaluates nearly all URL officers in one competitive category, aviators, infantrymen, and logistics/combat service support officers compete with one another for promotion opportunities, and the promotion system does not necessarily use promotion boards to reinforce specific career fields. The promotion system winnows the officer corps to promote competitive marines, rather than competitive aviators, infantrymen, tankers, or other specific MOSs.

To prevent skewing the percentage of those selected for promotion toward one MOS at the expense of another, Marine Corps promotion boards are composed of (relatively) equal representation among ground, support, and aviation officers. In practice, however, the Marine Corps officer corps is imbalanced among MOSs. For example, infantry officers typically promote at a higher rate than supply officers, and public affairs officers become increasingly underrepresented as a cohort promotes through the ranks of O-4 through O-6, largely because there is less need for that type of MOS at more senior levels. Figure 7.5 depicts overall promotion rates by career category by grade, and Figure 7.6 shows the breakdown of promotion rates by both grade and career type. As in other services, promotion rates from O-6 to O-7 are lowest compared with any other promotion, but infantry officers tend to be promoted to O-7 (and beyond) at higher rates than other career fields.

[557] Senior leader selection exercise notes, January 30, 2019, RAND Corporation, Arlington, Virginia.

Figure 7.5. Percentage of Marine Corps Officers Who Promote to the Next Grade, 2000–2010 Officer Cohorts

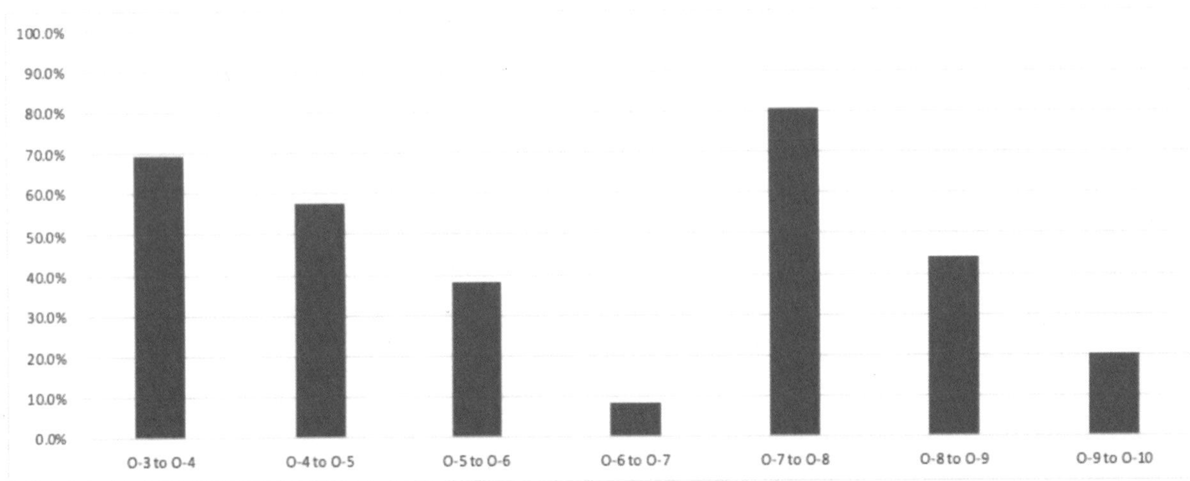

Source: Authors' analysis of DMDC data.
Note: These numbers represent the average progression rate for the 11 (overlapping) cohorts of Marine Corps officers present in each grade at the beginning of each year from 2000 to 2010, and reflect these officers' observed rates of reaching the next higher grade at any point up to the beginning of 2018, the last year for which we have data.

Figure 7.6. Percentage of Marine Corps Officers Who Promote to the Next Grade, by Grade and Career Type, 2000–2010 Officer Cohorts

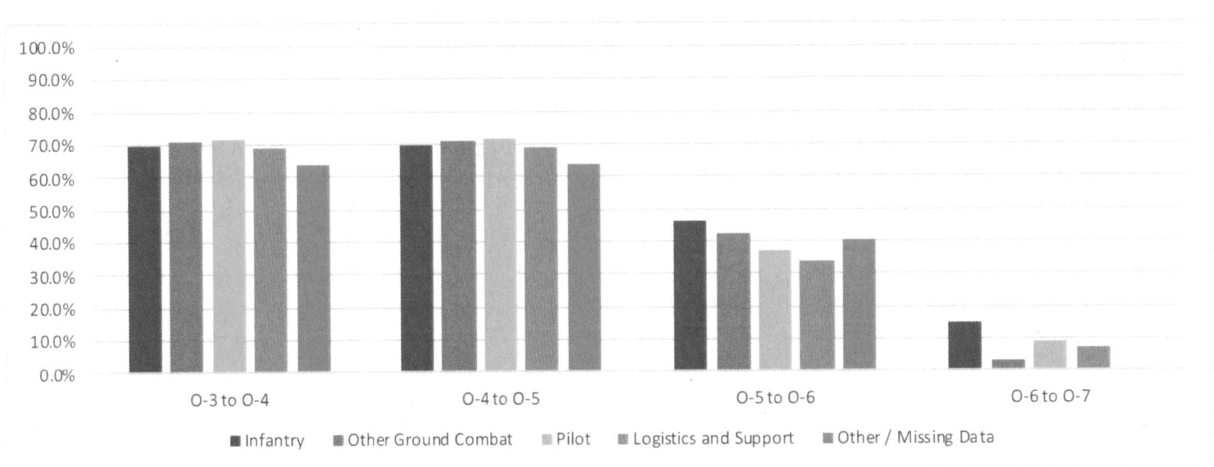

SOURCE: Authors' analysis of DMDC data.
NOTE: These numbers represent the average progression rate for the 11 (overlapping) cohorts of Marine Corps officers present in each grade at the beginning of each year from 2000 to 2010, and reflect these officers' observed rates of reaching the next higher grade at any point up to the beginning of 2018, the last year for which we have data. Officers are categorized by type using the primary service occupation codes assigned to each officer in any given year. When a Marine Corps officer is promoted to O-6, they are often assigned a generic senior officer primary occupation code. To correct for this, officers at the ranks of O-6 to O-10 are categorized by type using the last meaningful, nongeneric, primary service occupation code assigned to them as O-5s.

Rather than quotas, Marine Corps board precepts provide "skill guidance," or data on the percentage that the Marine Corps is currently short of a critical skill in a given grade. This guidance informs (but does not necessarily compel) a board to consider how the distribution of promotion rates from all MOSs might benefit the Marine Corps as a whole. The precepts still emphasize the need to select officers who are "best and fully qualified," but they ask the board to give "due consideration to the needs of the Marine Corps for officers with particular skills." The data can inform board decisionmaking if the strengths of two files are particularly similar but one officer provides a critical skill that the other may not have. In the FY 2018 O-7 promotion board, desired critical skills included the emerging field of unmanned aerial systems, public affairs, and acquisitions.[558] Since financial management officers are considered in their own competitive category, the board precepts include a maximum number of authorized promotions for that career field.[559]

Marine Corps board precepts also reinforce the centralized nature of the assignments process. The 2017 precepts for those individuals considered for promotion to O-5 in FY 2019 explicitly stated,

> The Marine Corps has not established an expected or preferred career pattern. . . . In your deliberations, you should consider that assignments are made in the best interests of the Marine Corps. Officers rarely have direct influence over their assignments.[560]

One critique of the precepts is that they end up prioritizing too many characteristics, in some ways rendering the guidance overwhelming or confusing. In the words of one interviewee, "If everything matters, nothing matters."[561]

Marine Corps promotion boards evaluate the strength of an officer's Official Military Personnel File (OMPF), which consists of the officer's service folder, commendatory/derogatory folder, and performance folder. The service folder largely captures administrative data used to determine time in service. The commendatory/derogatory folder tracks awards, education (military and civilian), court-martial information (if necessary), and "other material reflecting significant personal achievement or adversity." The performance folder contains FitReps. OMPFs are distributed to the board one week prior to a board convening.[562] As stated previously, Marine Corps boards value the official photo as a necessary part of the OMPF. If an officer does

---

[558] Assistant Secretary of the Navy (Manpower and Reserve Affairs), memo to Brigadier General Kevin M. Iiams, USMC (AVN), "Precept Convening the Fiscal Year 2019 U.S. Marine Corps Regular Unrestricted Lieutenant Colonel Promotion Selection Board, Regular Unrestricted Major Continuation Selection Board, Financial Management Lieutenant Colonel Promotion Selection Board, and Financial Management Major Continuation Selection Board," August 1, 2017a, p. 4.

[559] Assistant Secretary of the Navy (Manpower and Reserve Affairs), 2017b, p. 3.

[560] Assistant Secretary of the Navy (Manpower and Reserve Affairs), 2017b, p. 4.

[561] M7, active duty Marine Colonel, September 5, 2018.

[562] MARADMIN 196/18, *FY20 U.S. Marine Corps Officer Promotion Selection Boards*, Washington, D.C.: Headquarters Marine Corps, April 5, 2018.

not submit a current official photo, it signals to the board that the officer does not wish to be considered for promotion during the board convening.

Marine Corps officers are only promoted to the next grade after submitting a FitRep observing their performance in a key billet, which is typically marked by command billet (at the O-3 company command level) or a specific staff assignment (such as a battalion executive officer or operations officer at the O-4 grade).[563] Further, because all officers share the same career cycles and trajectories, it is easier to compare "like jobs to like jobs."[564] Because all Marine Corps officers structurally cycle between operating force positions and B-billets, no one officer is at a disadvantage in a promotion board for taking a B-billet assignment in due course. Additionally, there are no incentives for individual officers to pursue two subsequent key assignments at the expense of a B-billet assignment.

Certain factors appear to have an outsized influence on whether a marine will eventually be promoted to O-7. An officer's position on the lineal OML attained at TBS remains with an officer for the remainder of their career. While more data are necessary to determine the rate at which distinguished graduates go on to become GOs nearly 20 years later, it is highly likely that TBS performance correlates with future promotion.

Of particular importance to Marine Corps promotion boards is command experience. As noted previously, operational experience, particularly in combat roles, is highly regarded in the Marine Corps, and any marine who has not spent a substantial amount of time deployed in the past 18 years is generally less favorably considered for promotion. Attainment of and performance in command roles, combined with significant deployment time, are clear differentiating factors in promotion to O-7, according to SLSE participants.[565] Our review of Marine Corps GO biographies confirmed the observations from the exercise and from multiple interviewees: Command and operational experience features strongly throughout nearly all Marine Corps GOs' backgrounds.

The Minimal Influence of Personal Networks

In the Marine Corps, the egalitarian nature of the personnel management system dissuades against any one senior officer having the power to identify and groom certain individuals for a future role as a GO. Whereas other services value high-level endorsements from GOs, "A letter from the Commandant himself wouldn't carry a lot of weight in a Marine Corps promotion board."[566] Further, the typical officer career path—in which officers cycle through operational force tours and institutional support tours—decreases the likelihood that individual officers will

---

[563] Chad A. Buckel, "The Infantry Career Path: A Case for Changes," *Marine Corps Gazette*, Vol. 102, No. 2, February 2018.

[564] Senior leader selection exercise notes, January 30, 2019, RAND Corporation, Arlington, Virginia.

[565] Senior leader selection exercise notes, January 30, 2019, RAND Corporation, Arlington, Virginia.

[566] Senior leader selection exercise notes, January 30, 2019, RAND Corporation, Arlington, Virginia.

serve under the same superior for multiple assignments. Additionally, the network effects afforded to academy graduates in other services is not as prevalent in the Marine Corps; as stated previously, the Marine Corps GO corps more equitably represents officers who commissioned from ROTC, OCS, and the USNA. According to one retired Marine Corps GO, "Being a ring-knocker [academy graduate] might get you ahead in the Navy, but we don't do that in the Marine Corps."[567]

The locus of Marine Corps networks and influence is Quantico. Since all Marine Corps officers attend TBS at Quantico, all Marine Corps officers in a given cohort are assigned to the same location within the same network at the same time. Further, many attend Amphibious Warfare School (intermediate PME) and/or the Marine War College (senior service PME) in Quantico. These universal and near-universal experiences within the same cohort might further serve to minimize potential network effects on propensity to become a GO, though it is possible that superior officers are able to use these common experiences as a means to assess an officer's leadership skills against their peers.

Special Board: The Career Designation Board

Beginning in 2010, the Marine Corps re-instituted the CDB, held for all Marine Corps officers after 540 days of observed time after completing their MOS school.[568] Today, the CDB is intended to ensure that the service retains only the most competitive officers. The timing of the CDB allows the Marine Corps to have a significant observable period of the officer's performance and enables individual officers to demonstrate their leadership ability and technical proficiency. CDBs evaluate marines in five competitive categories: Combat Arms, Combat Service Support, Aviation Ground, Aviation Air, and Law.[569] The Manpower Management Officers Assignments office evaluates the current strength of each category and sets CDB target percentages for each competitive category in order to meet the requirement. Between 2010 and 2013, the CDB reduced the number of marines considered by nearly 30 percent, from 6,732 to 4,723.[570] The highly competitive nature of the CDB ensures that by the time a cohort reaches the

---

[567] Senior leader selection exercise notes, January 30, 2019, RAND Corporation, Arlington, Virginia.

[568] The CDB is used as a force shaping tool, enabling the Marine Corps to reduce the number of officers to meet manpower requirements. The Marine Corps had the authority to implement a CDB prior to 2010, but the need to expand the number of Marine Corps officers during the wars in Iraq and Afghanistan and high officer attrition trends in the 1990s rendered the force-shaping tool unnecessary. Marine Corps policy therefore allowed for all fully qualified officers to promote to the next higher grade. As a result of sufficient officer accession and retention in the post-9/11 era and end strength reductions occurring at the end of the official wars in Iraq and Afghanistan, the Marine Corps returned to a competitive CDB as a force shaping tool. See Raul P. Garza, *United States Marine Corps Career Designation Board: Significant Factors in Predicting Selection*, Monterey, Calif.: Naval Postgraduate School, 2014, p. 1.

[569] Garza, 2014, p. 9.

[570] Garza, 2014, p. v.

O-4 promotion board, its members have been thoroughly tested and vetted for expanded rank and responsibility.

The CDB is further meant to ensure that the Marine Corps "keeps faith" with those officers not selected for retention. The Marine Corps holds a belief that it would be unfair to keep a marine who is unlikely to promote to O-4 until after the ten-year mark, at which point the officer would have invested a significant amount of time in service to the Marine Corps but would have no access to retirement benefits, according to one of our interviewees.[571] Individuals who are not selected as career designees are therefore released from their service early enough in their careers to transfer their skills beyond the Marine Corps.

Other Factors That Matter in Marine Corps General Officer Selection

Aside from those detailed in the analysis of the Marine Corps' formal personnel management processes, other factors influence an officer's likelihood to be promoted to O-7. Some in the Marine Corps say that the distinction between most marine O-6s and those who make O-7 is simply the promotion itself. One interviewee told us that he overheard a three-star Marine Corps GO comment that he could fill, then crash, a C-130 filled with new marine O-7s, and repeat the process seven times with new waves of marine O-7s, before seeing a discernible difference in officer quality.[572] Further, SLSE participants reported that when a Marine Corps officer is promoted to the grade of O-7, they receive letters from other Marine Corps GOs including advice and a reminder that the distinction could just as easily been afforded to ten of their colleagues, and to take the responsibility of the rank seriously and humbly.[573] This not only underscores the Marine Corps' egalitarian culture, but points to the existence of less tangible, or even arbitrary, factors that can affect who becomes an O-7 in the Marine Corps.

Personality and Physical Characteristics

While all services offer potential officers a higher calling and the ability to test themselves physically and emotionally, the Marine Corps markets an extreme version of austerity and overcoming hardship. The question posed to Marine Corps recruits is "Do you have what it takes to be a Marine?" not "What can the Marine Corps do for you?" This messaging of eliteness helps to reinforce Marine Corps cultural values from the outset, as it likely attracts a specific subset of individuals interested in military service that has bearing on the ultimate makeup of the Marine Corps officer corps.

---

[571] M1, active duty marine O-6, July 15, 2018. It is worth noting that reforms to service member retirement benefits as a result to the Blended Retirement System (BRS), in which individuals will receive a 401k-type retirement benefit before 20 years of service, may affect the decision calculus in the future.

[572] M91, active duty field-grade officer, February 22, 2019.

[573] Senior leader selection exercise notes, January 30, 2019, RAND Corporation, Arlington, Virginia.

The centrally managed, prescribed pathway of the Marine Corps officer personnel management system tends to appeal more to individuals who are more comfortable with rule-following and who believe in the benevolence of organizational and institutional decisionmaking. Marine Corps culture therefore produces a paradox: Marine Corps officers are risk-takers in matters of physical performance and warfighting, but they tend to be risk-averse and resistant to change in matters of institutional management, as is evident in the Marine Corps' resistance to allowing women to serve in combat roles and to adopting some of the authorized personnel management changes in the FY 2019 NDAA.

Further, Marine Corps officers, perhaps more than those in other services, place a high value on professional and personal appearance. The Marine Corps publication *Leading Marines* ties physical appearance to combat effectiveness: "A Marine's professional appearance—backed by our formidable reputation—instills fear in our enemies and confidence in those we protect."[574] Physical appearance—whether marked by fitness, hygiene, or uniform presentation—serves as an external indicator of a marine's commitment to discipline.

Indistinguishable Career Experiences

Given the emphasis on performance at every echelon and the role of the career designation board at O-3, the Marine Corps loses competitive talent both through those it passes over for promotion and those who choose to leave the service. As stipulated in DOPMA, the maximum promotion rate from O-3 to O-4 (after passing the career designation board) is 80 percent; the promotion rate from O-4 to O-5 is 70 percent; and the promotion rate from O-5 to O-6 is 50 percent.[575] Therefore, many of those passed over for promotion at each subsequent level might still be high performers, who were identified at around five years of service as competitive marines. Moreover, the relative uniformity of experience across the entire officer corps, regardless of MOS, further makes it difficult to distinguish one high performer's record from another's. One interviewee, a former O-5 who performed well at every echelon, was passed over for promotion on his first look in the O-6 board. Upon being passed over, the officer volunteered for a deployment on a Special Purpose MAGTF in order to distinguish his file for his above-the-zone board the following year. The officer was then passed over a second time. In an interview, the officer indicated that while he was disappointed in the outcome, he also understood that every O-5 who was promoted to O-6 was promoted because they, too, were competitive. Even if he may have been more qualified than some of his peers, the difference was that he was "99.5 percent of the standard, while they were 99.4 percent of the standard. And really, to the Marine Corps, what is the difference?"[576]

---

[574] MCWP 6-11, 2014.

[575] Public Law 96-513, Defense Officer Personnel Management Act, December 12, 1980.

[576] M3, former Marine O-5, September 4, 2018.

Factors in Selecting Out

The Marine Corps also loses potential future GOs when they choose to leave of their own volition, and generally due to their own frustrations with the current personnel system. Given the more prescriptive nature of career paths in the Marine Corps, the lack of broadening opportunities outside the service and the lack of ability to pursue a graduate degree frustrate some high performers.[577] In particular, some Marine Corps officers leave after approximately ten to 12 years of service to pursue graduate degrees.[578] The Marine Corps commitment to linking graduate school to a specific requirement provides less flexibility than the other services, and generally sets the conditions such that Marine Corps officers are unable to attend graduate school until post-battalion-level command, or at the point of approximately 17–18 years of service.[579]

Summary

The Marine Corps' deeply egalitarian, tradition-based culture is readily observed in the service's personnel processes and typical pathways to O-7. Service-wide adherence to these common values tends to produce officers who are committed to upholding and maintaining the existing culture and who value discipline, the importance in abiding by established rules, and following orders.

Given the MAGTF structure and how Marine Corps personnel management systems stress the "every marine a rifleman" culture, the Marine Corps' career fields are fairly evenly represented in the GO corps at the O-7 rank, but infantry and aviation career fields tend to dominate as GO grades increase. Because of, and contributing to, this roughly equal distribution of MOSs in the GO corps, marines across MOSs share largely uniform career paths.

However, it is not necessarily the case that this representation across different MOSs means that diverse viewpoints characterize the Marine Corps GO cadre. Given the universal training that every marine receives through TBS, the small size of the force, and the Marine Corps' deliberately reinforced egalitarian culture, we found that many Marine Corps GOs share similar career experiences and appear to espouse similar leadership philosophies, regardless of career field.

Whereas service academy graduates are strongly represented in the G/FO corps of the other services, Marine Corps GOs largely come from OCS, given the high proportion of officers who commission through that source. NROTC graduates make up ground proportionally in the GO grades, while USNA graduates become GOs at roughly in proportion with their commissioning rates. In PME, marines are expected to fulfill the joint education requirements, but performance in those schools is not a factor in promotion decisions, which further reflects the Marine Corps'

---

[577] M1, active duty Marine O-6, July 15, 2018.

[578] David Barno and Nora Bensahel, "Can the U.S. Military Halt Its Brain Drain?" *The Atlantic,* November 5, 2015.

[579] Barno and Bensahel, 2015.

egalitarian culture. Graduate degrees can even hurt a marine's chances at promotion, as they are viewed as time away from leading marines. Deployments appear to be highly valued in O-7 promotion decisions, both because of the warfighting emphasis in Marine Corps culture and the egalitarian principle that all marines must contribute to the fight. Further, while the Marine Corps remains service-centric in many of its career assignments, it appears to be less averse institutionally to the concept of jointness as other services can be, perhaps in part because the small size of the force fosters reliance on other service capabilities.

Marine Corps GOs are, on average, older than their counterparts from other services. Additional years in service can bring additional experiences and potentially wisdom to a position; on the other hand, this average age difference might explain, or exacerbate, marine tendencies to be resistant to change. Because senior marines tend to have more years of experience than their counterparts in joint, OSD, and interagency assignments, there is a belief among marines that Marine Corps officers take on leadership roles naturally among their cross-service peers within joint assignments.[580]

At senior levels, positions on the NSC, on civilian staffs in OSD or the Department of the Navy, and joint positions (particularly aides to three- and four-star G/FOs) are seen as opportunities to demonstrate the value of the individual Marine Corps officer and the service as a whole—providing the "face of the Marine Corps" at strategic levels. Congressional fellowships are particularly valued among field-grade officer assignments, as those positions enable the Marine Corps to continue to foster strong relationships with Capitol Hill.

Finally, Marine Corps officers' performance in particular positions is of utmost importance when being considered for promotion. There are very few "kingmaker" positions, and officers are judged based on performance in a given assignment, rather than by strength of one's network or previous positions held. How these shared experiences and values observed in the typical Marine Corps pathways to GO might shape future Marine Corps officers' approaches to strategic-level advice and institutional leadership will be explored in Chapter 8.

---

[580] Senior leader selection exercise notes, January 30, 2019, RAND Corporation, Arlington, Virginia.

8. How General and Flag Officer Archetypes Might Advise and Lead

In the preceding chapters, we analyzed how the military services approach development and selection of G/FOs, and we identified, for each service, what career experiences and other characteristics are typical in many G/FOs as a result of those approaches and other related aspects, such as service culture. These factors likely help shape the advice that senior military officers provide to civilian officials, and the ways G/FOs lead and manage defense institutions. Ultimately, these factors might have significant impacts on how DoD responds to emerging threats and changes to the global strategic environment.

In this final chapter, we summarize common experiences, characteristics, and other trends we observed across each of the services' G/FOs, present G/FO archetypes for each service, and explain what the attributes of these archetypes might mean for the type of advice archetypical G/FOs provide, and the way they might approach leading organizations.

Archetypes are notional profiles that reflect the characteristics that are most consistently replicated among G/FOs in each service that we identified throughout the course of our research. The archetypes are not intended to be representative of all G/FOs within a particular service. Further, the archetypes are not intended to perfectly predict future trends. Rather, our research indicates that if status quo processes remain in place, future G/FO skills, traits, and experiences are likely to strongly resemble current G/FOs, particularly because the G/FOs of the future are already being developed and selected today.

We did not aim to be predictive, nor do we claim that our assessments of each of the service personnel management processes and cultural influences are fully explanatory of who is promoted to O-7 in any service. Much of the analysis in this chapter is based on our assumptions outlined in Chapter 2 and heavily informed by common themes within the literature, the data, our interviews, and the SLSE, captured throughout this report.

As noted in Chapter 2, we assumed that the way an officer is trained, educated, and gains experience through a service's personnel management system will be reflected in their approaches to leadership, management, and advice when they become a G/FO; that officers are shaped in their service's desired skills, traits, attributes, and experiences through personnel management systems and requirements, and also by observing the characteristics of those selected for G/FO; that officers are provided with the necessary training and education to succeed within their service and career field, but that intangible factors (and the assignment to specific career fields themselves) influence officers' potential for selection to G/FO; and that characteristics we observe to be consistently replicated provide information regarding a service G/FO's potential strengths and weaknesses.[581]

We did not attempt to quantify the amount of influence that professional experiences and other characteristics have on a G/FO's advice or approach to leadership and management, and, accordingly, we do not make claims about the degree of influence that any single factor might have. The hypotheses about approaches to leadership, management, and advice follow logically from the service profiles we identified, but the hypotheses were not empirically tested, as we did not have the data with which to do so. Further, we understand that a multitude of factors not captured in this report influence and shape senior military leaders' worldviews, strategic aptitudes, and approaches to institutional leadership and strategic-level advice. However, the findings from our qualitative and quantitative data analyses captured throughout the course of our research highlight certain patterns in the services' approaches to developing officers, patterns which are useful for senior civilian leaders to understand.

Service-Common Observations

Overall, we found that while the services each rely on certain career management processes mandated by law and shaped centrally by DoD, each of the service's unique cultures, missions, and institutional preferences work to create different incentives and rewards for specific innate or developed traits, career experiences, and other attributes. Despite these differences across the services, we did find several commonalities that define officer career development and selection in the Army, Navy, Air Force, and Marine Corps. That some commonalities exist is expected: After all, the services all support the same overarching U.S. national security goals, are subject to the same officer career management laws, and work in the same joint organizational structures. The following list summarizes these relevant commonalities among service personnel processes and the types of experiences and other characteristics that enhance an officer's promotability:

- **The value of command is universal.** Regardless of service, time and successful performance in command (particularly at the O-5 and O-6 grades) consistently serves as the chief signal to promotion boards that an officer is proficient in their specialty and has potential to excel at higher levels. Of course, this signaling is not exclusive to promotion boards; it can affect how peers and seniors view an officer as well—potentially affecting an officer's networks, evaluations, assignments, and more. Many career fields throughout the military do not offer command opportunities, so those officers are not evaluated on the same criteria—but, demonstrating the value the military overall places on command,

[581] Examples we highlighted in Chapter 2 include the following: We assume that a lack of training in and exposure to strategic analysis could mean that a G/FO's advice would not rely heavily on strategic analysis; that tactical training (and selection for promotion based on tactical performance) might lead to an officer being more likely to rely on tactical solutions, even beyond the tactical level; and that few or no assignments in civilian environments and/or nonservice assignments might lead to officers who are either initially uncomfortable or underprepared when the officer arrives at an interagency, policy, and/or civilian organization.

the vast majority of senior-most G/FO positions are filled by officers whose career fields do feature successful command assignments.

- **"Ducks pick ducks."** We were unable to obtain data on exact compositions and backgrounds of promotion board members in order to compare them with the backgrounds of the candidates they ultimately chose for promotion. But we heard repeatedly from interviewees in each service that there is a tendency for promotion boards to select officers whose career experiences are comparable to their own, and for senior officers to select officers with backgrounds similar to theirs for aide jobs, positions that serve as a signal of O-7 potential to board members and can provide access to powerful networks of G/FOs. We also observed this trend in the SLSE. The notion of "ducks picking ducks" serves to cyclically reinforce service culture by perpetuating the selection of officers who similarly reflect service goals and preferences. As far back as World War II, Morris Janowitz wrote about the propensity of senior military leaders to fill their staff roles (e.g., military assistant or executive officer) with people who could "speak the same language."[582] However, this observation does not mean that the officers who are selected for promotion by similar, more senior officers are necessarily less qualified; it is possible that the "ducks pick ducks" tendency in some cases occurs because well-qualified officers sitting on promotion boards are selecting for other well-qualified officers.
- **Many officers become O-7s with narrow, mostly service-specific experience.** Partly because of demanding career path timelines that do not afford future G/FOs ample time to pursue joint and broadening assignments, officers across the services tend to have mostly tactical or operational, service-specific experience, and relatively little joint or strategic experience. Further, we heard repeatedly from officers with promotion board experience that assignments outside of one's service or specialty are often looked upon less favorably. The narrow focus of these officer career paths means that many officers who become O-7s likely lack expertise in policy, strategic planning, budgeting, programming, and, significantly, working with other services and civilian organizations, such as OSD and the State Department. This can contribute to another observation many interviewees relayed to us: that strategic-level experience—frequently gained from broadening and joint positions—is more often acquired "on the job," after an officer becomes a G/FO.
- **Personnel systems discourage risk-taking in career management choices and in professional performance.** High-quality evaluations are critical in promotion decisions for officers across the services, and failure resulting from taking risks might not reflect well in an evaluation, even if those risks are innovative and forward-thinking. Because officers are rated in comparison to other officers (who might not have taken similar risks), even small failures might negatively affect one's prospects for promotion. Further, officers who want to promote might be less likely to take risks in pursuing unusual assignments for their career path. Together with the services' tendency for senior officers to select junior officers for promotion who are similar to themselves, the inclination to avoid risk-taking can drive even more similarities—likely across several dimensions—among G/FOs within each service.

---

[582] Danskine, 2001, p. 102.

Factors with Difficult-to-Measure Effects Also Influence Genera/Flag Officer Pathways

Some factors that influence how an officer becomes a G/FO are substantially challenging to isolate and characterize but are no doubt important—and potentially decisive. A few factors whose effects are difficult to measure that consistently emerged in our literature review, interviews, and SLSE are detailed below. Although we only briefly cover some of these factors in this report, their influence was clear throughout our research process, and more robust analyses of these factors are warranted.

- **Timing.** Promotions can be affected based on needs of a specific community in the service. For example, if a career field has a shortage of O-6s in 2019 but not in later years, more officers with relatively weaker files might be selected for promotion in 2019 than in later years. Similarly, an officer who happens to have a strong advocate on their behalf sitting on a board one year might be assessed differently in another year when the board composition is different. One key factor related to timing might simply be randomness: Sometimes an officer is slated in an assignment that sets him or her on a pathway to generalship or admiralship that cannot otherwise be explained.
- **Networks and personal connections.** Networks and personal connections appear to play a—sometimes significant—role in the development and selection of some G/FOs, but this likely varies depending on the service and on the community. These factors were mentioned repeatedly throughout our interviews, from observations that officers need an advocate on O-7 promotion boards to opinions that having a parent who served as a G/FO can increase an officer's chances of promotion. Further, although the effect of connections is notably difficult to measure, some studies have provided insights into the relevance they might have in career progression.[583] Although it is challenging to separate the effects of mentoring from other personnel management and human capital efforts, this research in both civilian and military communities suggests that this dynamic should be taken into account when considering promotion pathways.
- **Personality.** Related to the power of networks is another challenging factor to measure in career development: personality. Throughout our interviews, the SLSE, and our review of the literature, we found repeated references to personality traits that individuals observe are common among certain service G/FOs, or G/FOs who emerge from particular competitive categories or career fields within a service. The role that personality traits play in promotion decisions is not new: Indeed, General George C. Marshall famously evaluated officers on a number of characteristics, including personality traits such as optimism, energy, loyalty, and candor.[584] While it was beyond the scope of this report to measure and analyze personality, we assess that it likely influences an officer's career pathway.

---

[583] See, for example, Lyle and Smith, 2014; Suzanne C. de Janasz, Sherry E. Sullivan, Vicki Whiting, "Mentor Networks and Career Success: Lessons for Turbulent Times," *Academy of Management Perspectives*, Vol. 17, No. 4, 2003, pp. 78–91; and Romila Singh, Belle Rose Ragins, Phyllis Tharenou, "What Matters Most? The Relative Role of Mentoring and Career Capital in Career Success," *Journal of Vocational Behavior*, Vol. 75, No. 1, August 2009, pp. 56–67.

[584] Thomas E. Ricks, *The Generals: American Military Command from World War II to Today*, New York: Penguin Books, 2012; George C. Marshall Foundation, "George C. Marshall: A Study in Character," webpage, undated.

- **Appearance.** Interviewees noted that some services and communities tend to have G/FOs who share physical attributes. This is partially understandable, as some career specialties require particular physical abilities, and also because certain services, such as the Marine Corps, place value on appearance in the form of evaluating an officer's official photograph during promotion boards. However, the role of appearance might go beyond job requirements or the concept of military bearing. Several studies have found a connection between physical appearance and perceptions of leadership potential and trustworthiness, factors that have substantial bearing in officer promotion decisions.[585] For example, a 1984 study by Mazur et al. found that attractiveness was positively correlated with promotions throughout the careers of USMA's graduating class of 1950, noting the importance of "tallness, handsomeness, and athletic physique, which are associated with dominance, manliness, and leadership."[586] Yet the same study highlighted the difficulty of attributing personality traits to observable physical characteristics, saying that although athleticism was correlated with high rank, "Is it the athlete's physique, which fits our stereotyped image of the leader, or his personal traits of courage and coordination, or is it the symbolic value of contributing to West Point's prestige in competitive sports?"[587]
- **Gender, race, and ethnicity.** Although beyond the scope of this report, discussion with interviewees and at the SLSE highlighted the impact that diversity—of gender, race, and other attributes not analyzed in this report—has on the composition of each service's G/FO corps, its culture, and perhaps the advice offered to senior civilian leaders. We did not focus on these factors but acknowledge that they have bearing on the ultimate perspectives of G/FOs across the service.

Service G/FO Archetypes

In this section, we provide sketches of what professional experiences and other characteristics constitute an archetypical service G/FO profile, and an assessment of how these factors might shape the way these archetypical G/FOs could lead and manage institutions and advise senior civilian leaders. Leading and managing institutions and providing strategic-level advice are different actions, but they are related, as they derive in large part from an officer's same experiences and perspectives. Further, every G/FO's approach to institutional leadership and management and strategic-level advice will differ based on factors such as individual personality and preferences, but we attempt to capture potential implications of common

---

[585] See, for example, Alex L. Jones, Jeremy J. Tree, and Robert Ward, "Personality in Faces: Implicit Associations Between Appearance and Personality," *European Journal of Social Psychology*, Vol. 49, No. 3, 2018; and Lisa M. Korenman, Elizabeth L. Wetzler, Marjorie H. Carroll, and Elizabeth V. Velill, "Is It in Your Face? Exploring the Effects of Sexual Dimorphism on Perception of Leadership Potential," *Military Psychology*, Vol. 31, No. 2, 2019, pp. 107–116.

[586] Allan Mazur, Julie Mazur, and Caroline Keating, "Military Rank Attainment of a West Point Class: Effects of Cadets' Physical Features," *American Journal of Sociology*, Vol. 90, No. 1, 1984, p. 126.

[587] Mazur, Mazur, and Keating, 1984, p. 140.

attributes in the sections below, based on our analyses in the Chapters 3 through 7 and also informed by other reflections from the literature, our interviews, and the SLSE.

Despite DoD's efforts to forge operational and strategic jointness, the reflection of service culture in personnel management processes means that service preferences will inevitably shape each service's leaders, and the analysis and advice they provide. Senior civilian leadership can benefit from understanding the common professional backgrounds and attributes that characterize the services' archetypical G/FOs, and how those backgrounds and the service personnel processes that helped shape and select them might affect the way that G/FOs view problems, and advise on solutions to address them.

Throughout the following section, we repeatedly refer to *archetypes*. We use this term to describe a notional profile composed of the most common characteristics for each service that we identified throughout the course of our research. We do not intend to mean that all, or even most, service G/FOs will share the same backgrounds and other characteristics; rather, the archetype is simply a collection of the most common attributes we identified among G/FOs in each service.

In referring to future G/FOs, we do not attempt to define a specific time period, but rather some years into the future when today's junior and mid-level or field-grade officers, who are being currently shaped by the service's personnel processes, will be promoted to O-7 and beyond. We understand that this time period is roughly between five and 25 years from now, and furthermore that substantial social, legal and policy, technological, and geopolitical shifts can, and likely will, occur between now and that time. These factors could certainly have an impact on the professional experiences, viewpoints, and overall makeup of DoD's G/FO corps. Although our analysis does not attempt to account for those changes in developing current service archetypes, we do point out factors that could reshape the G/FO corps in the future.

The Army General Officer Archetype

The Army's current GO pathway tends to be tactically focused, command-centric, doctrine-based, and, especially for O-7 promotion decisions, influenced by an officer's reputation among Army senior leaders. In various official publications, the Army highlights its need to develop leadership experience at all levels, as well as proficiency in combined arms warfare. The Army also stresses other qualities in its formal documents, such as agility, adaptiveness, and ability to lead in joint, interagency, and international organizations, but it is difficult to identify the incentives that promote those same qualities throughout an officer's career development processes.

Typical Career Experiences

Using our analysis in Chapter 4, we found that the current archetypical Army GO features the professional experiences outlined in Tables 8.1 and 8.2. Three main officer career fields (infantry and armor, support, and other combat arms) dominate the O-7 grade, and many of their career experiences are shared despite different career fields.

Table 8.1. Army General Officer Archetype Career Experiences

Category	Career Experience
Career field	Infantry, armor, or support branch career fields at O-7; by O-9 and O-10, overwhelmingly infantry or armor
Time in grade and years in service	Somewhat likely to have been promoted early to O-4, O-5, or O-6; more time in grade at O-4
Commissioning source	ROTC or USMA graduate at O-7, and more likely a USMA graduate as GO rank increases
PME and graduate education	In-resident PME experience focused on military planning, but performance in PME will not have been weighed heavily; unlikely to have civilian master's degree/Ph.D.
Other factors	Demonstration of tactical excellence throughout their career; minimal experience in strategic analysis or financial management but strong familiarity with doctrine; strong networks in the GO community

Table 8.2. Army General Officer Archetype Duty Assignments and Related Experience

Duty Assignments	
Heavy experience in tactical and operational positions; service institutional assignments such as assignment officer with HRC, as an aide-de-camp to a GO, or in the 75th Ranger Regiment	
Leadership experience	Significant team leadership experience starting at junior grades; experience in command within their career field or in Army-heavy organizations
Broadening and joint experience	Minimal broadening or joint experience, and joint experience will rarely occur in commands where Army officers are in the minority
Deployment experience	Multiple combat tours, often in key tactical positions
High-visibility assignments	Post-brigade command assignment as a GO's executive officer or aide, with broad exposure to GOs who will serve on O-7 selection boards

The Archetypical Army General Officer's Approaches to Institutional Leadership and Management and Strategic-Level Advice

The Army GO archetype's professional experiences and characteristics, combined with other influences, such as service culture and institutional goals, could have bearing on the type of leaders they will be as GOs, and the ways they will advise and manage as senior leaders. This characterization of approaches is based on our analysis in Chapter 4.

Institutional Leadership and Management Approach

Due in large part to the archetype's career-field-specific assignment history and deployment experience, the Army GO archetype could bring an Army-centric view when leading institutions: combat-oriented and tactical in nature, hierarchical in structure, and heavily reliant on doctrine and military planning processes. This could mean the archetypical GO can work decisively in specific situations for which doctrine is established, and that the Army GO archetype thinks of leadership in terms of personnel led, and specifically small teams. Because of the service's emphasis on combat effectiveness, however, the archetypical Army GO does not have extensive experience in institutional leadership, which could mean that they rely on tactical and operational experiences to guide strategic-level organizations. They could also likely emphasize tactical performance in the personnel they oversee, given that tactical-level leadership performance is viewed as indicative of strategic-level potential in the Army.

Potentially further contributing to the Army-centric view of leadership is that the archetypical GO has served in very few positions where Army officers are the minority opinion. Army officers spend most of their career with other Army officers, even in joint commands: Standard joint tours might feature many other Army officers, and some joint commands might develop a culture very similar to that of the Army because of the high number of Army officers at those commands and because warfighting commands are frequently headed by Army GOs.

Additionally, the archetypical Army GO might have a lack of joint experience in field-grade ranks, particularly at O-7. This might cause challenges when the archetypical Army GO is operating in a joint organization where the Army is the minority opinion. However, in joint organizations, the emphasis on planning and the focus on understanding war in PME and in doctrine helps enable the archetypical Army GO to assume leadership roles in positions that the Army finds institutionally important, such as CCMD J-3s and J-5s.[588]

The Army GO archetype might also not have deep experience in civilian-led organizations or in strategic-level policy offices (such as OSD) that provide exposure to interagency policy processes or equities. This could mean that the archetypical Army GO might be initially challenged to navigate the strategic-level policymaking process and lead organizations in a way that prioritizes operational-level tasks over strategic implications. To this point, during the senior leadership selection exercise, one participant described some interactions of GOs with senior civilian officials as "shockingly dismissive."[589]

In summary, we assess that when leading large institutions, the archetypical Army GO might

- lead based on an Army-centric, ground combat–oriented perspective
- work decisively in situations for which doctrine exists
- rely on tactical and operational experiences to guide strategic-level decisions
- define leadership in terms of personnel management rather than platform management
- be unfamiliar working in organizations where the Army is not the majority, potentially affecting the Army GO archetype's effectiveness in joint organizations
- excel in J-3 and J-5 positions but be challenged to work in civilian-dominant organizations and to navigate strategic-level policy processes
- emphasize tactical performance.

---

[588] A82, Army general officer, September 24, 2018. J-3 positions are leadership positions in joint organizations that manage and oversee operations; J-5 positions are those that manage and generally oversee plans, policy, and strategy.

[589] Senior leader selection exercise notes, January 30, 2019, RAND, Arlington, Virginia.

Approach to Strategic-Level Advice

The Army GO archetype's viewpoint and advice is heavily informed by their operational experience and approach to planning. Additionally, military planning is probably central to the Army GO archetype's approach to advising. Because of the Army's heavy emphasis on doctrine and military planning, the archetypical Army GO might be an excellent planner of military operations at multiple levels, but might not be highly adaptable and creative, particularly when facing challenges for which doctrine does not exist. As one interviewee told us, the Army's focus on doctrine "makes us really, really good planners, but if it's something new and strategic and we don't have a manual for it yet? That's hard."[590]

Partly as a result of the Army's "muddy boots" culture, which is reinforced by common career experiences, Army GOs form a largely cohesive and uniform cadre. The archetypical Army GO has been incentivized to follow a narrow and specific developmental pathway, which drives officers to similar skill sets, jobs, units, and, potentially as a result, similar perspectives and advice. Further, the archetypical Army GO's strategic-level advice will likely be shaped in part by their significant combat deployment experience. This experience can provide a useful frame of reference for strategic-level advice but could also introduce biases formed from previous wars.

These factors might also serve to discourage innovative perspectives and advice. Indeed, Janowitz observed nearly a half-century ago that "officers who express too openly their desire to innovate or to criticize are not likely to survive."[591] As in the other services, incentives to avoid risking a poor performance evaluation are high in the Army, which could temper the archetypical Army GO's candor and discourage them from voicing controversial opinions.

Additionally, the Army's practice of discussing personal knowledge of O-7 candidates means that the archetypical GO will have taken one or more high-visibility, service-centric assignments that enable access to a wide range of GOs, which further supports the "ducks pick ducks" observation noted throughout this report. This heavy focus on personal reputation might also discourage the archetypical GO from providing advice that challenges their superiors for fear of negative repercussions in promotion decisions.

In summary, we assess that when advising senior leaders the Army GO archetype might

- base advice on formal military planning, meaning that the officer will be an excellent planner of military operations but might not be highly adaptable and creative, particularly when facing challenges for which doctrine does not exist
- share similar perspectives with other Army GO archetypes, based on the uniformity of their experience and lack of emphasis on strategic analysis in training and education
- rely on their combat deployment experience in providing advice, which can be a useful frame of reference but can also introduce biases formed from previous wars

---

[590] A01, Army field-grade officer, August 9, 2019.

[591] Janowitz, 1971, p. 17.

- be less likely to share innovative perspectives and advice in order to maintain strong support networks and strong evaluations from senior raters.

Potential Changes to Archetypal General Officers

If no major changes are made to current personnel management processes, the Army's future GOs will probably look quite similar to those produced today: tactically focused leaders effective in combat and military planning with minimal joint and/or broadening experience prior to O-7. Two specific factors might influence the future Army GO pool. First, the service's increased investment in civilian education will likely result in more Army GOs with nonmilitary degrees, which could potentially broaden GO perspectives on strategic issues. Second, a greater number of junior officers with experiences shaped heavily by deployments in Iraq and Afghanistan will become GOs. These operations bring with them the lessons—and biases—of counterterrorism- and counterinsurgency-focused wars that enabled a certain level of autonomy that potential future national security threats (such as near-peer focused, partnered operations) might not afford.

The Navy

Across the three main URL communities (aviation, surface warfare, and submarine warfare), the Navy's career development processes tend to emphasize self-reliance, technical expertise, and "Darwinian" competition. In the surface and subsurface communities especially, command at sea is emphasized. These values directly reflect Navy culture and help to create FOs who have substantial community-specific operational experience, are comfortable with executing operations independently from other services and with minimal oversight, and are used to working across multiple naval domains. Navy guidance on leadership and promotions stresses the essentiality of these attributes in its officers, and also names leader development, including mentoring, as its top priority. Specifically, the Navy's evaluation forms heavily weigh dimensions such as strategic thinking and ability to lead change, but it is unclear how those attributes are measured.

Typical Career Experiences

Based on our analysis of Navy FO pathways in Chapter 5, we found that the Navy FO archetype profile features the professional experiences summarized in Tables 8.3 and 8.4. Submarine warfare, surface warfare, and aviation officers compose the majority of O-7 officers, and while their career pathways are community-specific, all tend to emphasize similar development pathways.

Table 8.3. Navy Flag Officer Archetype Career Experiences

Category	Career Experience
Career field	Aviation, surface, or submariner communities, especially the latter at higher grades
Time in grade and years in service	Promoted in the primary zone at all grades; more years in service at O-6 grade than any other grade, or O-6 service counterparts
Commissioning source	USNA graduate, especially at O-9/O-10
PME and graduate education	Navy Nuclear Power School graduate; STEM expertise; completed ILE online; PME performance will not have been weighed heavily; any civilian degree will have been completed during free time
Other factors	Strong peer and FO networks, forged in part through USNA affiliation; potentially has other specific certifications, such as financial management

Table 8.4. Navy Flag Officer Archetype Duty Assignments and Related Experience

Duty Assignments	
Extensive command experience in their platform along a highly specialized, technical career path; focus on operating in a naval multidomain environment; on-the-job training gained through milestone assignments intended to weed out lower performers; emphasis on learning operational independence and self-reliance	
Leadership experience	More seasoned in platform management than personnel-focused leadership; extensive command experience within their community, but not in a joint environment; comfortable with taking initiative and operating with minimal oversight
Broadening and joint experience	Familiarity with naval multidomain operations; joint/broadening experience only as required, likely at USINDOPACOM or related command
Deployment experience	Significant operational sea duty, particularly in the Pacific theater, but limited combat experience
High-visibility assignments	Aide to a senior Navy FO, generally at O-5/O-6

The Archetypical Navy Flag Officer's Approaches to Institutional Leadership and Management and Strategic-Level Advice

The Navy FO archetype's career experiences could have bearing on the type of senior leaders they will be and the way they will advise and manage. This characterization of approaches is based on our analysis in Chapter 5.

Institutional Leadership and Management Approach

A central tenet of the Navy's leadership philosophy is command at sea, which is ingrained through many of its milestone command assignments, PME, and overall culture. Command at sea places a high degree of trust and autonomy in a commander to make critical decisions based on the commander's own judgment. This emphasis on this type of command at sea (or mission command) might mean that archetypical Navy officers are relatively comfortable with leadership and decisionmaking in ambiguous situations or relatively unfamiliar situations. It also might tend to drive self-reliance and initiative, which, in an institutional leadership capacity, could net positive attributes, such as driving needed strategic-level changes. Alternatively, it could influence a leader to rely only on their own judgment when making major decisions, rather than weighing others' opinions. This self-reliance denotes a certain amount of risk acceptance in operational decisions, but does not necessarily indicate that an officer can be careless. Because of the need to compete for both milestone assignments and promotions at each grade, which are heavily reliant on stellar FITREPs that require an officer to "break out" among their peers, the archetypical Navy FO still might weigh operational actions and leadership decisions carefully to avoid negative repercussions in the evaluations process. Further, the concept of command at sea is only relayed to ship commanders, not to all officers on a ship—and not necessarily in all warfighting communities. It is unclear how officers are prepared for such self-reliance in assignments preceding command.

Additionally, we found that Navy leaders are well versed in establishing, testing, improving, and strictly following rules-based procedures, at least for technical systems. But because of Navy culture's promotion of initiative and independence, they might be less likely to focus on formal, standardized procedures for executing strategic leadership tasks, preferring to rely on their own experience over doctrinal approaches.

Leadership experience for the archetypical Navy FO will probably be defined more by the platforms they have commanded than by the people they have led. As a result, the Navy FO might expect subordinates to excel in their positions and grow as leaders without substantial mentoring. The Navy's platform-centric approach to leadership might also have an influence on the ability of FOs to lead people in large organizations at the O-7 grade and above, especially as team leadership, like many other professional skills in the Navy, is expected to be learned on the job.

While the archetypical Navy FO does not have multiple tours in a joint environment, they are practiced in integrating naval capabilities across domains (air, surface, and subsurface). This could be particularly true as the Navy FO archetype has commanded a carrier strike group, which prompted a participant in the SLSE to remark that officers who have done so "have such competence . . . their experience commanding large military formations" in both air and surface domains is unique and there is "nothing like it anywhere else in the military."[592] This could mean that the archetypical Navy FO is familiar with leveraging communities with different equities to work together, but, consistent with Navy culture, probably still favors service autonomy—multidomain or otherwise—over jointness.

The Navy as an institution has, at times, been more resistant to change than other services, such as during Goldwater-Nichols deliberations, and particularly when Navy personnel perceive a threat to their ability to remain self-reliant masters of their maritime domain. It is possible that the archetypical Navy FO's service-centric training and education contributes to this type of inflexibility.

In summary, we assess that when leading institutions, the Navy FO archetype might

---

[592] Senior leader selection exercise notes, January 30, 2019, RAND, Arlington, Virginia.

- be relatively comfortable with decisionmaking in ambiguous situations or relatively unfamiliar situations
- demonstrate self-reliance and initiative, which could lead the officer to drive needed strategic-level changes; or alternatively, self-reliance and initiative could influence a leader to rely only on their own judgment when making major decisions, rather than weighing others' opinions
- be less risk-averse in operational decisions than G/FO archetypes in other services, though not careless—although this might be more true of archetypes with surface warfare and subsurface backgrounds
- utilize formal procedures for managing technical systems, but be less tied to standardized, doctrinal approaches in strategic leadership tasks
- define leadership more in terms of platforms the officer has commanded rather than by people the officer has managed
- see value in leveraging multiple communities with different equities to work together, but still favor service autonomy over jointness.

Approach to Strategic-Level Advice

The typical Navy FO potentially offers diversity in terms of perspectives and advice because a given officer will represent one of three different specialized URL communities. Within each URL community, however, the archetypical Navy FO has very similar career experiences to their peers, which is driven in part by the Navy's model in which communities control the process for selecting officers for milestone assignments. Given that these experiences across communities all heavily emphasize technical expertise and training, the archetypical Navy FO might gravitate toward platform-based (and, understandably, maritime-based) technical solutions to strategic problems. Further, given that the officer will have very limited joint experience and, moreover, very little experience outside of their career field overall, the archetypical Navy FO might have a narrow frame from which to draw advice for senior leaders.

The archetypical Navy FO's tight career development timeline features low prioritization of strategic analysis or performance in PME, which means the Navy FO archetype might not feature an extensive background in strategic education and might have to rely more on learning on the job once they make O-7. As such, archetypical Navy FOs might advise largely from experience and community-specific training learned throughout their careers, rather than drawing from strategic analysis.

Significantly, while the archetypical Navy FO has substantial operational deployment time at sea, it is most likely that the officer will not have served extensively in combat roles, given the Navy's smaller role in U.S.-involved wars over the past several decades. This carries several potential implications. On one hand, the archetypical Navy FO does not have the experience of being combat-tested that might serve officers well in high-pressure environments; on the other hand, the wars that current and future FOs will have to advise on and plan for are not likely to closely mirror those that other services' GOs have experience in. This means that the archetypical Navy FO, while less experienced in combat than their peers in the other services, might be able to offer advice that does not carry forward biases incurred from previous combat deployment experiences, and instead might offer fresh perspective to strategic challenges.

Because of the importance of personal networks, the archetypical Navy FO might endeavor to maintain good relations with peers and senior ranking officers, which might mean that they are hesitant to provide contrarian advice in an effort to maintain cordiality. Also, the Navy's strongly tradition-based culture tends to promote a cohesive officer cadre, which might affect an officer's willingness to offer minority opinions in a larger Navy group.

In summary, when advising at the strategic level, we assess the archetypical Navy FO might

- exhibit relative diversity in their perspectives across Navy FO archetypes because they will come from one of three distinct communities; however, within a community, they will likely provide technical advice based on very similar, narrow career pathways
- demonstrate a higher degree of risk acceptance in operational decisions than other services' G/FO counterparts, depending on which community the archetype represents
- provide more-intuitive advice that does not heavily incorporate strategic analysis
- offer fresh perspective and strategic advice that does not carry forward biases incurred from previous combat deployment experiences; however, the officer might not have firsthand understanding of how strategic-level decisions affect tactical and operational combat environments
- prioritize maintaining good relations with peers and senior ranking officers, which might mean that the officer is hesitant to provide contrarian advice in an effort to maintain cordiality.

Potential Changes to Archetypal Flag Officers

Many of the archetypical Navy FO career experiences and implications might remain the same into the future. However, we anticipate that a few changes could affect certain ways Navy FOs advise and manage in the future. First, the Navy is starting to prioritize leader development, which is a departure from its previous "sink or swim" approach to career progression. Part of this energized initiative is to place greater emphasis on graduate-level education, as it will be required for O-6 major command positions, and education overall through means such as establishing a chief learning officer position.[593] At the same time, there is also a renewed call for officers to spend even more time gaining technical expertise and platform-specific training, particularly following recent collisions in the Pacific, so the precise focus of the Navy's education efforts remains to be seen.

The Navy's practice of ordering certain promotions based on merit could also serve to incentivize talented leaders who might otherwise consider leaving the Navy to instead stay in the FO pipeline. Moreover, the service's greater focus on leadership accountability in the wake of recent events might create cultural shifts in the Navy—potentially even affecting the fundamental principle of autonomous command at sea—that could have bearing on future FOs.

---

[593] John Kroger, "Charting the Future of Education for the Navy-Marine Corps Team," *War on the Rocks*, November 4, 2019.

The Air Force

The Air Force's personnel management processes feature early identification of talent, compressed timelines due to emphasis on BPZ promotions, and greater importance placed on education and jointness relative to the other services. Given the Air Force's missions and culture, the archetypical GO is a pilot and, most frequently, a fighter pilot. The Air Force's official leadership development goals place a premium on technical mastery, strategic analysis, and developing its personnel.

Typical Career Experiences

Our Air Force analysis, detailed in Chapter 6, yielded several observations about what professional experiences and other attributes might characterize the archetypical Air Force GO. We summarize these experiences in Tables 8.5 and 8.6.

Table 8.5. Air Force General Officer Archetype Career Experiences

Category	Career Experience
Career field	Pilot background, especially a fighter pilot as grade increases
Time in grade and years in service	Promoted below the zone at least twice; fewer years in service than same-grade counterparts as mid-grade officers and GOs
Commissioning source	USAFA graduate, particularly at higher grades
PME and graduate education	Distinguished graduate from in-resident IDE; possibly a SAASS and/or Weapons School graduate; educated in strategic analysis
Other factors	Will have demonstrated excellence by O-3; has developed networks and mentor relationships; strong communications skills

Table 8.6. Air Force General Officer Archetype Duty Assignments and Related Experience

Duty Assignments	
Clearly defined, time-compressed pathway focused on developing skills needed at the senior GO level emphasizes tactical leadership, technical mastery, and communication and analysis skills; at least one staff-level position to increase visibility and awareness of strategic issues	
Leadership experience	More skilled in technical mastery than "people" leadership; minimal experience leading teams at junior levels; has held squadron, group, and wing command
Broadening and joint experience	Minimal joint/broadening experience due to tight timeline; strategic level exposure through staff and joint assignments at the O-4 through O-6 levels; possible experience in a resource management role at a joint command
Deployment experience	Multiple deployments, but might not have been directly involved in combat
High-visibility assignments	Executive officer or aide to a GO (Air Force or joint), Air Staff position that increased exposure to senior leaders

The Archetypical Air Force General Officer's Approaches to Institutional Leadership and Management and Strategic-Level Advice

The archetypical Air Force GO's professional experiences and other characteristics, in conjunction with factors such as service culture and institutional goals, might influence how the Air Force GO archetype will lead and manage at senior levels. This characterization of approaches is based on our analysis in Chapter 6.

Approach to Institutional Leadership and Management

The archetypical Air Force GO has spent the earlier parts of their career mastering weapon systems, rather than practicing small-team leadership. This could potentially influence the importance the Air Force GO archetype places on personnel leadership versus platform-based leadership and contribute to a more individualistic management approach. As one active duty GO we interviewed noted, "In the Army and Marine Corps, when you are leading men in the field, they are the technology. When you are piloting an F-16, you are out there on your own."[594] However, given the service's investment in mentoring at an early grade, the Air Force GO archetype might be predisposed to valuing officer development when they are in a leadership position.

The Air Force GO archetype might exhibit a rule-abiding approach based on careers spent managing multimillion-dollar (or in some cases multibillion-dollar) systems, which could lead the officer to perform well in leadership positions that require attention to detail and mastering complex information and executing tasks accordingly. This comfort with task execution could also mean that the archetypical Air Force GO might be less comfortable with "outside-the-box" ideas and in leadership positions that require decisions without the benefit of clear order and procedure. In those environments, the Air Force GO archetype might be prone to seeking guidance from others, rather than executing independently. In a joint or civilian-heavy organization, this tendency to value broader opinions could net positive benefits.

The Air Force GO archetype might have substantial awareness of resource constraints to leadership positions, given the GO's exposure to serving in a resource management position in a joint environment. The Air Force has shown institutional openness to change and willingness to adapt, such as in its focus on securing resource management positions in joint organizations as a way to wield substantial influence when coveted J-3 and J-5 positions were filled by other services, or in the strategic and personnel management changes currently being implemented in the service. Overall, the Air Force GO archetype might value jointness more than G/FO archetypes in other services, based on previous experiences and training that emphasizes the importance of jointness. However, retired GO interviewees stressed that the Air Force tends to

---

[594] AF75, active duty general officer, November 30, 2018.

favor officers with operational experience, but that does not always create a leader who can operate in the joint environment.[595]

In a leadership position, the archetypical Air Force GO might also exhibit strong communications and strategic analysis skills and could value broader perspectives in decisionmaking processes. These skills and approaches could have been developed in part during their time in high-visibility Air Staff positions, and throughout their PME experiences, because the Air Force aims to develop its future GOs to be able to lead in any function at senior-most levels, regardless of specialty. This is tied to the observation that "potentially, airmen could bring a three-dimensional perspective to the joint fight that might otherwise be lacking."[596]

In summary, we expect that, in institutional leadership roles, the Air Force GO archetype might

- emphasize technical, platform-based leadership over personnel leadership, but value officer development when they are in a leadership position
- be less comfortable with "outside-the-box" ideas and in leadership positions that require decisions without the benefit of clear order and procedure
- seek guidance and input from others, rather than executing independently, valuing broader perspectives in decisionmaking processes
- bring a keen understanding of resource constraints to leadership positions
- demonstrate openness to change and willingness to adapt
- value jointness more than G/FO archetypes in other services
- exhibit strong communications and strategic analysis skills.

Approach to Strategic-Level Advice

Overall, Air Force GOs tend to come from homogenous career backgrounds, which might mean that many senior Air Force GOs have similar training and professional experiences.[597] However, given the service's emphasis on strategic analysis—and the potential inclination to include multiple viewpoints in decisionmaking—typical Air Force GO approaches to leading and advising might be similar, but their ultimate analytic assessments might be less uniform than in other services. Additionally, despite Air Force GOs' narrow career field focus, the advice they draw from those perspectives might be balanced by their training and education in strategic analysis.

Further, based on their flying background, the Air Force GO archetype might bring a nonhierarchical view to planning and operations, given their familiarity with flatter command structures, but also might hesitate to deviate from an established course in their advice.

The Air Force GO archetype's preference for rule and order over taking risks and breaking norms might suggest that the archetypical Air Force GO might be somewhat uncomfortable with

---

[595] AF92, retired general officer, October 12, 2018; AF89, retired field-grade officer, October 26, 2018.

[596] Lee et al., 2017, pp. 14–15.

[597] For further discussion on Air Force-centric nature of promotions, see Lee et al., 2017, pp. 24–25.

challenging the status quo when they provide advice. As Air Force Colonel Jason Lamb noted in an interview with the *Air Force Times*,

> The Air Force really struggles with candor. . . . The entire system incentivizes risk avoidance. What we see as risk these days, really speaks to our problem with risk avoidance. When we stand up and applaud when a wing commander chooses not to abide by an Air Force Instruction because he thinks it's silly, that's seen as a huge victory.[598]

The archetypical Air Force GO might have been designated as a high-performing officer at O-3, and both mentored and assigned to specific technical, operational positions designed to develop the officer's ability to progress through the GO grades. These assignments could predispose the archetypical GO to focus on technological solutions to complex problems later in their career, despite the service's emphasis on strategic analysis.

Further, although innovation is one of the Air Force's cultural values—in terms of the development and utilization of technology—in practice, its emphasis on standardized training might lead to less innovative thinking in its archetypical GO, who has adhered to established guidelines over the course of their career. Further, a proclivity toward strategic analysis could make the archetypical Air Force GO more prone to favor incremental change over sudden or drastic change, and to weighing pros and cons when providing advice to civilian leaders regarding major changes. However, this emphasis on strategic analysis in assignments and PME might help enable the officer to understand broader implications about future fights and technological changes. This experience is focused on preparing Air Force officers to become GOs at O-9 and O-10, a longer view than the other services, which might prepare them well to provide strategic-level advice at the highest levels.

Additionally, the compressed pathway to GO will mean that officers in the Navy and the Marine Corps will have a few additional years of experience as compared with the archetypical Air Force GO, but, given the Air Force's different preparatory focus than the other services, it is unclear whether their relative seniority to the Air Force GO archetype introduces any advantages. However, the archetypical Air Force GO might feel pressured to counter the perception of having less experience than other G/FOs at their grade, which could have an effect on their advice.[599]

Finally, in accordance with Air Force institutional goals, the archetypical Air Force GO might advocate in their advice for a substantial role for Air Force capabilities in a campaign, but could be comfortable advising on ways to leverage Air Force capabilities in either a lead or a support role, given the service's interest in the former and recent familiarity with the latter. Based on the Air Force's desire to increase its role in joint leadership positions, the archetypical

---

598 Stephen Losey, "'Ned Stark' Unveiled: Colonel Who Wrote Viral Leadership Columns Has a Challenge for the Air Force," *Air Force Times*, May 13, 2019.

599 AF62, active duty field-grade officer, December 7, 2018.

Air Force GO might emphasize the service's criticality to a wide range of national security challenges in their advice to senior leaders.

In summary, when providing strategic-level advice, Air Force GO archetypes might

- provide analytic assessments that might be less uniform with one another than in other services
- apply analysis that combines strategic analysis skills with operational experience
- bring a nonhierarchical view to planning and operations, given their familiarity with flatter command structures
- hesitate to deviate from an established course in their advice
- be somewhat uncomfortable with challenging the status quo when they provide advice
- focus on technological solutions to complex problems
- rely on strategic analysis and understand broad implications of future fights and technological changes
- favor incremental change over sudden or large changes, and weigh pros and cons carefully
- advocate for a substantial role for Air Force capabilities in a campaign, but also be comfortable advising on ways to leverage Air Force capabilities in either a lead or a support role.

Potential Changes to Archetypal General Officers

The Air Force's archetypical GO might look somewhat different in the future, depending on the extent the service shifts institutionally toward space and cyber missions. It is possible that the next generation of Air Force GOs is more heavily characterized by officers with these non-aviation backgrounds, as the Air Force seeks to increase its primacy in these missions, or that the service's emphasis on advancing the careers of rated officers could mean a mismatch in the skills of the Air Force's GOs with these emerging missions. Given the "ducks promote ducks" tendency in the promotion system, a retired GO we interviewed offered that the service is not likely to undertake whole-cloth reforms to its promotion system devoid of a forcing function.

New competitive categories carved out of the LAF category might create additional focus on and opportunities for nonpilots, which would mean that officers with different leadership experiences and tactical focus could rise to senior levels. In *Rare Birds*, the authors found that the Air Force tends to groom its GOs for key positions within the service.[600] It is likely that, regardless of career path, the Air Force's increasing emphasis on developing leaders capable of leading in a joint environment—and in specific positions—will continue.

Regardless of these changes, it is likely that pilots will continue to compose a substantial number of GO positions in the Air Force. One important related issue to that point is pilot retention. According to February 2018 congressional testimony, the Air Force was 1,937 pilots short in FY 2018, with the fighter pilot inventory most adversely affected.[601] Additionally,

---

[600] Lee et al., 2017.

[601] Kelly, 2019, p. 5.

several opinion pieces published in recent years have suggested that personnel challenges might be exacerbated because the Air Force fosters a system that promotes managers, not leaders, and supports a culture that avoids addressing leadership issues head-on.[602] One option the Air Force considered to retain pilots is an aviation-only career track that eliminates many non-operational duties so a pilot can focus on flying, but the long-term effects of this program are unknown.[603]

The Marine Corps

Across Marine Corps career fields, the officer development process is highly prescriptive and performance-based, and common experiences serve to reinforce the Marine Corps' egalitarian culture and create a highly cohesive Marine Corps GO corps. Officers are promoted to O-7 by career field roughly in proportion to commissioning rates, but career pathways remain similar regardless of specialty. Official service guidance emphasizes the leadership and development of marines, tactical competence, and discipline.

Typical Career Experiences

Our analysis of Marine Corps GO pathways, detailed in Chapter 7, highlighted several specific professional experiences and other characteristics the archetypical Marine Corps GO would feature. We summarize these most commonly observed of these in Tables 8.7 and 8.8.

Table 8.7. Marine Corps General Officer Archetype Career Experiences

Category	Career Experience
Career field	At O-7, could represent one of several career fields; most likely aviation and infantry as officers approach O-10
Time in grade and years in service	Promoted on time, not BZ; selected to O-7 later than other services; more years in service than other service counterparts, particularly after O-7
Commissioning source	OCS graduate, in line with commissioning rate
PME and graduate education	Location and performance in PME will not have been weighed heavily; civilian graduate degree, if any, will be directly related to Marine Corps requirements
Other factors	Known for military bearing, discipline, and command presence; experiences focused on tactical leadership and team over self; multiple screening processes weed out lower performers early

---

[602] See, for example, Jack McCain, "A Navy Pilot's Take: The Air Force Doesn't Have a Pilot Crisis, It Has a Leadership Crisis," ForeignPolicy.com, April 24, 2017, and Colonel Ned Stark, "Commentary: The Air Force Is Not Designed to Produce Good Leaders," *Air Force Times*, July 31, 2018.

[603] Charlsy Panzino, "New in 2018: AMC Pushes for Aviation-Only Career Track," *Air Force Times*, December 29, 2017.

Table 8.8. Marine Corps General Officer Archetype Duty Assignments and Related Experience

Duty Assignments	
Career pathway is MAGTF-centric, focused on leading marines and developing discipline and tactical expertise at every grade; performance will be exceptional in every position, but very few "kingmaker" positions exist	
Leadership experience	Tactical leadership experience starting at junior grades; personnel leadership emphasized over platform management; command assignments are paramount
Broadening and joint experience	Minimal joint experience outside of the Marine Corps, but will have gained cross-service institutional knowledge in valued B-billet assignment; assigned to a congressional fellowship to advance Marine Corps needs
Deployment experience	Significant overseas assignments and multiple combat tours
High-visibility assignments	Congressional fellowship will denote excellence, but no other specific signaling assignments

The Archetypical Marine Corps General Officer's Approaches to Institutional Leadership and Management and Strategic-Level Advice

The archetypical Marine Corps GO's career experiences and other characteristics might shape the ways they will advise and manage. This characterization of approaches is based on our analysis in Chapter 7.

Approach to Institutional Leadership and Management

The concept of "team before self" is probably central to the archetypical Marine Corps GO's leadership philosophy. Their entire Marine Corps experience will emphasize the importance of developing and leading marines, and the Marine Corps GO archetype will have extensive experience in personnel-based leadership. At the same time, the Marine Corps GO archetype might equate effective leadership with understanding how to also be a good, disciplined follower—of rules, and of other leaders. These principles could translate directly to the way the marine would lead an organization as a GO: expectation of order and adherence to a hierarchical chain of command, but also a strong focus on developing and utilizing the capabilities of its personnel.

The Marine Corps GO archetype might be experienced and educated in tactical leadership, with minimal exposure to joint leadership roles until later GO grades. Based on the value the Marine Corps places on B-billets and working across career fields in the Marine Corps, the Marine Corps GO archetype might have previous experience in recognizing and leveraging the utility of a wide range of groups within an organization and might bring that perspective to a joint environment.

The archetypical Marine Corps GO will have undergone the Marine Corps' unique screening processes, such as the CDB, that serve to refine the quality of the officer pool at various stages, and will be accustomed to strict valuation of performance rather than signaling positions. This additional screening could mean that the Marine Corps GO archetype closely matches the service's vision of what a Marine Corps officer—and leader—should be. At the same time, the focus on performance versus future potential could skew Marine Corps evaluations to weigh tactical performance more heavily, which is not necessarily an indicator of strategic excellence. These factors could result in a more tactically focused, but highly disciplined, leader.

Additionally, the Marine Corps' egalitarian approach to personnel development, which features common training experiences across all marines and forced distribution of talent in initial entry assignments, could lead the archetypical Marine Corps GO to understand that talent exists across an organization (including the reserve component) and thus value career fields other than their own in the organization they are leading.

However, the archetypical Marine Corps GO's service-specific experience, combined with the cultural emphasis on the unique talents and contributions of marines, might lead them to favor Marine Corps perspectives and capabilities over others. This belief in the singularity of Marine Corps talent is summarized by Marine Corps Commandant David H. Berger in the 2019 Commandant's Planning Guidance: "I believe in my soul that Marines are different. Our identity is firmly rooted in our warrior ethos. This is the force that will always adapt and overcome no matter what the circumstances are. We fight and win in any clime and place."[604]

The Marine Corps GO archetype might chafe at institutional reform efforts, particularly with respect to personnel policy. For example, in recent years, the service has been hesitant to adapt DoD policies integrating women into combat arms.[605] The Marine Corps has also been slow to recognize the potential utility of new officer management flexibilities provided in the FY 2019 NDAA, which would enable more variable career paths.[606] This resistance to institutional reform could be attributed in part to the high valuation of tradition in the service, and could be reflected in archetypical Marine Corps GO's approach to leading organizations charged with undertaking institutional reforms.

Despite this resistance to institutional change, the Marine Corps has shown itself to be highly adaptive to operational change. During the post-9/11 wars, the service demonstrated its ability to engage in sustained ground combat operations despite its amphibious missions. As the United States evolves its national defense strategy to emphasize the threats presented by near-peer competitors, the Marine Corps is developing new concepts and doctrines to contribute to the joint fight.[607] These shifts denote the Marine Corps' ability and commitment to evolving operational approaches to meet rising threats, particularly those posed by near-peer competitors, and could be reflective of the operationally adaptive nature of its archetypical GOs.

In summary, we assess that, when leading institutions, the Marine Corps GO archetype might

- define leadership as personnel-based, rather than platform-based

---

[604] U.S. Marine Corps, *Commandant's Planning Guidance, 2019*, Washington, D.C., 2019.

[605] Shawn Snow, "Where Are the Female Marines?" *Marine Corps Times,* March 5, 2018.

[606] Albert A. Robbert, Katherine L. Kidder, Caitlin Lee, Agnes Gereben Schaefer, and William H. Waggy II, *Officer Career Management: Steps Toward Modernization in the 2018 and 2019 National Defense Authorization Acts*, Santa Monica, Calif.: RAND Corporation, RR-2875-OSD, 2019.

[607] U.S. Department of Defense, 2018.

- emphasize the importance of developing and leading marines
- equate effective leadership with understanding how to also be a good, disciplined follower—of rules, and of other leaders
- expect order and adherence to a hierarchical chain of command, but also focus on developing and utilizing the capabilities of its personnel
- be able to recognize and leverage the utility of a wide range of groups within an organization
- emphasize tactical performance
- value career fields other than their own in an organization the officer is leading, but still favor Marine Corps perspectives and capabilities over others
- initially chafe at sudden or large institutional reform efforts, particularly with respect to personnel policy
- demonstrate adaptiveness to operational change and commitment to evolving operational approaches to meet rising threats.

Approach to Strategic-Level Advice

Overall, Marine Corps GOs exhibit substantial uniformity in career paths, which we found marines tend to believe is an asset, as it provides a unified voice in their advice and thought processes in the joint environment.[608] This uniformity is supported by the Marine Corps' egalitarian culture, which discourages early promotions, so cohorts are standardized from commissioning through GO grades. This, combined with the Marine Corps' small size and service-wide training in TBS, means that most marines in a specific year group will know one another, further contributing to cohesiveness across the service. Indeed, we found in our research that marines are more likely to identify as a marine than by MOS. These factors together likely extend to uniform advice from Marine Corps GO archetypes.

This uniformity in experience across career fields provides the Marine Corps with a highly qualified pool of officers from which to select future GOs, which can create a culture in which marines are seen as interchangeable. This relative lack of specialization could yield a shortage of specific skill sets necessary to meet the needs of the future Marine Corps or joint force, but it could also foster a wider range of experiences from which to base one's perspectives and advice.

The Marine Corps GO archetype might value discipline over risk-taking, having been taught that the commitment to discipline ensures successful, fluid warfighting advantages when engaging in hostile environments. However, the commitment to discipline might also mean the archetypical Marine Corps GO is averse to questioning assumptions underlying existing processes, strategies, and orders. Of note, however, the Marine Corps' FitRep emphasizes "avoiding zero defects"—an attribute that could influence the service's acceptance—and potentially the archetypical Marine Corps GO's acceptance—of risk in order to foster initiative, assertiveness, and innovation.

---

[608] Senior leader selection exercise notes, January 30, 2019, RAND, Arlington, Virginia.

Although the Marine Corps GO archetype might be broadened in terms of understanding the range of Marine Corps capabilities, the officer might lack key preparatory broadening experiences for providing advice in senior-level joint billets, given the lack of Marine Corps emphasis on joint assignments. The archetypical Marine Corps GO's tactically focused assignments and limited focus on PME might further contribute to a relatively narrow perspective in decisionmaking and advising, particularly in joint environments.

The Marine Corps officer's career path tends to be slower than those of their service counterparts. As such, the archetypical Marine Corps GO will have a longer service record and potentially more assignments than their counterparts by the time they make O-7. Their added experience might provide them with increased breadth and/or depth of judgment informing the quality of advice they are able to provide to civilian leadership, but it also might further entrench specific analytic biases and restrict their flexibility.

Given the Marine Corps' long-standing tradition as an expeditionary force, the service has a bias toward forward presence. Archetypical Marine Corps GOs have had significant overseas experience, whether serving in contingency operations, on a MAGTF afloat, or with an overseas MEF, and might place a high value on the contribution forward-stationed marines provide. Their experience might influence the advice they provide to civilian leadership about the value of forward engagement.

The archetypical Marine Corps GO also has substantial deployment and combat-deployment time. This experience might provide the archetypical Marine Corps GO perspective and training in high-pressure environments, but could introduce bias toward advice to approach warfighting based on the models of those they have previously fought in.

Additionally, the archetypical Marine Corps GO might advise in accordance with the Marine Corps' role in the joint force. To ensure that the Marine Corps is capable of injecting into a hostile environment to set conditions for the other services, particularly the Navy, the Marine Corps must have enough organic capabilities to survive and persist before the joint force is able to reach a given theater. As such, the Marine Corps GO archetype might favor acquisition investments enabling Marine Corps autonomy in order to contribute to the joint force. The archetypical Marine Corps GO might advocate for these types of capabilities so as to guarantee marines' freedom of maneuver without the assistance of other services. For example, in the current strategic environment, Marine Corps advocacy for the F-35B and certain elements of organic cruise missile defense reflect the service's pursuit of autonomy.[609]

In providing advice on the strategic level, archetypical Marine Corps GOs might

- provide advice representing the Marine Corps as a whole, rather than being narrowly focused on career field requirements
- value discipline over risk-taking

---

609 Zimmerman et al., 2019, p. 105; Shawn Snow, "Why the Corps Needs a System to Shoot Down Russian and Chinese Cruise Missiles," *Marine Corps Times*, February 11, 2019.

- be averse to questioning assumptions underlying existing processes, strategies, and orders
- lack key preparatory broadening and joint experiences for providing advice in senior-level joint billets
- rely on experience in tactically focused assignments
- have increased years of experience compared with other service G/FOs on which to base advice, which could add breadth and/or depth of judgment, or could further entrench specific biases and inflexibility
- place a high value on forward presence
- view warfighting strategy based on the models of those they have previously fought in
- favor investments that enable Marine Corps autonomy.

Potential Changes to Archetypal General Officers

The 2019 Commandant's Planning Guidance directs the investigation of several initiatives that, if fully implemented, would represent fundamental changes to the Marine Corps' approach to talent management, force organization, and institutional change. Some of these potential initiatives include extended maternity leave, use of BZ promotions, and increasing the weight of PME in FitReps.[610] However, as this guidance was published as this report was being written, it is too soon to tell what the impact of these investigations, and potential subsequent initiatives, might be. In any case, the Marine Corps' deeply valued culture will prove to be hard to change quickly, so we do not expect radical changes to the archetypical Marine Corps GO's typical career experiences or advisory tendencies in the near future.

Importance of Specific Experiences and Characteristics Across Services

Although this report does not seek to conduct comparative analysis of the utility of each service's approach to developing and selecting G/FOs, we include Table 8.9 for illustrative purposes. While other specific experiences matter for promotion to O-7 depending on the service, we highlight selected types of experience here to show the range of promotion criteria valuation across the services. We base our determinations on the totality of our research described in this report and define the range of values as "not important," "minimally important," "somewhat important," and "very important." Of note, the importance of some of these factors change beyond the grade of O-7, but Table 8.9 shows the importance of these experiences only in terms of each service's pathway up to O-7. The cells which are designated as "very important" are highlighted.

We observe some key areas of comparison in Table 8.9—many of which align with aspects of each service's culture. First, the only characteristic that is weighed with equal importance across all of the services is command experience. Second, the Navy and the Marine Corps highly value a smaller range of experiences in promotion decisions than the Army and the Air Force, concentrating value in just a few factors, but not the same ones. Third, what the Marine Corps

---

[610] U.S. Marine Corps, 2019.

values most—command experience, combat-related deployments, and personnel-based leadership—are among the same experiences as what the Army values most, which is unsurprising given both services' ground-centric cultures. Additionally, the Army also values high-visibility assignments and personal networks very highly, while the Marine Corps does not, a distinction that also aligns with Marine Corps culture.

Table 8.9. Importance of Specific Experiences for Promotion to O-7, by Service

	Army	Navy	Air Force	Marine Corps
Commissioning source	Somewhat important	Very important	Somewhat important	Minimally important
Joint experience	Minimally important	Minimally important	Somewhat important	Minimally important
Command experience	Very important	Very important	Very important	Very important
Below the Zone promotions	Minimally important	Not important	Very important	Not important
Combat-related deployments	Very important	Not important	Somewhat important	Very important
Type of PME and PME performance	Somewhat important	Not important	Very important	Not important
High-visibility assignments	Very important	Very important	Very important	Minimally important
Personnel-based leadership	Very important	Somewhat important	Somewhat important	Very important
Experience in strategic analysis	Not important	Not important	Very important	Not important
Personal networks	Very important	Very important	Very important	Minimally important

Areas for Further Research

Throughout the course of our analysis, we identified several key questions about the implications of service personnel approaches that were beyond the scope of this study but that merit further research. All of them provide further insights to the same broader policy concern underlying the research contained in this report—that is, whether the services need to change the way they are developing their G/FOs so that these senior leaders have the right development and experiences to effectively respond to rising threats and a changing global strategic environment. Accordingly, we recommend research in the following areas:

- **Can these hypotheses about archetype approaches to leadership, management, and advice be tested empirically?** While the potential approaches identified in this chapter are logical derivations of the service-specific archetype profiles, further studies with access to more data could test our hypotheses, and potentially measure the degree to which specific career experiences or other characteristics affect a G/FO's propensity to lead, manage, or advise in certain ways.

- **What are the experiences and professional characteristics required for success in key service and joint positions in the future, and are the services producing officers who will have those experiences and characteristics?** A study addressing this question would establish the demand signal for officer experiences and other characteristics, and help DoD understand whether the services' personnel management processes are sufficient for the future trajectories of national security challenges. Further, it could help DoD better understand which potential candidates for specific joint positions might be better prepared to fulfill those responsibilities, and how to select officers for key positions that require specific backgrounds and perspectives.
- **Is it possible to predict which mid-grade officers will become G/FOs based on available career experience data?** We found that certain professional experiences, depending on the service, tend to be more common in officers who later become G/FOs. Although other factors have significant impact on whether an officer will be promoted to O-7, it could be the case that professional experiences account for enough of an officer's promotion potential that forecasting future officers earlier in their careers is possible. If viable, such predictions could help the services assess which professional experiences they *want* to define future G/FOs, and which officers they want to further develop for G/FO potential.
- **What changes should DoD overall, and the services in particular, make to existing personnel processes to better develop and select for the characteristics they desire in senior leaders, and feasibility and trade-offs of those changes?** We did not attempt in this study to analyze how service processes could be changed to better align with DoD and service needs, but enough data exist to pursue this area of inquiry. Such a study could analyze informal selection mechanisms identified in this report, formal DoD and service policies, and federal legislation. This type of research could also analyze policy proposals, such as the development of separate officer tracks for strategy, warfighting, and other specialties, and also consider whether any military or civilian roles in the personnel management process should change.
- **How might future changes in the geostrategic landscape challenge personnel management processes?** Topics could include trade-offs that would need to be made in training and education in order to focus on more technical or innovative skills, whether jointness will continue to be valued as it currently is, and whether the ongoing strategic shift to focus on near-peer competition might stress the services' traditional practices.
- **What is the role of networks and personal connections in promotions?** We found that personal networks can play a significant role in officer career development, but we were unable to further explore their precise impact in promotion decisions to O-7 and beyond. Further research could establish methods to better understand how these personal connections, including accession source networks, mentors, senior raters, and more, shape the nation's G/FO corps.
- **How can this analysis be applied to specific communities that compose a minority of G/FO positions but remain critical to executing national security strategy?** This study focused on the most common archetypes of G/FOs in each service, generally representing a subset of career fields, but other G/FO archetypes from smaller career fields—such as special operations, intelligence, and cyber professionals—also tend to

have strategic impact, and their impact could increase in the future. Understanding service preferences for characteristics and experiences in those communities would provide greater understanding to senior civilians in DoD about what approaches to advice and institutional leadership these officers would bring to G/FO positions.

- **What are service and joint preferences for G/FO characteristics in the O-9 and O-10 ranks, and for specific joint positions, such as CJCS, CCMD commanders, and other key roles?** As shown in this report, service preferences for selection to O-7 (largely based on operation command) have direct effects on the future pool of candidates for O-9 and O-10 leadership, as they are drawn directly from former O-7s who are promoted. An exploration of the skills required of O-9 and O-10 leadership could shift priorities for service selection at O-7.
- **How could the SLSE method be applied to military personnel management questions about the joint force?** The exercise could be expanded to examine the needs and preferences of the joint force. Future research could identify ways in which specific service cultures might generate comparative advantages for specific joint G/FO billets, or could better inform the services how to develop and select officers to meet the needs across the full range of joint G/FO billets.

Conclusion

Looking forward, we expect that the professional experiences and characteristics that tend to define each service's G/FO corps and that might drive their management and advisory approaches will largely remain the same in the near to mid-term, given the length of military careers and how long major changes to personnel management processes can take. Although adjustments to officer development processes, and responses to changes in the geopolitical environment, will certainly occur, the institutional traditions and cultures of each service are strong and entrenched, and therefore will evolve slowly.

Most current G/FOs have well more than 30 years of service. The length of time it takes to become a G/FO means that only in the past few years has the G/FO corps included officers who spent their entire career in the post–Goldwater Nichols joint military environment. Similarly, the Navy and Air Force opened up many of their most high-profile career fields to women in the 1990s, but only now are the women who were able to enter those fields at the beginning of their military career (rather than transferring later than usual) becoming eligible for promotion to G/FO. Changes to how the U.S. military overall and the individual services develop and select their G/FOs often take a long time to fully take effect, sometimes even taking a generation or more to reach their full impact, at least partially because of the time it takes officers to move up through the ranks.

Certain trends suggest inevitable evolution in the G/FO corps, however. The requirements of major ongoing military operations since 2001, as well as technological development and the changing nature of war itself, will help shape leadership development. Because of a long period of major deployments to Iraq and Afghanistan, many officers have gained extensive warfighting experience, particularly in the career fields that are most combat-oriented and are often most well represented in the G/FO corps in certain services. At the same time, special operations, cyber warfare, space, and other missions have increased in prominence and will continue to do so, increasing the demand for G/FOs with experience in those specific fields.

Current efforts across the services to reform military personnel processes, such as allowing career intermissions during which to pursue civilian education and increasing merit-based promotions, might have value, but the impacts of these changes will take years to ascertain. Other efforts, such as reducing the number of G/FOs across the force, could have lasting implications on officer development, but, again, it will be years before the impact will be known. For example, one potential implication of the reduction in G/FOs is a corresponding reduction or downgrading in certain preparatory assignments. Some of the positions targeted for cuts are staff director, deputy, and chief of staff assignments—positions that are frequently leveraged as professional development opportunities to prepare a junior GO for a position of greater responsibility. Further, G/FO reduction efforts could also result in lowering morale across the officer corps as leadership opportunities diminish, which could affect officer retention and performance.

Despite these potential effects on officer development, the very nature of culture means that efforts to change the development, training, and experiences of G/FOs in each of the services will take time and substantial effort, given the strong ties between officer development processes and military culture. As DoD determines whether adjustments to current officer personnel management processes are merited and feasible, senior leaders can use this research as a guide to understand how an officer's career experiences and service culture might converge to shape the way senior military officers approach management and leadership challenges and provide advice.

Appendix A. Detailed Description of DMDC Data Analysis

The primary data set we used was the DMDC Active Duty Master File, which provides individual-level data on all active duty military personnel on a monthly basis. We collected the these files for January in each of the years for which data were available, 1995 to 2018, and used them to create a single person-year level database, with separate entries for each individual in each year they were recorded on active duty.

We compiled active-duty officer numbers by service and grade using this database and then checked these numbers against those found in DMDC's public reports on active duty officers by service and grade for January of each year and found them to be identical or nearly identical (less than 0.2 percent difference).[611] The data were then processed and cleaned, with a small number (less than 1 percent of total) of National Guard and Reserve component officers on active duty removed from the database, together with an even smaller number (less than 0.01 percent of total) of records with duplicate unique identifiers (scrambled social security numbers). We augmented this database with three additional DMDC datasets, on active duty pay, educational and training history, and training courses.[612]

We also used the DMDC Formal Course Database to identify course identifiers for two courses of particular importance for senior leader development: Ranger School for the Army and Weapons School for the Air Force. We then examined the DMDC Individual Training History Files, which contain individual-level data on all military education and training courses completed by active duty military personnel, to identify which officers had graduated from these courses and when. These data were then joined to our master database, with each person-year record now indicating whether that officer had graduated from Ranger School or Weapons School.

This final database allowed us to group officers by grade, career field, commissioning source, course completion, and other relevant characteristics. We then compared the distribution of these groups across each of the services and examined these various officer groups' characteristics related to career progression. Career experiences we analyzed from this database were time in grade, years in service, accession source, career field, and course completion.

---

[611] Defense Manpower Data Center, 2018.

[612] Since we did not have available data on combat-related deployment time, we approximated time by extracting data on combat-related pay from the DMDC active duty pay files. This data provided individual-level pay on all active duty military personnel on a monthly basis from 1995–2018. We counted an individual as deployed for each month that they received the combat zone tax exclusion and/or received "hostile fire/imminent danger pay." However, we found that using this method to approximate combat deployments was unreliable across the services and did not include it in our analysis.

To capture how officers are distributed across grades, and career paths, we averaged data over the period from calendar years 2008 to 2018. This multiyear focus served to even out annual variations that could skew findings based on a single year's data and allowed us to eliminate earlier years for which more data were missing. We often analyzed the characteristics of all officers in a given grade in each of these years, but some analyses were conducted just on the cohort of officers who had recently been promoted to that grade in the prior calendar year. This latter approach allowed us to avoid double-counting officers and to more precisely understand the experience of specific officer grade cohorts up through their prior grade. For example, examining a recently promoted Army O-4 cohort provided insights into the O-1 to O-3 experiences that led to the O-4 promotion. We found this to be a much cleaner methodology rather than lumping all officers of a given rank together regardless of their time in grade.

The person-year level database we used for our analysis contained separate records for each officer for every year they were on active duty. Each of these person-year records contained information on that officer's status at the time the data were collected (January of each year), as well as the officer's most recent promotion rate. We used these records to compile a set of information on characteristics of that officers' overall career, including calculations of how long they remained in each grade and what grades they eventually did or did not reach. We then associated these career-long officer characteristics with the snapshot-in-time person-year records for that officer, allowing us to examine an officer's status at the beginning of any given year and place this into the context of that officers' past and future overall career.

The fact that our data set ends in 2018 meant that we had to carefully choose the baseline time periods examined when conducting forward-looking analyses of officer careers. For example, when calculating the percentage of officers at a particular rank who are later promoted to the next higher grade, we used 2000 to 2010 as the baseline time period for our analysis. All officers of a given rank in any of these years would be expected to either promote to the next higher grade or retire from active duty prior to 2018, the final year of our data set, because of the military's "up or out" approach to career progression. If we included a more recent year in our baseline, such as 2014, we would find that many officers at the grade of O-3 and higher were still at the same rank four years later in 2018; only in future years' data will it become clear whether or not they promote to the next grade.

Because of the scope of our study, we were not able to analyze all available data, nor analyze it in certain ways. For example, one limitation within the DMDC data as provided was that we were able to pull it either by accession source or MOS; we were not able to cross-tabulate in order to see whether there were any interaction effects between the two (though we recognize that there would be a utility in such analysis). In this case, we made the decision to analyze the data by MOS, as we determined that would yield richer observations because MOS is so closely related to many educational, training, and duty assignments.

Appendix B. Service Personnel Basics

In this appendix, we provide background on select service personnel basics relevant to our discussion of G/FO selection: pay grade structure, end strength and the size of the officer corps, and the distribution of officers across the services.

Pay Grade Structure

Military officers in each of the services are separated by pay grades. Junior officers are those in the grades of O-1 through O-3, and field-grade officers are O-4s through O-6s. G/FO grades begin at O-7 and end at O-10. Official ranks that correspond to pay grades are the same for officers in the Army, Air Force, and Marine Corps, but the Navy's differ, as noted in Table B.1.

Table B.1. Officer Pay Grades and Rank by Service

Pay Grade	Army	Navy	Air Force	Marine Corps
O-1	Second Lieutenant	Ensign	Second Lieutenant	Second Lieutenant
O-2	First Lieutenant	Lieutenant Junior Grade	First Lieutenant	First Lieutenant
O-3	Captain	Lieutenant	Captain	Captain
O-4	Major	Lieutenant Commander	Major	Major
O-5	Lieutenant Colonel	Commander	Lieutenant Colonel	Lieutenant Colonel
O-6	Colonel	Captain	Colonel	Colonel
O-7 (one-star)	Brigadier General	Rear Admiral (Lower Half)	Brigadier General	Brigadier General
O-8 (two-star)	Major General	Rear Admiral (Upper Half)	Major General	Major General
O-9 (three-star)	Lieutenant General	Vice Admiral	Lieutenant General	Lieutenant General
O-10 (four-star)	General	Admiral	General	General

End Strength and Total Officers by Service

Congress determines each service's end strength, or total authorized personnel, in a given year. The Army's end strength is largest, given the service's size and requirements of its inherently ground-based mission, while the Marine Corps is smallest. The Marine Corps also has the smallest percentage of officers compared with its overall force—10.3 percent—and the Air Force has the highest, at 19.2 percent.

The number of G/FOs in each service closely corresponds to the total number of officers in each service. As shown in Table B.2, G/FOs make up a very similar proportion of the total officer corps, ranging from a low of 0.40 percent in the Army to 0.47 percent in the Air Force. Yet the number of G/FOs and the number of officers as a proportion of total active duty military strength varies somewhat by service. G/FOs compose just 0.046 percent of the Marine Corps, but 0.090 percent of the Air Force—a small number, but nearly double the percentage. In addition, while the Air Force has 2 percent fewer active military personnel than the Navy, it has 30 percent more G/FOs.

Table B.2. Active Duty Military Strength, Officer Totals, and Funding by Service, as of January 2018

	Army	Air Force	Navy	Marine Corps
Military strength	468,161	318,869	320,552	183,833
Officers	76,555	61,222	52,449	19,067
Total number of G/FOs	308	286	215	85
Officers as % of total service end strength	16.4%	19.2%	16.4%	10.3%
G/FOs as % of total service end strength	0.066%	0.090%	0.067%	0.046%
G/FOs as % of total officers by service	0.40%	0.47%	0.41%	0.45%
Funding (FY 2018, in millions)	158,354	170,239	(Department of the Navy combined numbers) 172,992	
Total funding (in millions) divided by total G/FOs	514	595	576	

SOURCES: Military strength: DMDC, 2018. Funding: Office of the Under Secretary of Defense (Comptroller), Chief Financial Officer, *Defense Budget Overview: U.S. Department of Defense Fiscal Year 2019 Budget Request*, February 2018, pp. 8-1, 8-7, 8-12.

Such differences are primarily due to the number of congressionally authorized officer billets and G/FO requirements for each service, but they do affect service culture and approaches to officer development and selection. These authorizations themselves take into account a number of factors, including the services' different manpower levels and their differing levels of responsibility for nonmanpower resources.[613] As shown in Table B.2, the Air Force's budget of $170 billion in FY 2018 is the highest of all the services, given the cost of the various platforms

[613] For more on congressionally authorized G/FO requirements by service, see Harrington et al., 2018, pp. 13–20.

at the heart of the service, and is nearly as high as the combined Navy and Marine Corps' budget of $172 billion.[614]

Officer Distribution by Service

Distribution of officers by grade is shaped in part by federal law. There is no statutory limit on officers in grades O-1 to O-3, but from grades O-4 to O-6, 10 U.S.C. Section 523 specifies limits by grade based on the overall size of the service's officer corps.[615] Other legal limitations on officer progression and on G/FO officer caps are described in Appendix C.

The distribution of officers by grade for each service, as depicted in grade "pyramids" in Figure B.1, show roughly similar proportions of officers at each grade, though there are some differences between the four services. One obvious difference occurs at the junior-most grades. While the junior-most officers in the Air Force, Navy, and Marine Corps all spend roughly equal amounts of time (24 months) in the grades of both O-1 and O-2, in the Army they spend just 18 months as O-1s and more time as O-2s, leaving the Army with fewer O-1s than O-2s.

The proportion of active duty O-3s to other officers within the same service is fairly similar across all of the services, ranging from 33 to 36 percent, as is the proportion of O-4s, which ranges from 20 to 22 percent.[616] However, the proportions diverge somewhat at O-5. Here the Marine Corps' pyramid narrows, with O-5s composing just 9.9 percent of officers, while the Air Force's O-5s compose 15.7 percent of officers, and the Navy and Army percentages fall in between the two. The Navy, Army, and Air Force pyramids then converge again, with O-6s composing 5.5 to 6.3 percent of each service's officer corps, while the equivalent figure for the Marine Corps stays low at 3.5 percent.

---

[614] Office of the Under Secretary of Defense (Comptroller), 2018, pp. 8–7, 8–12.

[615] For more information on officer grade limitations, including exceptions to the grade caps, see 10 U.S. Code, Section 523, Authorized Strengths: Commissioned Officers on Active Duty in Grades of Major, Lieutenant Colonel, and Colonel and Navy Grades of Lieutenant Commander, Commander, and Captain.

[616] Although the services' grade structure is pyramid-shaped in terms of diminishing numbers of officers promoted to subsequent higher grades, the time spent in grade is greatest at the O-3 and O-4, and to a lesser extent at the O-5 and O-6.

Figure B.1. Officer Pyramids, by Grade and Service, Average, 2008–2018

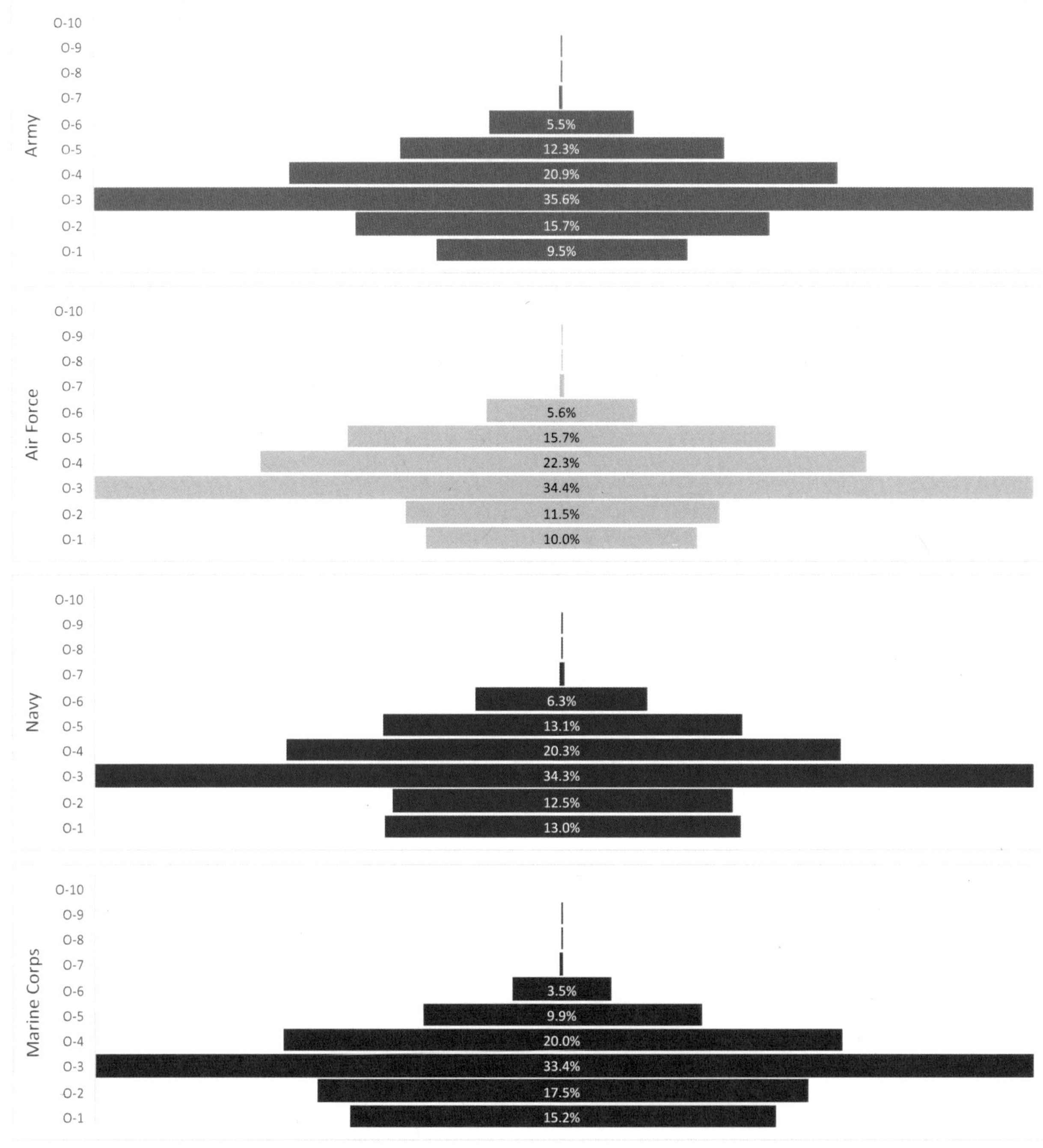

SOURCE: Authors' analysis of DMDC data.

For G/FOs specifically, the percentages across O-7, O-8, O-9, and O-10 reveal interesting patterns. In Figure B.2, we see that the Air Force has the greatest percentage of O-7s as compared with the other G/FO grades, but the smallest percentage of O-9s relative to the other services. This might reflect that the Air Force has many O-7 level requirements that need to be filled, but that it is not required to fill as many O-9 billets, many of which are joint, as other services do. The Marine Corps has the highest percentage of both O-9s and O-10s relative to the other services, which is related to the number of high-level joint and service requirements that service is selected to lead despite the Marine Corps' small number of GOs. The Army has the smallest percentage of O-10s compared with the other services, which is likely because the Army's GO corps is larger than the others, but O-10 positions are very limited.

Figure B.2. General/Flag Officer Grade Distributions, by Service, Average Percentage, 2008–2018

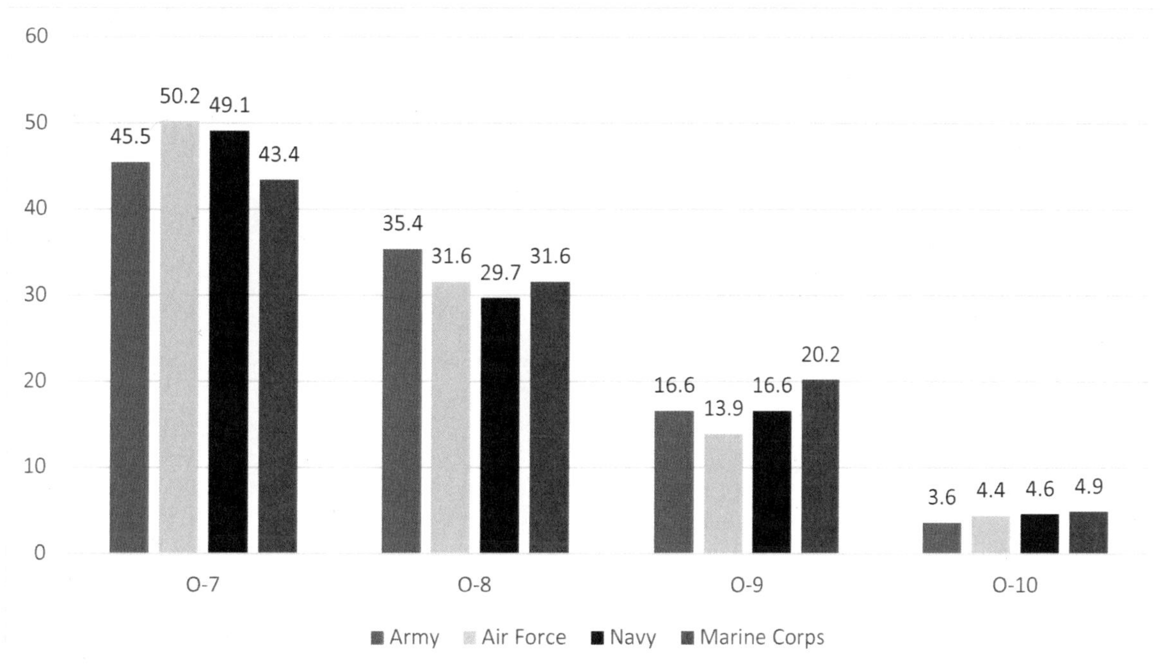

Grade	Army	Air Force	Navy	Marine Corps
O-7	45.5	50.2	49.1	43.4
O-8	35.4	31.6	29.7	31.6
O-9	16.6	13.9	16.6	20.2
O-10	3.6	4.4	4.6	4.9

SOURCE: Authors' analysis of DMDC data.

Appendix C. Key Legislation Governing Military Officer Personnel Management Processes

Congress actively exercises its oversight responsibilities with regard to military personnel matters by establishing limits on military budgets, end strength, and force structure, all of which affect personnel matters, and also by regularly reviewing the laws that specifically govern military personnel management. While many laws and statutes have a role in military personnel management, three key measures in particular have had the most widespread and lasting effect on officer career paths.[617] These laws provide fundamental underpinnings to the existing military personnel system, and they also create mechanisms to ensure congressional oversight into specific military personnel matters. Though these laws do not define the military's personnel management systems in their entirety, they do have foundational impact on the most significant aspects of each service's processes and procedures. These three pieces of legislation that most affect military officer career management from O-1 to O-10 are summarized in this appendix.

The 1947 Officer Personnel Act

In the years immediately following World War II, Congress focused on reforming traditional officer management practices across the Department of the Army and the Department of the Navy. Prior to World War II, the two departments managed officer careers independently, leading to discrepancies in promotion practices. Additionally, full mobilization of the U.S. military and rapid growth of the officer corps fostered stagnation throughout the officer corps as older officers remained in service stunting junior officers' ability to promote. In 1947, Congress passed the Officer Personnel Act (OPA). The act standardized officer career paths across the services and established the "up-or-out" system in place of the seniority-only based system, emphasizing a "young and vigorous" force requires an officer to either perform well enough to be promoted or else separate or retire.[618] OPA left a lasting legacy on the current personnel system: The foundation of modern officer career management, the competitive up-or-out system, remains in current statute and policy.

---

[617] For example, Congress has played a role in ensuring that acquisition professionals are adequately represented in senior officer ranks. For more information, see Albert A. Robbert, Tara L. Terry, Paul Emslie, and Michael Robbins, *Promotion Benchmarks for Senior Officers with Joint and Acquisition Service,* Santa Monica, Calif.: RAND Corporation, RR-1447-OSD, 2016, p. ix; Department of Defense Instruction 5000.66, *Defense Acquisition Workforce Education, Training, Experience, and Career Development Program*, Washington, D.C., U.S. Department of Defense, July 27, 2017, p. 12.

[618] Bernard Rostker, Harry Thie, James Lacy, Jennifer Kawata, and Susanna Purnell, *The Defense Officer Personnel Management Act of 1980: A Retrospective Assessment*, Santa Monica, Calif.: RAND Corporation, R-4246-FMP, 1993.

Defense Officer Personnel Management

In 1980, Congress passed DOPMA, a broad framework of rules and regulations through which the military services manage the careers of their officers. While each of the military services has a certain degree of autonomy in designing its military personnel management systems, DOPMA's requirements, many of which were based on processes used since World War II and the passage of OPA, provide the basis for these processes as a whole. DOPMA defined several aspects of today's officer personnel management system that are central to this study:

- **Uniform promotion system.** DOPMA provided a baseline for officer training, appointment, promotion, separation, and retirement across all four services. It further provided a requirement for "advanced education" of all officers.[619]
- **Competitive categories.** Officers compete for promotion among others in a competitive category, which is the grouping of officers who compete against each other for promotion.[620] Competitive categories, in practice, consist of one or multiple career fields for one or more ranks, although the law allows for other distinctions.[621] Competitive categories allow the services to manage the career development and promotion of groups of officers whose career fields make separate career management desirable in order to ensure that certain skill sets remain in the service and are not narrowed out by competition with larger communities (such as combat arms).[622] The services determine the specific composition of competitive categories. One consideration is that a small number of competitive categories might disadvantage noncombat career fields, as a financial officer may not be as competitive if placed in the same category as a fighter pilot, for example.[623]
- **Time-in-grade requirements and year groups.** DOPMA's time-in-grade requirements depicted earlier in this chapter define how long an officer must serve at a particular pay grade before they can be considered for promotion to the next pay grade.[624] These time in

619 Rostker et al., 1993, p. 7.

620 10 U.S. Code, Section 621, Competitive Categories for Promotion.

621 For instance, a military service could establish a competitive category for officers in the rank of O-5 who are fluent in a foreign language, regardless of career field. No service uses this option, but it would be allowable under the statute.

622 Department of Defense Instruction 1320.12, *Commissioned Officer Promotion Program*, Washington, D.C.: U.S. Department of Defense, September 27. 2015.

623 Sydney J. Freedburg Jr., "SASC Pushes Officer Promotion Changes; HASC Not So Much," *Breaking Defense*, May 25, 2018. Each of the services approaches competitive categories differently, which will be explored in later chapters. For example, the Marine Corps, finding that Financial Management Officers were not promoting in adequate rates to the more senior grades when competing with Combat Arms officers, established a separate competitive category for Financial Management Officers while all other officers compete in one separate competitive category. The Navy, for instance, uses 20 competitive categories. The Army, by comparison, starts most officers in one large competitive category for promotion to O-3, breaks that competitive category into four smaller competitive categories for O-4 to O-6 promotions, and then merges those four back into one competitive category for the O-7 promotion board.

624 10 U.S. Code, Section 619.

grade requirements effectively create "year groups," or officer categorizations based on year of commissioning that determine when officers are considered for promotion. This policy and practice enables the services to centrally manage cohorts, but this year-group construct can effectively select against "late bloomers" whose performance potential is realized later in their careers or whose professional skill contributions are more highly valued at higher ranks, sometimes past the point that a particular service identifies officers who are G/FO material. G/FOs in the ranks of O-8 through O-10 have no time-in-grade requirements.

- **Up-or-out system.** Building on provisions from the OPA, DOPMA continues the up-or-out model, preventing stagnation and ensuring that those officers promoted are the best qualified. The up-or-out model limits the amount of time an officer may spend in a particular grade and requires officers to either promote to the next grade within their primary or secondary promotion board for the grade or leave the service. Officers twice passed over for promotion may opt into a selective continuation board, remaining on active duty in their previous grade. However, officers who are not selected for promotion may be subject to involuntary separation, creating the competitive up-or-out system.[625] The up-or-out requirements ensure that officers of a similar year group progress through a military career at roughly the same pace. The predictability of the system allows the military services to develop career pathways that fit within specified career windows. DOPMA therefore results in standard career lengths, ranging from the voluntary retirement option at 20 years of service and mandatory retirement for non-G/FOs by 30 years of service.[626]
- **Promotion board composition.** Promotion boards must be composed of at least five officers from the same military service of higher rank.[627] To ensure a degree of equity, DOPMA also specified that promotion boards should, when possible, include at least one officer from each competitive category being considered for promotion.[628] DOPMA further defines the role of the Secretary of Defense, who is authorized to set regulations regarding which information should be made available to promotion boards, and the role of the service secretaries, who determine the maximum number of promotions by grade and competitive category.[629] The intent of these requirements is to ensure that all highly qualified officers have an equal chance that their knowledge, skills, and experiences will be evaluated by officers who understand the merit associated with those attributes. However, in practice, it is less likely that a representative from an officer's career field will be present on a promotion board in services with fewer competitive categories.

---

[625] 10 U.S. Code, Section 632, Effect of Failure of Selection for Promotion: Captains and Majors of the Army, Air Force, and Marine Corps and Lieutenants and Lieutenant Commanders of the Navy.

[626] Task Force on Defense Personnel, *Defense Personnel Systems: The Hidden Threat to a High-Performance Force*, Washington, D.C.: Bipartisan Policy Center, 2017, p. 10; U.S. Department of Defense, "Modernizing Military Pay: Report of the First Quadrennial Review of Military Compensation," The Military Estate Program (Appendices), Vol. V, 1969, pp. Appendix I, 111-4, 5.

[627] 10 U.S. Code, Section 612, Composition of Selection Boards.

[628] 10 U.S. Code, Section 612. Additionally, beginning in 1986, and as a result of Section 402 of the Goldwater-Nichols Act, boards for more senior grades where joint duty assignments are considered are required to include at least one officer currently serving in a joint assignment. The Marine Corps may waive the requirement.

[629] 10 U.S. Code, Section 615, Information Furnished to Selection Boards.

Overall, senior military leadership and the military departments continue to believe that, for the most part, the basic tenets of DOPMA provide an effective way to manage officer careers.[630] However, as the services compete for talent in emerging fields and as shifts occur across larger workforce dynamics, notable attention has been paid to reforming officer personnel management, including basic tenets of DOPMA in recent years.[631] While the officer management system created by DOPMA remained largely intact, criticisms have been leveled against the DOPMA's inflexibility. These include that cohort-based management does not recognize high performers, talent cannot be accessed from the civilian sector at senior levels, and the military cannot capture returns from senior officers at the peak of their performance.[632] Several efforts aimed at addressing these criticisms have occurred in recent years. The Force of the Future initiative, championed by then–Secretary of Defense Ash Carter and then–Acting Under Secretary of Defense for Personnel and Readiness Brad Carson, attempted to identify ways in which DoD could adapt officer career management policies within the limitations outlined in DOPMA.[633] Congress and service leadership were not initially receptive to personnel management reforms as suggested in Force of the Future, but recent provisions in the FY 2019 NDAA provide flexibilities within statute enabling the services to recruit and retain critical skill sets within the DOPMA construct, as detailed in the following section.[634]

Officer Personnel Management Flexibilities Provided for in the FY 2019 NDAA

The FY 2019 NDAA introduced changes to officer personnel management that could have substantial impact on officer career pathways. Broadly, the reforms

- remove a previous age restriction at time of commissioning
- allow for additional constructive service credit at commissioning
- standardize temporary promotion authority across military departments
- allow resequencing of promotion lists based on merit
- allow officers to opt out of promotion consideration under some circumstances
- allow selective consideration of more junior officers

---

[630] Robbert et al., 2019, p. xix.

[631] For additional information on DOPMA and the necessity and implications of potential DOPMA reforms, see Rostker et al., 1993, and Robbert et al., 2019.

[632] Barno et al., 2013; Tim Kane, *Bleeding Talent: How the US Military Mismanages Great Leaders and Why It's Time for a Revolution*, New York: Palgrave Macmillan, 2013; Colarusso and Lyle, 2014.

[633] Under Secretary of Defense for Personnel and Readiness, *Force of the Future Final Report: Reform Proposals, Version 2.0*, U.S. Department of Defense, August 24, 2015; Andrew Tilghman, "Pentagon's Quiet Push for Military Personnel Reform," *Military Times*, May 11, 2015.

[634] For more information on these changes to DOPMA, see Public Law 115-232, John S. McCain National Defense Authorization Act for Fiscal Year 2019, August 13, 2018.

- provide an alternative promotion framework for officers in designated competitive categories.[635]

The changes maintain the overall DOPMA framework for most officer career paths but enable service secretaries a degree of flexibility in targeting officers with critical skill sets for recruitment and retention. Further, the provisions enable the recruitment of older officers and those with significant experience to commission at grades associated with mid-career officers, and the provisions enable the services to work around the tenets of the up-or-out system, if necessary, in order to meet service requirements. For example, the service secretary may approve an individual's request to opt out of a promotion board if the officer was not able to fulfill key promotion requirements, such as PME, because they were meeting a service requirement in an assignment that prohibited their participation. The service secretary could therefore remove the stigma associated with being "passed over" for promotion. The service secretaries are also granted the authority to create additional alternative competitive categories with varying promotion timelines, addressing particular competitive categories that would benefit from faster promotion paths (such as cyber career fields, which may need to keep pace with the private sector) or slower promotion paths (such as foreign area officers, who might benefit from more time at the grade of O-4 in order to complete all necessary education, training, and key assignments).

Despite these flexibilities, the changes might not influence the core qualities or timelines of future G/FOs. The services, consistent with their cultures, developed models of ideal behavior and experience that are well adapted to aspects of DOPMA that did not change. Further, it is likely that many of the FY 2019 NDAA provisions will not apply to officers who select out of a typical G/FO career path, and instead benefit officers in niche specialties, limiting potential impact on the most common pathways to generalship.

1986 Department of Defense Reorganization Act (Goldwater-Nichols)

Goldwater-Nichols directed substantial changes to DoD's organizational structure to ensure that the President, the NSC, and the Secretary of Defense receive the best military advice from the Joint Chiefs of Staff (JCS). The act specifically established joint duty prerequisites for all military officers, requiring joint assignments prior to promotion to G/FO.[636] Recognizing that the services prioritized key assignments within their service rather than in joint billets, particularly for their most competitive officers, the act further laid forth the expectation that officers in joint assignments should promote at comparable rates to their peers in assignments within their service—thus ensuring that officers were not penalized for fulfilling a joint assignment. The main Goldwater-Nichols components of officer management are as follows:

---

[635] Public Law 115-232; Robbert et al., 2019, pp. xviii–xix.

[636] Public Law 99-433, Goldwater-Nichols Department of Defense Reorganization Act of 1986.

- **Joint officer management.** Officers are selected for joint service by the Secretary of Defense with the advice of the CJCS. Service secretaries nominate competitive individuals for joint assignments, beginning at the grades of senior O-3 through O-4. A joint duty assignment requires three and a half years to qualify, though the Secretary of Defense has the option to provide a waiver for individuals with at least two years of joint duty.
- **Promotion procedures for joint officers.** Goldwater-Nichols specifies that selection boards must include at least one officer currently serving in a joint duty assignment.
- **Consideration of joint duty in senior G/FO appointments and advice on qualifications.** As part of the nomination process to the grade of O-9, the CJCS must submit an evaluation of the officer's performance in other joint duty assignments. The Secretary of Defense must also inform the President of the necessary joint qualifications required of the officer promoted to the O-9 position.
- **Joint duty assignment as a prerequisite for promotion to G/FO.** Officers may not be selected for promotion to the grade of O-7 if they have not previously served in a joint duty assignment. [637]

Goldwater-Nichols reforms were intended to create a more-joint force led by senior officers practiced in interservice operations. As a consequence of the additional requirements, however, service-specific experience suffered, and officers were required to meet additional requirements within stringent career timelines. Particular career fields, including Navy aviators and Air Force pilots, reported in interviews that they often struggle to meet required training and operational time within their service.[638] Additionally, the timeline for joint assignments begins after the tenth year of service, often at the same time that highly competitive officers are competing for leadership positions in command assignments within their own service.[639] Acknowledging these challenges, then–Secretary of Defense Ash Carter proposed that the qualifying period of joint duty should be shortened from three years to two years to ensure that the most competitive officers had the flexibility to pursue command and broadening experiences in addition to meeting the intent of the Goldwater-Nichols joint duty requirement.

---

[637] For additional information on the impacts of Goldwater-Nichols on joint qualification, including joint professional military education, for example, see Kamarck, 2016.

[638] Robbert et. al, 2019, p. 21.

[639] Bernard D. Rostker, "Reforming the American Military Officer Personnel System," testimony before the Senate Armed Services Committee, Santa Monica, Calif.: RAND Corporation, CT-446, December 2, 2015.

Appendix D. General and Flag Officer Management Processes

G/FOs fill the positions of greatest authority, responsibility, and importance among uniformed officers in DoD. They are few in number, relative to the size of the overall military and officer corps, and have the most experience. To become a G/FO, an officer must progress through the ranks to O-6 and then be chosen by their service for promotion to O-7, in an extremely selective process.[640] Accordingly, this promotion is much different than those in previous grades and represents a significant step in an officer's career.

This promotion is not only representative of the increased responsibilities in senior leadership positions in the military, but it is also highly symbolic. Thomas Ricks described the transformative promotion from an Army perspective in *The Generals*, though it is true across the services.

> The promotion from colonel to brigadier (or one-star) general is one of the largest psychological leaps an officer can take. It is richly symbolic: The promoted officer removes from his or her collar the insignia of an Army branch . . . and puts on a single star. As brigadier generals, the newly promoted officers are instructed in a special course—they no longer represent a part of the Army, but now are the stewards of the entire service. As members of the Army's select few, they are expected to control and coordinate different branches, such as artillery, cavalry, and engineers—that is, to become generalists.[641]

Reflecting this major leap, G/FO responsibilities, personnel, and positions overall are tightly managed within DoD and overseen by Congress. In the following sections, we will discuss how G/FO requirements are determined, and how G/FO positions are filled, authorized and managed.

General/Flag Officer Requirements, Roles, and Responsibilities

A small number of G/FO positions, such as combatant commanders, service chiefs, and the CJCS, are specifically required by federal statute. All other G/FO requirements are designated by DoD and the services, which take a shared overall approach to choosing which positions are of sufficient importance to require filling with a G/FO. Each service, the Joint Staff, and OSD have GO and/or FO management offices that are tasked with balancing available G/FO inventory and DoD requirements with congressional authorizations and limitations.

---

[640] Just as with field-grade officers, promotion objectives at O-7 and O-8 include the requirement that officers are joint-qualified. For more information on joint qualification for G/FO ranks, see DoDI 1300.19, 2018. Further, O-9s and O-10s are subject to a substantively different evaluation and promotion selection process. Officers are not promoted to the grade of O-9 or O-10 as such; instead, these positions are requirements driven and officers must be nominated by the President and approved by the U.S. Senate to fill a specific position. Further, O-9s and O-10s do not receive formal evaluation reports.

[641] Ricks, 2012, p. 9.

DoD's approach to establishing G/FO requirements was described by then–Under Secretary for Personnel and Readiness Clifford Stanley in 2011. He stated:

> They assess any statutory requirements; the nature of the position's duties and magnitude of its responsibilities; the span of control and scope of resources managed; and the significance of actions and decisions required by the position along with the importance of the position's mission accomplishment to national security and other national interests.[642]

The following criteria are used in these determinations of G/FO requirements:[643]

- nature, characteristics, and function of the position
- grade and position of superior, principal subordinates, and lateral points of coordination
- degree of independence of operation
- official relations with other U.S. and foreign governmental positions
- magnitude of responsibilities
- mission and special requirements
- number, type, and value of resources managed and employed
- forces, personnel, value of equipment, total obligation authority
- geographic area of responsibility
- authority to make decisions and commit resources
- development of policy
- national commitment to international agreements
- impact on national security and other national interests
- effect on the prestige of the nation or the armed force.

Of course, once requirements are established, the G/FO management offices need to determine which available G/FOs should fill these requirements. Some G/FO positions require specific experiences or special designations, such as for acquisition professionals and non-acquisition science and technology. At the more senior levels, G/FOs serving in certain positions are required by law to hold certain grades or have previously held specific assignments, such as the CJCS, who must have served previously as the Vice Chairman of the Joint Chiefs of Staff (VCJCS), a service chief, or a combatant commander.[644]

---

[642] Clifford L. Stanley and William E. Gortney, "General and Flag Officer Requirements," testimony before the Subcommittee on Personnel, Senate Armed Services Committee, Washington, D.C., September 14, 2011, pp. 62–63.

[643] Congressional Research Service, *General and Flag Officers in the U.S. Armed Forces: Background and Considerations for Congress*, Washington, D.C., February 1, 2019, pp. 3–4. Also see Harrington et al., 2018, pp. 3–4, 34–36.

[644] However, the President can waive this law. See 10 U.S.C. Section 152. For more information on statutory requirements and management procedures for general and flag officers, see Chairman of the Joint Chiefs of Staff Instruction 1331.01D, *Manpower and Personnel Actions Involving General and Flag Officers,* Washington, D.C.: U.S. Department of Defense, August 1, 2010; Department of Defense Instruction 1320.04, *Military Office Actions Requiring Presidential, Secretary of Defense, or Under Secretary of Defense for Personnel and Readiness Approval or Senate Confirmation*, Washington, D.C.: U.S. Department of Defense, January 3, 2014.

In other cases, G/FO positions are intended to be filled by leaders with a wide range of experience and backgrounds. This is particularly true in joint G/FO positions, which are filled by G/FOs from each of the services. G/FOs serving on the Joint Staff, for example, must be roughly equally sourced by the Army, the Air Force, and the Navy and Marine Corps (representing one department).[645] As we will see later in this report, certain career fields in each of the services tend to dominate the G/FO grades, particularly at the O-9 and O-10 grades. In general, the number of G/FO positions available for certain career fields, such as JAG, medical personnel, and administrative specialists, tend to be very few in number.

General and Flag Officer Requirements, Authorizations, and Distributions

In addition to the key legislative acts described earlier, Congress also directs several aspects of G/FO management, establishing specific positions, confirming nominees for particular roles and promotions, and authorizing the total number of G/FOs in DoD and by service. The 2018 RAND report *Realigning the Stars: A Methodology for Reviewing Active Component General and Flag Officer Requirements* summarizes Congress's role in controlling the number of DoD G/FOs as follows:

> - The overall authorized strength, for the maximum number of G/FOs that DoD could potentially employ.
> - The allocation of those authorizations across the services; for example, how many go to the Army, the Navy, the Air Force, for the Marine Corps, and the pool of officers serving in joint duty positions.
> - The distribution of those officers in officer grades O-7 through O-10.[646]

One specific aspect of G/FO officer authorizations that concerns Congress is managing the proportion of G/FOs relative to the overall size of the total force. Congress establishes the total authorized number of G/FOs in the U.S. military as well as the number of G/FO positions allocated to each service and their distribution across the O-7 through O-10 grades.[647] Congress periodically reviews and changes these authorized numbers. As a recent Congressional Research Service report stated, "A frequent tension during these reviews has been DoD requests for additional GFOs versus congressional concerns that there are too many GFOs."[648] Congressional concerns about the military being top-heavy with G/FOs have been particularly pronounced during periods when the military is downsizing, such as after the end of the Vietnam War, after

---

[645] 10 U.S. Code, Section 155, Joint Staff.

[646] For additional information, see Harrington et al., 2018, p. 13. For more information on the specific sections of the U.S. Code that govern these authorizations and distributions, see Harrington et al., 2018, pp. 13–20, 157–183.

[647] For specific sections of U.S. Code that govern these authorizations and distributions, see Harrington et al., 2018, pp. 13–20, 157–183.

[648] Congressional Research Service, 2019, p. 1.

the Cold War, or after the more recent end of major deployments in Iraq and Afghanistan.[649] These concerns informed the 2017 NDAA, which set the current statutory levels of G/FO authorizations and called for a reduction in their number by the end of 2022.

As of November 2018, the number of total authorized G/FO positions was 963. This includes service-specific as well as joint G/FO positions. The current service-specific G/FO authorizations by grade and service are depicted in Table D.1.

Table D.1. General/Flag Officer Authorization by Service and Grade

Grade	Army	Navy	Air Force	Marine Corps
O-10 maximum	7	6	9	2
O-9 and O-10 combined maximum	46	33	44	2
O-8 maximum	90	50	73	22
O-7 minimum	95	79	81	23
Total	231	162	198	62

NOTE: 10 U.S. Code, Section 525, Distribution of Commissioned Officers on Active Duty in General Officer and Flag Officer Grades; 10 U.S. Code, Section 526, Authorized Strength: General and Flag Officers on Active Duty. For more information on service-specific authorizations and allocations of G/FOs by grade, see Harrington et al., 2018. 10 U.S.C. 525 provides the total number of G/FOs by service, further specified as those serving in the grade of O-10, those serving in grade O-9 plus O-10, and those serving in the grade O-8. Remaining G/FO authorizations are the minimum number of O-7s.

Additionally, Congress specifies authorizations for G/FOs serving in joint positions, collectively called the "joint pool." These 310 positions, which are not subject to the same statutory limitations as service-specific positions, are broken down by grade in Table D.2.

Table D.2. Authorizations for Joint General/Flag Officer Positions

Grade	Total
O-10	20
O-9	68, minus total O-10s
O-8	144
O-7	310, minus total O-8s—O-10s

NOTE: The allocation of the joint pool by service is defined in 10 U.S.C. 526(2).

As mentioned earlier, Congress implemented a series of changes to reduce total G/FO authorizations in the FY 2017 NDAA. As of December 31, 2022, DoD is required to reduce its G/FO totals to 620 service positions and 232 joint positions, a total reduction of 110 G/FO

[649] Congressional Research Service, 2019, p. 1.

positions.[650] These reductions are being implemented differently in each of the services, so total positions will continue to decrease at varying rates until that date.

[650] 10 U.S.C. 526.

Appendix E. Methodology and Findings from the Senior Leader Selection Exercise

To support our efforts to develop and test profiles based on our evaluation of the typical professional backgrounds and other relevant attributes of G/FOs in each service, RAND hosted a SLSE in January 2019. The purpose of the three-stage, full-day exercise was to examine which professional characteristics and experiences mattered most in selection for promotion to the grade of O-7. Retired officers from the rank of O-6 to O-10 participated in the exercise. The findings from the exercise address the following question: What factors in an individual's career path matter most to their service when being considered for promotion to the grade of O-7 and why? In this chapter, we summarize the structure and findings of the exercise, including key points taken from facilitated discussions. We also assess ways the exercise structure could be applied to other policy questions.

Game Structure

The specific purpose of the exercise was to reveal certain common preferences for profile characteristics related to O-7 selection decisions in each service, including education level, commissioning source, career field, assignment history, and PME experience, and help test the profiles that we developed over the course of our research. The exercise provided a mechanism to isolate which factors or combinations of factors were most prevalent in those selected (and those not selected) for O-7 in each service. Further, the exercise provided secondary observations for use in our overall research on the mechanics of service personnel processes, dynamics at play within board proceedings, and how service culture affects preferences for officer experiences, traits, and abilities in each service.

To isolate the role of various factors, we divided the exercise into three separate stages with numbers of selectees constrained or unconstrained in each scenario. In two stages, participants worked individually; in the third stage, they worked in service-specific groups. We conducted one facilitated discussion following the conclusion of the individual participation stages, and one following the group participation session to further understand why certain factors mattered or did not matter in the selection of G/FOs. We also included a "self-identification question" that asked individuals to circle the number of the profile they felt most closely matched their career path. After the conclusion of the exercise, we analyzed which profile the participant selected as most similar to their own and tabulated the ranking that the participant had given to that profile in the unconstrained stage.

Participants

We invited retired officers at the grades of O-6 through O-10 from the four services to compare the preferences of those who were promoted to G/FO and those who were either not selected for promotion or chose to leave the service before promotion to O-7. Selection exercise participants were a separate group of individuals from those we included in interviews. Thirty participants attended the event: seven former Navy officers, six former Air Force officers, eight former Army officers, and nine former Marine Corps officers. Every service group featured at least one former G/FO. To generate an environment in which all service representatives felt they could participate equally, ranks were not included in participant materials. The exercise observed the Chatham House Rule to enable participants to speak freely without fear that they would be associated publicly with their comments.[651] We used both individual and service-based team structures to draw out participants' choices and feedback regarding their service's preferences.

Notional Profiles

We developed 50 profiles of officers at the grade of O-6 for each service, for a total of 200 profiles, using a spreadsheet matrix. We developed the profiles based on our overall study analysis of DMDC quantitative data, information gleaned from a review of current active duty G/FO biographies, our review of literature, and subject-matter interviews. Professional experiences in the profiles included

- career field
- in-residence ILE versus correspondence
- commissioning source
- quality and type of graduate education
- special training schools
- specific O-5 command/command-select positions
- specific O-6 command/command-select positions
- specific O-6 post-command billets, service and joint.

To develop realistic billets and test for preferences, we based professional characteristics on the actual rates by career field, in-residence versus correspondence ILE, commissioning source, and special training schools within the specific service. Further, if a specific training was deemed a prerequisite for a specific assignment, we ensured that the profile contained the relevant training (for example, an Army officer could only serve in the elite 75th Ranger Regiment if they were a Ranger School graduate). With respect to graduate education, each of the services was assigned the same number of civilian master's degree programs with the same distribution of quality (for example, assigning some officers a master's degree from Georgetown University,

---

[651] Under the Chatham House Rule, "participants are free to use the information received, but neither the identity nor the affiliation of the speaker(s), nor that of any other participant, may be revealed." Chatham House, "Chatham House Rule," undated.

and others a master's degree through the University of Phoenix) in order to compare the value of graduate education both within and across the services. We also included O-6 post-command billets that were designated as three-star and four-star executive and staff positions, headquarters staff positions within a service, CCMD staff positions, and Joint Staff positions at roughly the same rates across the services. Further, we introduced BZ promotions at rates reflective of service utilization: 8 percent in the Army, 4 percent in the Air Force, 1 percent in the Navy, and 0 percent in the Marine Corps.[652]

Within the profiles, we also included randomized qualitative variables, which were consistent across the services. First, we included a category articulating whether the service representative knew the officer's rater. If the service representative knew the rater, we further delineated between whether the representative trusted the rater or did not trust the rater. These randomized variables were not intended to be perfectly representative, but rather to serve as a proxy for the role relationships might play for an individual serving on a board. Additionally, to spur conversation regarding the role of relationships and network effects, we introduced a randomized variable into four profiles in each service for whether an officer's parent was a G/FO.

Game Parameters

While individual preferences provide useful information, the exercise was intended to reveal systemic preferences within individual services. To capture system dynamics, we asked participants to roleplay, providing the guidance that they should select individuals they thought the average board member from their service would select. The roleplaying guidance allowed for further discussion of the differences between personal preference and "typical" board member preference during the facilitated discussions. Participants were provided with five major assumptions:

- All notional candidates have been evaluated as high quality and the best of all their peers, or "1 of N," in their evaluations at each grade through O-6
- There are no adverse actions in any files.
- For any required extra schooling or test performance specific to a billet that was not included, the officer has exceeded the standard at each point.
- Where specific information is included such as named units or commands (e.g., the 75th Ranger Regiment), it is intended to be significant.
- Where general information is provided (for example, "O-5 operational command"), a due-course assignment or PME opportunity would have followed.
- All are joint-qualified.

---

[652] Authors' analysis of DMDC data; Marx, 2014, p. 14. In the Army, fewer people are promoted BZ multiple times over a career than in the Air Force, but more are promoted just once. In the Air Force, it is more likely that the same individuals are promoted BZ to O-4 and later to O-5 or O-6. The percentage of individuals promoted BZ is lower in the Air Force, but those officers who are promoted BZ are promoted to BZ multiple times in their career.

The game assumed that all notional candidates had similarly high-performance evaluations in order to capture that all individuals seriously being considered for G/FO must have sustained superior performance. The assumption further enabled us to isolate consistent factors beyond exceptional performance that serve as discriminating factors between those who were selected for promotion and those who were not. These discriminating factors illuminate what the services value, providing insights into the archetypical G/FO within the service.

Limitations

We designed this exercise to socialize and validate the project's in-progress findings regarding the importance of qualitative and quantitative factors in considering which individuals are selected to the grade of O-7 in each service. While it had significant utility in this regard, the exercise presents several limitations.

We did not intend to use the exercise as a scientific validation of our findings, but rather to test our assumptions in discussion with subject-matter experts. Additionally, we did not intend for the results of the exercise to be predictive. The exercise provided us with the ability to characterize which qualities and experiences the services value when selecting for G/FO, and the implications for future G/FO selection if the current trends continue. Further, while we did include a few proxies for networks and relationships, the exercise could not truly replicate the role that relationships play in selection for promotion. Moreover, to simplify the exercise process, we intentionally removed key evaluation feedback that a board would otherwise have—specifically, rater comments. Although we asked participants to assume that all files represented the same exceptional rater feedback, we recognize that for all services (some more than others), these comments are critical in the decisionmaking process. We also did not include mock photos in the profiles, which some services use as a distinguisher during a promotion board. Additionally, although we examined throughout the course of the broader study why the services decide to promote or separate individuals, we did not consider the reasons competitive individuals might choose to separate from the service before promoting to the G/FO ranks in this exercise. Lastly, in the interest of allowing free-flowing discussion, we did not assign anyone to the role of board president, which could present a different set of dynamics than those that exist in a true board.

Stage-Specific Results

The exercise was designed to facilitate comparison of the different results from each stage across all three stage. Accordingly, we provide our conclusions based on collective findings from all three stages, the self-identification exercise, and the facilitated discussion.

For Stages 1 and 2 of the game, participants' selections were weighted based on position. Each participant's first choice was assigned ten points, their second choice was assigned nine points, and so on until their tenth choice which was assigned one point. We then combined the assigned points per profile to calculate the top ten profiles for each service. For Stage 3 of the game, the participants assigned the same weighting guidelines outlined in the first two stages rubric internal to their deliberations and delivered their collective top-ten selections.

Stage 1: Unconstrained Individual Rank-Ordering

During the first stage of the exercise, individuals were provided with all 50 profiles for their service and given one hour to rank-order the profiles from 1 to 50. We proposed a theoretical legislative mandate whereby promotions were not constrained by quotas or caps by career field. Given the time constraint, most participants approached the exercise by quickly reviewing all profiles once before reordering accordingly. Participants then individually filled out a promotion exercise table, rank-ordering all 50 profiles. Participants were asked not to discuss their determinations with anyone else on their team. We then tabulated the individual rankings by group and identified the top ten most commonly selected profiles in each service.

Findings from Stage 1

Some common themes emerged across the services. Having held a command position at O-5 and O-6 was the most important prerequisite for promotion to O-7. Confirming our previous research, every profile among the top ten selections for each service had commanded at O-5 and O-6. However, other indicators, such as PME and graduate school, broadening assignments, or specific training schools, carried different weight across the services. The analysis below focuses on the top ten profiles selected by participants in each service, where we did see some consensus among participants' choices within the service-specific groups. However, we saw very little consensus in who participants ranked in the bottom ten, where several profiles were only selected by one participant.

Army

Of the top ten profiles selected by participants, nine had civilian master's degrees. Three of the top ten selected profiles obtained Ph.Ds: an operations research and systems analysis (ORSA) officer, a military intelligence officer, and an engineer. Eight of the top ten most selected profiles were four-star executive officers in their post-O-6 command assignment. Seven of the profiles earned their joint qualification during a deployment. Four of the ten most selected profiles spent time as USMA instructors, though only two of the top ten commissioned through USMA. Of the eight Army participants, seven selected Profile 2 in their top ten; six participants selected Profile 2 in their top three. Profile 2 represented an infantry officer, commissioned through OCS, with Ranger School, served in the 75th Ranger Regiment, had a civilian master's degree, and had in-residence ILE (Table E.1).

Table E.1. Army Stage 1 Top Ten Profiles (Individual, Unconstrained)

Profile	Commissioning Source	Career Field	Training	Graduate Education	Post O-6 Command Assignment
2	OCS	Infantry	Ranger School	M.A., in-residence, Georgetown	4-star executive officer
30	ROTC	Armor	SAMS School	MBA, Columbia University	4-star executive officer
10	USMA	FA 49 (ORSA)	Airborne School	Ph.D., in-residence	4-star executive officer
36	ROTC (military college)	Special Forces	Ranger School	M.A., University of Texas	4-star executive officer
39	ROTC	Engineer	JCWS	M.A., in-residence, Massachusetts Institute of Technology	4-star executive officer
46	USMA	Information Operations	Airborne School	M.A., Massachusetts Institute of Technology	4-star executive officer
48	ROTC (non-elite school)	Infantry	Ranger School	M.A., correspondence, University of Phoenix	4-star executive officer
29	OCS	Civil Affairs	Ranger School	M.A., PME	4-star executive officer
41	OCS	Engineer	Airborne School	Ph.D., in-residence, University of Tennessee	3-star executive officer
14	ROTC	Military Intelligence	Ranger School	Ph.D., in-residence	Division chief of staff

NOTES: M.A. = master of arts; JCWS = Joint and Combined Warfighting School; MBA = master of business administration.

Table E.1. Army Stage 1 Top Ten Profiles (Individual, Unconstrained) — continued

Profile	Intermediate PME	Senior Service PME	Joint Experience	Early Career Broadening	Promotion Below the Zone	Number of Deployments
2	In-residence ILE, Ft. Leavenworth	Army War College	Deployment	Ranger Regiment		3
30	Satellite	Joint senior service college	Deployment	USMA Instructor		3
10	Satellite	Sister service college	CJCS Staff	USMA Instructor		2
36	Satellite	Sister service college	CJCS Staff	USMA Instructor	BZ to Major	3
39	In-residence ILE, Ft. Leavenworth	Sister service college	Deployment			4
46	Satellite	Army War College	Deployment	USMA Instructor		2
48	In-residence ILE, Ft. Leavenworth	Joint senior service college	OSD/NSC Staff			4
29	Satellite	Sister service college	Deployment		BZ to Major	2
41	Satellite	Senior Service College Fellowship	Deployment	ROTC Instructor		3
14	Correspondence	Army War College	Deployment	HRC		2

Navy

Navy participants had a high degree of consensus in the most-selected profiles. The top five candidates all attended Navy Nuclear Power School. Eight of the top ten profiles had a civilian master's degree, many of them in physics or engineering (though we did not differentiate between whether a civilian master's degree was completed on one's own time, which we found that overall is much more common in the Navy than a master's degree completed on the Navy's time). Fifty percent of the top ten profiles attended in-residence intermediate PME, and only three of the top ten profiles selected attended the Naval War College for senior service college, while the remainder attended sister service colleges or completed a senior service college fellowship. Three profiles included time as a four-star executive officer post-O-6 command, and two completed a sequential command at sea. All seven participants selected profile 25 and profile 47 in their top ten selections, though neither appeared as the number one profile for any one individual. The two profiles both represented officers from the aviation community (an aviator and an aviation officer), attended Nuclear Power School, commanded at sea, and attained civilian master's degrees (Table E.2).

Table E.2. Navy Stage 1 Top Ten Profiles (Individual, Unconstrained)

Profile	Commissioning Source	Career Field	Training	Graduate Education	O-6 Post-Major Command
25	NROTC (non-elite school)	Aviator	Nuclear Power School	MBA	4-star executive officer
47	OCS	Aviation Officer	Nuclear Power School	M.S., physics	Sequential command at sea
20	NROTC (military college)	Submarine Warfare Officer	Nuclear Power School	M.S., engineering	4-star executive officer
23	NROTC (non-elite school)	Aviator	Nuclear Power School	M.S., engineering	Sequential command at sea
41	OCS	Submarine Warfare Officer	Nuclear Power School	M.S., physics	Military assistant to Secretary of the Navy
16	OCS	Surface Warfare Officer	Acquisition Professional	M.S., engineering	CNO executive officer
11	USNA	SEAL		M.A., PME	Joint Staff
34	USNA	Surface Warfare Officer	Nuclear Power School	M.A., PME	3-star executive officer
10	USNA	Surface Warfare Officer	Afghanistan-Pakistan Hands Program	M.S., engineering	Commander, Afghanistan Provincial Reconstruction Team
17	NROTC (military college)	Surface Warfare Officer	Financial Management Subspecialty	M.A., strategic studies, Stanford	4-star executive officer

NOTE: M.S. = master of science.

Table E.2. Navy Stage 1 Top Ten Profiles (Individual, Unconstrained) — continued

Profile	Intermediate PME	Senior Service PME	Joint Experience	Promotion Below the Zone	Significant Time at Sea
25	In-residence	Sister service college	CCMD staff		Yes
47	Not in-residence	Sister Service college	CJCS staff		Yes
20	In-residence	Naval War College	CJCS staff		Yes
23	Not in-residence	Naval War College	CCMD staff		Yes
41	Not in-residence	Senior service college fellowship	Deployment		Yes
16	Not in-residence	Sister service college	OSD/NSC staff		Yes
11	Not in-residence	Naval War College	OSD/NSC staff		Yes
34	In-residence	Senior service college fellowship	CCMD staff	BZ to O-4 and O-6	Yes
10	In-residence	Sister service college	CJCS staff		Yes
17	In-residence	Joint senior service college	CCMD staff		Yes

Air Force

Of the top ten profiles, four profiles included civilian graduate education, and one profile included a civilian Ph.D. Five of the top ten profiles included time as a four-star executive officer post-O-6 command. Seven of the most-selected profiles completed their intermediate IDE via correspondence. All six Air Force participants selected Profile 1 and Profile 45 in their top three. The two profiles overlapped across a range of indicators. Both profiles were pilots (fighter and bomber); each attended Air War College in-residence for their senior service college and served on CCMD staffs post-O-6 command. Finally, both profiles were promoted early to both O-4 and O-5 (Table E.3).

Table E.3. Air Force Stage 1 Top Ten Profiles (Individual, Unconstrained)

Profile	Commissioning Source	AFSC	Training	Graduate Education	Post O-6 Command Assignment
10	USAFA	12FX Fighter Combat Systems Officer	Squadron Officer School	MA, PME	4-star executive officer
45	ROTC (elite school)	11FX Fighter Pilot	RED FLAG	SAASS	U.S. Army Cyber Command
1	USAFA	11BX Bomber Pilot	Weapons School	MA, PME	Air Staff
36	ROTC (military college)	13CX Special Tactics Officer	Weapons School	No graduate degree	4-star executive officer
14	ROTC	13BX Air Battle Manager	Weapons School	Ph.D., in-residence	Air Staff
2	OTS	11EX Experimental Test Pilot	Squadron Officer School	M.A., in-residence, Georgetown	4-star executive officer
29	OTS	11UX Remotely Piloted Aircraft Pilot	Weapons School	MA, PME	4-star executive officer
48	ROTC (non-elite school)	11RX Reconnaissance Pilot	Squadron Officer School	M.A., correspondence, University of Phoenix	4-star executive officer
3	ROTC (elite school)	11FX Fighter Pilot	Weapons School	M.A., PME	3-star executive officer
13	ROTC (non-elite school)	12RX Reconnaissance/ Surveillance Combat Systems Officer	Weapons School	M.A., correspondence, University of Phoenix	CCMD staff

Table E.3. Air Force Stage 1 Top Ten Profiles (Individual, Unconstrained) — continued

Profile	Intermediate PME	Senior Service PME	Joint Experience	Promotion Below the Zone	Number of Deployments
10	Correspondence	Sister service college	CJCS staff	BZ to O-5	2
45	Correspondence	Air War College	CCMD staff	BZ to O-4 and O-5	4
1	In-residence IDE	Air War College	CCMD staff	BZ to O-4 and O-5	1
36	Correspondence	Sister service college	CJCS staff	BZ to O-4	4
14	Correspondence	Air War College	Deployment		3
2	In-residence IDE	Air War College	Deployment		2
29	Correspondence	Sister service college	Deployment		2
48	In-residence IDE	Joint senior service college	OSD/NSC staff		1
3	Correspondence	Sister service college	CJCS staff		2
13	Correspondence	Sister service college	CCMD staff		2

Marine Corps

The Marine Corps participants had less consensus in their individual, unconstrained choices than the other services. No single profile was selected by more than four of the seven Marine Corps participants within their top ten selections. Notably, no profiles in the top ten represented individuals with civilian graduate education. All profiles selected had between two and four deployments, with the top four profiles completing two deployments. The profiles selected represented diverse commissioning sources: four NROTC, three USNA, and three OCS/PLC commissions (Table E.4).

Table E.4. Marine Corps Stage 1 Top Ten Profiles (Individual, Unconstrained)

Profile	Commissioning Source	Career Field	Training	Graduate Education	Post O-6 Command Assignment
17	NROTC (military college)	Aviation Maintenance Officer		M.A., PME	CCMD staff
21	USNA	Infantry		M.A., PME	COE staff
4	USNA	Infantry		M.A., PME	CCMD staff
19	OCS	LAAD Command and Control Officer		M.A., PME	CAG staff
25	NROTC (non-elite school)	Adjutant Officer		M.A., PME	CCMD staff
30	NROTC	Field Artillery		M.A., PME	4-star executive officer
39	NROTC	Combat Engineer Officer		M.A., PME	4-star executive officer
1	USNA	Infantry		M.A., PME	Division chief of staff
2	PLC	Aviation/Fixed Wing		M.A., PME	4-star executive officer
5	OCS	Infantry		M.A., PME	Division Chief of staff

NOTE: LAAD = Low Altitude Air Defense; CAG = Commander's Action Group.

Table E.4. Marine Corps Stage 1 Top Ten Profiles (Individual, Unconstrained) — continued

Profile	Intermediate PME	Senior Service PME	Joint	Number of Deployments
17	Expeditionary Warfare School, in-residence	Joint senior service college	NATO staff officer	2
21	Expeditionary Warfare School, in-residence	Joint senior service college	USTRANSCOM staff officer	2
4	Expeditionary Warfare School, distance	Sister service college	USEUCOM staff officer	2
19	Expeditionary Warfare School, in-residence	Marine War College	CJCS staff officer	2
25	Expeditionary Warfare School, in-residence	Sister service college	USNORTHCOM	3
30	Expeditionary Warfare School, in-residence	Joint senior service college	USINDOPACOM staff officer	3
39	Expeditionary Warfare School, distance	Sister service college	UN Command-Korea staff officer	4
1	Expeditionary Warfare School, distance	Marine War College	USINDOPACOM staff officer	2
2	Expeditionary Warfare School, distance	Marine War College	USCENTCOM staff officer	3
5	Expeditionary Warfare School, distance	Marine War College	USINDOPACOM staff officer	3

NOTE: USTRANSCOM = U.S. Transportation Command; USNORTHCOM = U.S. Northern Command.

Stage 2: Constrained Individual Rank-Ordering

In the second stage, we added constraints and asked individuals to rank-order their top ten profiles under the new conditions. The constraints were constructed using realistic guidelines from each of the services. Where precepts or board instructions were publicly available (the Navy and Marine Corps), they were used to guide the distribution of career fields. Where precepts or board instructions were not publicly available (Army and Air Force), we developed proportions based on the service's FY 2018 promotions to O-7 as seen in the DMDC data. Participants were required to select profiles representing career fields in specific numbers as follows:

- Army: six combat arms officers, three combat service/combat service support officers, one functional area officer
- Air Force: six pilots, two combat systems officers, two acquisitions or logistics officers
- Navy: two aviators or aviation officers; one surface warfare officer; one submarine officer; three officers from the URL (any community), and three officers from the non-URL community
- Marine Corps: Reflecting Marine Corps precept structure, the marines were provided ten positions from any MOS. However, they were provided with guidance regarding understrength skill sets, including intelligence, communications, and signal fields.

Findings from Stage 2

Across each of the services, the selections had at least some changes from Stage 1 to Stage 2. Nearly every individual maintained a combination of the top six to seven profiles from the unconstrained exercise. However, they did vary their later top ten selections in order to accommodate the new constraints. The differences between the profiles selected in the unconstrained stage (largely operators) and the profiles selected in the constrained stage (a forced combination of operators and support) demonstrate that, in the absence of constraints, participants preferred combat-focused career fields over support career fields.

Army

In part, the diversity of backgrounds represented in Army participants' selections in Stage 1 led to a reordering of the initial choices rather than a wholesale replacement of individual selections. For example, the two civil affairs officers represented in the stage 1 selections remained on the list but gained more votes in stage 2. Profile 39, an engineer, remained from Stage 1 to Stage 2, and was selected in seven participants' top ten (as compared with five participants' top ten in Stage 1). Participants selected an ORSA profile in stage 1, and the profile remained in the overall top ten for Stage 2. Army participants added an aviator and an infantry officer. One engineer and an information operations officer dropped off, while a second engineer (Profile 39) appeared in seven participants' top ten rated profiles (an increase from the three participants' selections in stage 1). Among all choices in Stage 2, seven profiles with post-O-6 command assignments were four-star executive officers. Three were promoted BZ to major, and three spent time as USMA instructors. Nine of the top ten profiles selected in Stage 2 attained civilian master's degrees (Table E.5).

Table E.5. Army Stage 2 Top Ten Profiles (Individual, Constrained)

Profile	Commissioning Source	Career Field	Training	Graduate Education	Post O-6 Command Assignment
30	ROTC	Armor	SAMS School	MBA, Columbia University	4-star executive officer
39	ROTC	Engineer	JCWS	MA, in-residence, Massachusetts Institute of Technology	4-star executive officer
2	OCS	Infantry	Ranger School	MA, in-residence, Georgetown	4-star executive officer
48	ROTC (non-elite school)	Infantry	Ranger School	MA, correspondence, University of Phoenix	4-star executive officer
29	OCS	Civil Affairs	Ranger School	MA, PME	4-star executive officer
19	OCS	Aviation	Ranger School	M.A., Nights and weekends, Kansas State University	COE Staff
36	ROTC (military college)	Special Forces	Ranger School	M.A., University of Texas	4-star executive officer
31	USMA	Civil Affairs	Airborne School	M.A., correspondence, University of Phoenix	3-star executive officer
34	USMA	Infantry	SAMS and Ranger School	MPA, Harvard University	HQDA Staff
10	USMA	FA 49 (ORSA)	Airborne School	Ph.D., in-residence	4-star executive officer

NOTE: SAMS = School of Advanced Military Studies; COE = Center of Excellence; MPA = master of public administration; HQDA = Headquarters, Department of the Army.

Table E.5. Army Stage 2 Top Ten Profiles (Individual, Constrained) — continued

Profile	Intermediate PME	Senior Service PME	Joint Experience	Early Career Broadening	Promotion Below the Zone	Number of Deployments
30	Satellite	Joint senior service college	Deployment	USMA Instructor		3
39	In-residence ILE, Leavenworth	Sister service college	Deployment			4
2	In-residence ILE, Leavenworth	Army War College	Deployment	Ranger Regiment		3
48	In-residence ILE, Leavenworth	Joint senior service college	OSD/NSC Staff			4
29	Satellite	Sister service college	Deployment		BZ to Major	2
19	In-residence ILE, Leavenworth	Army War College	Deployment		BZ to Major	2
36	Satellite	Sister service college	CJCS Staff	USMA Instructor	BZ to Major	3
31	In-residence ILE, Leavenworth	Joint senior service college	OSD/NSC Staff			4
34	Correspondence	Senior Service College Fellowship	CCMD Staff			4
10	Satellite	Sister service college	CJCS Staff	USMA Instructor		2

Navy

Under the Navy's constrained model, participants added a supply corps officer, an engineering duty officer, and an aerospace engineering officer to the most-selected profiles. Two surface warfare officers and an aviator who appeared in the top ten selections during Stage 1 no longer appeared in the top ten. Of the three new profiles added to the top ten in Stage 2, both the supply corps officer and the aerospace engineering officer spent their post-O-6 command at a Major Acquisition Shore Command. Of the top ten profiles in Stage 2, nine of the profiles represented an officer with a civilian or Naval Postgraduate School (NPS) master's degree (Table E.6).

Table E.6. Navy Stage 2 Top Ten Profiles (Individual, Constrained)

Profile	Commissioning Source	Career Field	Training	Graduate Education	O-6 Post-Major Command
16	OCS	Surface Warfare Officer	Acquisition Professional	M.S., Engineering	CNO Executive Officer
23	NROTC (non-elite school)	Aviator	Nuclear Power School	M.S., Engineering	Sequential Command at Sea
25	NROTC (non-elite school)	Aviator	Nuclear Power School	MBA	4-star executive officer
20	NROTC (military college)	Submarine Warfare Officer	Nuclear Power School	M.S., Engineering	4-star executive officer
47	OCS	Aviation Officer	Nuclear Power School	M.S., Physics	Sequential Command at Sea
9	NROTC	Supply Corps Officer		M.S., Engineering	4-star executive officer
41	OCS	Submarine Warfare Officer	Nuclear Power School	M.S., Physics	Military assistant to Secretary of the Navy
39	NROTC	Engineering Duty Officer	Acquisition Professional	M.A., NPS	Major Acquisition Shore Command
11	USNA	SEAL		M.A., PME	Joint Staff
44	OCS	Aerospace Engineering Officer	Navy Test Pilot School	MBA	Major Acquisition Shore Command

Table E.6. Navy Stage 2 Top Ten Profiles (Individual, Constrained) — continued

Profile	Intermediate PME	Senior Service PME	Joint Experience	Promotion Below the Zone	Significant Time at Sea
16	Not in-residence	Sister service college	OSD/NSC Staff		Yes
23	Not in-residence	Naval War College	CCMD Staff		Yes
25	In-residence	Sister service college	CCMD Staff		Yes
20	In-residence	Naval War College	CJCS Staff		Yes
47	Not in-residence	Sister service college	CJCS Staff		Yes
9	In residence	Joint senior service college	Deployment		Yes
41	Not in-residence	Senior Service College Fellowship	Deployment		Yes
39	Not in-residence	Naval War College	Deployment		No
11	Not in-residence	Naval War College	OSD/NSC Staff		Yes
44	In-residence	Naval War College	Deployment		Yes

Air Force

Air Force participants largely maintained their consensus on the top profiles (pilots) between Stage 1 and Stage 2, with less consensus on nonpilot positions. Because of this lack of consensus, the Stage 2 selections resulted in an air battle manager, a nuclear and missile operations officer, and a space operations officer being removed from the top ten overall selections. Between Stage 1 and Stage 2, Air Force participants newly selected a training pilot and a second fighter pilot to their top ten selections. Seven of the top ten Air Force selections represented pilots, with two fighter combat systems officers and a special tactics officer. Of the top ten profiles selected in Stage 2, five profiles represented officers who served as four-star executive officers post-O-6 command; four attained civilian graduate degrees, and four commissioned through the Air Force Academy. Five of the ten were promoted BZ at least once in their career, with the top two profiles selected representing officers who promoted BZ to both O-4 and O-5 (Table E.7).

Table E.7. Air Force Stage 2 Top Ten Profiles (Individual, Constrained)

Profile	Commissioning Source	AFSC	Training	Graduate Education	Post O-6 Command Assignment
45	ROTC (elite school)	11FX Fighter Pilot	RED FLAG	SAASS	U.S. Army Cyber Command
1	USAFA	11BX Bomber Pilot	Weapons School	M.A., PME	Air Staff
25	ROTC (non-elite school)	11KX Training Pilot	RED FLAG	MPA, Harvard University	CCMD Staff
29	OTS	11UX Remotely Piloted Aircraft Pilot	Weapons School	M.A., PME	4-star executive officer
2	OTS	11EX Experimental Test Pilot	Squadron Officer School	M.A., in-residence, Georgetown University	4-star executive officer
36	ROTC (military college)	13CX Special Tactics Officer	Weapons School	No graduate degree	4-star executive officer
48	ROTC (non-elite school)	11RX Reconnaissance Pilot	Squadron Officer School	M.A., correspondence, University of Phoenix	4-star executive officer
10	USAFA	12FX Fighter Combat Systems Officer	Squadron Officer School	M.A., PME	4-star executive officer
24	USAFA	11FX Fighter Pilot	Weapons School	No graduate degree	3-star executive officer
31	USAFA	12FX Fighter Combat Systems Officer	Squadron Officer School	M.A., correspondence, University of Phoenix	3-star executive officer

Table E.7. Air Force Stage 2 Top Ten Profiles (Individual, Constrained) — continued

Profile	Intermediate PME	Senior Service PME	Joint Experience	Promotion Below the Zone	Deployments
45	Correspondence	Air War College	CCMD Staff	BZ to O-4 and O-5	4
1	In-residence IDE	Air War College	CCMD Staff	BZ to O-4 and O-5	1
25	Correspondence	Sister service college	CCMD Staff	BZ to O-4	2
29	Correspondence	Sister service college	Deployment		2
2	In-residence IDE	Air War College	Deployment		2
36	Correspondence	Sister service college	CJCS Staff	BZ to O-4	4
48	In-residence IDE	Joint senior service college	OSD/NSC Staff		1
10	Correspondence	Sister service college	CJCS Staff	BZ to O-5	2
24	Correspondence	Senior Service College Fellowship	Deployment		2
31	In-residence IDE	Joint senior service college	OSD/NSC Staff		4

Marine Corps

Between Stage 1 and Stage 2, Marine Corps participants selected a very different slate of officers in their collective top ten. In part, the turnover between the stages reflects the lack of consensus among selections in both stages. In Stage 2, the top ten selections included one signals intelligence officer, two financial management officers, and a logistics officer that were not reflected in the Stage 1 selections. Among the top ten profiles selected in Stage 2, one had a civilian graduate degree (an increase from the Stage 1 selections). The top nine selections attended Expeditionary Warfare School in-residence, and the tenth attended via correspondence. A diversity of experiences were represented in their post-O-6 command assignments: Two were assigned to Commander's Action Group (CAG) staffs; two were assigned to CCMD staffs; one was assigned to Headquarters Marine Corps (HQMC) staff; one served as an executive officer to an O-10, and one served as a three-star executive officer. Similar to Stage 1, all profiles in the collective top ten had between two and four deployments (Table E.8).

Table E.8. Marine Corps Stage 2 Top Ten Profiles (Individual, Constrained)

Profile	Commissioning Source	Career Field	Training	Graduate Education	Post O-6 Command Assignment
21	USNA	Infantry		M.A., PME	CAG Staff
17	NROTC (military college)	Aviation Maintenance Officer		M.A., PME	CCMD Staff
37	USNA	Signals Intelligence Officer		M.A., PME	3-star executive officer
25	NROTC (non-elite school)	Adjutant Officer		M.A., PME	CCMD Staff
28	USNA	Logistics		M.A., PME	Joint Staff
33	NROTC (non-elite school)	Financial Management Officer		M.A., PME	Flag officer–led Air Defense Command
12	OCS	Communications Officer		M.A., PME	HQMC Staff
10	USNA	Financial Management Officer		M.A., PME	4-star executive officer
44	OCS	Infantry		M.A., PME	CAG Staff
38	OCS	Combat Engineer Officer		M.A., security studies, Georgetown University	USASOC Staff

Table E.8. Marine Corps Stage 2 Top Ten Profiles (Individual, Constrained) — continued

Profile	Intermediate PME	Senior Service PME	Joint	Number of Deployments
21	Expeditionary Warfare School, in-residence	Joint senior service college	USTRANSCOM staff officer	2
17	Expeditionary Warfare School, in-residence	Joint senior service college	NATO staff officer	2
37	Expeditionary Warfare School, in-residence	Marine War College	USSOCOM staff officer	4
25	Expeditionary Warfare School, in-residence	Sister service college	USNORTHCOM	3
28	Expeditionary Warfare School, in-residence	Senior Service College Fellowship	USCENTCOM staff officer	3
33	Expeditionary Warfare School, in-residence	Marine War College	USSOCOM staff officer	3
12	Expeditionary Warfare School, in-residence	Sister service college	USEUCOM staff officer	2
10	Expeditionary Warfare School, in-residence	Sister service college	USINDOPACOM staff officer	2
44	Expeditionary Warfare School, in-residence	Marine War College	CJCS staff officer	3
38	Expeditionary Warfare School, Distance	Sister service college	USNORTHCOM staff officer	2

Self-Identification Question

After Stage 2, but before moving to the facilitated discussion, we moved to the self-identification question. We expected that the retired G/FO participants to have found their career path within their top ten, with more variance among the terminal O-6s. Our results demonstrate that five of the ten retired G/FO participants who responded identified their career path within one of their top ten selections, one of whom (a retired Air Force pilot) identified most with their number one selection. All G/FOs identified their career path within the top twenty profiles. Among retired O-6s, six of the seventeen who responded identified their career path within one of their top ten selections; four identified their career path within the bottom ten of their selections; and seven ranged in between (Table E.9).

It is noteworthy that all former G/FO participants recognized their pathways within the top half of their selections. The fact that many terminal O-6s recognized themselves in the top half of their service selection might reflect the competitive nature of each service; while they were not promoted to G/FO ranks, it does not necessarily mean that they were not competitive in the process. They could have selected out themselves rather than not having been chosen by the service for O-7.

Table E.9. Ranking of Self-Identified Most-Similar Profile

Service	Grade	Career Field	Similar Profile Ranking
Navy	O-6	Aviator	48
Navy	O-6	Aviator	7
Navy	O-6	Surface warfare officer	49
Navy	O-6	Aviator	3
Navy	O-6	Surface warfare officer	19
Navy	O-6	Aviator	35
Navy	O-8	Flight officer	12
Air Force	O-8	Mobility pilot	10
Air Force	O-6	Reconnaissance/surveillance/ electronic warfare pilot	48
Air Force	O-6	Fighter pilot	8
Air Force	O-9	Bomber pilot	1
Air Force	O-8	Fighter pilot	8
Air Force	O-6	Acquisition	28
Army	O-7	Intelligence	18
Army	O-7	Maintenance	9
Army	O-6	Chemical	35
Army	O-7	Field Artillery/Perm Prof	19
Army	O-6	Special Forces	31
Army	O-6	Field artillery	27
Army	O-9	Logistician	(commented that no profiles matched)
Army	O-6	Special Forces	8
Marine Corps	O-6	(not provided)	12
Marine Corps	O-10	(not provided)	8
Marine Corps	O-8	(not provided)	(not provided)
Marine Corps	O-7	(not provided)	13
Marine Corps	O-6	Pilot	8
Marine Corps	O-6	(not provided)	11
Marine Corps	O-6	Ground intelligence	42

Stage 3: Constrained Group Rank Ordering

For the third and final stage of the exercise, all representatives were divided into groups based on service. The teams were provided with the same profiles and constraints provided in the second individual stage of the exercise but were required to come to a collective consensus on the top ten profiles for their service. While some profiles were selected by many or all participants in the individual stages of the exercise, each service demonstrated different group dynamics in developing the top ten group ranking.

Findings from Stage 3

Service-specific findings from Stage 3 are detailed in the following section. Beyond the profile selections themselves, this stage also allowed us to observe that each group made collective decisions differently when given limited guidance as to how selections must be made. While these proceedings likely reflect the participants' own preferences when working in a group setting, participants were also role playing how their service's board members would interact, so we viewed these different interactions as relevant to our research.

Army

In Stage 3, Army participants selected six of the same profiles reflected in the most common profiles selected in Stage 2. The four new profiles selected included a public affairs officer, a military police officer, a field artillery officer, and a special forces officer. Of the new officers, one had served as a general's aide earlier in their career, and the field artillery officer had been promoted BZ to O-6. Of the overall group constrained selection, four profiles represented Ranger School graduates, six had civilian master's degrees, four served as four-star executive officers, and three served as three-star executive officers (Table E.10).

In this stage, the Army team came to consensus quickly. One dynamic of note was the fact that if an individual's choice was not selected, they quickly accepted the consensus candidate as a viable strong alternative. The Army participants appeared fair and egalitarian in their methods, reflecting Army culture, and participants weighed their recommendations equally across the proceedings. For example, if an individual's third choice did not make it into the group top ten, no concern was voiced.

Table E.10. Army Stage Three Top Ten Profiles (Group, Constrained)

Profile	Commissioning Source	Career Field	Training	Graduate Education	Post O-6 Command Assignment
48	ROTC (non-elite school)	Infantry	Ranger School	M.A., correspondence, University of Phoenix	4-star executive officer
2	OCS	Infantry	Ranger School	M.A., in-residence, Georgetown	4-star executive officer
19	OCS	Aviation	Ranger School	M.A., nights and weekends, Kansas State University	COE Staff
30	ROTC	Armor	SAMS School	MBA, Columbia University	4-star executive officer
31	USMA	Civil Affairs	Airborne School	M.A., correspondence, University of Phoenix	3-star executive officer
29	OCS	Civil Affairs	Ranger School	M.A., PME	4-star executive officer
28	USMA	Public Affairs	SAMS School	MBA, nights and weekends, Georgetown University	Joint Staff
5	OCS	Field Artillery	Airborne School	M.A., PME	Division Chief of Staff
37	USMA	Special Forces	Pathfinder	M.A., PME	3-star executive officer
18	USMA	Military Police	Mountain Warfare School	M.A., PME	3-star executive officer

Table E.10. Army Stage Three Top Ten Profiles (Group, Constrained) — continued

Profile	Intermediate PME	Senior Service PME	Joint Experience	Promotion Below the Zone	Number of Deployments
48	In-residence ILE, Leavenworth	Joint senior service college	OSD/NSC staff		4
2	In-residence ILE, Leavenworth	Army War College	Deployment		3
19	In-residence ILE, Leavenworth	Army War College	Deployment	BZ to O-4	2
30	Satellite	Joint senior service college	Deployment		3
31	In-residence ILE, Leavenworth	Joint senior service college	OSD/NSC staff		4
29	Satellite	Sister service college	Deployment	BZ to O-4	2
28	Correspondence	Senior Service College Fellowship	CJCS staff		3
5	In-residence ILE, Leavenworth	Army War College	Other Joint Staff	BZ to O-5	3
37	Satellite	Army War College	Deployment		4
18	In-residence ILE, Leavenworth	Senior Service College Fellowship	CCMD staff		2

Navy

As a group, Navy participants' constrained selections fully matched the top ten profiles selected by individuals in Stage 2. The group quickly reached agreement on what the Navy values for promotion, especially for URL officers, including both what was valued (time commanding at sea) and what was less valued (educational performance and institution). There was a bit more discussion required to reach agreement on what the Navy values for promotion for non-URL officers (RL and staff). Some disagreement occurred on whether the Navy's values for promotion are really the ones that should be guiding promotion. Participants differed on the degree to which education should be regarded more than it is currently, for example, or whether broadening assignments such as an assignment to NATO should be encouraged (Table E.11).

Regarding group dynamics and simulated board proceedings, the unofficial board chairperson proposed that a simple average score to match their ranking for each candidate be calculated based on all participants' scores as a starting point, and then moved through the list of top candidates one by one to initiate discussion on whether everyone was comfortable with where that average ranking put someone, and eliciting opinions when candidates were close to each other. When someone had a major difference in how they scored a candidate, the disagreement was brought up as a matter of course, either during initial discussions or during the stage when an average score for that candidate was calculated. One participant ranked top RL candidates higher than top URL candidates, unlike all the other participants, and was asked to make a case for why this was. The participant's explanation was heard, but it was set aside as a somewhat philosophical, unresolvable difference. Breaking ties on otherwise similar candidates resulted in a fair bit of discussion, with a mix of participants volunteering their opinions (often from the particular community in question, as they were often deferred to for those particular candidates). Opinions were elicited by the chairman from those who were speaking up a bit less. Sometimes officers changed their minds on their original scores, other times they simply did an informal voice vote, in order to break the tie.[653]

Table E.11. Navy Stage Three Top Ten Profiles (Group, Constrained)

Profile	Commissioning Source	Career Field	Training	Graduate Education	O-6 Post-Major Command
16	OCS	Surface Warfare Officer	Acquisition professional	M.S., Engineering	CNO executive officer
23	NROTC (non-elite school)	Aviator	Nuclear Power School	M.S., Engineering	Sequential command at sea
41	OCS	Submarine Warfare Officer	Nuclear Power School	M.S., Physics	Military assistant to Secretary of the Navy
20	NROTC (military college)	Submarine Warfare Officer	Nuclear Power School	M.S., Engineering	4-star executive officer
47	OCS	Aviation Officer	Nuclear Power School	M.S., Physics	Sequential command at sea
25	NROTC (non-elite school)	Aviator	Nuclear Power School	MBA	4-star executive officer
11	USNA	SEAL		M.A., PME	Joint Staff
39	NROTC	Engineering Duty Officer	Acquisition professional	M.A., NPS	Major Acquisition Shore Command
44	OCS	Aerospace Engineering Officer	Navy Test Pilot School	MBA	Major Acquisition Shore Command
9	NROTC	Supply Corps Officer		M.S., Engineering	4-star executive officer

NOTE: NPS = Naval Postgraduate School.

[653] Senior selection exercise notes, January 30, 2019, RAND Corporation, Arlington, Virginia.

Table E.11. Navy Stage Three Top Ten Profiles (Group, Constrained) — continued

Profile	Intermediate PME	Senior Service PME	Joint Experience	Promotion Below the Zone	Significant Time at Sea
16	Not in-residence	Sister service college	OSD/NSC Staff		Yes
23	Not in-residence	Naval War College	CCMD Staff		Yes
41	Not in-residence	Senior Service College Fellowship	Deployment		Yes
20	In-residence	Naval War College	CJCS Staff		Yes
47	Not in-residence	Sister service college	CJCS Staff		Yes
25	In-residence	Sister service college	CCMD Staff		Yes
11	Not in-residence	Naval War College	OSD/NSC Staff		Yes
39	Not in-residence	Naval War College	Deployment		No
44	In-residence	Naval War College	Deployment		Yes
9	In-residence	Joint senior service college	Deployment		Yes

Air Force

Of the Air Force group's top ten selections, nine reflected the overall top ten profiles selected by individuals in Stage 2. Three individuals selected Profile 31 in Stage 2 and debated its merits against Profile 30 in the group selection process. The group ultimately decided that the Profile 30's time as a four-star executive officer was seen as a benefit, Profile 31's correspondence master's degree from the University of Phoenix was seen as a detractor.[654] Overall, six of the top ten profiles selected by the group served as four-star executive officers, while one more served as a three-star executive officer. Fighter pilots held the plurality of pilot positions, and a fighter combat systems officer, a bomber combat systems officer, and a special tactics officer were represented in the nonpilot selections. Four of the top ten profiles selected by the group attended Weapons School. Four of the profiles represented officers with civilian graduate education. Two of the top ten group selections were promoted BZ to O-4, one was promoted BZ to O-5, and two were promoted BZ to both O-4 and O-5 (Table E.12).

Overall, the Air Force participants generally agreed on which candidates to promote in the pilot and combat systems officer categories. However, substantial debate characterized who to promote out of the "other" category. Ultimately, the group chose the best-qualified candidates who could grow the service into the space and nuclear and missile operations domains, demonstrating an inclination to grow the Air Force's core missions. When distinguishing between candidates, serving as an executive to a three- or four-star general was an important

[654] Senior selection exercise notes, January 30, 2019, RAND Corporation, Arlington, Virginia.

discriminator because participants felt as though those positions allowed candidates to understand what generalship requires up close, and could emulate positive behaviors if asked to perform at that level.

Table E.12. Air Force Stage Three Top Ten Profiles (Group, Constrained)

Profile	Commissioning Source	AFSC	Training	Graduate Education	Post O-6 Command Assignment
45	ROTC (elite school)	11FX Fighter Pilot	RED FLAG	SAASS	U.S. Army Cyber Command
1	USAFA	11BX Bomber Pilot	Weapons School	M.A., PME	Air Staff
48	ROTC (non-elite school)	11RX Reconnaissance Pilot	Squadron Officer School	M.A., Correspondence, University of Phoenix	4-star executive officer
25	ROTC (non-elite school)	11KX Training Pilot	RED FLAG	MPA, Harvard University	CCMD Staff
29	OTS	11UX Remotely Piloted Aircraft Pilot	Weapons School	M.A., PME	4-star executive officer
2	OTS	11EX Experimental Test Pilot	Squadron Officer School	M.A., in-residence, Georgetown	4-star executive officer
24	USAFA	11FX Fighter Pilot	Weapons School	No graduate degree	3-star executive officer
10	USAFA	12FX Fighter Combat Systems Officer	Squadron Officer School	M.A., PME	4-star executive officer
30	ROTC	12BX Bomber Combat Systems Officer	Squadron Officer School	MBA, Columbia University	4-star executive officer
36	ROTC (military college)	13CX Special Tactics Officer	Weapons School	No graduate degree	4-star executive officer

Table E.12. Air Force Stage Three Top Ten Profiles (Group, Constrained) — continued

Profile	Intermediate PME	Senior Service PME	Joint Experience	Promotion Below the Zone	Deployments
45	Correspondence	Air War College	CCMD staff	BZ to O-4 and O-5	4
1	In-residence IDE	Air War College	CCMD staff	BZ to O-4 and O-5	1
48	In-residence IDE	Joint senior service college	OSD/NSC staff		1
25	Correspondence	Sister service college	CCMD staff	BZ to O-4	2
29	Correspondence	Sister service college	Deployment		2
2	In-residence IDE	Air War College	Deployment		2
24	Correspondence	Senior Service College Fellowship	Deployment		2
10	Correspondence	Sister service college	CJCS staff	BZ to O-5	2
30	Correspondence	Joint senior service college	Deployment		2
36	Correspondence	Sister service college	CJCS Staff	BZ to O-4	4

Marine Corps

The Marine Corps group made different choices collectively than they had as individuals. Three of the top ten profiles selected by the group in Stage 3 were similar to the constrained choices made by individuals in Stage 2. Among the group choices were three logistics officers, two infantry officers, a signals intelligence officer, a communications officer, a financial management officer, and a field artillery officer. As a group, the participants debated the merits of officers meeting a critical skills gap (three billets) up front and came to a consensus on the financial management officer, communications officer, and signals intelligence officer. Two of these three profiles (the communications officer and the signals intelligence officer) did not have enough support from individuals during Stage 2 to rank in the overall top ten. However, when their merits were debated and discussed by the group, the three profiles gained consensus support quickly. Of the final ten constrained profiles selected by the group, three served as four-star executive officers, one served as a three-star executive officer, two served as CCMD staff officers, two served within the Marine Corps at HQMC and on a CAG, and two served on the Joint Staff. Only one officer in the top ten had one deployment; all others deployed between two and four times. None of the top ten selected by the group had a civilian master's degree (Table E.13).

In terms of group dynamics, when considering the operational profiles, each participant listed their top five candidates under the constraints, and apportioned points to each candidate (five for a first choice through one for the fifth choice). For all profiles except two, there was near consensus on who should be in the top ten. However, when discussing competing values for two individuals on the cusp, most participants valued a high-level joint three- or four-star executive officer position over an extra deployment or deployments.

Table E.13. Marine Corps Stage Three Top Ten Profiles (Group, Constrained)

Profile	Commissioning Source	Career Field	Training	Graduate Education	Post O-6 Command Assignment
30	NROTC	Field Artillery		M.A., PME	4-star executive officer
10	USNA	Financial Management Officer		M.A., PME	4-star executive officer
39	NROTC	Combat Engineer Officer		M.A., PME	4-star executive officer
12	OCS	Communications Officer		M.A., PME	HQMC staff
37	USNA	Signals Intelligence Officer		M.A., PME	3-star executive officer
21	USNA	Infantry		M.A., PME	CAG staff
25	NROTC (non-elite school)	Logistics		M.A., PME	CCMD staff
4	USNA	Infantry		M.A., PME	CCMD staff
28	USNA	Logistics		M.A., PME	Joint Staff
45	NROTC (elite school)	Logistics		M.A., PME	Joint Staff

Table E.13. Marine Corps Stage Three Top Ten Profiles (Group, Constrained) — continued

Profile	Intermediate PME	Senior Service PME	Joint	Number of Deployments
30	Expeditionary Warfare School, in-residence	Joint senior service college	USINDOPACOM staff officer	3
10	Expeditionary Warfare School, in-residence	Sister service college	USINDOPACOM staff officer	2
39	Expeditionary Warfare School, distance	Sister service college	UN Command-Korea staff officer	4
12	Expeditionary Warfare School, in-residence	Sister service college	USEUCOM staff officer	2
37	Expeditionary Warfare School, in-residence	Marine War College	USSOCOM staff officer	4
21	Expeditionary Warfare School, in-residence	Joint senior service college	USTRANSCOM staff officer	2
25	Expeditionary Warfare School, in-residence	Sister service college	USNORTHCOM	3
4	Expeditionary Warfare School, distance	Sister service college	USEUCOM staff officer	2
28	Expeditionary Warfare School, in-residence	Senior Service College Fellowship	USCENTCOM staff officer	3
45	Expeditionary Warfare School, in-residence	Marine War College	NATO staff officer	1

Facilitated Discussion

We also gained valuable insights from the facilitated discussions after the first set of two stages and the third stage. During these discussions, we posed questions to each group in order to draw out the rationale behind their choices. Additionally, we asked follow-up questions on underlying assumptions arising from the research for the broader study. Facilitated questions included the following:

- When weighing various factors, which single indicator mattered most in your approach?
- Were indicators included that did not factor into your decisionmaking?
- What factors did you expect to see, but did not?
- When comparing the 1–50 list with the top ten individuals selected under the constraints, did you make different selections? Who was promoted in the top ten list under the constraints who you did not promote without constraints?
- Did you see your own career path reflected (or not reflected) in certain profiles? How did that affect your decisions?
- When comparing the individual top ten selections with constraints to the group selections with constraints, was there widespread agreement or variance?
- How did the service team selections differ from individual selections?

Further, although not the topic of our formal questions during the SLSE, discussion during the SLSE elicited useful information into how these experiences affect the way service G/FOs approach strategic advice, leadership, and management; preparation to perform in interagency environments; value of joint assignments and jointness overall; and reflections of service culture in personnel processes. We incorporated these observations throughout the main body of this report.

Summary of Findings

Upon the completion of the exercise, we synthesized our findings across the stages and from both the facilitated discussions and observations of group dynamics throughout the exercise. Below, we summarize the characteristics that the SLSE participants appeared to value most, as well as our assessments of how service culture impacts those choices.

The exercise provided valuable insights and perspectives from service representatives, who are effectively subject-matter experts on their own service's values. Their experience and knowledge of service culture, preferences, and processes enhanced our understanding of key factors for promotion to G/FO and largely confirmed the characteristics and experiences we had identified in each of the service profiles. In addition, participants provided us with valuable insights we had not previously uncovered that helped to refine our service profiles.

Notably, participants from across the services provided feedback regarding how they perceived the veracity and effectiveness of the characteristics and experiences put forward in the exercise profiles. Participants from all four services noted that our inclusion of whether a given officer's parent was a G/FO did not matter at all in their decisionmaking. However, the inclusion of the characteristic did generate meaningful conversation within each of the groups, as it was noted that, in their experience, the representation of those with a G/FO parent within the G/FO ranks was perhaps higher than might be anticipated with all other factors being considered equally. Participants indicated that potential reasons for this representation were less specifically related to the fact that the individual's parent was a G/FO, and more a factor of deeper existing relationships and networks with senior leaders and/or better preparation for the requirements of a career as an officer from a young age.

Feedback across the services varied on specific characteristics included in the exercise, reflecting differences in service promotion board proceedings and the attributes each service tends to emphasize in the process. Marine Corps participants indicated that many of the factors we included, while influencing their decisions for the purposes of the game, were not the factors that matter most in a true board, such as accession source and location of PME attendance. Marine Corps participants reported that the most important factors at a given board were the most recent performance reviews, and that the assumption that all participants shared the same quality of performance reviews was not realistic to a true board.

Navy participants noted that, while we presented profiles with specific types of major commands at sea, there exists a distinction between certain geographic commands (such as Norfolk, San Diego, and Pearl Harbor) that were not captured by the exercise.

While their notional profile rankings indicated that USAFA commissioning was an important factor in promotion to O-7, Air Force participants said that an academy commission did not matter in and of itself. Rather, it had the potential of providing a head start, but it matters what an officer did with that head start that mattered.

Army participants noted that our inclusion of whether or not a board member knew the rater was not necessarily a significant factor for evaluation. Overall, participants' feedback provided us with valuable perspectives for analysis and future iterations of a similar exercise.

Across all services, we found that O-5 and O-6 commands (or command-select positions) were the most important factor for selection to the grade of O-7. These results conformed with observations from our other research efforts. However, representatives from across the services reported that command is not a distinguishing factor for promotion, but rather a prerequisite. Superior performance in a command assignment does not guarantee promotion to G/FO. Beyond the role of command, observations varied across the services.

Army

The Army group agreed through individual and group rankings on discriminators required to even be considered for promotion to O-7: meeting career gates, including O-5 command and O-6 command, along with the requisite PME at the intermediate and senior service levels. In-residence PME selection mattered greatly to the Army representatives, even for ILE. The finding was surprising given the weight afforded to O-5 and O-6 commands (assigned after ILE), and the length of time between completing ILE and an individual's selection to the grade of O-7 (approximately 10 years).

Participants indicated that post-O-6 command positions also mattered significantly. Both four-star and three-star executive officer assignments were viewed as highly competitive, with no notable distinction between aide jobs to joint or service three- or four-stars. Those assigned to division-level chief of staff positions provided a slight advantage, and no other assignments were viewed as advantageous.

Participants stated that for the most part, one to two deployments did not offer a competitive advantage, but three or four deployments (or more, in theory) were viewed as beneficial.

When asked which factors did not matter, Army representatives posited that an officer's commissioning source did not have a direct effect in selection to GO. Participants also noted that the perception of the rater did not affect their considerations. Lastly, participants also noted that Ranger School was not a discriminator—though being assigned to the 75th Ranger Regiment was. The participants wanted more details about nominative assignments, highlighting that in the Army, some specific assignments are seen as more valuable or detrimental than others.

When asked about the comparison between their choices in the unconstrained stage to the constrained stage, some participants met their full slate of requirements (six combat arms officers, three combat service/service support officers, and one functional area officer) without having to change any of their selections from the unconstrained stage. The finding indicated that, in the absence of constraints, not all individuals would exclusively select operators.

Overall, the rankings and the discussion points raised in the Army group substantially agreed with the profiles Army participants reinforced in an earlier finding that, in addition to command, the post-O-6-command assignment is critical in differentiating candidates for promotion to O-7.

One area of observation differed from our original profile development. Army participants provided insights regarding the consideration afforded to in-residence ILE, even when presented with competitive files for O-5 and O-6 commands. While our other research accounted for the importance of in-residence ILE, it was surprising to learn the weight afforded to the experience ten to 12 years prior to an O-7 board.

Navy

The Navy group indicated that high-visibility positions throughout an officer's career created the most-competitive candidates. An aide assignment to a four-star admiral indicated that an individual was both vetted based on past performance and was exposed to a high-level network while in the assignment. Serving in a CCMD instead of within the service resulted in officers being "pushed aside almost immediately," unless the individual was an information warfare or intelligence officer, where CCMD assignments aligned with their career path priorities.[655] Similarly, participants mentioned that broadening experiences outside of the Navy were not viewed as providing value to the Navy.

The participants highlighted that sea experience mattered in different ways for the URL and RL. All URL officers were expected to have significant time at sea in order to even be considered for promotion to FO; while important, it was (to some degree) a necessary box to check. For those in the RL, significant time at sea provided a discriminator for selection to FO. Sea time for the RL indicated that an individual had a broader awareness of what was required across the service.

Participants indicated that more granularity on specific command assignments would have been helpful, noting that commands at certain bases signaled more importance than others. For example, commands out of Norfolk, San Diego, and Pearl Harbor were seen as more competitive than commands at other geographic locations.

When moving from the unconstrained stage to the constrained stage, participants stated that they did have to reconsider many of their initial selections in order to choose from RL staff, who were largely placed further down the list. The necessity of a new approach in the constrained stage indicates a more natural preference or inclination to select for operators within the Navy.

Participants' selections indicated that education was not considered as a key factor in promotion to FO, noting that commissioning source did not affect their choices—an interesting finding given that 39 percent of all incoming Navy O-7s and 60 percent of all incoming O-9s and

---

[655] Senior leader selection exercise notes, January 30, 2019, RAND Corporation, Arlington, Virginia.

O-10s in FY 2019 commissioned through the USNA.[656] Graduate school was not considered a discriminator, and both intermediate and senior PME were viewed merely as boxes to check.

When asked to reflect on the way the participants' own career paths might have affected their selections, Navy participants did note a particular affinity toward certain candidates whose professional experiences mirrored their own. One participant noted, "I think it's easier to recognize people with that experience because you understand what is required."[657]

During the group exercise, the Navy team was able to come to consensus quickly. While not all Navy participants selected the same top ten in the same order, many of them selected the same combination of individuals within their top ten. This high degree of consensus around the same characteristics across individuals could mean that there is little variance across the Navy in what experiences are most valued.

Navy participants validated the service preference for assignments within the service over joint staff assignments when considering officers for promotion to FO. They also confirmed the limited role PME plays in selection for promotion. Further, participants reinforced that the use of BZ promotions in the Navy is requirements-driven and broadly applied to a competitive category rather than an indicator of individual success.

One observation that we had not anticipated in our initial analysis was that decisionmaking processes when considering RL officers for promotion indicated that acquisition experience was perhaps the most valuable skill for officers from that population.

Air Force

Air Force participants confirmed initial research findings, emphasizing the role of successful wing command as the single indicator signaling future success as a GO. Air Force participants further emphasized the significance of BZ promotions in signaling future potential. The group described a certain path dependence in officer careers beginning at the grade of O-4, wherein those with future GO potential are promoted BZ and then afforded the requisite opportunities (specific commands and training) to ensure their competitiveness at the O-7 board. Although we attempted to provide a realistic proportion of individuals promoted BZ to O-5 and O-6, Air Force participants noted that the "profiles are a little artificial because in reality, all of these successful officers would likely have been BZ."[658]

Regarding specific positions at O-5 and O-6, command experience was of utmost importance to the Air Force group, just as with other services. However, one distinct experience that appeared to be valued much more highly among the Air Force participants than the other service participant groups was joint experience. Participants noted that the Air Force prized joint experience and ability to operate in joint and interagency environments given their longer-term

---

[656] Authors' analysis of DMDC data.

[657] Senior leader selection exercise notes, January 30, 2019, RAND Corporation, Arlington, Virginia.

[658] Senior leader selection exercise notes, January 30, 2019, RAND Corporation, Arlington, Virginia.

focus on developing GOs for strategic, four-star positions that demand deftness in skills gained from those types of experiences as a more junior officer.

Graduate education mattered for Air Force participants, both in location and in performance. When distinguishing between candidates, in-residence PME and master's degrees from prestigious universities were important discriminators when decisions were close. The group inferred a level of commitment from pursuing a master's degree that may not be inherent in taking correspondence courses.

The Air Force participants noted that commissioning sources did not play a role in their individual decisions. However, the group identified a pattern in the individuals selected and recognized that USAFA graduates were highly represented. The group discussed different reasons why, even though the commissioning source was not important, those who were commissioned through the USAFA might be selected at a higher rate. For some, a USAFA commission demonstrated a greater commitment to become an Air Force officer early on, and therefore made officers more driven to demonstrate success early and pursue greater options for success. Participants also surmised that USAFA graduates might also benefit from extensive networks.

As in the other services, the data and observations gained from this exercise largely confirmed the profiles we had developed on typical Air Force GOs. One point in particular that was underscored was that Air Force participants confirmed the role BZ promotions have historically played in signaling future leadership potential beginning at the promotion to O-4.

An observation we had not expected was the extent to which Air Force participants emphasized the importance of in-residence graduate education and the quality of the degree as a discriminator. While previous research did account for the role of these factors, the exercise highlighted how much more weight the Air Force afforded to graduate education than the other services.

Marine Corps

Marine Corps participants emphasized the importance of command in selection to the grade of O-7 (and at every promotion consideration point in their career). The Marine Corps participants also strongly emphasized that the basis for promotion comes largely in the form of FitRep narrative remarks due to similarity of career experiences, and thus challenged the notion that they would make selections based on the information provided in the profiles. Marine Corps participants noted that many of the factors provided, such as commissioning source, intermediate and senior PME, and training, were viewed as simple boxes to check; the way in which an officer achieved them did not matter. However, as the exercise evolved, and relying on the assumptions laid forth at the outset that each candidate represented a "1 of N" officer, the team did agree that certain factors, such as assignments to high-visibility positions, mattered more than others in selection to O-7. However, in a real-world scenario, we acknowledge that these factors would likely matter much less than rater notes.

Many of the participant comments confirmed findings from the course of the study. Underpinning the Marine Corps' reliance on FitRep narratives is the notion that "the Marine Corps has an embarrassment of riches" and that "the most difficult point in a board is when you start to realize that those not selected for GO are just as competitive of those who were selected."[659] Moreover, at each promotion point beginning at O-4, marines prefer the term *not selected* as opposed to *passed over* when an individual is not promoted. The distinction was important to the Marine Corps participants, who commented that because Marine Corps requirements drive promotion considerations and there are such small numbers promoted to O-7 each year, it is generally not a reflection of any kind of personal failure if an officer does not attain the rank of brigadier general.

In terms of education, commissioning source did not factor into the Marine Corps group's selections. No one afforded any extra credibility to USNA graduates. Graduate school experience was also not positively valued in their considerations. Higher education was seen as reflecting individual desires rather than service-driven requirements. If an individual completed a master's degree on nights and weekends, it was "noted but not weighted." If a marine took time out of the fleet to complete a master's degree, it was viewed in some ways as a lack of commitment to the service and as taking the officer away from their roles and responsibilities leading marines.

As we expected from our previous research, Marine Corps participants emphasized the importance of the service's egalitarian culture and performance-based selection. The team confirmed that no individual Marine Corps leader is viewed as a being on a specific path to generalship above others. They further confirmed that these same service culture values drive the very low rate of BZ promotions at any grade, and thus does not predetermine that any individual is on a GO pathway.

Avenues for Future Application

The exercise enabled our team to test our in-progress findings and assumptions and provided us with a valuable opportunity to gain insights into why and how the services might prefer certain professional experiences and other characteristics in its G/FOs. Building on this utility, the structure and methodology of this exercise could be adapted to address future research questions. For example, the approach developed through this exercise could be applied to analysis of

- preferred characteristics of officers in specific communities within each service, for positions in the joint force, or for senior civilian positions in the U.S. government
- preferred characteristics for high-level joint staff and/or CCMD positions
- impact of network and relationship effects in evaluation of officer profiles. While we included proxies for network and relationship effects, the scope of this exercise was

---

[659] Senior leader selection exercise notes, January 30, 2019, RAND Corporation, Arlington, Virginia.

limited from truly testing the role relationships and personal knowledge of candidates may play within board considerations.

- each service's requirements and preferences for promotion to the grades of O-9 and O-10, which function differently from prior promotions.

Appendix F. Interview Protocol

Leadership and Generalship Philosophy

- Describe a typical G/FO in [service].
- How would you characterize [service's] approach to who can become a general, and how?
- What does it mean to be considered a successful G/FO in [service]?
- What is [service's] concept of leadership?
- How do you think [service's] culture is reflected in its concept of generalship?

Pathway(s) to Generalship

General Questions

- What is the typical pathway to generalship in [service]? Are there multiple pathways to generalship? (Competitive categories, career field, two ways to get to G/FO in the same career field, etc.) [If yes]: What are they?
- At what point does your service identify potential G/FOs, formally and informally?
- How does [service] signal G/FO potential? (E.g. assignments, BZ or double BZ promotions)
- *Likely for more senior interviewees*: Can you identify individuals who haven't followed the normal pathway who still became G/FOs? If so, what was their career path? (no need to name names; just describe path)
- *Likely for more senior interviewees*: What are common attributes/experiences of those that are promoted to G/FO on a non-traditional path?
- *For interviewees who have sat on promotion or command selection boards:* What are the formal criteria and processes [service] uses to determine readiness for promotion to [rank of promotion boards he/she sat on]/command selection?
- What are the criteria that end up being most important?
- *For interviewees that were not promoted to G/FO or were not promoted to O-8, O-10*: Why do you think you didn't you make it?
- What differentiates you from those that did?

Career Fields and Special Designators

- What career fields are most common in [service's] G/FO corps?
- Are there certain training qualifications (i.e., Ranger tab) that increase likelihood of making G/FO?

Assignments

- What assignments are considered the "plum assignments" in [service]?

- Include type of assignment (aide, operations officer, etc.); staff jobs vs. operational jobs vs. broadening assignments; specific units; specific bases/posts; deployments
- How are joint billet assignments perceived within your service?
- How are broadening assignments used and viewed? E.g., as retention tools, as a reward, directly tied to requirements?
- What assignments are considered career enders?
- What types of professional assignments (specific jobs, kinds of jobs such as military assistant to a senior official, combat tours, command assignments) are typical among G/FOs in [service]?

Education and Commissioning Source

- Do commissioning sources play a role? (Academy, OCS, ROTC)
- What PME experiences lead to successful consideration for G/FO in [service, and in pathway]? (E.g. fellowships, civilian education, in residence PME, senior service college location, cross service, interagency)
- What level of educational achievement is typical among G/FOs in service (top graduate in PME courses, Ph.D., etc.)?

Networks

- What sort of networks are most influential in making G/FO in [service]?

Personal Characteristics

- What types of personal characteristics (temperament, physical activity, work ethic, risk aversion, etc.) are associated with a typical G/FO in [service]?
- What career timeline milestones (BZ, double BZ, certain assignments held at the right time before a promotion) are associated with G/FOs in [service]?

Pathway Sufficiency

- Earlier you described [service's] typical G/FO. How does that characterization differ from what the service needs?
- Is the pipeline satisfactory for service needs? [If not, what is lacking?]
- Is the pipeline satisfactory for key joint jobs? [If not, what is lacking?]

References

9th Marine Corps District, "Staying Marine: Example Career Progression—Officer," website, June 2008. As of July 29, 2019: https://www.9thmcd.marines.mil/Portals/82/Docs/Mod%208-Staying%20Marine%20Section.pdf

AFDD—*See* Air Force Doctrine Document.

AFI—*See* Air Force Instruction.

Air Force Doctrine Document 1-1, *Leadership and Force Development*, Washington, D.C.: Department of the Air Force, 2011.

Air Force Form 707, *Officer Performance Report*, Washington, D.C.: Department of the Air Force, July 31, 2015, version 1.

Air Force Instruction 36-2110, *Assignments*, Washington, D.C.: Department of the Air Force, June 8, 2012, p. 30.

Air Force Instruction 36-2110, *Total Force Assignments*, Washington, D.C.: Department of the Air Force, October 5, 2018.

Air Force Instruction 36-2406, *Officer and Enlisted Evaluation Systems*, Washington, D.C.: Department of the Air Force, November 8, 2016.

Air Force Instruction 36-2406, *Officer and Enlisted Evaluation Systems*, Washington, D.C.: Department of the Air Force, May 10, 2019.

Air Force Instruction 36-2501, *Officer Promotions and Selective Continuation*, Washington, D.C.: Department of the Air Force, July 16, 2004.

Air Force Instruction 36-2611, *Officer Professional Development*, Washington, D.C.: Department of the Air Force, July 26, 2018.

Air Force Instruction 36-2640, *Executing Total Force Development and Management*, Washington, D.C.: Department of the Air Force, August 30, 2018.

Air Force Policy Directive 36-26, *Total Force Development and Management*, Washington, D.C.: Department of the Air Force, March 18, 2019.

Allen, Charles D., and George J. Wood, "Developing Army Enterprise Leaders," *Military Review*, July–August 2015.

Anastasi, Anne, "Evolving Trait Concepts," *American Psychologist*, Vol. 38, No. 2, 1983, pp. 175–184.

Army Directive 2017-08, *Competitive Categories for Commissioned Officers and Warrant Officers Serving on the Active Duty List and the Reserve Active Status List*, Washington, D.C.: Department of the Army, February 15, 2017.

Army Doctrinal Publication 6-22, *Army Leadership and the Profession*, Washington, D.C.: Department of the Army, 2012.

Army Regulation 350-1, *Army Training and Leader Development*, Washington, D.C.: Department of the Army, 2017.

Army Regulation 623-3, *Evaluation Reporting System*, Washington, D.C.: Department of the Army, 2015.

Assistant Secretary of the Navy (Manpower and Reserve Affairs), memo to Brigadier General Kevin M. Iiams, USMC (AVN), "Precept Convening the Fiscal Year 2019 U.S. Marine Corps Regular Unrestricted Lieutenant Colonel Promotion Selection Board, Regular Unrestricted Major Continuation Selection Board, Financial Management Lieutenant Colonel Promotion Selection Board, and Financial Management Major Continuation Selection Board," August 1, 2017a.

Assistant Secretary of the Navy (Manpower and Reserve Affairs), memo to Brigadier General Kevin M. Iiams, U.S. Marine Corps (AVN), "Precept Convening the Fiscal Year 2019 U.S. Marine Corps Selection Board," August 11, 2017b.

Barnett, Roger W., *Navy Strategic Culture: Why the Navy Thinks Differently*, Annapolis, Md.: Naval Institute Press, 2009.

Barno, David, "How One General Interprets the Army's Selection of New One-Stars: Too Much Infantry, and Way Too Many Exec Assts," *Foreign Policy,* June 9, 2011.

Barno, David, and Nora Bensahel, "Can the U.S. Military Halt Its Brain Drain?" *The Atlantic,* November 5, 2015.

Barno, David, Nora Bensahel, Katherine Kidder, and Kelley Sayler, *Building Better Generals*, Washington, D.C.: Center for A New American Security, 2013.

Barrick, Murray R., Terence R. Mitchell, and Greg L. Stewart, "Situational and Motivational Influences on Trait-Behavior Relationships," in Murray R. Barrick and Anne Marie Ryan, eds., *Personality and Work: Reconsidering the Role of Personality in Organizations*, Vol. 20, John Wiley & Sons, 2004.

Barrick, Murray R., and Anne Marie Ryan, eds., *Personality and Work: Reconsidering the Role of Personality in Organizations*, Vol. 20, New York: John Wiley & Sons, 2003.

Barron, Tom., "To Retain Today's Talent, the DoD Must Support Dual-Professional Couples," Center for a New American Security, January 7, 2019. As of January 21, 2019:

https://www.cnas.org/publications/commentary/to-retain-todays-talent-the-dod-must-support-dual-professional-couples

Bastian, Nicole V., "The Problem with Becoming an Irreplaceable Marine Officer," Task and Purpose, December 9, 2015. As of January 12, 2019: https://taskandpurpose.com/the-problem-with-becoming-an-irreplaceable-marine-officer

Blair, Dave, "Seven Stories for Seven Tribes," *Over the Horizon: Multidomain Operations and Strategy*, April 9, 2018. As of January 20, 2019: https://othjournal.com/2018/04/09/seven-stories-for-seven-tribes/

Borman, Walter C., Daniel R. Ilgen, and Richard J. Klimoski, eds., *Handbook of Psychology*, Vol. 12: *Industrial and Organizational Psychology*, Hoboken, N.J.: John Wiley & Sons, 2003.

Brennan, Edward, *Leading Airmen: Taking Leadership Development Seriously*, Maxwell Air Force Base, Ala.: Air University, School of Advanced Air and Space Studies, June 2012.

Bryant, Susan, and Heidi A. Urben, *Reconnecting Athens and Sparta: A Review of OPMS XXI at 20 Years*, Arlington, Va.: Institute of Land Warfare, No. 114, October 2017.

Buckel, Chad A., "The Infantry Career Path: A Case for Changes," *Marine Corps Gazette*, Vol. 102, No. 2, February 2018.

Builder, Carl, *The Masks of War: American Military Styles in Strategy and Analysis,* Baltimore, Md.: Johns Hopkins University Press, 1989.

BUPERSINST—*See* Bureau of Naval Personnel Instruction.

Bureau of Naval Personnel Instruction 1610.10D, Change Transmittal 1, *Navy Performance Evaluation System*, Washington, D.C.: Chief of Naval Personnel, February 25, 2016.

Burks, William H., *Blue Moon Rising? Air Force Institutional Challenges to Producing Senior Joint Leaders*, Fort Leavenworth, Kan.: U.S. Army Command and General Staff College School of Advanced Military Studies, 2010.

Carter, Ashton, *Force of the Future: Maintaining Our Competitive Edge in Human Capital*, Washington, D.C.: U.S. Department of Defense, November 18, 2015.

Carter, Walter E. Jr., "President's Forum," in "Winter 2014 Review," *Naval War College Review*, Vol. 67, No. 1, 2014, pp. 18–19.

Cattell, Raymond, *Intelligence: Its Structure, Growth, and Action*, New York: Houghton Mifflin, 1971.

Chairman of the Joint Chiefs of Staff Instruction 1331.01D, *Manpower and Personnel Actions Involving General and Flag Officers*, Washington, D.C.: U.S. Department of Defense, August 1, 2010.

Chairman of the Joint Chiefs of Staff Instruction 1800.01E, *Officer Professional Military Education Policy*, Washington, D.C.: U.S. Department of Defense, May 29, 2015.

Chatham House, "Chatham House Rule," webpage, undated. As of February 28, 2020: https://www.chathamhouse.org/chatham-house-rule

Chief of Naval Operations, "The Navy Leader Development Strategy," 2013.

Chief of Naval Operations, "Navy Leader Development Framework: Version 1.0," January 2017.

Chief of Naval Operations, "Leadership Development Framework: Version 2.0," April 2018.

Chief of Naval Personnel, Public Affairs, "Leader Development Framework Implementation Plan Announced," March 10, 2017.

Chief of Naval Personnel, Public Affairs, "Navy Announces 2018 Stockdale Award Recipients," September 4, 2018.

Clark, Colin, "Hyten Likely Air Force Chief of Staff Nominee; Carlisle Next," Breaking Defense, March 2, 2016. As of January 20, 2019: https://breakingdefense.com/2016/03/hyten-likely-air-force-chief-of-staff-nominee-carlisle-next/

Colarusso, Michael J., and David S. Lyle, *Senior Officer Talent Management: Fostering Institutional Adaptability*, Carlisle Barracks, Pa.: Strategic Studies Institute, 2014.

Collins, Brian J., *The United States Air Force and Profession: Why Sixty Percent of Air Force General Officers Are Still Pilots When Pilots Comprise Just Twenty Percent of the Officer Corps*, doctoral thesis, Georgetown University, August 2006.

"Command Excellence and the Wardroom," Naval Leadership and Ethics Center, Naval War College, undated, p. 10. As of February 14, 2019: https://dnnlgwick.blob.core.windows.net/portals/16/NLECCourses/Command-Excellence-and-the-Wardroom.pdf?sr=b&si=DNNFileManagerPolicy&sig=KCgmRZTtVB3U%2B71AUdOR5qNTV5S%2Fb3rNhphS6VoEPUk%3D

Congressional Research Service, *General and Flag Officers in the U.S. Armed Forces: Background and Considerations for Congress*, Washington, D.C., R44389, February 1, 2019.

Currie, Karen, John Conway, Scott Johnson, Brian Landry, and Adam Lowther, *Air Force Leadership Study: The Need for Deliberate Development*, Maxwell Air Force Base, Ala.: Air University Press, 2012.

Dailey, Ryan T., *Leading Factors Determining Lateral Transfer Success*, Monterey, Calif.: Naval Postgraduate School, March 2013.

Danskine, Wm. Bruce, *Fall of the Fighter Generals: The Future of USAF Leadership*, School of Maxwell Air Force Base, Ala.: Advanced Air Power Studies, Air University, June 2001.

Davis, Stephen L., and William W. Casey, "A Model of Air Force Squadron Vitality," *Air and Space Power Journal*, January 2018.

Defense Manpower Data Center, "Department of Defense, Active Duty Military Personnel by Rank/Grade, January 1, 2018," January 1, 2018. As of February 26, 2019: https://www.dmdc.osd.mil/appj/dwp/dwp_reports.jsp

de Janasz, Suzanne C., Sherry E. Sullivan, and Vicki Whiting, "Mentor Networks and Career Success: Lessons for Turbulent Times," *Academy of Management Perspectives*, Vol. 17, No. 4, 2003, pp. 78–91.

Department of Defense Instruction 1300.19, *DoD Joint Officer Management (JOM) Program*, Washington, D.C.: U.S. Department of Defense, April 3, 2018. As of February 26, 2019: https://www.esd.whs.mil/Portals/54/Documents/DD/issuances/dodi/130019p.pdf

Department of Defense Instruction 1320.04, *Military Office Actions Requiring Presidential, Secretary of Defense, or Under Secretary of Defense for Personnel and Readiness Approval or Senate Confirmation*, Washington, D.C.: U.S. Department of Defense, January 3, 2014. As of February 10, 2020: https://www.esd.whs.mil/Portals/54/Documents/DD/issuances/dodi/132004p.pdf

Department of Defense Instruction 1320.12, *Commissioned Officer Promotion Program*, Washington, D.C.: U.S. Department of Defense, September 27, 2015.

Department of Defense Instruction 5000.66, *Operation of the Defense Acquisition Workforce Education, Training, Experience, and Career Development Program*, Washington, D.C.: U.S. Department of Defense, July 27, 2017. As of February 10, 2020: https://asc.army.mil/web/wp-content/uploads/2019/11/DoDI-5000.66.pdf

Department of the Army Pamphlet 600-3, *Commissioned Officer Professional Development and Career Management*, Washington, D.C.: Department of the Army, April 3, 2019.

Department of the Army Memo 600-2, *Policies and Procedures for Active-Duty List Officer Selection Boards*, Washington, D.C.: Department of the Army, September 25, 2006.

Deputy Chief of Naval Personnel, "Order Convening the FY-20 Surface Commander Command Screen Board," November 28, 2018.

DoDI—*See* Department of Defense Instruction.

Douthit, Gina, "Command and Staff College Distance Education Program," *DISAM Journal*, September 2008, p. 9.

Evans, Lee, and Ki-Hwan Bae, "Simulation-Based Analysis of a Forced Distribution Performance Appraisal System," *Journal of Defense Analytics and Logistics*, Vol. 1, No. 2, 2017, pp. 120–136.

Fanning, Eric K., Secretary of the Army, *Memorandum of Instruction—FY17 Brigadier General, Army Competitive Category, Promotion Selection Board—Change 1*, Washington, D.C.: Department of the Army, January 12, 2017.

Faram, Mark D., "Here's How the Navy Is Revolutionizing Officer Career Paths," *Navy Times*, February 28, 2019.

Freedburg, Sydney J., Jr., "SASC Pushes Officer Promotion Changes; HASC Not So Much," Breaking Defense, May 25, 2018. As of February 17, 2020: https://breakingdefense.com/2018/05/leaders-matter-most-sasc-reforms-how-military-promotes-officers/

Friedman, B. A., "The End of the Fighting General," *Foreign Policy*, September 12, 2018.

Friedman, Norman, "The Navy Needs People Even More Than Ships," *U.S. Naval Institute Proceedings*, Vol. 144, No. 7, July 2018.

Funder, David C., *The Personality Puzzle*, 2nd edition, New York: Norton, 2001.

Garza, Raul P., *United States Marine Corps Career Designation Board: Significant Factors in Predicting Selection*, Monterey, Calif.: Naval Postgraduate School, 2014.

Geaney, David, "We Ask Too Much of Our Air Force Pilots," *Foreign Policy*, June 1, 2017.

George C. Marshall Foundation, "George C. Marshall: A Study in Character," webpage, undated. As of February 17, 2020: https://www.marshallfoundation.org/marshall/essays-interviews/george-c-marshall-study-character/

Gerras, Stephen J., and Leonard Wong, *Changing Minds in the Army: Why It Is So Difficult and What to Do About It*, Carlisle Barracks, Pa.: U.S. Army War College Press, 2013.

Goldfein, David L., "The Air Force Chief Responds: Keep Writing, Col. 'Ned Stark," and Join My Team," *War on the Rocks*, August 21, 2018. As of February 20, 2020: https://warontherocks.com/2018/08/the-air-force-chief-responds-keep-writing-col-ned-stark-and-join-my-team/

Graham-Ashley, Heather, "3rd ACR Transitions to Strykers, Changes Name," U.S. Army website, November 30, 2011. As of March 4, 2019: https://www.army.mil/article/70060/3rd_acr_transitions_to_strykers_changes_name

Granville, Anna, "4 Reasons I Am Resigning My Commission as a Naval Officer," Task & Purpose, April 13, 2015. As of February 14, 2019: https://taskandpurpose.com/4-reasons-i-am-resigning-my-commission-as-a-naval-officer/

Hardison, Chaitra, Susan Burkhauser, Lawrence M. Hanser, and Mustafa Oguz, *How Effective are Military Academy Admission Standards?* Santa Monica, Calif.: RAND Corporation, RB-9905-OSD, 2016. As of February 20, 2020: https://www.rand.org/pubs/research_briefs/RB9905.html

Harrington, Lisa M., Bart E. Bennett, Katharina Ley Best, David R. Frelinger, Paul W. Mayberry, Igor Mikolic-Torreira, Sebastian Joon Bae, Barbara Bicksler, Lisa Davis, Steven Deane-Shinbrot, Joslyn Fleming, Benjamin Goirigolzarri, Russell Hanson, Connor P. Jackson, Kimberly Jackson, Sean Mann, Geoffrey McGovern, Jenny Oberholtzer, Christina Panis, Alexander D. Rothenberg, Ricardo Sanchez, Matthew Sargent, Peter Schirmer, Hilary Reininger, and Mitch Tuller, *Realigning the Stars: A Methodology for Reviewing Active Component General and Flag Officer Requirements*, Santa Monica, Calif.: RAND Corporation, RR-2384-OSD, 2018. As of February 27, 2020: https://www.rand.org/pubs/research_reports/RR2384.html

Hayes, James H., *The Evolution of Military Officer Personnel Management Policies: A Preliminary Study with Parallels from Industry*, Santa Monica, Calif.: RAND Corporation, R-2276-AF, August 1978. As of February 17, 2020: https://www.rand.org/pubs/reports/R2276.html

"Hobson's Choice," *Wall Street Journal*, May 14, 1952.

Holt, Michael S., *Evolution of the Marine Corps Officer Promotion System: A Re-Evaluation of the Current Marine Corps Officer Promotion System*, Quantico, Va..: Marine Corps University, 2005.

Hosek, Susan D., Peter Tiemeyer, M. Rebecca Kilburn, Debra A. Strong, Selika Ducksworth, and Reginald Ray, *Minority and Gender Differences in Officer Career Progression*, Santa Monica, Calif.: RAND Corporation, MR-1184-OSD, 2001. As of June 6, 2019: https://www.rand.org/pubs/monograph_reports/MR1184.html

Hough, Leatta M., and Adrian Furnham, "Use of Personality Variables in Work Settings," in Walter C. Borman, Daniel R. Ilgen, and Richard J. Klimoski, eds., *Handbook of Psychology*, Vol. 12: *Industrial and Organizational Psychology*, Hoboken, N.J.: John Wiley & Sons, 2003.

Jaffe, Greg, and David Cloud, *The Fourth Star: Four Generals and the Epic Struggle for the Future of the United States Army*, New York: Crown Publishers, 2009.

Janowitz, Morris, *The Professional Soldier: A Social and Political Portrait*, New York: The Free Press, 1971.

Johnson, David E., *Preparing Potential Senior Army Leaders for the Future*, Santa Monica, Calif.: RAND Corporation, IP-224-A, 2002. As of December 3, 2019: https://www.rand.org/pubs/issue_papers/IP224.html

Joint Publication 3-35, *Deployment and Redeployment Operations*, Washington, D.C.: U.S. Joint Chiefs of Staff, January 10, 2018. https://www.jcs.mil/Portals/36/Documents/Doctrine/pubs/jp3_35.pdf

Jones, Alex L., Jeremy J. Tree, and Robert Ward, "Personality in Faces: Implicit Associations Between Appearance and Personality," *European Journal of Social Psychology*, Vol. 49, No. 3, April 2019, pp. 658–669.

Kamarck, Kristy N., *Goldwater-Nichols and the Evolution of Officer Joint Professional Military Education (JPME)*, Washington, D.C.: Congressional Research Service, R44340, January 13, 2016.

Kane, Tim., *Bleeding Talent: How the US Military Mismanages Great Leaders and Why It's Time for a Revolution*, New York: Palgrave Macmillan, 2013.

Keleher, Katherine, "B-Billets Boost Marines' Careers," U.S. Marine Corps Training and Education Command, February 6, 2009.

Kelly, James, "Strengthening Our Naval Profession Through a Culture of Leader Development," *Naval War College Review*, Vol. 67, No. 1, Winter 2014, pp. 12–16.

Kelly, Brian T., *FY20 Posture Statement*, Department of the Air Force presentation to the Subcommittee on Personnel Committee on Armed Services, U.S. Senate, February 27, 2019. As of March 25, 2019: https://www.armed-services.senate.gov/imo/media/doc/Kelly_02-27-19.pdf

Korenman, Lisa M., Elizabeth L. Wetzler, Marjorie H. Carroll, and Elizabeth V. Velilla, "Is It in Your Face? Exploring the Effects of Sexual Dimorphism on Perception of Leadership Potentia," *Military Psychology*, Vol. 31, No. 2, 2019, pp. 1–10.

Kroger, John, "Charting the Future of Education for the Navy-Marine Corps Team," *War on the Rocks,* November 4, 2019. As of November 6, 2019: https://warontherocks.com/2019/11/charting-the-future-of-education-for-the-navy-marine-corps-team/?utm_source=WOTR+Newsletter&utm_campaign=1ad7ecd6c4-EMAIL_CAMPAIGN_10_30_2018_11_23_COPY_01&utm_medium=email&utm_term=0_8375be81e9-1ad7ecd6c4-33477585

Laing, Kelly L., *Leadership in Command Under the Sea*, Maxwell Air Base, Ala.: Air Command and Staff College, Air University, April 2009.

Lander, Natasha, "The Air Force," in S. Rebecca Zimmerman, Kimberly Jackson, Natasha Lander, Colin Roberts, Dan Madden, and Rebeca Orrie, *Movement and Maneuver: Culture and the Competition for Influence Among the U.S. Military Services*, Santa Monica, Calif.: RAND Corporation, RR-2270-OSD, 2019, pp. 77–94. As of February 17, 2020: https://www.rand.org/pubs/research_reports/RR2270.html

Lee, Caitlin, Bart E. Bennett, Lisa M. Harrington, and Darrell D. Jones, *Rare Birds: Understanding and Addressing Air Force Underrepresentation in Senior Joint Positions in the Post–Goldwater-Nichols Era*, Santa Monica, Calif.: RAND Corporation, RR-2089-AF, 2017. As of June 26, 2019: https://www.rand.org/pubs/research_reports/RR2089.html

Light, Mark F., "The Navy's Moral Compass," *Naval War College Review*, Vol. 65, No. 3, Summer 2012.

Losey, Stephen, "Air Force: Commanders, Not Promotion Boards, Now Pick Officers for Developmental Education," *Air Force Times*, July 13, 2017. As of February 17, 2020: https://www.airforcetimes.com/news/your-air-force/2017/07/13/air-force-commanders-not-promotion-boards-now-pick-officers-for-developmental-education/

Losey, Stephen, "'Ned Stark' Unveiled: Colonel Who Wrote Viral Leadership Columns Has a Challenge for the Air Force," *Air Force Times*, May 13, 2019.

Lyle, David S., and John Z. Smith, "The Effect of High-Performing Mentors on Junior Officer Promotion in the US Army," *Journal of Labor Economics*, Vol. 32, No. 2, April 2014.

Lynes, Jerome, Deputy Director Joint Staff, Joint Education and Doctrine, "Framing the Problem: Strategic Guidance and Vision," briefing, October 31, 2018. As of February 26, 2019: https://www.jcs.mil/Portals/36/Documents/Doctrine/MECC2018/framing_brief.pdf?ver=2018-10-26-084404-533

MacFarland, Sean, "It's Time to Invest in Armored Forces Again," *ARMY Magazine*, Vol. 68, No. 11, November 2018. As of January 21, 2019: https://www.ausa.org/articles/it%E2%80%99s-time-invest-armored-forces-again

Mack, Russell L., *Creating Joint Leaders Today for a Successful Air Force Tomorrow*, Maxwell Air Force Base, Ala.: Air Force Research Institute, 2010.

Madden, Dan, "The Marine Corps," in S. Rebecca Zimmerman, Kimberly Jackson, Natasha Lander, Colin Roberts, Dan Madden, and Rebeca Orrie, *Movement and Maneuver: Culture and the Competition for Influence Among the U.S. Military Services*, Santa Monica, Calif.: RAND Corporation, RR-2270-OSD, 2019, pp. 95–123. As of February 17, 2020: https://www.rand.org/pubs/research_reports/RR2270.html

MARADMIN—*See* Marine Administrative Message.

Marine Administrative Message 548/16, *Official Military Personnel File (OMPF) Photograph Guidance*, Washington, D.C.: Headquarters Marine Corps, October 17, 2016.

Marine Administrative Message 196/18, *FY20 U.S. Marine Corps Officer Promotion Selection Boards*, Washington, D.C.: Headquarters Marine Corps, April 5, 2018.

Marine Administrative Message 308/18, *FY19 Manpower Management Officer Assignments (MMOA) Command Visit*, Washington, D.C.: Headquarters Marine Corps, June 4, 2018.

Marine Corps Doctrinal Publication 1, *Marine Corps Operations*, Washington, D.C.: Headquarters Marine Corps, 2011.

Marine Corps Doctrinal Publication 1, *Warfighting*, Washington, D.C.: Headquarters Marine Corps, April 4, 2018.

Marine Corps Doctrinal Publication 6, *Command and Control*, Washington, D.C.: Headquarters. Marine Corps, October 4, 1996.

Marine Corps Order 1500.61, *Marine Leader Development*, Washington, D.C.: Headquarters Marine Corps, July 28, 2017.

Marine Corps Order 1553.4B, *Professional Military Education*, Washington, D.C.: Headquarters Marine Corps, January 25, 2008.

Marine Corps Order 1610.7, *Performance Evaluation System*, Washington, D.C.: Headquarters Marine Corps, February 13, 2015.

Marine Corps Tactical Publication 6-10A, *Sustaining the Transformation*, Washington, D.C.: Headquarters Marine Corps, May 2, 2016.

Marine Corps Technical Publication 6-10B, *Marine Corps Values: A User's Guide for Discussion Leaders*, Washington, D.C.: Headquarters Marine Corps, 2016.

Marine Corps University, "Expeditionary Warfare School," webpage, undated. As of February 20, 2020:
https://www.usmcu.edu/EWS/

Marine Corps University, "Expeditionary Warfare School Distance Education Program," webpage, undated. As of February 20, 2020:
https://www.usmcu.edu/CDET/officer-seminar-ews/

Marine Corps University, *Student Handbook*, Quantico, Va., 2017. As of July 23, 2019:
https://www.usmcu.edu/Portals/218/SchoolFiles/Student%20Handbook%20(Final)%207%20Feb%2017.pdf?ver=2018-10-02-085104-033

Marine Corps Warfighting Publication 6-11, *Leading Marines*, Washington, D.C.: Headquarters Marine Corps, August 1, 2014.

Markel, Wade M., Henry A. Leonard, Charlotte Lynch, Christina Panis, Peter Schirmer, and Carra S. Sims, *Developing U.S. Army Officers' Capabilities for Joint, Interagency, Intergovernmental, and Multinational Environments*, Santa Monica, Calif.: RAND Corporation, MG-990-A, 2011. As of February 17, 2020: https://www.rand.org/pubs/monographs/MG990.html

Marx, Aaron, *Rethinking Marine Corps Officer Promotion and Retention*, Washington, D.C.: Brookings Institution, 2014.

Matthews, Lloyd J., "Anti-Intellectualism and the Army Profession," in Don M. Snider, project director, and Lloyd J. Matthews, ed., *The Future of the Army Profession*, 2nd edition, New York: McGraw Hill, 2005.

Maucione, Scott, "New Study Shows Grim Outlook for Future of Air Force Pilot Shortage," Federal News Network, April 15, 2019. As of April 20, 2019: https://federalnewsnetwork.com/dod-personnel-notebook/2019/04/new-study-shows-grim-outlook-for-future-of-air-force-pilot-shortage/

Mayberry, Paul W., William H. Waggy II, and Anthony Lawrence, *Producing Joint Qualified Officers: FY 2008 to FY 2017 Trends*, Santa Monica, Calif.: RAND Corporation, RR-3105-OSD, 2019. As of August 19, 2019: https://www.rand.org/pubs/research_reports/RR3105.html

Mazarr, Michael J., *Developing Senior Leaders for the Reserve Components*, Santa Monica, Calif.: RAND Corporation, PE-194-OSD, 2017. As of June 6, 2019: https://www.rand.org/pubs/perspectives/PE194.html

Mazur, Allan, Julie Mazur, and Caroline Keating, "Military Rank Attainment of a West Point Class: Effects of Cadets' Physical Features," *American Journal of Sociology,* Vol. 90, No. 1, 1984, pp. 125–150.

McCain, Jack, "A Navy Pilot's Take: The Air Force Doesn't Have a Pilot Crisis, It Has a Leadership Crisis," ForeignPolicy.com, April 24, 2017. As of January 22, 2019: https://foreignpolicy.com/2017/04/24/a-navy-pilots-take-the-air-force-doesnt-have-a-pilot-crisis-it-has-a-leadership-crisis/

McConville, James C., and Debra S. Wada, *U.S. Army Talent Management Strategy: Force 2025 and Beyond*, Washington, D.C.: Department of the Army, September 20, 2016.

McCrae, Robert R., Paul T. Costa, Jr., and Catherine M. Busch, "Evaluating Comprehensiveness in Personality Systems: The California Q-Set and the Five Factor Model," *Journal of Personality*, Vol. 54, No. 2, June 1986, pp. 431–446.

MCDP—*See* Marine Corps Doctrinal Publication.

McInnis, Kathleen J., *Goldwater-Nichols at 30: Defense Reform and Issues for Congress*, Washington, D.C.: Congressional Research Service, June 2, 2016.

MCTP—*See* Marine Corps Tactical Publication.

MCWP—*See* Marine Corps Warfighting Publication.

"Meet the Monitors," *Marine Corps Gazette*, Vol. 70, No. 1, January 1986.

Middleton, Ryan, and William Wagstaff, "Promoting What We Value: Weapons School and Talent Management in the Air Force," *War on the Rocks*, December 5, 2018. As of January 21, 2019: https://warontherocks.com/2018/12/promoting-what-we-value-weapons-school-and-talent-management-in-the-air-force/

Military Leadership Diversity Commission, *Issue Paper #23: Military Occupations and Implications for Racial/Ethnic and Gender Diversity*, March 2010.

Moore, David W., and B. Thomas Trout, "Military Advancement: The Visibility Theory of Promotion," *American Political Science Review*, Vol. 72, No. 2, 1978, pp. 452–468.

Mullen, Michael, and Robert Natter, "We Can Fix the SWO Career Path," *U.S. Naval Institute Proceedings*, Vol. 144, No. 4, April 2018.

Murray, Williamson, "Is Professional Military Education Necessary?" *Naval War College Review*, Vol. 67, No. 1, Winter 2014, pp. 150–157.

NAVADMIN—*See* Naval Administration Message.

Naval Administration Message 060/17, *Navy Leader Development Framework Implementation Plan*, Washington, D.C.: Chief of Naval Operations, March 9, 2017.

Naval Administration Message 263/18, *Update to Navy Graduate Education Program*, Washington, D.C.: Chief of Naval Operations, October 25, 2018.

Naval Doctrine Publication 6, *Naval Command and Control*, Washington D.C.: Department of the Navy, May 19, 1995.

Naval History and Heritage Command, "Chiefs of Naval Operations," undated.

Navy Marine Corps 1200.1C, *Military Occupational Specialties Manual*, Washington, D.C.: Headquarters Marine Corps, April 17, 2017.

Navy Personnel Command, "FY-18 Active Line Officer Community Brief," undated a.

Navy Personnel Command, "FY-20 Active Line Officer Community Brief," undated b.

Navy Personnel Command, "Officer Community Management and Detailing: Officer," undated c.

Navy Personnel Command, "Let's Talk Timing," undated d.

Navy Personnel Command, "Active Duty O3 Line," undated e. As of February 14, 2019: https://www.public.navy.mil/bupers-npc/boards/activedutyofficer/03line/Pages/default.aspx

Navy Personnel Command, "FY-18 Active-Duty Navy Lieutenant Commander Line Promotion Selection Boards," undated f.

Navy Personnel Command, "Board Membership, FY-18 Active-Duty Navy Captain Line Promotion Selection Boards," undated g. As of February 14, 2019: https://www.public.navy.mil/bupers-npc/boards/activedutyofficer/06line/Documents/FY-18%20AO6L%20CONVENING%20ORDER%20MEMBERSHIP.pdf

Navy Personnel Command, "Flag Aide," undated h.

Navy Personnel Command, *Manual of Navy Officer Manpower and Personnel Classifications*, Vol. 1, Part A: *Billet and Officer Designator Codes*, January 2019a.

Navy Personnel Command, "Career Intermission Program," April 10, 2019b. As of August 31, 2019: https://www.public.navy.mil/bupers-npc/career/reservepersonnelmgmt/IRR/Pages/CIP.aspx

NDP—*See* Naval Doctrinal Publication.

Nolan, Jr., Steven T., and Robert E. Overstreet, "Improving How the Air Force Develops High-Performing Officers," *Air and Space Power Journal*, Summer 2018, pp. 21–36.

Office of the Under Secretary of Defense (Comptroller), Chief Financial Officer, *Defense Budget Overview: U.S. Department of Defense Fiscal Year 2019 Budget Request*, February 2018.

Olson, Craig R., *Naval Leadership: Developing Operational Leaders for the 21st Century*, Newport, R.I.: Naval War College, May 4, 2009.

O'Rourke, Ronald, *Navy Force Structure and Shipbuilding Plans*, Washington, D.C.: Congressional Research Service, October 19, 2018.

Orsi, Douglas., "Professional Military Education and Broadening Assignments: A Model for the Future," *Joint Forces Quarterly*, Vol. 86, 3rd quarter, 2017.

Panzino, Charlsy, "New in 2018: AMC Pushes for Aviation-Only Career Track," *Air Force Times*, December 29, 2017. As of January 22, 2019: https://www.airforcetimes.com/news/your-air-force/2017/12/29/new-in-2018-amc-pushes-for-aviation-only-career-track/

Pierce, James G., *Is the Organizational Culture of the U.S. Army Congruent with the Professional Development of Its Senior Level Officer Corps?* Carlisle Barracks, Pa.: U.S. Army War College Press, 2010.

Powers, Rod, "Air Force Assignment System," The Balance Careers, December 17, 2018. As of February 14, 2019: https://www.thebalancecareers.com/air-force-assignment-system-3331731

Public Law 96-513, Defense Officer Personnel Management Act, December 12, 1980.

Public Law 99-433, Goldwater-Nichols Department of Defense Reorganization Act of 1986, October 1, 1986.

Public Law 103-160, Section 921, National Defense Authorization Act for Fiscal Year 1994, November 30, 1993.

Public Law 115-232, John S. McCain National Defense Authorization Act for Fiscal Year 2019, August 13, 2018.

Public Law 114-328, National Defense Authorization Act for Fiscal Year 2017, December 23, 2016.

RAND Corporation, "RAND DOPMA/ROPMA Policy Reference Tool: Promotion Timing, Zones, and Opportunity," webpage, undated. As of January 20, 2019: http://dopma-ropma.rand.org/promotion-timing-zones-and-opportunity.html

Rex, Travis D., *Speed Trap: The USAF 24-Year Pole to General Officer*, Carlisle Barracks, Pa.: U.S. Army War College, April 2015.

Rhodes, Daniel C., "Moral and Ethical Leadership: The Challenges of Implementing the Appropriate Training," *Marine Corps Gazette*, Vol. 93, No. 5, May 2009, pp. 54–56.

Ricks, Thomas, *The Generals: American Military Command from World War II to Today*, New York: Penguin Books, 2012.

Riker-Coleman, Erik Blaine, *"Positions of Importance and Responsibility": U.S. Four-Star Military Leaders in a Changing World, 1968–2000*, dissertation, University of North Carolina, 2006.

Robbert, Albert A., Katherine L. Kidder, Caitlin Lee, Agnes Gereben Schaefer, and William H. Waggy II, *Officer Career Management: Steps Toward Modernization in the 2018 and 2019 National Defense Authorization Act*, Santa Monica, Calif.: RAND Corporation, RR-2875-OSD, 2019. As of February 17, 2020: https://www.rand.org/pubs/research_reports/RR2875.html

Robbert, Albert A., Steve Drezner, John E. Boon, Jr., Lawrence M. Hanser, Craig Moore, Lynn Scott, and Herb Shukiar, *Integrated Planning for the Air Force Senior Leader Workforce: Background and Methods*, Santa Monica, Calif.: RAND Corporation, TR-175-AF, 2004. As of July 2, 2019: https://www.rand.org/pubs/technical_reports/TR175.html

Robbert, Albert A., Tara L. Terry, Paul Emslie, and Michael Robbins, *Promotion Benchmarks for Senior Officers with Joint and Acquisition Service*, Santa Monica, Calif.: RAND Corporation, RR-1447-OSD, 2016. As of June 06, 2019: https://www.rand.org/pubs/research_reports/RR1447.html

Roberts, Colin, "The Navy," in S. Rebecca Zimmerman, Kimberly Jackson, Natasha Lander, Colin Roberts, Dan Madden, and Rebeca Orrie, *Movement and Maneuver: Culture and the Competition for Influence Among the U.S. Military Services*, Santa Monica, Calif.: RAND Corporation, RR-2270-OSD, 2019, pp. 47–75. As of February 17, 2020: https://www.rand.org/pubs/research_reports/RR2270.html

Rosen, Stephen Peter, *Winning the Next War: Innovation and the Modern Military*, Ithaca, N.Y.: Cornell University Press, 1991.

Rostker, Bernard D., "Reforming the American Military Officer Personnel System," testimony before the Senate Armed Services Committee, December 2, 2015. As of February 17, 2020: https://www.rand.org/pubs/testimonies/CT446.html

Rostker, Bernard D., Harry J. Thie, James L. Lacy, Jennifer H. Kawata, and Susanna W. Purnell, *The Defense Officer Personnel Management Act of 1980: A Retrospective Assessment*, Santa Monica, Calif.: RAND Corporation, R-4246-FMP, 1993. As of June 06, 2019: https://www.rand.org/pubs/reports/R4246.html

Sackett, Anna L., Angela Karrasch, William Weyhrauch, and Ellen Goldman, *Enhancing the Strategic Capability of the Army: An Investigation of Strategic Thinking Tasks, Skills, and Development*, Fort Belvoir, Va.: U.S. Army Research Institute for the Behavioral and Social Sciences, 2016.

Salmoni, Barak A., Jessica Hart, Renny McPherson, and Aidan Kirby Winn, "Growing Strategic Leaders for Future Conflict," *Parameters*, Spring 2010.

Saucier, Gerald, and Lewis R. Goldberg, "The Structure of Personality Attributes," in Murray R. Barrick and Ann Marie Ryan, eds., *Personality and Work: Reconsidering the Role of Personality in Organizations*, San Francisco, Calif.: Jossey-Bass, 2003.

Scales, Bob, *Scales on War: The Future of America's Military at Risk*, Annapolis, Md.: Naval Institute Press, 2016.

Scales, Robert H., *Are You a Strategic Genius? Not Likely, Given Army's System for Selecting, Educating Leaders*, Arlington, Va.: Association of the United States Army, October 13, 2016.

Scales, Robert H., "Ike's Lament: In Search of a Revolution in Military Affairs," *War on the Rocks*, August 16, 2017. As of February 10, 2020:

https://warontherocks.com/2017/08/ikes-lament-in-search-of-a-revolution-in-military-education/

Schmidt, Frank L., John E. Hunter, and Alice N. Outerbridge, "Impact of Job Experience and Ability on Job Knowledge, Work Sample Performance, and Supervisory Ratings of Job Performance," *Journal of Applied Psychology*, Vol. 71, No. 3, 1986, pp. 432–429.

Schmitt, Eric, Thomas Gibbons-Neff, and Helene Cooper, "Navy Collisions That Killed 17 Sailors Were 'Avoidable,' Official Inquiry Says," *New York Times*, November 1, 2017.

Schmitt, Neal, Jose M. Cortina, Michael J. Ingerick, and Darin Wiechmann, "Personnel Selection and Employee Performance," in W. C. Borman, D. R. Ilgen, and R. J. Klimoski, eds., *Handbook of Psychology*, Vol. 12, *Industrial and Organizational Psychology*, Hoboken, N.J.: John Wiley & Sons, 2003, pp. 77–105.

Schneider, Benjamin, "The People Make the Place," *Personnel Psychology*, Vol. 40, No. 3, 1987, pp. 437–454.

Schneider, Benjamin, D. Brent Smith, Sylvester Taylor, and John Fleenor, "Personality and Organizations: A Test of the Homogeneity of Personality Hypothesis," *Journal of Applied Psychology*, Vol. 83, No. 3, 1998.

Schogol Jeff, "Two-Star Fired for 'Treason' Rant Against A-10 Supporters," *Air Force Times*, April 10, 2015. As of January 21, 2019: https://www.airforcetimes.com/news/your-air-force/2015/04/10/two-star-fired-for-treason-rant-against-a-10-supporters/

Schogol, Jeff, "Where Have All the Combat Vets Gone?" *Marine Corps Times*, August 14, 2017.

SECNAVINST—*See* Secretary of the Navy Instruction.

Secretary of the Air Force, Public Affairs, "Air Force Simplifies Promotion Recommendation Forms for Officers," May 8, 2019. As of June 21, 2019: https://www.af.mil/News/Article-Display/Article/1841404/air-force-simplifies-promotion-recommendation-forms-for-officers/

Secretary of the Navy, "FY-18 Active-Duty and Reserve Navy Flag Officer Promotion Selection Board Precept," September 19, 2016a.

Secretary of the Navy, "Order Convening the FY-18 Promotion Selection Boards to Consider Officers in the Line and Staff Corps on the Active-Duty List of the Navy for Permanent Promotion to the Grade of Rear Admiral (Lower Half)," October 11, 2016b.

Secretary of the Navy, "FY-18 Active-Duty and Reserve Navy Officer and Chief Warrant Officer Promotion Selection Board Precept," December 12, 2016c.

Secretary of the Navy, "Order Convening the FY-18 Promotion Selection Boards to Consider Officers in the Line on the Active-Duty List of the Navy for Permanent Promotion to the Grade of Captain," January 5, 2017a.

Secretary of the Navy, "Order Convening the FY-18 Promotion Selection Boards to Consider Officers in the Line on the Active-Duty List of the Navy for Permanent Promotion to the Grade of Commander," February 13, 2017b.

Secretary of the Navy, "Order Convening the FY-18 Promotion Selection Boards to Consider Officers in the Line on the Active-Duty List of the Navy for Permanent Promotion to the Grade of Lieutenant Commander," May 2, 2017c.

Secretary of the Navy Instruction 1401.3A, *Selection Board Membership*, Washington, D.C.: Department of the Air Force, December 20, 2005.

Secretary of the Navy Instruction 1420.1B, *Promotion, Special Selection, Selective Early Retirement, And Selective Early Removal Boards for Commissioned Officers of the Navy and Marine Corps*, Washington, D.C.: Department of the Air Force, March 28, 2006.

Shaw, Ronald R., Jr., "Now Hear This—Let Talented Officers Opt-In for Early Promotion," *U.S. Naval Institute Proceedings*, Vol. 142, No. 3, March 2016.

Sicard, Sarah, "Air Force Expands Sabbatical Leave for Up to 3 Years if Airmen Stay in," Task & Purpose, September 26, 2017. As of August 31, 2019: https://taskandpurpose.com/air-force-expands-sabbatical-leave-3-years-airmen-stay

Simons, Anna, *21st-Century Challenges of Command: A View from the Field*, Carlisle Barracks, Pa.: U.S. Army War College Press, 2017.

Singh, Romila, Belle Rose Ragins, and Phyllis Tharenou, "What Matters Most? The Relative Role of Mentoring and Career Capital in Career Success," *Journal of Vocational Behavior*, Vol. 75, No. 1, 2009, p. 56–67.

Slavin, Erik, "Navy's Promotion System Struggling to Root Out Unfit Commanders," *Stars and Stripes*, May 16, 2010.

Snodgrass, Guy, Ben Kohlmann, and Chris O'Keefe, *2014 Navy Retention Study*, September 1, 2014. As of February 10, 2020: http://www.dodretention.org/results

Snow, Shawn, "Where Are the Female Marines?" *Marine Corps Times*, March 5, 2018.

Snow, Shawn, "Why the Corps Needs a System to Shoot Down Russian and Chinese Cruise Missiles," *Marine Corps Times*, February 11, 2019.

Stanley, Clifford L., and William E. Gortney, "General and Flag Officer Requirements," testimony at hearing before the U.S. Senate Armed Services Committee, Subcommittee on Personnel, September 14, 2011.

Stark, Ned, list of commentaries, *War on the Rocks*, undated. As of January 22, 2019: https://warontherocks.com/author/ned-stark/

Stark, Ned, "Commentary: The Air Force Is Not Designed to Produce Good Leaders," *Air Force Times*, July 31, 2018. As of September 1, 2019: https://www.airforcetimes.com/opinion/commentary/2018/07/31/commentary-the-air-force-is-not-designed-to-produce-good-leaders/

Steele, Robert G., Kelly E. Fletcher, William F. Nadolski, Emily Ann Buckman, and Stephen W. Oliver, Jr., *Competency-Based Assignment and Promotion to Meet Air Force Senior Leader Requirements*, Maxwell Air Force Base, Ala.: Air University Press, 2006.

Task Force on Defense Personnel, *Defense Personnel Systems: The Hidden Threat to a High-Performance Force,* Washington, D.C.: Bipartisan Policy Center, 2017.

Thie, Harry J., Margaret C. Harrell, Roland J. Yardley, Marian Oshiro, Holly Ann Potter, Peter Schirmer, and Nelson Lim, *Framing a Strategic Approach for Joint Officer Management*, Santa Monica, Calif.: RAND Corporation, MG-306-OSD, 2005. As of June 26, 2019: https://www.rand.org/pubs/monographs/MG306.html

Thornhill, Paula, "To Produce Strategists, Focus on Staffing Senior Leaders," *War on the Rocks*, July 20, 2018. As of February 18, 2020: https://warontherocks.com/2018/07/to-produce-strategists-focus-on-staffing-senior-leaders/

Thornton, David, *Navy Education Overhaul Creates New CLO, Community College*, Federal News Network, February 15, 2019. As of July 2, 2019: https://federalnewsnetwork.com/navy/2019/02/navy-education-overhaul-creates-new-clo-community-college/

Tice, Jim, "Army Seeks Officers for Elite Military Studies Doctoral Program," *Army Times*, February 15, 2016. As of March 4, 2019: https://www.armytimes.com/news/your-army/2016/02/15/army-seeks-officers-for-elite-military-studies-doctoral-program/

Tilghman, Andrew, "Pentagon's Quiet Push for Military Personnel Reform," *Military Times*, May 11, 2015. As of May 4, 2019: http://www.militarytimes.com/story/military/pentagon/2015/05/11/personnel-reform-push/70895094/

Tortora, Robert, "Unrestricted Line Officer Promotions: Best and Fully Qualified?" July 2014.

Triandis, Harry C., "Individualism-Collectivism and Personality," *Journal of Personality*, Vol. 69, No. 6, 2001.

Under Secretary of Defense for Personnel and Readiness, *Force of the Future Final Report: Reform Proposals, Version 2.0*, Washington, D.C.: U.S. Department of Defense, August 24, 2015.

U.S. Air Force, *Air Force Core Doctrine*, Vol. II: *Leadership*, Maxwell Air Force Base, Ala.: Curtis E. Lemay Center for Doctrine Development and Education, 2015.

U.S. Air Force, Air Force Personnel Center, "Officer Promotions," undated. As of November 27, 2018:
https://www.afpc.af.mil/Promotion/Officer-Promotions/

U.S. Army Public Affairs, "Department of the Army Announces Force Structure Decisions for Fiscal Year 2017," June 15, 2017. As of February 14, 2019:
https://www.army.mil/article/189082/

U.S. Army War College, Department of Command, Leadership and Management, *Strategic Leadership Primer*, 2nd edition, Carlisle Barracks, Pa., 2004.

U.S. Code, Title 10: Armed Forces; Section 152: Chairman: Appointment; Grade and Rank, as amended through December 23, 2016. As of June 26, 2019:
https://www.law.cornell.edu/uscode/text/10/152

U.S. Code, Title 10: Armed Forces; Section 155: Joint Staff, as amended through December 23, 2016. As of June 26, 2019:
https://www.law.cornell.edu/uscode/text/10/155

U.S. Code, Title 10: Armed Forces; Section 3013: Secretary of the Army, as amended through August 13, 2018. As of June 26, 2019:
https://www.law.cornell.edu/uscode/text/10/3013

U.S. Code, Title 10: Armed Forces; Section 523, Authorized Strengths: Commissioned Officers on Active Duty in Grades of Major, Lieutenant Colonel, and Colonel and Navy Grades of Lieutenant Commander, Commander, and Captain.

U.S. Code, Title 10: Armed Forces; Section 525: Distribution of Commissioned Officers on Active Duty in General Officer and Flag Officer Grades, as amended through December 23, 2016. As of June 26, 2019:
https://www.law.cornell.edu/uscode/text/10/525

U.S. Code, Title 10: Armed Forces; Section 526: Authorized Strength: General and Flag Officers on Active Duty, as amended through December 23, 2016. As of June 26, 2019:
https://www.law.cornell.edu/uscode/text/10/526

U.S. Code, Title 10: Armed Forces; Section 612: Composition of Selection Boards, as amended through January 7, 2011. As of June 26, 2019: https://www.law.cornell.edu/uscode/text/10/612

U.S. Code, Title 10: Armed Forces; Section 615: Information Furnished to Selection Boards, as amended through January 7, 2011. As of June 26, 2019: https://www.law.cornell.edu/uscode/text/10/615

U.S. Code, Title 10: Armed Forces; Section 619: Eligibility for Consideration for Promotion: Time-in-Grade and Other Requirements, as amended through August 13, 2018. As of June 26, 2019: https://www.law.cornell.edu/uscode/text/10/619

U.S. Code, Title 10: Armed Forces; Section 621: Competitive Categories for Promotion, as amended through December 12, 1980. As of June 25, 2019: https://www.law.cornell.edu/uscode/text/10/621

U.S. Code, Title 10: Armed Forces; Section 632: Effect of Failure of Selection for Promotion: Captains and Majors of the Army, Air Force, and Marine Corps and Lieutenants and Lieutenant Commanders of the Navy, as amended through August 13, 2018. As of June 26, 2019: https://www.law.cornell.edu/uscode/text/10/632

U.S. Code, Title 10: Armed Forces; Section 661: Management Policies for Joint Qualified Officers, as amended through December 12, 2017. As of June 26, 2019: https://www.law.cornell.edu/uscode/text/10/661

U.S. Code, Title 10: Armed Forces; Section 668: Definitions, as amended through December 23, 2016. As of June 26, 2019: https://www.law.cornell.edu/uscode/text/10/668

U.S. Code, Title 10: Armed Forces; Section 8013: Secretary of the Navy, as amended through August 13, 2018. As of June 26, 2019: https://www.law.cornell.edu/uscode/text/10/8013

U.S. Code, Title 10: Armed Forces; Section 9013: Secretary of the Air Force, as amended through August 13, 2018. As of June 26, 2019: https://www.law.cornell.edu/uscode/text/10/9013

U.S. Department of Defense, *Modernizing Military Pay: Report of the First Quadrennial Review of Military Compensation*, Vol. V, *The Military Estate Program (Appendices)*, 1969.

U.S. Department of Defense, *Summary of the 2018 National Defense Strategy of the United States of America: Sharpening the American Military's Competitive Edge*, Washington, D.C., 2018. As of February 18, 2020:

https://dod.defense.gov/Portals/1/Documents/pubs/2018-National-Defense-Strategy-Summary.pdf

U.S. House of Representatives, 115th Congress, H. Report 115-676 to H.R. 5515, National Defense Authorization Act for Fiscal Year 2019, 2018.

U.S. Marine Corps, "Becoming a Marine: Marine Corps Officer: Officer Eligibility," webpage, undated. As of March 11, 2020: https://www.marines.com/becoming-a-marine/officer.html

U.S. Marine Corps, *Commandant's Planning Guidance, 2019*, Washington, D.C., 2019. As of August 13, 2019: https://www.hqmc.marines.mil/Portals/142/Docs/%2038th%20Commandant%27s%20Planning%20Guidance_2019.pdf?ver=2019-07-16-200152-700

U.S. Marine Corps Concepts and Programs, "Types of MAGTFs," U.S. Marine Corps, undated.

U.S. Marine Corps Fitness Report (1610), "Commandant's Guidance," NAVMC 10385, revised July 2011.

U.S. Marine Corps, Office of Legislative Affairs, "Congressional Fellowship Program," webpage, undated. As of February 20, 2020: https://www.hqmc.marines.mil/Agencies/Office-of-Legislative-Affairs/Congressional-Fellowship-Program/

U.S. Marine Corps Training and Education Command, "RP 0103-Principles of Marine Corps Leadership," undated.

U.S. Marine Corps Training Command, "Fitness Reports I," in *Fitness Reports B3K3738 Student Handout*, Basic Officer Course student handout, Camp Barrett, Va., undated a. As of July 30, 2019: https://www.trngcmd.marines.mil/Portals/207/Docs/TBS/B3K3738%20Fitness%20Report.pdf?ver=2015-03-26-102052-153

U.S. Marine Corps Training Command, "The Basic School," website, undated b. As of February 20, 2020: https://www.trngcmd.marines.mil/Northeast/The-Basic-School/

U.S. Naval Academy, "Class of 2017 Statistics," May 30, 2017. As of February 20, 2020: https://www.usna.edu/NewsCenter/2017/05/class-of-2017-statistics.php

U.S. Naval Academy, "Class of 2018 Statistics," May 25, 2018. As of February 14, 2019: https://www.usna.edu/NewsCenter/2018/06/Class%20of%202018%20Statistics.php

U.S. Naval Academy News Center, "Class of 2019 Receives Service Assignments," November 19, 2018. As of February 25, 2019:

https://www.usna.edu/NewsCenter/2018/11/Class_of_2019_Receives_Service_Assignments.php

U.S. Navy, "United States Navy Biographies," webpage, undated. As of March 11, 2020: https://www.navy.mil/navydata/bios/bio_list.asp

U.S. Senate, 115th Congress, S. Report 115-262 to S. 2987, the John S. McCain National Defense Authorization Act for Fiscal Year 2019, 2018.

Vice Chief of Naval Operations, "Memorandum for all Flag Officers: Standards of Conduct," August 12, 2008.

Vice Chief of Naval Operations, "Raising Our Standards," *Navy Live*, April 12, 2018.

Vick, Alan, David Orletsky, Bruce Pirnie, and Seth Jones, *The Stryker Brigade Combat Team: Rethinking Strategic Responsiveness and Assessing Deployment Options*, Santa Monica, Calif.: RAND Corporation, MR-1606-AF, 2002. As of February 17, 2020: https://www.rand.org/pubs/monograph_reports/MR1606.html

Vitelli, Romeo, "Can You Change Your Personality?" *Psychology Today*, September 7, 2015.

Wardynski, Casey, David S. Lyle, and Michael J. Colarusso, *Talent: Implications for a U.S. Army Officer Corps Strategy*, West Point, N.Y.: U.S. Army War College Strategic Studies Institute, October 28, 2009.

Watson, Zach N., Brian C. Babcock-Lumish, and Heidi A. Urben, "The Value of Broadening Assignments," *ARMY Magazine*, Vol. 66, No. 12, December 2016. As of January 21, 2019: https://www.ausa.org/articles/value-broadening-assignments

West Point Association of Graduates, "Branch Night 2018," website, undated. Last accessed September 6, 2019 from: https://www.westpointaog.org/branchnightclassof2019

Wilhelm, Charles E., Wallace C. Gregson, Jr., Bruce B. Knutson, Jr., Paul K. Van Riper, Andrew F. Krepinevich, and Williamson Murray, *U.S. Marine Corps Officer Professional Military Education 2006 Study and Findings*, Quantico, Va.: Marine Corps University, PCN 50100121000, 2006. As of February 10, 2020: https://www.marines.mil/Portals/1/Publications/U.S.%20Marine%20Corps%20Officer%20Professional%20Military%20Education%202006%20Study%20and%20Findings.pdf

Wilson, James, *Bureaucracy: What Government Agencies Do and Why They Do It*, New York: Basic Books, 1989.

Worden, Mike, *Rise of the Fighter Generals: The Problem of Air Force Leadership 1945–1982*, Maxwell Air Force Base, Ala.: Air University Press, 1998.

Yingling, Paul, "The Failure of Generalship," *Armed Forces Journal*, May 10, 2007.

Zimmerman, S. Rebecca, "The Army," in S. Rebecca Zimmerman, Kimberly Jackson, Natasha Lander, Colin Roberts, Dan Madden, and Rebeca Orrie, *Movement and Maneuver: Culture and the Competition for Influence Among the U.S. Military Services*, Santa Monica, Calif.: RAND Corporation, RR-2270-OSD, 2019, pp. 21–46. As of February 17, 2020: https://www.rand.org/pubs/research_reports/RR2270.html

Zimmerman, S. Rebecca, Kimberly Jackson, Natasha Lander, Colin Roberts, Dan Madden, and Rebeca Orrie, *Movement and Maneuver: Culture and the Competition for Influence Among the U.S. Military Services*, Santa Monica, Calif.: RAND Corporation, RR-2270-OSD, 2019. As of June 13, 2019: https://www.rand.org/pubs/research_reports/RR2270.html

Zirkle, Robert Allen, *Communities Rule: Intra-Service Politics in the United States Army*, doctoral thesis, Cambridge: Massachusetts Institute of Technology, 2008.